THE ETHNIC FRONTIER

THE ETHNIC FRONTIER

Essays in the History of Group Survival in Chicago and the Midwest

edited by

MELVIN G. HOLLI
and
PETER d'A. JONES

William B. Eerdmans Publishing Company

Copyright © 1977 by Wm. B. Eerdmans Publishing Co.
255 Jefferson Ave. S.E., Grand Rapids, Mich. 49503
Printed in the United States of America

Library of Congress Cataloging in Publication Data

The Ethnic frontier.
  Includes index.
  1. Minorities — Illinois — Chicago — History. 2. Chicago — Race relations.
3. Minorities — Middle West — History. 4. Middle West — Race relations. I. Holli,
Melvin G. II. Jones, Peter d'Alroy.
F548.9.A1E86   301.45'0977311   77-2746
ISBN 0-8028-1705-X

in memory of
one special product of the American cauldron

GILBERT OSOFSKY
(1935-1974)
Jewish boy from Brooklyn
pioneer historian of black America
passionate scholar
inspiring teacher
mensch

Contents

6   Contents

THE STRUGGLE CONTINUES

List of Illustrations

Introduction

PETER d'A. JONES AND MELVIN G. HOLLI

The Cauldron of American Values

> *All is race; there is no other truth.*
> —Benjamin Disraeli

> *I have ever hated all nations, professions and communities, and all my love is towards individuals.*
> — Jonathan Swift

ETHNIC VARIETY HAS BEEN ACKNOWL-edged as a major shaping force in American history. Ethnicity itself, however, is more complex than many Americans have been prepared to admit. What precisely *is* ethnicity? Much work and thought is still needed before this question can be answered adequately. This book of research essays examines examples of ethnic communities past, present, and ongoing, and provides fresh insights into community dynamics and values. We have avoided those simplistic, too easily grasped, polarized scenarios such as "Black" versus "White," "WASP" versus "ethnic," "host" society versus "immigrant," in favor of a more sophisticated and realistic approach. Dualistic mental sets and simple adversary categories have proved uncreative and intellectually barren in ethnic history. After all, one cannot expect confrontationist political slogans, however justifiable or effective in their day, to serve well as analytical research concepts. Even that hallowed polarity "Indian" versus "White Man" is shot through with ambiguity and difficulty in the more complex world of historical research. American history offers very few clear and simple moral battles.

What we might term "ethnic democracy"* in a polycultural, ideologically egalitarian society such as ours emerges only with painful slowness over the years, as group after group jockeys for position. Some true sense of pluralism, or acceptance of many differences, emerges from struggles both

*We include "racial" in the general word "ethnic" to avoid clumsiness, and because as social historians we are concerned with black Americans as a cultural group and not with those minor genetic attributes such as color or particular physical characteristics. Sociologically, it is redundant to speak of "ethnicity *and* race" in American life.

external and *internal* to ethnic groups, and from tensions between and among a great variety of such groups. The bipolar adversary model simply does not fit.

An adversary framework would also reduce ethnic history to a mere local argument or dialectic, a battle for "freedom" against "prejudice"; the richness and variety of ethnic life would be obscured or ignored. In *The Ethnic Frontier* we are indeed concerned with prejudice and freedom, but we seek an ethnic history for its own sake, a richly detailed and informing portrait, warts and all, of various ethnic communities, their values, social structures, inner dynamics, and everyday lifestyles. For example, most of us would readily recognize the indefensibility of a distinction between "host" and "immigrant" in our society, given the overwhelming number of immigrants and their varying origins over time. But other lessons have been more difficult to grasp — such as the fact that each ethnic group has been and is itself complex: there is no such mythic, abstract creature as "the" Negro, "the" white, "the" Indian, "the" Jew, or "the" Catholic in American history.* Divisions and tensions *within* ethnic groups, Poles or Jews, for instance, are fully illustrated in the following pages.

The inner complexity of each group is perhaps more readily imparted nowadays because the concept of the "melting pot" has been abandoned. In the present age of "ethnic revival" and neonationalism, the melting pot, with its assumption (usually unspoken) that the newcomers would melt into an "Anglo-Saxon" matrix, is an inept metaphor, false in historical fact and misleading in social theory. The immigrants did not "melt" in the expected manner. Yet value conflict and adjustment, rejection, alienation, and mediation have been and are major themes of ethnic history. America has been a cauldron of values.

The Ethnic Frontier addresses itself directly to these themes. The essays have been written expressly for this

---

*On the ethnic group as itself a pluralistic phenomenon, see Arthur Mann's "The City As a Melting Pot" in Indiana Historical Society Lectures (1971-72), *History and the Role of the City in American Life* (Indianapolis: Indiana Historical Society, 1972). This introduction owes a great deal to many years of discussion with Professor Mann.

book; they are original, freshly researched, and often path-breaking in their findings. The authors emphasize group folkways and the problems of identity, acceptance, and survival in the very heartland of the American popular democracy — the Midwest. They seek to convey some of the real concerns of the American peoples (perhaps the word makes more sense in the plural), and to transfer some feeling for the living material of ethnic life. The book also brings together two major American concepts and experiences — ethnicity and the frontier — and illustrates their interaction.

A deep sense of geographic and physical place, and a sensitivity to the texture of everyday life, is evident in Jacqueline Peterson's fluent and evocative study of frontier Chicago, which opens the book and sets the scene. Highly advanced societies can ignore, obviate, or even reshape their geography; for pioneer Chicago the physical setting was paramount and it is skillfully portrayed here. Peterson's microsocial history of the founding families, their homes, occupations, systems of social status, concerns, and lifestyles provides a unique picture of an early frontier settlement. Under the profit-seeking aegis of the American Fur Company, many sorts of folk were tolerated and accepted: Indians, French, Anglos, *métis,* and other mixed-bloods. For a few brief frontier years the society was casually multiracial. Then this mixed culture vanished under the impact of the invasion of Yankees. The newcomers, with their built-in, inner-directed sense of linear "progress," their capacity for deferred gratification, and their readiness, as Peterson puts it, to "cheat the present," swept everything before them. The clash of values is seen clearly with the example of Mark Beaubien, owner of the Sauganash tavern, soon surrounded by a growing Chicago, who carelessly gave away potentially valuable lots, observing with nonchalance: "Didn't expect no town."

Parallel attitudes are seen elsewhere in the Midwest, in French Detroit, surgically laid open in Chapter II by Melvin G. Holli. Detroit also experienced the Yankee invasion, but here the Yankees met *feudal* values. We witness French *habitants* failing to rise to the occasion and make money from rising land values. A combination of "didn't expect no town" apathy or culture shock and, as Holli makes clear, traditional peasant land-hunger — unwillingness either to part with land or to view it as a commodity of trade — help to explain this failure.

It may be true that the idea of America's having "no feudal past" has been overdrawn and that feudal contributions to our culture are in need of reassessment. But in Detroit, at least, early French *seigneurial* modes were rapidly swamped once the Yankees came. Holli's chapter exposes for us the outer dimensions that delimited the nonbourgeois, precommercial, and fundamentally archaic social system of French Detroit. Yet as an historian he is also sensitive to many of those folk values that got in the way of "modernization," noting for instance the *habitant's* ability to "coexist with nature." The image of Joseph Campau will stick in the reader's mind: that Detroit-born, French slave-owning gentleman merchant refused to accept compensation from the growing city when it built Griswold Street across his property, because he could not bring himself to recognize the city's authority. Perhaps there is a quiet message to would-be ethnic nationalists in this chapter, where Professor Holli singles out the absence of French schools, of newspapers, and of a literary ambience in Detroit; the French cultural tradition was rich, but mainly oral.

Hugo P. Leaming's study of a racially mixed "nation" is a truly exciting and remarkable rediscovery and re-identification of a lost people. The result of at least ten years of painstaking field work, archival searches, and the sifting of fragmentary and elusive literary sources, this chapter is a fine example of reconstructive history. Racial mixing has not been a large element in American life, and whatever mixed groups did exist were lost to history. Leaming identifies, and portrays as fully as his present research allows, a significant triracial (African-Native American-poor white) tribe, the Ben Ishmaels, a tight seminomadic community that came to number about 10,000 souls.

The doleful and distressing story of the growing harassment of the tribe from the 1840s on, and their eventual threatened sterilization and dispersal by the state of Indiana in the early 1900s, is synthesized here. Leaming categorizes the confrontation of the Ben Ishmaels with American society as a fundamental culture conflict between a migratory hunting-fishing group and a settled commercial society. The latter's racism is vividly portrayed in the personal vendetta against the tribe by the Reverend Oscar C. McCulloch, the "liberal," social gospel Congregational minister whose harsh proposals included ending all charity for the group and taking away their children. After five generations of "shiftlessness," the tribe was regarded as "biologically degenerate" and became a horrible warning example in "eugenics" textbooks. The "Indiana Plan" of 1907, which gave that state the world's first compulsory sterilization law — supported by Progressive reformers — was, we can now see, directed at the Ben Ishmaels.

Leaming's fresh study has even more insights to offer. He confirms the suspicions of a few earlier scholars that the Ishmaels of James Fenimore Cooper's *The Prairie* were an historic people. Scholars of American literature, American Studies, and Western Americana must now revise their accounts accordingly. Beyond this, Leaming provides an added bonus in the suggestion that the people of this dispersed tribe were early examples for the Black Muslim religion — with their Islamic names and styles. Leaming's observations cross over into literature, religion, and anthropology. By piecing together an overview of the tribe's economy, beliefs, and way of life in a masterly fashion, he virtually adds an "ethnic group" to the known American list.

A study of the role of ethnic group leaders by Victor Greene rounds out the first section of the book and leads into the middle section, which focuses on the history of four major ethnic groups in Chicago: Poles, blacks, Jews, and Chicanos. While Peterson, Holli, and Leaming have dealt with groups and value structures that vanished or were dispersed, Greene makes a special comparative study of the leaders of later groups that survived intact within the composite culture; it is thus an attempt to understand to some degree the very processes of group survival. He finds that his model leaders — Swedish ministers, Polish priests, Italian *padrone*-bankers, and Jewish editors — acted as "cultural brokers" for their peoples, oiling and managing the mechanisms of group accommodation to American values, such as the cult of success and social advancement. The voluntary institutions of the ethnic communities, led by conscious role-playing leaders ("traditional modernists" Greene calls them), made possible a large degree of cultural assimilation to American norms *across* ethnic boundaries, without destroying ethnicity. Professor Greene's conclusions throw serious doubts on certain revisionist interpretations which view American society from the late nineteenth century onward as tending toward increasing fragmentation.* He suggests, very usefully, one of the ways in which America *held together* over the years.

The middle section of *The Ethnic Frontier* concerns the frontier in the late nineteenth- and early twentieth-century American city, in particular Chicago, where ethnicity did more than survive — it flourished. Edward R. Kantowicz, in his insightful and original study of the survival of Chicago's large Polish community, has selected one of the most culturally bonded, in-group peoples to be found anywhere. In Europe, Poles survived as Poles over many decades when there was politically no Polish nation. This deep, tenacious attitude toward national identity the Poles brought with them to America and did not lose in the streets of Chicago or Milwaukee. Thus Kantowicz's theme is "Survival Through Solidarity."

Yet there is a price to pay for a group's singlemindedly internalizing its energies. The Poles of Chicago achieved a

---

*In particular Robert Wiebe's *The Segmented Society*, which, though published in 1975, was the result of ideas developed in Wiebe's other writings from the 1960s. The peculiar conditions of the late 1960s in American life, the general turbulence which Arthur Mann has called a sense of "multicrisis" and of the "ungluing" of American society, has passed. Perhaps historians will now begin seeking to explain the centripetal as well as the centrifugal forces in society.

greater sense of wholeness than most ethnic groups, no doubt; but, as Professor Kantowicz indicates, the cost was a diminished influence in the wider non-Polish community. Building from within, Polish Americans created a solid *Polonia*, a nation within a nation, on the basis of their churches, their superb building and loan associations, their parochial schools, and their fraternal associations. Even the major division within the group — between the nationalists and religionists — was milder than splits within comparable groups, such as Lithuanians and Bohemians. (Here, as throughout his chapter, the author makes cross-ethnic comparisons, noting for example that Italians, unlike Poles, were content to use the public school system.) The price Poles paid for commitment to separate treatment within the Catholic Church, and their insistence on Polish priests and parishes, for example, was low general influence in the higher levels of the Church, which lacked Polish leaders. The same was true in the secular realm of city, and for that matter, state and national, politics. There are lessons here, as Professor Kantowicz suggests, not only for future Polish-American leaders but for other ethnic groups as well.

In contrast to the separatism of the Polish community, most black Americans* in Chicago, during the years before the Great Migration of World War I and the 1920s, would have chosen as much local and national political influence as they could win — if circumstances and white politics had permitted. Charles Branham describes and explains the nature of black politics and the choices open to would-be leaders in Chicago at this time. From John Jones, the first black American to hold public office in Illinois, down to Edward H. Wilson, politician of the early 1900s, leaders stood — in varying degrees — for accommodationist politics, for working within the system, following party needs and "delivering the

---

*We have adopted the lower case "b" for "black" in this book. Nothing is intended by this except convenience (considering the great number of times the word appears) and avoidance of the need to capitalize "white" also. The editors believe people should be called what they want to be called, according to their own spelling; in the matter of capitalization of "black," there seems to be no consensus at present among black Americans.

goods," particularly at election time. In this respect the role of black leaders was not so different from that described by Victor Greene of the Swedish, Polish, Italian, and Jewish leaders who acted as cultural brokers or buffers between their own people and the general society. For blacks, however, the choices were even more limited and racially circumscribed. Like the other groups, blacks generally chose to work within the system; but the system paid them less.

Charles Branham's much-needed research on black politics in Chicago between Reconstruction and the Great Migration not only fills a gap in our knowledge of black history for that period, describes the considerable political activity among black Americans, portrays some of their leaders, and indicates the issues with which they were concerned; it also illustrates the abiding faith in America which so many blacks have maintained throughout the worst years of trial and doubt. Professor Branham points to two dominant features of the politics of black Chicago: a general faith in the efficacy of the party system and the "essentially defensive nature" of black politics during this era. There were changes to come.

The Great Migration of blacks from the deeper South to northern cities was, of course, a major turning point in many ways. Not the least of its consequences was the tension it would create between older black residents of cities like Chicago and the newer, less educated, less worldly-wise, rural blacks with southern drawls. Catholic Americans also experienced tensions between the first-comers, Germans and Irish, who dominated the Church, and late-comers like the Poles. Similarly, Jews passed through a period of adjustment when the settled, mainly Germanic and Ashkenazic Jews found themselves facing mass immigration of Yiddish-speaking, synagogue-building, religiously conservative — and sometimes politically radical — Jews from Poland, Hungary, Romania, Russia and elsewhere, the so-called "orientals." Edward Mazur analyzes this division in Chapter VII. Mazur describes the building of the first Chicago Jewish community in the pre-Civil War years, its tightly knit character, its fraternal organizations, its self-confidence ("there were no millionaires ... but all felt independent"), and its Germanic tastes. As early as 1852, however, German-Polish Jews broke away to form their own group. The literary societies, the newspapers, and the various rival social clubs were indicative of the many factions within the Jewish community.

The big challenges, moreover, were still to come, with the arrival of East European Jews in large numbers beginning in the 1880s. Unlike the German-Jews, the newcomers were entering a Chicago which was by now a fully developed industrial-commercial metropolis, and they served the machine economy as factory hands and tailors. They created the ghetto and labor organizations; they brought with them the Yiddish theater and a streetlife of their own. Professor Mazur illustrates the tensions between these *Ostjuden* and the older, settled Jewish communities in the city, as well as the changing residential patterns of Jews, before examining the consequences of this division for politics.

One man managed to straddle the Jewish groups and produce a more or less unified constituency for himself: Henry Horner, a Chicago-born lawyer and probate court judge, was governor of Illinois from 1933 until his death in 1940. Horner's ability to fashion a unified constituency and his various political achievements throw light on the nature of ethnic politics in general, as well as the role of political brokers, and link this chapter with earlier ones, particularly Victor Greene's.

A pioneer scholar of Chicano America, Louise Año Nuevo Kerr, has written the last of the four Chicago chapters in the middle section of the book. As part of her broader work on the Chicago Chicano community, Kerr offers a special study here of how the assimilation process for Chicanos was aborted during World War II and the immediate postwar years. The large influx of *bracero* workers from Mexico brought by government agreement and induced by industrial and railroad recruiting, the subsequent split between these *braceros* and Chicanos long settled in the city, and the emergence of more overt prejudice against "Mexicans" in general during the war years were the historical forces aborting assimilation. Professor Kerr shows that with the coming of peace, the previously solicitous official attitude toward *braceros* faded and the program was phased out. Even so the number of Chicanos in Chicago continued to grow, as legal immigrants and growing numbers of "illegals" swelled the numbers of early residents and ex-*braceros* who managed to stay. Ethnic tensions in Chicago produced surveys and projects concerning the Chicanos, including the Mexican Social Center, which opened in 1945. Yet, Kerr concludes, after a decade of activity in which Chicanos had looked beyond the limits of their settlements in Chicago toward each other, and outwards toward assimilation with the larger community, the process faltered and waned.

The argument summarized here has some very interesting implications, and Professor Kerr's essay contains much more: there are comparisons among Chicanos, Poles, and Italians of income and education in the city, and hints of areas where future research will be needed, such as the recent trend of direct immigration from Mexico and Texas *to the suburbs* — an idea with striking implications.

The problems of group survival and identity have not diminished in more recent decades, and in our final section, "The Struggle Continues," we have deliberately chosen only one major example: the ethnic jockeying for housing. Arnold Hirsch, an imaginative and resourceful young scholar, selects an allegedly "quiescent" period of Chicago history (1940-1960) to illustrate the continuing struggle: the existence during that period of persistent, day-to-day tension and sometimes unrecorded violence over housing. Can we see in these battles over living space a radically transformed — but ancient — peasant land-hunger, the residue of a half-forgotten past that continues to express itself in terms of ethnic and neighborhood solidarity? One is tempted to find atavistic remnants in these struggles, which were begun and carried on by the descendants of European immigrants (WASP names are noticeably absent in the riots). What Hirsch uncovers is a broad community participation in housing "riots"; according to the evidence he marshals, these were not disturbances created or led by "outside agitators" but were communal protests in defense of the neighborhood against undesired "intruders" and would-be settlers.

The well-known riot analyses of the late sixties and the official studies of urban violence always emphasized the role of young unmarried males. Hirsch, in contrast, finds women playing roles during the earlier period, children joining in as aides, and older people fully participating, in what he terms "a grim parody of a community sing," such as the 1949 disturbance at Park Manor. Insofar as whites were successful during the late forties and fifties in excluding blacks from preferred housing, white violence *paid:* was this a direct lesson for the bigger disturbances of the 1960s?

The unfamiliar role of the press in those days — imposing what sometimes amounted to a virtual news blackout on items of racial violence — was in such strong contrast to the media role in the riotous 1960s and later that one must ask the question: why this massive change of policy on the part of the media? The mere spread of television itself in the 1950s, its first decade of real coverage, is part of the answer; but there is more to be said, and future work is needed here. In any event, these earlier housing riots did not enter the living rooms of the nation. As the late Mayor Richard Daley often said, Chicago is a city of neighborhoods. The disturbances of the forties and fifties were kept largely within the ken of those neighborhoods, with the help of a cooperative press.

In Hirsch's study of housing battles we can find all the complexities and ambiguities of the American commitment to egalitarian ideals at loggerheads with the "dream of success" and of a materially better tomorrow in a polycultural society. It is thus a fitting final chapter — not, of course, in any sense a "conclusion" — to *The Ethnic Frontier*.

* * * * *

Conclusions are a long way off. Metaphors for American society seem to be of little help. The "melting pot" has had to go. Israel Zangwill, who did more to popularize the metaphor than anyone, with his melodrama of that name in 1908, turned to music for the source of another metaphor. The young Russian-Jewish hero of his play, David Quixano, yearned to write the "great American symphony." As an amalgamationist (albeit temporarily), Zangwill meant this to imply that the instruments of the orchestra blend together as one voice. It is interesting and ironic that Zangwill's major intellectual opponent, Horace Kallen, champion of "cultural pluralism" and ethnic separatism, also turned to music for his metaphor, speaking of a possible "orchestration of mankind." Presumably, in his orchestration each musical instrument would maintain the integrity of its separate sound and identity.

One image, two opposing lessons: assimilation or fragmentation, melting pot or cultural pluralism. But Americans cannot seek aid in metaphors, however fitting or clever they may be. The Founding Fathers were genuinely confused about America's ethnic future, and though they agreed to admit all and sundry, they had no way of realizing in what great numbers the immigrants would come and how this would transform America. We have still not made up our minds: we fluctuate between separatism and "Americanization," between "desegregation" and "Black Power," between antidiscrimination laws and fears of "affirmative discrimination." The cauldron of American values bubbles on.

Yet America has always been more than the sum of its sometimes warring parts. The vantage point of the social historian, as participant observer, may yet prove useful in the years ahead.

DIVERSE ROOTS

Chapter I

JACQUELINE PETERSON

"Wild" Chicago:
The Formation and Destruction of a Multiracial Community on the Midwestern Frontier, 1816-1837

> *If we write histories of the way in which heterogeneous people arrived on a frontier, come to form themselves into a community . . . we shall be writing something complementary to histories of disintegration. We shall be writing the history of becoming whole.*
>
> — Robert Redfield,
> *The Little Community*

1

Have you built your ship of death, O have you?
O build your ship of death, for you will need it.

And die the death, the long and painful death
that lies between the old self and the new.

— D. H. Lawrence,
"The Ship of Death"

RIDING FROM THE EAST TOWARD
Chicago, a visitor today can see, even in bright midday, the
hulking steel mills of Gary burning miles off in the distance.
Orange and black clouds hang heavily in the sky as if to warn
of some terrible pestilence. Travelers grimly lock themselves
in airtight spaces away from the stench of sulphur, and hurry
by.

Rising with the Chicago Skyway bridge, one wonders what
kind of unheavenly vision William B. Ogden, early
nineteenth-century industrialist and railroad maker, could
have had. A century after him, the corroded assemblage of
steel girders, rail tracks, foundries, breweries, and shipping
cranes fans out below the bridge like a giant black erector set
devastated in a fiery holocaust. Humans do not easily belong
here.

Beyond the curve of the bridge is Wolf Lake. The vision is
startling, for there in the midst of angry waste and decay —
and Wolf Lake itself is an industrial sewage dump — is a
scene which has eluded time: the grassy marshes, frozen in
winter, which swell and flood the lowlands in spring; the

26

shallow lakes and ponds broken only by narrow glacial or man-made ridges; the stunted scrub oak, poplar, and pines; the reed-covered banks lying low in the water so that a canoe need only be pushed up a foot or two to rest on the shore. It is all there, except for the stillness and the wild rice of the marshes.[1]

This neglected landscape is what Chicago must have looked like as late as 1833. It was an inhospitable spot. Its sloughs defied the cart and buggy: "No Bottom" signs marked much of what was later to become a bastion of straight-laced skyscrapers; ladies "calling" in long silk dresses were often seen wading barefoot in the knee-deep mud. Only canoes or hollowed-out skows made their way with ease across the wet grasslands or wound a path through the wild rice blanketing the Chicago River's branches and streams.[2]

The desolation of the unbroken prairie stretching to the south as far as the eye could reach — as far as Springfield — inspired dread and, only occasionally, admiration. The interminable vista reduced people to miniature stature. The gnawing loneliness did not come from a lack of human company; it came rather from the land, a terrain which took nothing in halfway measure.[3]

Old settlers, army scouts, fur trappers, and the Indians before them waited in the silent heat of summer for the brown prairie grasses to burst into flame in the momentary blaze of fusion of sun and horizon. They listened on white winter nights to the thunder of a nor'easter lashing and breaking the frozen piles on the shore and sending the ice-clogged waters of the Chicago River scurrying backward to ravage its tributary banks. Wolves howled at the shore, and weeks without sun or moon made the inhabitants as blindmen whose only guide was the sound of the wind.[4]

It would later occur to easterners that a way to shut out the lonesome vastness was to reshape the landscape. These town builders, less innovative than in need of psychological fortification, laid the imprint of a grid for city streets and in so doing cut through hill, stream, and forest, drained scores of marshes, raised buildings a full story above lake level, and absorbed a population of more than 4,000 within four short years of incorporation (1833-37), whose members filled the more subtle fortresses of judicial, political, religious, and social organization.[5] The master planners had conceived a blueprint for the systematic production of civilization. But it was unnatural; it could have been anywhere.

Its place name was *Checagou*, and that, at least, we owe to its earliest inhabitants. Archaeological diggings at the end of the nineteenth century indicated that prior to the European invasion there were at least twenty-one major Indian villages in Chicago's environs, all located on waterways: the Chicago River and its branches, the Des Plaines, the DuPage, the Calumet, and the lakeshore. In early historic times, the rolling Illinois and Wabash country was held by bands of the Miami and Illinois tribal confederations. The Miami maintained permanent summer residence at Chicago, where native women planted, harvested, and stored maize, squash, and beans. Miami hunters tracked the southern Illinois plains in search of buffalo. In spring and summer whole bands gathered to construct fresh mat-covered houses, to kindle a new fire for the coming year, to attend clan feasts, and to open and bless the sacred medicine bundles. By winter the Miami and the Illinois split into family hunting units to farm the waterways for muskrat and beaver.[6]

The Miami tribe was one of nine major Great Lakes Indian groups which developed, between 1600 and 1760, a distinctive tribal identity and culture. They numbered only 4,000 on the eve of the great white migration, a scant percentage of the approximately 100,000 natives who occupied the region. Living far to the north on the upper shores of Lake Michigan and Lake Superior, the numerically dominant Ojibway (25,000-30,000), adventurers and nomadic hunters, were to become the prototypes for the white fur traders. To the south, along the western shore of Lake Michigan, camped the seminomadic Fox, Sauks, Winnebago, and the Menomini wild rice gatherers. Along the eastern shore lived the farming-hunting Potawatomi and the highly structured urban communities of the Huron and Ottawa farmers. At the bottom bowl of the lake were the Miami and the Illinois tribes.[7]

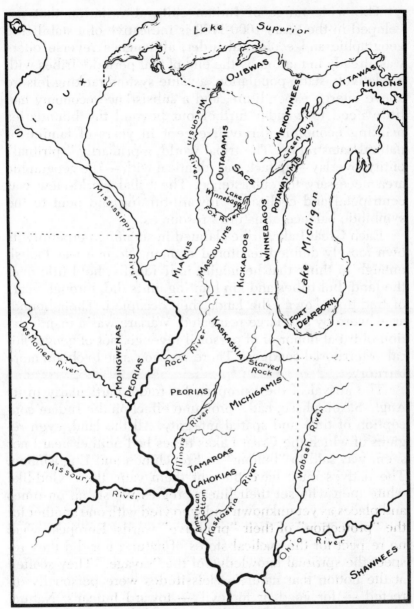

The first inhabitants: Indian tribes of the Great Lakes

The wide range of Indian cultural variation that developed in the years 1600-1760 is indicative of a stabilizing geographic and ecological order, although a reverse effect was already in motion by the end of that period.[8] Tribes with a relatively static population, a value system ranking leisure above energy expenditure, and a subsistence economy had little need to wander further out beyond the boundaries marking economic survival, except in years of famine or natural catastrophe. The tribal world, a primarily "spiritual" entity, overlay — in fact, was identical with — the geographic area necessary for subsistence. The tribal world-view was centripetal and cyclical — inward-turning and bent to the symbiotic balance of nature's resources.

Each Great Lakes tribe claimed in seeming perpetuity its own loosely defined territorial domain. No one was foolish enough to think that he might, individually, hold title over the land; but tribes and kin hunting units did, through years of tradition, "own" the lands they occupied. Their boundaries were by and large respected. Warfare was a manifestation of tribal honor or of personal revenge, not of geographical or territorial conquest. There was no cause to obtain more territory.

The arrival of the European fur trade, particularly in its Anglo-Saxon phase, had a profound effect on the Indian conception of time and spatial integrity. All the land, even regions of which the Great Lakes tribes had neither heard nor seen, was said to "belong" to Frenchmen and Englishmen. The natives must have thought them vain, these God-like white men who set their linear-progressive stamp on times and places as yet unknown and who vied with one another for the "protection" of their "primitive" wards. Europeans had no respect for the cyclical stores of nature; nor did they respect the spiritual knowledge of the "savage." They scoffed at the notion that nature's vicissitudes were personally directed — for good or for evil — toward humans. Natural phenomena were to be understood and then controlled.

Perhaps — although current research signals otherwise — the native momentarily accepted the "superior" notion that a land which had seemed only comfortably to support a population ratio of one per square mile was suddenly limitless in its abundance. Indeed, for the Indian hunter the land was not without limits, and the diminishing herds of elk, caribou, and deer led the natives, already increasingly dependent on European material culture, away from the maize fields into the vast stretches of forest and finally onto the trails of the white fur-trader. These trails, long used by Indian messengers, heavy with wampum and running to announce war, death, birth, or high council, had never been avenues of ingress. They crossed boundaries never surveyed, but which insured the integrity of distinct tribal cultures. With the coming of the fur trade, the ancient roads became highways of destruction.[9]

Competition for hunting grounds and trade routes had by 1800 despoiled most of the diversity and autonomy of the Great Lakes tribes. Early nineteenth-century residents of and visitors to Chicago regarded their Indian neighbors as little more than stray dogs — vermin-infested scavengers. These were, of course, insensitive observers; but a direct result of the fur traffic had indeed been the emergence between 1760 and 1800 of a Pan-Indian culture in the Lakes region, one which mimicked the peripatetic, band-oriented Chippewa social structure and which depended heavily on imported trade goods. The art of pottery-making was lost around 1780. Maize cultivation, once an activity central to the unity of village life, was now carried on primarily for white consumption. Ironically, years of famine brought on by the depletion in game reserves, found Chicago-area Potawatomi buying back at grossly inflated prices corn meal which they had earlier cultivated.[10]

The rapid transition to a fur-trading culture by all of the Great Lakes tribes was propelled by a mistaken supposition that a white-Indian alliance might prove reciprocally enriching. Unfortunately, the disintegration of stable and coexisting tribal structures was the necessary price of the formation of a new social order. Tribal disintegration, even in its earliest stages, had devastating consequences. The tearing of a social fabric woven by oral tradition left the individual native defenseless in the face of a more sophisticated technology.

Indian magic lost face to the gun.

The importation of European goods and foodstuffs destroyed the meaningful division of labor between the sexes. Potters, weavers, basket-makers, stoneworkers, and planters lost their occupations and status rank. Time, once the gentle discipline behind seasons, duties, and ritual, became an albatross. Intricate patterns of consanguineous and affineal recognition and avoidance were destroyed by intermarriage with whites, who refused to "avoid" certain relatives, tantamount to incest. Acceptance of "half-blood" chiefs confused, fragmented, and ultimately defused the potency of clan identification. Above all, the never-ending search for peltry broke up villages and kin groupings and clouded recognition of tribal boundaries. The result was prolonged intertribal war.[11]

Ancient runners' trails from the north, south, and east crossed at Chicago. With the establishment of fur-trading centers at St. Louis, Green Bay, Detroit, Fort Wayne, and Sandusky, the Miami and Illinois saw their hunting grounds invaded from three sides. From the north and west came the Sauk, Fox, and Kickapoo, and from the east marauding Iroquois bands. By the time Fort Dearborn was first built in 1803, the Miami had largely been driven toward the Wabash Valley.[12]

The Potawatomi were already bending under white influence. Earlier habitation near Detroit and Green Bay had exposed their members to intimate contact with French and British traders. Considerable intermarriage had occurred; dark-skinned daughters of mixed marriages were often trained and educated in French-Canadian homes, while sons were encouraged to enter the trade with their fathers. Signs of a metal age were everywhere: elaborate silver breast plates, crosses, earbobs, and crescent-shaped gorgets; iron spear- and arrowheads; copper cooking utensils; copper studs ornamenting the avenging end of tribal war clubs; and finely crafted tomahawks and hatchets.[13]

The influence of educated mixed-bloods within the tribe increased out of all proportion to their actual numbers. By 1833, on the eve of Potawatomi removal, a fair number of

Ancient runners' trails and waterways met at Fort Dearborn (Chicago).

mixed-blood leaders had assumed, by American appointment, "chiefly" status. Such "chiefs" and their followers came eventually into the villages to live side by side with British and French traders, sharing food, equipment, and advice. They built one- or two-room log and bark huts, and in language, dress, and material wealth they took on the trappings of European civilization. Their social movement between white and Indian lifestyles seems to have been fluid. Their services were at least temporarily needed – as buffers between antagonistic cultures.[14] The majority of Potawatomi, meanwhile, still camped in band villages along streams and rivers. Their mat-covered, dome-shaped wigwams did not impinge on the landscape but followed its curves and hollows, forming a loose circle on high, level ground. They retained the language of their ancestors, traditional religious beliefs, tribal authority, and social structure. However, their lives, like those of their mixed-blood leaders, had been irreparably altered. They had become part of a larger community.[15]

No member of the fur-trade world — either white or native — escaped the anguish dealt by the extinction of the "occupation" and the transition to a highly organized and stratified society launched by the Yankee invasion of the Old Northwest. Most white traders were neither prosperous nor urban in outlook. Rather, they blended into the Pan-Indian culture developing in the Great Lakes region, learning Ojibway, the *lingua franca* of the trade, as their Indian counterparts learned a French *patois*. They adopted many of the customs and habits of the tribes with whom they wintered. They too were the victims of lavishly financed entrepreneurial ventures emanating from New York and Montreal, which culminated in a regionwide monopoly between 1811 and 1834 led by John Jacob Astor's American Fur Company.[16] When Astor's profits dipped sharply between 1828 and 1834, he merely sold his Great Lakes holdings and moved the trade beyond the Mississippi. His white and Indian employees — clerks, traders, *voyageurs*, and *engagés* — were left behind to stagger into the new world rising from the East.

Traditionally, the lower Great Lakes fur trade has been divided into pre-Astor entrepreneurial and post-Astor monopoly phases. The division implies that prior to the formation of the American Fur Company access to the trade was open to anyone with gumption, and that profitable competition was carried on by small French-Canadian, British, and mixed-blood traders throughout the region. However, this does not appear to have been the case. Few people of little means realized profits from the fur trade; most lived barely above the subsistence level and were perpetually in debt to supply agencies at Detroit, Montreal, or Michilimackinac. In collusion with British investors, Astor's Southwest Fur Company held a virtual monopoly over the Chicago region prior to the War of 1812, which forced his partners to sell their American interests. A reorganized "American" Fur Company was the result.

What actual competition existed prior to the AFC consisted of eastern capitalists who supplied local middlemen traders through their personal agents at Detroit and Michilimackinac. Such high-level competition survived throughout the Astor regime. The Detroit houses of Conant & Mack and William Brewster financed the ventures of two of the most successful traders at Chicago between 1820 and 1828.[17] The local traders themselves were never able to compete successfully. They lacked both capital and the respect of their employers. Despite a wealth of field experience, such men were regularly refused promotion into the inner executive chambers of the great trading houses. Most seriously, prices of pelts and trade goods were fixed in the East and abroad.[18]

The Chicago of 1816-1834 was thus a community of such middlemen traders and their employees — clerks, *voyageurs*, and *engagés* of French, British, American, Indian, and mixed extraction. They existed for the most part under the aegis of the AFC. Their work, social aspirations, and group solidarity revolved around the profit-and-loss ledger kept by Astor's chief assistants at Michilimackinac, Ramsay Crooks and Robert Stuart, and the annual trek to the "great house" on that island. Thus, in the following discussion of early Chicago lifeways, one must not forget the hidden specter of a ruling class looking sternly down Lake Michigan from its storehouse at Mackinac. Entrance to this ruling class was closed to local men. The exclusion of Chicago residents between 1816 and 1834 meant that they were already accustomed to taking orders from outsiders when the eastern speculators arrived. It also meant that the natural instinct of men to acquire status, dignity, and personal gain would exercise itself in other spheres. This was as true for the Potawatomi as for the British, French-Canadian, and "métis" employees of the trade.

The multiracial settlement of the early 1800s at Chicago was no utopian paradise, though exchanges between Indian and white culture had produced perhaps a less sophisticated ordering of financial and social status than that of the eastern newcomers. Slander, theft, moral outrage, extravagant competition, hints of petty squabbling, and even murder marked the social lives of the old settlers. But they were also marked by the security of clan; a tenuous kind of racial harmony; an easy, enveloping spirit that gathered in the entire village; and a peaceful, irreverent disdain for "progress."

II

The earth keeps some vibration going
There in your heart, and that is you.
And if the people find you can fiddle,
Why fiddle you must, for all your life.

— Edgar Lee Masters,
"Fiddler Jones"

Chicago, on the eve of the Fort Dearborn garrison's second coming in 1816, lay fallow, as it had lain for centuries, awaiting the imperceptible retreat of Lake Michigan's glacial waters to dry out its sandy bottom. Riders on horseback, skirting the sand dunes of the lower bowl of the lake, must have been struck, as they took the northward curve, with the notion that they were treading on ground already claimed. Such men were not geologists, but when they saw the blue mist veiling the high hill in the distance, they named it Blue Island. This mound and its less auspicious neighbor, Stony Island, were by some chance of nature built of sturdier bedrock than the surrounding terrain. The mounds had been spared the leveling scrape of the last glacier. And when American soldiers arrived in 1816, the triple arms of the Chicago River still embraced much of the land for six months of the year.[19]

The lifeways of Chicago's early nineteenth-century inhabitants were of necessity waterways. A liquid boundary arc stretched from Wilmette (*Ouillmette*) at the northern lakeshore, down the north branch of the Chicago River to Wolf Point, following the river's south branch to what became 35th Street, and then cutting across to the southern lakeshore. Within this arc were scattered at least fifteen families whose lives were interdependent — united by blood, occupational survival, common values, and the river. As if by instinct, residents set their log and bark cabins and barns on the high bank and let their lives lean to the current. Such houses rarely had more than one or two rooms and fewer windows, but their inhabitants chose, without need of plat, the level ground and placed their doors toward the river road and the yellow sun-down prairie.

The human landscape was as careless as the meandering river, but was not without design. A respect for space and the needs of field and stable kept households apart; but there was another meaning to the sprawl. Long before a greedy state legislature — anticipating an Illinois-Michigan Canal — put Chicago on the map, and lots, streets, and ward boundaries were platted, the settlement had its geographic divisions. In addition to the Yankee garrison ensconced on the south bank of the main river branch, four other kin groups or clans had claimed their "turf": the British (Mc)Kinzies and their south-ern relatives Clybourne and Hall on the north side; the French-Indian Ouillmette, Beaubien, and LaFramboise families on the far north, west, and south sides.

So dispersed was the settlement that it was impossible for the eye to encompass in a single sweeping glance from the fort's blockhouse, which occupied the highest ground. To an outsider accustomed to the comforting spectacle of shelters huddled together, Chicago seemed hardly to exist at all. United States Army Engineer William H. Keating recorded "but a few huts, inhabited by a miserable race of men, scarcely equal to the Indians from whom they are descended . . . [whose] log or bark houses are low, filthy and disgusting." Yet the town probably had a stable population of more than 150 outside the garrison prior to 1831. By its own enduring admission it was a community.[20]

The view to the south of the fort covered a wide grassy plain that stretched for several miles beyond the garrison's orchards and corn fields at the foot of the stockade. A half-mile down the lakeshore lay several scattered shanties used by the fort and the American Fur Company and a commodi-ous, though jerrybuilt house occupied by Jean Baptiste Beaubien, AFC agent, and his mixed-blood family. To the west the plain was interrupted by a thin stand of trees lining the south branch of the river. Hidden among the timber was the establishment called Hardscrabble.[21]

The name Hardscrabble, perhaps derived from limestone outcroppings in the vicinity, is suggestive of a single farm but actually included at least ten cabins, a major house and post, and sleeping quarters for *voyageurs* spread out along the river bank. Title to this establishment, as to almost every other dwelling in the community, was obscure. Located at the entrance to Mud Lake, the spring portage route to the Des Plaines, Illinois, and Mississippi rivers, Hardscrabble rivaled Beaubien's cabin at the lakefront as a trading location. While Beaubien, as well as American Fur Company agents before him, had the advantage of intercepting the first shipments of trade goods from Detroit and Michilimackinac in late summer, the traders at Hardscrabble were the first to see the *bâteaux* returning heavy with pelts in the spring.

Although Hardscrabble was most consistently occupied by the LaFramboise clan and other mixed-blood traders like Alexander Robinson, it became from time to time the seat of serious competition with the AFC. Prior to being bought out by Astor in 1824, John Crafts, representing Conant & Mack of Detroit, conducted his business there. Afterwards, when Crafts had taken over the lakefront store for the AFC, William H. Wallace of Detroit traded at Hardscrabble until his death in 1827. Antoine Ouillmette, whose home and trading store hugged the lakeshore ten miles north of the principal settlement, also had a connection with the place. Wallace was paying him rent in 1827.[22]

"Improvements" at Chicago lacked the value easterners would later assign to them. Lots and houses were swapped for as little as a cord of wood and a pair of moccasins, or changed hands as the casual winnings off a fast pony or a shrewd card game. Residents almost never registered their property at the early Wayne and Crawford county seats. Their rudely fashioned cabins did not weather the winds or the damp; and the thatched or bark-shingled roofs inevitably invited fire. Like the portable wigwams of their Indian neighbors, such houses had little material worth. However, that is not to say that the early residents did not value permanence and stability; rather, their sense of community was not embodied in a tidy row of whitewashed domiciles legally bound and named.[23]

The "Kinzie mansion" was an exception. Although the Kinzie title is still unrecovered, presumably the house on the north bank opposite the fort was the same property which Jean Baptiste Point du Sable registered and sold in 1800 to Jean Lalime, post interpreter and Kinzie's rival. Lalime resided in the house prior to 1804, when the vituperative red-beard Kinzie arrived and immediately took firm possession.[24]

By 1831 the family had abandoned the mansion to a tenant postmaster. Perched on a sandhill, it had seen fifty years of storm and drift and seemed impatient to slide into the river. In its heyday, the house had been an impressive example of the French *habitant* architecture of the Mississippi Valley, the *poteaux en terre*. It had five rooms — a spacious salon with a small room off each corner — and a wide piazza run-

Typical métis home, *poteaux en terre,* showing the bark-covered upright log structure and French picket fence

Courtesy of The Newberry Library

ning the length of the river side. Behind were stables, a bakehouse, huts for employees, and, characteristically, a garden and orchard fenced by a palisade. Although it was presumably similar to other dwellings in the vicinity, the Kinzie mansion was certainly the largest, and the only house with a palisade.[25]

Smaller homes of similar construction were indiscriminately lumped with "log cabins" by early travelers. However, the typical American "log cabin" of Swedish-Finnish origin was formed of logs set horizontally, with a fireplace at one end of the building. Cabins of this style were not unknown at Chicago, but prior to 1820 they were vastly outnumbered by houses of a primitive French-Canadian design, the *pieux en terre*, whose origins probably owe something to the Huron longhouse.[26] Typically, the French-Canadian dwelling was constructed of roughhewn logs set vertically into a trench and chinked with grass and mud mortar. The thatched or shingled roof was peaked high to facilitate runoff; the fireplace sat astride the roof's center. Ordinarily, the logs were covered with bark slabs, but when the timber was clean-shaven and whitewashed, the structure took on the appearance of stone or frame. It is not surprising that Mark Beaubien's "pretentious" two-story, blue-shuttered tavern, the Sauganash, was mistaken for a New England frame house. There is no evidence, however, that the "I" frame, with its central hall, preceded the Yankee influx of 1833.[27]

Fanning out beyond the "mansion," the numerous members of the Kinzie clan populated the wooded sloughs along the north bank and east of the north branch of the Chicago River. The north side was barely habitable: a dense growth of trees, knee-deep in water, choked out the sunlight, and the bogs were unfit for cultivation. When William B. Ogden's brother-in-law purchased the better part of the "Kinzie Addition" on speculation in the early 1830s, he was forced to initiate an extensive drainage program to render it fit for settlement. Yet from the very beginning this gloomy marsh spelled status, as did the Kinzie name.[28]

Viewed variously as the "father of Chicago" and as a common horse thief, Kinzie in fantasy obscures Kinzie in fact.

Courtesy of Chicago Historical Society

John Kinzie — "Father of Chicago"

A British subject and native of the Grosse Pointe district, Detroit, John Kinzie entered the fur trade early, after developing a fair skill as a silversmith. Ruthlessly ambitious, he soon wormed his way into the Detroit circle of merchant agents and found a patron for his Sandusky, Maumee, and St. Joseph trading "adventures." He apparently realized the potential value of territory in advance of the line of settlement. In 1795, he, his half-brother Thomas Forsyth, and other Detroit entrepreneurs almost succeeded in a conspiracy to grab title to Indian lands in Michigan and Indiana before General Anthony Wayne could finalize the Treaty of Greenville.[29]

Between 1804 and 1812, Kinzie at Chicago and Forsyth at Peoria together carved out a small empire in northern Illinois. Kinzie was unquestionably the most powerful man at Chicago during this period, outranking even the garrison officers who were humbled monthly by Kinzie currency advanced to cover their overdue military pay. Most of the French-Indian inhabitants — the Mirandeaus, Ouillmettes, LaFramboises, and Robinsons — worked for Kinzie and Forsyth during these years, although it might well be a mistake to label them simply *voyageurs* or *engagés*. At least one mixed-blood, Captain Billy Caldwell, son of an Irish officer and a Mohawk mother, served as clerk, a position of some responsibility.[30] But whatever the aspirations of local residents, guile, intimidation, and the soporific effects of British rum were devices Kinzie used to ensure that renegade trappers thought twice before embarking for Detroit to strike a separate bargain for their beaver pelts. Kinzie's recorded malevolence is limited to the murder of Jean Lalime in 1812, but hints of other threats abound.[31]

Despite Kinzie's local influence, he never escaped the pecuniary grasp of the Detroit merchants. Caught in the vast financial octopus that spread its tentacles to Montreal, London, and as far as Peking, Kinzie owed his livelihood to George McDougall, supply agent at Detroit, who in turn made his commission off trade goods sold by Forsyth and Richardson in Montreal. Imprisoned after the Fort Dearborn Massacre in 1812 for his British sympathies, Kinzie's credit collapsed, and he was forced to sell all his real property. His debt to George McDougall alone was a hefty $22,000.[32]

When the second Fort Dearborn garrison returned to rebuild the post in 1816, an aging Kinzie followed. The wrath of the Potawatomi had been aimed at the Americans; thus the Kinzie place, Hardscrabble, J. B. Beaubien's house on the southern lakeshore, and other assorted cabins stood unchanged. Even the scattered remains of the massacre victims, left to rot on the beach, had settled comfortably into temporary sandy graves. The bleached bones seemd an ominous omen, and the garrison hastily shoved them into wooden coffins and dropped them into higher ground. But for John Kinzie it was a homecoming.

Time had been a visitor. The Kinzie family reclaimed its place on the north bank, but John never recovered his former status. The fort, more self-assured after the recent United States victory, had little need for a quarrelsome old trader whose past allegiances were suspect. Still, from a Yankee perspective, a Britisher was more comely than a Frenchman, and before his death in 1828, Kinzie did manage to wangle brief appointments as interpreter and subagent (the latter a gratuity extended by his Indian agent son-in-law).[33]

The American Fur Company took him more seriously. An established trader, well known among the Potawatomi and mixed-blood *voyageurs*, Kinzie was viewed by Ramsay Crooks at Michilimackinac as the new company's key to the consolidation of the Illinois country. However, Kinzie failed to meet Crooks' expectations. Although reinforced by a second AFC trader, J.B. Beaubien, Kinzie's efforts to overwhelm the competition at Chicago were in vain. In desperation, Astor bought out his competitor's agent, John Crafts, and turned control of the Chicago trade over to him. After Crafts' death in 1825, Kinzie again assumed control, with Beaubien retaining one-third share. The Creole Beaubien, who had an Indian wife, received short shrift at the hands of Ramsay Crooks and Robert Stuart at the big house. Beaubien was treated as a perpetual "second" man, even though his lines of connection with the mixed-blood trappers ran deeper than Kinzie's. When Kinzie died, Astor, plagued by a diminishing return, sold his Illinois interests to Gurdon Hubbard, the American Fur Company agent on the Wabash.[34]

The Chicago settlement in Kinzie's day was dependent to a man on the fur trade. The social hierarchy, therefore, tended to coincide with rank in the occupation, at least in the eyes of the Detroit and Michilimackinac suppliers. The Kinzie family stood at the top of the social pyramid, closely followed by the Beaubiens, and then the mixed-blood families of La-Framboise, Ouillmette, Mirandeau, Billy Caldwell, and Alexander Robinson. The Indian *engagés* and hunters occupied the base. Or so the Kinzies would have said. Whether their version of the community structure was accurate, however, was largely unimportant. The subtle mechanisms that draw human beings together are for the most part unspoken; the sum of individual visions that converge to form a collective consciousness is never large enough to explain the whole. The view from the bottom of the social ladder would no doubt have been considerably different. The Beaubiens and LaFramboises were well-loved by the Potawatomi; and Billy Caldwell and Alexander Robinson carried political weight within the local bands.[35]

With the ebb of the "occupation," the struggle for power and position began anew. The Kinzies would quite naturally choose to align with the fort. The Yankee garrison was the self-styled "bringer of civilization," and the Kinzies had always felt culturally superior to their French Creole and Indian neighbors. They had paid the bad debts of their Indian employees and sheltered numerous children of the Ouillmette and Mirandeau lines, who, while serving as maids and stableboys, were given the opportunity to observe Anglo-Saxon manners and virtues. Still, a turn to the fort was a sharp shift in allegiance; the garrison had always seemed alien, an intrusion upon the measured rhythm of the Chicago community.[36]

At some imperceptible point around 1820, however, the fort merged with the community to become for a brief period its ruling class. Why the inhabitants of Chicago allowed this to happen is unknown. It may have been the unconscious drift of a people who had lost their moorings. Direction had always floated down from Detroit or Mackinac, and when — simultaneously — Ramsay Crooks began to pack his bags and the fur boats came home empty, residents panicked. The paternal symbolism of the fort became, at that point, too obvious to resist.

Union with the fort took two forms. For most of Chicago's inhabitants it was a simple matter of making the best use of the fort's presence. A garrison at the northern mouth of a new state would mean the influx of people, though in numbers more vast than the enterprising Beaubiens ever imagined. Overnight, a number of trading cabins were hastily converted to taverns, hostelries, and food-supply stores.[37]

The Kinzies beat a more direct path. Treating the garrison like a territorial clan, they marched through the front gate and brought home as relatives the highest ranking officials. Kinzie's elder son, John Harris, married Connecticut-born Juliette Magill, niece of the government Indian agent, Alexander Wolcott; his daughters· Ellen Marion and Maria Indiana married Alexander Wolcott and Captain (later General) David Hunter, respectively; and his younger son, Robert Allen, married Gwinthlean Whistler, daughter of the com-

mandant of the fort. As added insurance, both John Harris
and Robert Allen became Army officers. These were calculated moves to retain status, and they succeeded. The family's prestige had been on the wane between 1816 and 1828,
but in the eyes of the first Yankee arrivals in 1832-33, Kinzie
was once again the foremost name in Chicago.[38]

Juliette Kinzie was aware of that fact when, on a grey
winter night in 1831, she first stood with her new husband on
the threshold of Elijah Wentworth's trading store and some-
time inn at Wolf Point and looked down the main branch of
the river flowing eastward toward Lake Michigan. To her
right she could make out the silhouette of the two bastions of
Fort Dearborn nestled in the elbow of the river's sharp bend
to the south; to her left, directly across the river from the fort,
was the old Kinzie home hidden somewhere in the darkness
among the sand hills. It was Juliette's initial visit, but she
already knew her place.[39]

A few hours earlier, on the last leg of a three-day journey
on horseback, she, John Harris, and their company of
French-Canadian employees and guides had stumbled up
the frozen bank of the Des Plaines River to warm themselves
in front of Bernardus Laughton's fireplace. Mrs. Kinzie was
shocked to find a stove and carpet in the middle of the Illinois
wilderness. However, her hostess, Mrs. Laughton, was not
comforted by such accoutrements of civilization. Like so
many women — and men — set adrift on the prairie, she
waited nervously, with her arms tightly folded, for the westward advance of her "Eastern family" to catch up.[40]

Mrs. Kinzie had more romantic illusions, born in part of
her husband's success as an Indian agent at Fort Winnebago
and his unusual apprenticeship to Robert Stuart at
Michilimackinac, and in part by her own sense of *noblesse
oblige*. Although she had never been to Chicago, she understood her rank in the social order. With the old trader Kinzie
gone, she and John Harris Kinzie were the acknowledged
leaders of the clan. In view of their Anglo-Saxon ancestry,
they presumably were the leaders of the community as
well.[41]

A new Kinzie kin group began to trickle into the north

Family historian Juliette Kinzie, an easterner with a sense of *noblesse oblige*

side as early as 1816: this was a bastard southern line fathered during the American Revolution by the elder John Kinzie; the mother was a young white woman who had been an Indian captive. Juliette Kinzie and other family historians chose to ignore it. However, its importance for early town development was great indeed, and its numbers, even if unacknowledged, served to reinforce the hegemony of the Kinzie name. The anxious adoption of Yankee values by John Kinzie's legitimate second crop of children must be given a fair share of the credit for the testy snubbing, feuding, and in-house squabbling that marked the relations of the two branches between 1816 and 1833. Unofficial marriages and separations were common enough in unorganized territory, and children of different mothers were usually united without stigma or anguish. When threatened by outside competition or family death, the two sets of Kinzie children could act as a unit, but the alliance was tenuous and easily broken.

In the late 1770s, John Kinzie and a trading companion, Alexander Clark, had either ransomed or been "given" two Giles County, Virginia girls whom Tecumseh's Shawnees had captured in a raid. Margaret and Elizabeth Mackenzie set up housekeeping with John Kinzie and Alexander Clark near Sandusky. Over the next decade John Kinzie had three children: James, William, and Elizabeth. Clark fathered a son, whom he named John Kinzie Clark for his friend.[42]

After the war, the elder Mackenzie, hearing of his daughters' residence at Detroit, rode north to fetch them and their children. For whatever cause — a brutish John Kinzie, a distaste for the northern frontier, or the fear of reprisal due their British husbands — Elizabeth and Margaret fled to Virginia with their children and in short order married Jonas Clybourne and Benjamin Hall, also of Giles County.[43]

As early as 1816, however, a renegade James Kinzie had sought out his natural father and was trading in Chicago. Kinzie apparently took his son in and treated him kindly. His wife Eleanor undoubtedly harbored reservations: as the eldest Kinzie, James threatened the succession rights of John Harris and his younger brother, Robert Allen. Ironically, in terms of native habits and inclinations James was the obvious inheritor of John Kinzie's prairie domain. While Kinzie's daughters were acquiring polish at schools in Detroit and the East, and John and Robert were clerking for the AFC, James and his father worked the trade, chased wolves, raced horses, and got roaring drunk together. Had the rowdy old man lived until 1833, he might well have been a source of embarrassment to his own "refined" children. As it turned out, John Kinzie became a legend; James became the embarrassment.[44]

The southern contingent kept arriving. Word from James of fertile land and a burgeoning Illinois population brought his sister Elizabeth and his mother's and aunt's new families, the Halls and Clybournes. Others who came included John Kinzie Clark (thenceforth known as "Indian Clark"); the Caldwells, relatives of the Halls; and the Virginia-bred Miller brothers, one of whom married Elizabeth Kinzie. By 1829 they were at least twenty strong, too large a population to ignore.[45]

The southerners introduced a diversity of occupations unknown in early Chicago, breaking down the monolithic clutch of the fur trade several years before the easterners brought their crockery and sewing needles. The first attempts were at tavern-keeping, but by 1829 the southern members of the Kinzie clan were also engaged in butchering, tanning, intensive farming, ferrying, and blacksmithing. In addition, it seems clear that the Halls and Clybournes operated a still, Kentucky whiskey having replaced British rum as the liquid staple after 1812. The entire group built their log cabins on the east side of the north branch, running from the forks up to Rolling Meadows, and they settled in, in an uneasy harmony with their northside relatives and neighbors.[46]

The territorial space in which all families met — both occupationally and socially — was Wolf Point, a sort of "free zone." Located on the western, prairie side of the juncture between the two river branches, the Point was about midway between Hardscrabble and Clybourne's cattle yard at Rolling Meadows. A natural intersection, it served for nearly twenty years as the hub of village life — the scene of frolicking, trade, religion, education, and politics.

The territorial space in which all families met, Wolf Point was a sort of "free zone," the hub of village life for twenty years.

The Potawatomi were camping there after 1816, and they did not bother to move when stores and cabins were erected. By 1820 the LaFramboise brothers, mixed-blood "chiefs" Alexander Robinson and Billy Caldwell, and James Kinzie were operating out of trading huts at the Point. Shortly thereafter, James Kinzie built the Wolf Tavern and the Green Tree Tavern, which sported a false second-story front and a gallery, because Kinzie said he "wanted a white man's house." By 1828 the itinerant Methodist preachers Jesse Walker and William See were exhorting audiences weekly in a meeting-house used irregularly as a school for Chicago French-Indian children.[47]

That same year, Mark Beaubien, younger brother of Jean Baptiste Beaubien, was running a tavern which was later expanded into the famed "Sauganash," named for Billy Caldwell, on the bank opposite the Point to the south. Archibald Clybourne and Sam Miller also managed a tavern on the riverbank to the north. A few years later, David Hall and Robert Kinzie erected their own trading stores at the Point; Miller and Hall's tannery operated to the north of Miller's tavern. The Point was, by 1832, a bustling paradise of exotica. Races and accents mingled freely, as if the mere place had momentarily destroyed the compartments in people's minds and the territorial divisions of the town.[48]

Next to survival, "frolicking" was the major preoccupation of the town. No one expected to make a fast buck; that heady prospect had not yet presented itself. Instead, winter and summer, residents spent a part of their day and uncounted evenings at the Point, swapping tales, playing at cards, racing on foot or horseback, trading, dancing, and flying high on corn "likker," rum, and French brandy. Social class and clan affiliation had no bearing here; it was physical prowess, a witty tongue, or a graceful step that brought people into community.

Full-blooded Indian employees of the Kinzies, who were barred from the dinner table, could hold the whole village captive by the gymnastic fluidity of the Discovery Dance at Wolf Point. The French-Indian Beaubien and LaFramboise girls, who had the gayest feet on earth, found admiring partners among the Virginia farmers, who were just as willing as they to dance until dawn. Whiskey was the official solvent. Everyone — even the women — drank, often from the same bottle. It probably was not only the "dissipated" Indians who camped out on the prairie; Virginia boys, too, hitched their ponies and rolled in the long grass to sleep off a night's hilarity. No wonder easterners and ministers were shocked to find a people so ignorant of the healthful, refreshing qualities of water. Liquor was a "problem" all over the state — over the whole region, for that matter.[49]

Perhaps whiskey was seen as a device to break down the barriers between strangers who seemed to have little in common. Or its fantasy-producing properties may have lent a rosier cast to otherwise grey and frightened lives, going nowhere but into the grave. Outwardly, liquor was called a tonic, a body-builder, and a daily necessity for many frontiersmen. That Mark Beaubien's tavern, the Sauganash, was the focal point of the community, therefore, should not seem odd. Its opening in 1826 coincided with several important changes. A declining fur trade threatened the occupational

Courtesy of Chicago Historical Society: Charles D. Mosher, photographer

Mark Beaubien "kept tavern like hell."

security of many of Chicago's earliest residents, and the population was suddenly growing: the Clybournes, Halls, Galloways, Scotts, Sees, more Mirandeaus, and John K. Clark had already arrived; and the children of the first families — the Kinzies and Beaubiens — were returning, fully grown, from school and looking for mates.

There was more to the convergence at Beaubien's place than social need. There were other taverns: Barney Laughton's on the "Aux Plaines," for example, was a favorite resort of the younger Kinzies. Since hospitality was a primary avenue to status, there was always a drinking circle at John Kinzie's, Hardscrabble, and at J.B. Beaubien's house at the lakeshore. But Mark Beaubien, at a pivotal juncture in Chicago's history, offered more: entertainment and a defiant middle finger to the world.[50]

Beaubien joked that he "kept tavern like hell," and he evidently did. From 1826 until 1835, several years after the Yankee flood, when Mark tried a new venture, the Beaubien house was bursting its seams nightly. Mark boarded and slept upwards of twenty or thirty travelers and single townsmen at a time; by 1834 meals and blankets were being served in shifts. No one complained. After his bustling, round wife, the former Monique Nadeau, had cleared the table, Mark commenced the show. He played the fiddle like a madman, and full-blooded Potawatomi, French Creoles, Yankees, and Virginians could not keep from dancing.[51]

Dancing was a principal amusement among French *habitants;* it became, next to drinking, the most significant community-binding ritual at Chicago. Everyone came and everyone danced. Besides the graceful French-Canadian cotillions, residents learned southern reels, the athletic War and Discovery dances, and the sedate social dances of the Potawatomi. There was hardly a man in Chicago in 1832 who did not know how to paint his body, decorate his hair with eagle feathers, and leap in frenzied exultation, terrorizing effete easterners. When town dances were formalized and limited by invitation in the 1830s, they were called *wabanos* or Grand Wa-ba-nos, a reference to an Indian medicine society noted for its all-night revelries. The name retained

the native flavor. But something had changed: the Potawatomi and most of the mixed-bloods were noticeably absent
from the guest lists.[52]

Mark Beaubien liked everyone, and the feeling was
mutual. Among the Yankee reminiscences of Chicago's early
years, the stories of Mark are the most poignant — filled with
memories of handsome Creole charm, mirth, and abundant
kindness to Indians and Yankees alike. His first loves were
fiddle playing, horse racing at the Point (or later across a
rickety bridge erected in front of the Sauganash in 1831,
which he was supposed to be "tending" as toll collector), and
propagation. The most prolific man in town, he fathered
twenty-three children, many of them named after early
settlers he esteemed. He gave away to friends valuable lots
he had purchased when the first Michigan-Illinois Canal
lands were platted and sold; the only land he apparently pos-

**Dancing was a principal amusement among French *habitants;* next
to drinking it was the most important community-binding ritual in
Chicago.**

Courtesy of the Illinois State Historical Library

sessed when Chicago was incorporated as a city in 1837 was a sixty-four-acre tract at the mouth of the Calumet River, which the Indians had given to "their good friend Mark Beaubien" in the 1833 cession.[53]

The Sauganash was more than a watering hole and ballroom; it also saw its share of the meetings of the Chicago Debating Society (J.B. Beaubien presiding in 1831) and of local politics, seen in the chartering of the town. Chicago's incorporation in 1837 was largely a response to outside interest in the Canal and the downstate need for a local county seat. The village had certainly been large enough to incorporate earlier, but it had evidently not occurred to residents to legalize their community status. However, the early settlers were not unmindful of politics and government: when the area was still part of Peoria County between 1825 and 1831, Chicago men, particularly the Virginians, had avidly sought political office.[54]

Prior to 1827, when the Chicago precinct was organized, all offices were appointive. The commissioners at Peoria gave preference to the men of rank in Chicago, but they also appointed men who appeared eager for position. Old John Kinzie and Jean Baptiste Beaubien were made justices of the peace in 1825 (Alexander Wolcott to replace the deceased Kinzie in 1828), and the southern newcomers Archibald Clybourne and John K. Clark received the nod for constable in 1825 and 1827. Local notables also recommended Billy Caldwell's appointment as justice of the peace, and he was installed April 18, 1826.[55] Until 1828, Beaubien, John Kinzie, and Alexander Wolcott, the Indian agent, presided as election judges. James Kinzie later replaced his deceased father in that office. The job of election clerk was in fact that of messenger; the trip to and from Peoria with the voting returns paid $16.00, and that office went to John K. Clark in 1825; Alexander Robinson and Henley Clybourne for the two years following; and the Reverend Jesse Walker in 1832.[56]

A surprisingly large turnout participated in nine elections between 1825 and 1831. Thirty-five men registered in the first general election in 1826; thirty-three in 1828; and thirty-two in 1830. Nearly all of the available Kinzies (Canadian and southern) participated, as did most of the French Creole and mixed-blood men of the south and west sides. No political preference emerged during these three elections; the most obvious comment that can be made of the returns is that the village voted with the fort.[57]

Beginning in 1828, however, local elections were of a different species. Chicagoans took a provincial view of politics, and when the candidates were familiar a high-spirited campaign ensued. The election in 1830 to replace Wolcott as justice of the peace, for instance, drew fifty-six voters. The southerners clamored for office. In 1828, Henley Clybourne was elected constable, along with David Hunter; together they represented the Kinzie clan and the fort. Archibald Clybourne tried unsuccessfully in 1828 and 1830 to win election as justice of the peace, and in 1832 he ran as an Independent for Congress, losing to the Democratic candidate from Jacksonville. But he did manage to win appointment, along with Samuel Miller, in 1828, as trustee for the school section land sale and as treasurer of the First Court of Cook County Commissioners. James Kinzie was elected first sheriff of Cook County in 1831, but in 1832 he was beaten by Stephen Forbes, a Yankee schoolteacher.[58]

Despite the small trickle of Yankees into Chicago by 1832, Forbes' election was the first clear indication that Chicago's old settlers were about to lose the control they had exerted over their own political destinies. The experiment in political and occupational independence had been too brief to test whether Chicagoans could flourish apace with the rest of the state, under their own leadership. Their confusion and fear of autonomy was still manifest in 1833: when given the opportunity to elect a president of the town trustees, they chose Thomas J.V. Owen, the government Indian agent. A month later, Owen concluded, as United States commissioner, a land cession treaty between the united Potawatomi, Ottawa, and Chippewa nations and the government, which in effect disfranchised half of Chicago's residents. J.B. Beaubien's mixed-blood son Madore was a member of Owen's Board of Town Trustees in 1833, and John H. Kinzie was elected president in 1834. Thereafter, not one old settler held a position of importance in town or city government. Early residents simply could not compete with the horde of Yankees who descended on the prairie village between 1832 and 1836.[59]

The problem was not one of wits. Early Chicago settlers placed a surprisingly high value on education. Despite the historical impression that Yankees brought to a spiritually and educationally impoverished hinterland a fully developed cultural matrix, the cornerstone of which was the school, Chicago residents were already remarkably well educated, though somewhat less than godly.

Perhaps because Chicago was in many ways an extension of urban Detroit (Kinzie and the Beaubien brothers were raised in the same Grosse Pointe district), many of the early settlers were more enlightened than their rural counterparts downstate. However, the southern branch of the Kinzie clan certainly lacked literary and scientific polish. No poets, orators, or physicians rose from their ranks; the most prominent Virginian was the lay Methodist exhorter William See, who flapped his long blacksmith arms like a scarecrow when he preached and ended his delivery with something between a curtsy and a bow. See organized the first church meeting at the Point, but he always became so entangled in the web of his own scattered thoughts that he failed to bring many sinners to Christ.[60]

Bereft of formal religion until 1833, the Catholic French Creoles and mixed-bloods and the Episcopal Kinzies turned to the secular world. They packed their sons and daughters off to Detroit boarding and finishing schools or to Isaac McCoy's Indian mission school at Niles, Michigan. The Kinzie family connection was presumably with Mrs. Pattinson's establishment at Detroit, since John Kinzie, desperately in debt in 1815, had sold his Grosse Pointe farm to Mrs. Pattinson's husband. Kinzie's legal sons both attended school in Detroit, and his daughters went on to college in Middletown, Connecticut.[61] Some of the LaFramboise children studied in Detroit, as did the daughters of the Beaubien brothers. Madore and Charles Henry Beaubien, Jean Baptiste's sons by his first marriage to an Ottawa woman, after a stint at McCoy's Indian school were sent to Hamilton College and Princeton.

Captain Billy Caldwell, son of a British army officer, was highly literate, an eloquent speaker, and received a Catholic education at Detroit.[62]

Periodically, the early settlers tried to induce private tutors to come to Chicago. Most of these attempts were ill-fated. Family tutoring was a common means of working one's way west or locating a husband, and most teachers did not last the year. Female teachers paid by the town as late as 1837 still had to be recruited semiannually. The Kinzies and Beaubiens turned to family members: for example, John Harris Kinzie first studied under his father's half brother, Robert Forsyth, and when Charles Henry Beaubien returned from Princeton, he ran a school at home for the Beaubien-LaFramboise children.[63]

The first Yankee schoolteacher arrived unsolicited in 1830. A native of Vermont, Stephen Forbes was received with a mixture of apprehension and curiosity by those who had met his sister, the priggish Mrs. Laughton. Yet there was dire need for his services: the Beaubien and LaFramboise roosts were bursting. Forbes taught in the Beaubien house for a year and then quit to become sheriff. Perhaps he disliked his clientele; the pupils were overwhelmingly of mixed blood. The southerners did not send their offspring to Forbes' school; in fact, there is no indication that children on the north branch received any education at all until the town school districts were formed in 1837.[64]

In 1832, Thomas Watkins taught in the meeting-house at the Point. His pupils, again, were largely French-Indian, although a growing number of Yankee families sent their children. Watkins apparently also agreed to take full-blooded Indian children into the school. Billy Caldwell, convinced that literacy was a key to native survival, offered to pay the tuition of any Potawatomi child who would wear European clothing. None accepted his offer.[65]

The year 1833 was pivotal in the annals of Chicago religion and education, as it was in almost every other sphere. The return of the Fort Dearborn garrison during the Black Hawk War of 1832 brought an eastern Presbyterian minister, the Reverend Jeremiah Porter, and a schoolmarm from

Michilimackinac with dreams of a female academy. Chicago's ungodliness scandalized Porter, but he quickly formed a church group around a coterie of eastern arrivals of 1831-32 and members of the garrison. Porter's group was not so much pious or devout as it was conscious of a need for formality. Porter shared the meeting-house at the Point with the Methodists for a brief time, but the congregation pushed for a separate church building. Porter's first communion was embellished with the use of Major Wilcox' silver service. The new six-hundred-dollar church opened its doors six months later. Unfortunately, women filled out the congregation while their men caused "a wanton abuse of the holy day by ... sin[ning] against clear light and abus[ing] divine compassion and love." On that communion Sunday enterprising Yankee males were busy unloading two vessels in the new harbor.[66]

The Methodists still operated at the Point, reinforced in 1831 and 1833 by the Reverends Stephen Beggs and Jesse Walker, both southerners. By 1834 a revivalistic spirit produced a host of new members, primarily of southern origin, who erected a church on the north side. At the time, it seemed a logical place to build, since most of the Kinzie-Clybourne-Hall clan had settled on the north branch. However, it was not long before the Methodists felt "outclassed" by the wealthy Yankees settling in Ogden's improved "Kinzie's Addition." The congregation bodily moved its church across the river in 1836 to the area just west of the fort, Chicago's new "free zone."[67]

Although Baptists, Catholics, and Episcopalians each established a church in 1833, religion exerted little control over the everyday social and moral lives of most residents. An exception was the devout collection of Episcopalian Methodists who met at the home of Mark Noble on Thursday evenings for prayer and discussion. The group organized the first Sunday School in 1832, which was interdenominational in character.[68] Noble's enthusiastic followers represented in their piety and temperance the only persons in town — with the possible exception of some of Porter's "highfalutin" Presbyterians — who resisted the understandably attractive urge to accommodate themselves to the casual transcultural life-

Sauganash Tavern—favorite haunt of Chicago pioneers

style around them. They did not join Beaubien's Debating Society; nor did they frequent the favorite haunts of early residents, the Sauganash and Laughton's Tavern. Instead, they performed charitable acts, nourishing the school system and church attendance, and, though books were scarce, promoting an interest in literature. Mark Noble carried his entire library to the Sunday School wrapped in his pocket handkerchief. Noble's own timber built the Methodists' northside chapel. Arthur Bronson, East Coast financier and cohort of William B. Ogden, was so impressed with Noble's endeavors that he shipped one hundred free books to the school.[69]

Eighteen thirty-three was a time of ambivalence and guarded optimism. The population had doubled since 1831. There was talk of a canal, of pre-emption, of a land cession, and of the official incorporation of Chicago as a county seat, with all the legal and social trappings. But no one was sure any of this would come about. Lots in the emerging central business district on the south side, formed by the sale of the township's school section, were still going for as little as $200 and were traded away with nonchalance. The Yankee influx had been gradual, so gradual that one easterner's assimilation into the lifeways of the older settlers was accomplished before his next potential ally against the reigning social order arrived.[70]

The Yankee influence was felt in institutional ways: there were churches and classical academies; there were also ordinances for fire, garbage disposal, vagrant cattle, shooting, and horse-racing; and lawyers predominated among the arrivals of 1833. But the more subtle matrix of social habits and relations had not been significantly altered. Hospitality (rather than privacy and exclusivity), essential to the native, French Creole, and southern prestige systems, was still an unspoken requirement. Personal antagonisms that might generate complex patterns of avoidance in private life were inappropriate when the community gathered to act out its wholeness. There were no "private" parties. One's home, more than just a compartment for the family and one's prejudices, displayed the extent of one's generosity. A spacious house, able to fit the whole crowd under its rafters, was a distinct social attribute.[71]

The first Yankees did not build spacious homes; in fact, most rented back rooms or boarded at the Sauganash or at one of James Kinzie's taverns. In a way they became adopted relatives who danced, drank, and caroused until dawn, and sometimes through the following day with the rest. Eastern visitors were startled to see dark-skinned maidens with beaded leggings under their black stroud dresses jigging with army officers, and genteel ladies twirling on the arms of southern hayseeds. All under the merry auspices of Mark Beaubien and his fiddle.[72]

Wolf-hunting, horse-racing, card-sharking, and shooting matches were still in vogue, although mostly removed beyond the town limits. Army officers and later "pillars of the city" met weekly — on Wednesday morning — at the Sauganash for a bracer, before heading out over the wolf-bedeviled prairie with Madore Beaubien, in brilliant headdress, whooping at the forefront. Jeremiah Porter noticed, to his chagrin, that there were as many Yankees as French-Canadians gambling at cards on the Sabbath (a reputable Sunday pastime for French *habitants*). French *carioles* raced across the ice in winter, and those who lacked a sleigh built their own rude version from timber cut on the north side. Ice-skating by moonlight was a favorite community activity, concluded, as usual, by a rowdy warming at the Sauganash.[73]

Chicago residents did not need holidays to celebrate. However, New Year's Eve warranted something spectacular, particularly for the French-Canadians. In the early years the *Guignolée* and the *Reveillon* enlivened New Year's festivities all over the territory. Around 1833, Madore Beaubien and the "boys" fitted up the garrison's sizable skow with runners and made the rounds of village houses, adding sleigh party revelers at each stop. By the end of the evening the excitement was so out of hand that the group completely broke up a local tavern. The next morning, the "boys" paid $800 in damages without blinking an eye.[74]

There was something frenetic about the village scene. An unhoped-for material prosperity was in the wind, and residents rocked nervously on their heels — waiting. But there was also the scent of death. Black Hawk was defeated. His people, pushed into the turbulent Mississippi, fell like straw before the American scythe. Stragglers on the shore were dying of starvation or at the hands of the Sioux. What were white folks to do? What was anyone to do, in 1833, but wait?[75]

III. EPILOGUE

> . . . If lost to honor and to pride
> Thou wilt become the white man's bride
> Then go within the strong armed wall
> Partake the pomp of brilliant hall
> And wreath above thy maiden brow
> The sparkling gems to which they bow.
>
> — "The Muse of the Forest"
> Written for *The Chicago Democrat*,
> February 18, 1834

Chicago's future was secured by the tail end of summer 1833. The town received its corporate seal, elected its first set of trustees, and let it be known that the school section was to be auctioned off in order to raise funds for civic improvements, notably a courthouse. Settlers were notified of their pre-emption rights, and there was a dash — at least by some — to register their homesteads. The United Potawatomi, Chippewa, and Ottawa nation ceded all its land east of the Mississippi in exchange for 5,000,000 acres of promised soil west of the Missouri.*[76]

The year 1833 began with a sigh of relief. The Indian war was over, and the cholera that left a hundred army graves on the south bank had spent its malignancy in the winter freeze. General Scott's remaining troops were on their way east to spread the news about a lush green wilderness in Wisconsin and northern Illinois. Food, rationed during the Black Hawk scare, was once more in adequate supply. People got back to the normal business of running their small industries and drinking it up at Beaubien's.[77]

But it was not quite the same. The Yankee stream continued, increasing its breadth and current. The newcomers were primarily young men, single and ambitious, whose main goal in life was not to amass great wealth (although many would change their minds when given the opportunity), but to find a place that suited them and their talents, a place with which to grow. Chicago was not the first stop for many, nor the last for a few. The majority probably agreed, however, that Chicago was an advantageous place to settle during the 1830s. All occupational classes were arriving. Whereas the 1831-32 migration had seen a lopsided preponderance of merchants and a few professionals, 1833 witnessed a flock of lawyers and tradesmen who anticipated a growing urban center.[78]

In small numbers the New Englanders seemed to have been assimilated. Yet one by one they added cement to a structurally different world-view. Linear progress, historians

*A surprising number of French-Indians and non-Indian husbands went west with the Potawatomi. Over half of the registered voters between 1828 and 1830 were, or were thought to be, in Indian country during the 1850s.

would later call it: the belief that the future was only attaina-
ble by cheating the present, by conserving time, currency,
energy, and emotion, and by walking a straight line. The
Indians did not think people's lives should be bottled up like
so much stale spring water. Nor did the French or the southerners (or Old John Kinzie when he lived). The Indians
thought rather that the circle was the more natural version of
things. The sun was round, the year was round, and if a hill
was round, what sense did it make to cut a straight line
through it?

Nineteenth-century Yankees, obsessed with their right-
ness, could not wean the native and his French sympathizer
away from such notions. The simultaneous disappearance of
the French, the Canadian métis, and the Indian from Illinois
indicates a similarity in world-view and survival technique
not generally granted significance. The lack of Yankee initiative among *habitants* of the Mississippi valley may be
traced to more than an enslaving land system. The New Englanders had more success with the Kinzies and their southern
kinsmen, although the latter had difficulty adjusting to
Yankee aloofness and smug moralism as the years passed.[79]

The transition seemed relatively simple in 1833. Many of
the town elders were dead: Francis LaFramboise, John Kinzie, Benjamin Hall, and Alexander Wolcott. Young men remained: like their Yankee counterparts, most were under
thirty-five, and a fair share of those were under twenty-five.
Before the horde of speculators arrived briefly in 1833 for the
sale of the school section, and came to stay during the
Illinois-Michigan Canal sales of 1835, Chicago was a town of
"boys."

There was something innocent, almost naive, about the
young men's optimism. Robert Allen, John Kinzie's youngest
son, pre-empted 160 acres on the north bank, but rejected an
opportunity to register land at the Point because the family
would never use all they had acquired. Early in 1833, while
on an eastern buying trip for his trading store, the same young
man was flabbergasted when he was offered $20,000 — by a
shrewder judge of land values than he, Mr. Arthur Bronson —
for his tract of swamp. In 1835, Bronson sold the acreage to

Mark Beaubien: "Didn't expect no town" — Chicago, 1840.

his silent partner, Samuel Butler, for $100,000. In late sum-
mer of the same year, William B. Ogden, newly arrived to
dispose of his brother-in-law's property, sold one-third of the
property for the same amount. Ogden was not impressed at
the time. But Robert Allen Kinzie was; his family might have
been millionaires had they known.[80]

Mark Beaubien, only thirty-three and one of the "boys"
himself, continued to pack travelers into the Sauganash, put-
ting up curtains as sleeping partitions. When they laid out the
town in 1831, his tavern sat in the middle of the street.
"Didn't expect no town," he said; and the ease with which he
continued to give away his lots suggests that he didn't care if
it came.[81] Madore Beaubien took a Yankee partner, John
Boyer, and married his daughter. The store foundered, but
Madore had a high time selling fancy vests, hats, and laces to
his Indian friends while the venture lasted. Like his uncle
Mark, he sold his lots too early to share in any of the wealth.
And he lost his Yankee wife; Madore married, secondly, a

Potawatomi woman.[82]

The southerners expanded their cattle raising, butchering, and tanning operation at Rolling Meadows and cashed in on the eastern demand for beef. The newly dredged harbor begun in 1833 turned meatpacking into Chicago's most profitable business in the 1830s, with the exception of platting and selling "paper towns." Archibald Clybourne, the man probably least admired by the old settlers, was easily the most successful in the later city. This negative relationship held true for John H. Kinzie as well, who retained his former prestige as leader of the north side's first family until his death, even though he proved a financial lightweight.[83]

Chicago's French-Indian families and Kinzie's employees appeared to resent his growing air of condescension. Even in the early years, when Kinzie was Indian agent at Fort Winnebago, the habitually sly, joking French-Canadian *engagés* referred to him as "Quinze Nez." Creole *voyageurs* made an art of the French-English double entendre: they called the

Judge of Probate, for example, "le juge trop bête." Always sniffing for a way up, Kinzie did not fool his employees. Worse yet was Kinzie's romance-stricken wife, who reveled in her husband's noble attention to the poor "savage."[84]

The route an old settler had to take to rise in the increasingly eastern social milieu, and the amount of selling out that had to occur, is best illustrated by Kinzie's use of his wife's illusions. During the 1830s easterners in Chicago took a fancy to the finer aspects of Indian culture. Yankees were not particularly interested in seeing the display firsthand, but they welcomed Kinzie's tales of the wilderness, his rendition of sacred Potawatomi legend, his war paint, and his mock stag dance. Incredibly, he was so brash as to take an Indian show (in which he was the principal star) to the 1834-35 state legislature at Jacksonville for the purpose of "delighting" the delegates into passing a bill funding the proposed canal which was to cross land more or less taken from the Indians only a year earlier. Madore Beaubien must have burned down to his toes.[85]

The unmarried Yankee men lived together at the several boarding houses in a manner akin to rival fraternities. They gave in for the most part to the wilder ways of the young early settlers. John Wentworth, one of the "boys" for a time, and later mayor, claimed that he had never seen so much smoking and drinking. He found that the early churches also resembled fraternities, and he urged all of his friends to attend the Baptist services, where the best crowd gathered. The more contemplative Yankees, not so much averse to as timid about the drinking and shouting, were seated nightly in one or the other dry goods store playing checkers. Such games provided a political forum for the numerous young lawyers in town, who immediately swept novice officeholders like James Kinzie, Madore Beaubien, and Samuel Miller off their feet and out of the governmental door.[86]

Aside from politics, there was still in 1833 a healthy rapport among the young men. The Yankees relished a horse race as much as the early residents, and Mark Beaubien's daughters, as well as the dapper gentleman himself, drew the Yankees in as if magnetized. The old territorial divisions of the town were in a state of confusion, and new lines of class and race demarcation had not yet been drawn. Nearly all the Yankees lived on the near south side, the "free zone" which had replaced the Point as the central community meeting place. The boarding houses provided a kind of protective limbo, around which the bewildering array of conflicting values clashed but did not affect the people's lives. They were in the eye of the storm, and Mark Beaubien was Peter Pan. The "boys" were never going to grow up.[87]

The town found its adulthood abruptly and painfully. In early September 1833, the newly elected president of the town board, Robert C.V. Owen, called a grand council of the chiefs and headmen of the United Indian nations to discuss treaty arrangements for their removal west of the Mississippi. Owen, acting in his capacity as United States Government Commissioner, opened the proceedings by explaining to the assembly that he had heard that they wished to sell their lands. This was a blatant untruth; but the Indians unfortunately had no precedent for supposing that they would be allowed to keep their territory, even if they chose to. They deliberated.[88]

The 5,000 men, women, and children took their time, however, spending nearly three weeks at Chicago. They camped along the lakeshore and at the Point and enlarged their already mammoth debts to the local white traders, Robert Allen Kinzie among them. The bulk of the traffic was in liquor — alcohol enough to put them all in a drunken stupor for a week. Tipsy families wept together beside their tents, and in the sober morning there was still the wailing.[89]

On September 26 the treaty was concluded. Under a spacious open shed, specially constructed on the north side of the river for the occasion, the officers and spectators gathered. The chiefs did not arrive until the sun was red in the sky, and again they delayed while two old chiefs, wobbling with whiskey, made incoherent rebuttals. Then they signed. The commissioners sat with the sundown blaze in their faces, appearing, ironically, as brothers of the men they were herding away. Facing east, the Indians huddled in darkness.[90]

The spectacle rocked the inner heart of the town. Yankees were horrified at so pagan and slovenly a group; sympathy gave way to disgust. "Half-breeds" who had been raised as part of the community shunned their previous friends. By order of the court in 1834, Justice of the Peace Beaubien publicly posted a "no trespassing" sign at Hardscrabble. White traders, new and old, hustled the sales while they could and then went home to estimate the amount of indebtedness the tribe had accumulated. The treaty allotted $150,000 to settle past liens, but the final settlement was $175,000. Undoubtedly many traders inflated the sum due; it seems that every white man in Chicago got a slice. The American Fur Company received an outrageous $20,000. The various members of the Kinzie family, including some of the Forsyths, received the next largest payment.[91]

In addition to the land west of the Missouri and the allotment to collectors, the treaty provided for cash payment in lieu of reservations, which was requested by innumerable "mixed-bloods" who wished to remain in Chicago. However, only three applicants' reservations were granted; the rest were given a pittance, ranging downward from $1800. A hungry Kinzie family again received a sizable grant, far exceeding the sums distributed among the French-Indians. The fourth and fifth clauses of the treaty provided for a twenty-year annual payment of $14,000, and $100,000 in goods to be distributed after ratification.[92] Goods worth $65,000 were presented to the nation on October 4. In preparation, the traders had ordered vast stores of whiskey; one trader alone asked for fifteen barrels. Fortunately, a prevailing south wind hindered ship passage up the river, and the traders were forced to content themselves with selling the supply on hand, as well as overpriced trinkets, blankets, knives, and so forth.[93]

It was black Sunday. Worshipers did the only thing respectable people knew how to do: they hid within their churches from the drunken shouting, wailing, and fleecing. And they prayed. An old Indian stood playing a "jew" harp at the Reverend Jeremiah Porter's door, unaware that he was

Hamilton-educated, the mixed-blood Madore Beaubien was one of Chicago's "golden youngsters."

interrupting a religious service. When the payment was concluded, high winds and a driving rain sent the traders fleeing
back into their cabins. The Indians went back to their camp at
the Aux Plaines with $30,000 in silver. Porter thought that
someone's prayer had been answered.[94]

In the months to come, the numerous mixed-blood residents
at Chicago wrenched their hearts over whether to remove
with their Potawatomi kinsmen or stay. Many wanted to remain; the sacred ground in which their grandfathers were
buried meant more to people of native extraction than to the
Yankees who were about to gain the territory. But the breach
was irreparable. Indians and mixed-blood settlers willing to
forgive were treated as some ghastly sore, too horrible to look
at. The sore would not heal; it festered because the source
of the disease was inside the Yankee eye. In time the Indian
became the real evil in people's minds.[95]

Typical of the educated "mixed-bloods," Madore Beaubien was no fool. One of Chicago's "golden youngsters," he
had wanted his share of power. Years later, as he wasted away
on a reservation in Kansas, he explained that he had yearned
for recognition in the white world. Denied that, he sought
prestige within the tribe. Beaubien and most of his cohorts
joined the local Potawatomi bands in 1835. Painted in the
colors of death, they made their final turn through the streets
already covering the ancient trails and fields, dancing their
way out of vision, their shrieks sticking in the Americans'
ears.[96]

In 1835 the land sales — and one of the most incredible
heights of speculative fancy the West had ever seen — began.
Chicago was again a one-horse town; everyone dealt in lots.
But the land bore a stigma: by 1838 the majority of Chicago's
newer residents, as well as a few old ones who had managed
to keep their heads long enough to see the six-figure totals,
were bankrupt.[97]

It would be easy to suggest that William B. Ogden was
elected the first mayor of Chicago, incorporated in 1837, because wealth was the measure of power. However, it seems

just as likely that residents could not stand to face someone more familiar in their midst. New blood, clean blood, a new family, a new community might root and bloom in the desecrated land and make it whole once more.

Chapter II

MELVIN G. HOLLI

French Detroit: The Clash of Feudal and Yankee Values

I listen in vain for the melodies which were once the prelude to many joyous hours of early manhood. But, instead, my ear is larumed by the shriek of the steam-whistle and the laborious snort of the propeller. All announce that on these shores and waters the age of the practical, hard-working, money-getting Yankee is upon us, and that the careless, laughter-loving Frenchman's day is over.

— Bela Hubbard,
Reminiscence (1872)

$\mathbf{F}$OUNDED IN 1701 BY ANTOINE DE LA Mothe Cadillac, Detroit remained a fur-trading post and a garrison town for the first century and a quarter of its existence. Much of Detroit's entrepôt importance derived from her presence on one of the continent's longest inland waterways and on one of the eighteenth century's most important lines of commerce reaching into the North American interior. Her name "de troit," which translates as "strait," described the narrow connecting waters between Lakes Erie and Huron, which were of military significance for checking the incursions of the English and Iroquois Indians into the French fur domain. The French had hoped to attract to the Detroit garrison friendly Indians who would make summer camps as well as more permanent abodes there, and from which they would radiate forth to trap and gather valuable furs for transshipment to the European market. The French had penetrated deep into the interior of the continent and had engrossed much of the rich peltry trade. Yet English and Dutch interlopers were a continual threat to the French, with their lower priced goods and sometimes superior quality. Cadillac theorized that by establishing a French military presence on the lower lakes at a strategic bottleneck, which the French measured as "one gunshot" across, they could interdict the unwelcome incursions of outsiders.[1]

The first century and a quarter of Detroit's social history stems not from the Yankees of New England or the cavaliers of Virginia but from the *seigneurs* of New France. Although the historical process that dictated the founding of Detroit flowed generally from commercial and bourgeois motives on the part of French policymakers, this was not the case with

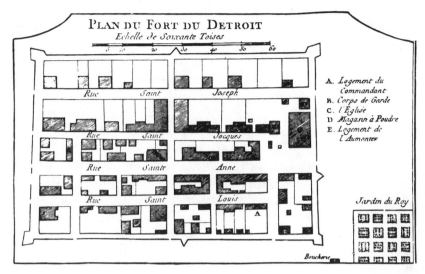

From *Bellin's* Atlas of 1764

French military presence in Detroit, 1763

the actual inhabitants of Detroit. The *habitants* were not full-fledged members of a bourgeois culture, nor was their economic behavior shaped significantly by the market.[2] Quite the contrary. The evidence clearly shows that the French *habitant,* though an important link to the capitalism of western Europe, did not share fully in the economic ethic that pervaded the Atlantic community of the eighteenth century or even the hill country of contemporaneous New England. Very little of the new business culture rubbed off on him. He was in effect the forest harvester of a one-crop economy that was controlled and regulated by a rigid governmental licensing system and a system of political control that discouraged almost any form of enterprise that did not directly support the peltry traffic. Physical isolation alone cannot account for the retrogressive social and economic behavior later displayed by the French, but their culture can: it was precommercial and immobilized by an archaic social system — *seigneurialism.*

Ironically, while *seigneurialism* was showing signs of

decay in seventeenth-century France, it was to be given a new vitality by the French colonizers of Canada. Its decline in France has often been attributed to the passing of military necessity and the growth of absentee proprietorships of *seigneurialism*, which helped to sever the "personal nexus" which had held the vassal to his lord. It was precisely these elements that breathed new life into old forms in the New World. Warlike Indians to the north and west, and hostile Dutchmen and Englishmen to the south revived its military aspect, and the reinstallation of the *seigneur* on his estate as resident proprietor restored that paternalistic and vital "personal nexus." Both gave the system a "new lease on life," which enabled it to "outlive its parent stem in France." The *seigneurialism* of French Canada bore a "closer resemblance to French feudalism of an earlier period than to French *seigneurialism* of the seventeenth and eighteenth centuries," wrote the noted authority William B. Munro.[3] And for good reason: Canada of the seventeenth and eighteenth centuries faced conditions which, though no longer found in France, were similar to those that had prompted feudalism in the France of an earlier age. Thus "the twilight of European feudalism" was more prolonged in French Canada than in any other part of North America.[4]

Seigneurialism's burdens in New France were not radically different from those of the old country and familiar to students of European history. The chief dues were *corvée*, *centes et rentes*, and *lods et ventes*, which obligated the tenant to work the *seigneur's* land a specified number of days each year, to pay both a fee and annual rent for the plot he occupied on the *seigneur's* estate, and to share one-twelfth of the sale price of his land when it passed to other than his direct relatives.[5] The two dominant forms of land tenure, *en fief et seigneurie* and *en rôture* drew with them other ancient appendages of feudalism, such as the royal *corvée*, which obligated the *habitant* to work on roads and fortifications, particularly the latter since they were so essential to French survival during the colonial wars of the eighteenth century. One of the feudal obligations common throughout New France was the duty of the tenant to have his grain ground in

the lord's mill, upon pain of a double toll or even confisca-
tion. The *habitant* was also required to give formal homage to
his *seigneur* and to submit litigation and disputes for the
seigneur's judgment.[6]

The "*seigneurial* drama" was also enriched by the church,
which acknowledged the *seigneur's* special status and ac-
corded him honorary privileges denied to ordinary laymen.
On large Canadian *seigneuries* the curé often resided at the
manor house, and the parish boundaries frequently coincided with those of the lord's estate. The *seigneur* was generally the pre-eminent layman and was given a special pew
on the right hand side of the main entrance of the church,
near the altar rail. He was also offered special prayers and
was the first to receive the sacraments as well as palms and
ashes on holy days. In all religious processions he took pre-
cedence immediately after the priest. It was at the door of the
church that the *seigneur* reminded his *habitants* each fall that
their dues and rents were payable to him on St. Martin's Day.
On New Year's Day the *habitants* generally called at the
seigneur's manor to receive his blessing for the new year.
Although the ecclesiastical privileges and status granted to
the *seigneur* were not particularly burdensome to the *habitants*, they served in an important way to symbolically link
the spiritual and temporal lords of the domain.[7] This then
was the feudal social model transplanted to the new world.

Not only did *seigneurialism* impart to New France an archaic social organization, but the all-important fur trade and
contact with the Indian also tended to draw the *habitants*
further from the bourgeois ideal of society. The sons of
habitants who became rangers in the "bush" cut even further
their links to contemporary Western society. General Thomas
Gage lamented to Jeffry Amherst in 1762 that the colony lost
men irretrievably to the voyageur system: "Nothing was more
common, than for the Servants whom the Merchants hired to
work their Boats, and assist in their Trade, through long habit
of Indian manners and customs, at length to adopt their way
of life, to intermarry with them and turn Savages." Some
"hundreds" of men, he supposed, "will never return to their
country." Even the *habitants* in the more settled portions of

the domain were affected by the Indian. Detroiters in 1765, according to George Croghan, were "in imitation of the Indians, whose manners and customs they have entirely adopted, and cannot subsist without them. The men, women, and children speak the Indian tongue perfectly well."

The entire lifestyle of the *habitant* in Detroit was profoundly influenced by the fur trade.[8] His canoe, his snowshoe, his moccasin or bootpac, his route of travel, and his techniques for catching beaver were taken from the Indian trapper. In exchange the *habitant* gave the Indian metal traps and guns, steel knives and pots — the benefits of an iron-age civilization. The *habitant,* unlike the English settler but like the fur-trapping Indian, seldom ventured inland from the waters, and his strip villages hugged the shores and rivers of the Great Lakes. The waterways were his highways. Road-building was not his forte. Pursuing fur-bearers by canoe to the headwaters of river systems was.

Detroit as a part of New France and then Upper Canada shared all of the disabilities — or privileges, if one prefers — of the *ancien régime.* Lamothe Cadillac's installation in 1701 and 1707 as commandant, *seigneur,* and fur factor in Detroit is a classic example of the imposition of a premodern social system on a people and a large geographic area at a time when northwestern Atlantic nation-states had advanced well into the first important phases of social and economic modernization. Cadillac had authority to monopolize, license, and restrict all classes of trade and prescribe classes of work for the inhabitants of a large hinterland stretching a thousand miles to the north and west of Detroit. He granted lands by feudal tenure, required from his vassals the customary prerequisites and emoluments, engrossed the feudal monopolies of the gristmill, and licensed and regulated all commerce and trade. This imposition of an archaic social system occurred a half century after Yankee settlers of Massachusetts had abandoned communal land tenure and were moving toward a modernized form of holding land wealth, namely, freehold tenure.[9] These two different modes of holding the community's most tangible forms of wealth, of organizing society, and of conducting commerce clearly capture some of the most vital and important differences between modernizing and premodern societies.

Seigneurialism in Detroit also adjusted to the Indian trade. By engrossing its most lucrative aspect, the fur traffic, the *seigneur*-commandant was also given a monopoly on the sale of gunpowder, wine, and brandy and was authorized to regulate the flow of peltries by licenses to the beaver country as well as permissions to Montreal for provisions. The result was that almost all beaver pelts moved under the seal of the commandant and his associates or later successors. Residents of Detroit were banned from trafficking in goods from Montreal, except for their own consumption and some incidental Indian trade. The *habitant's* least encumbered right was that of raising food for his own subsistence. On his fief the right to minerals, timber, firewood, and stone were reserved by the *seigneur* or the king. The raw muscles and backs of voyageurs did not escape exaction either. They were required by their permits to carry in each canoe one hundred fifty pounds of freeload cargo for the fort commandant from Montreal.[10]

After the conquest of New France in 1760, the British left much of the structure of the *ancien régime* undisturbed. Worship in the Catholic church, French civil law or the Custom of Paris, and *seigneurial* land tenure were permitted to continue as in the past and were given statutory sanction in the Quebec Act of 1774. With this measure the British abandoned any attempt to impose English institutions uniformly upon the colonies, and in the case of Canada returned to a prescriptive and "feudal authoritarian system." The promise of self-government, English law, and freehold tenure were all relinquished. Ironically, this program was promulgated in the interests of the French-speaking masses, or as one scholar put it, "unprecedented generosity toward a conquered people .... generosity in the interest of reaction."[11] But the flight of American Loyalists to Canada in the post-Revolutionary period placed new strains on *seigneurialism* and brought these émigrés into collision with feudal land-tenure and nonrepresentative institutions. As a concession to

From Le Detroit des Grandes Adventures *(Detroit, 1928)*

Detroit, French stockaded city in 1818

the Loyalists, an elective assembly, English civil law, and freehold tenure were granted in Upper Canada in 1791. Yet the existing *seigneurial* system was left intact, as were French privileges in law, language, and religion. The feudal system of land ownership was not completely abolished in Canada until the 1850s.

Customs and habits of the *ancien régime* lasted in Detroit well into the nineteenth century. Although *seigneurial* obligations in land tenure had ended in Detroit in 1796 with American occupation, older modes of life that had been generated and shaped by the system continued. Not until 1806 and later were the ancient land titles proved, and not until 1810 was the legal legacy of French custom, British law, and ancient usages cleared away and replaced by American territorial law. The economic mainstay of the *ancien régime*, the fur trade, continued as Detroit's leading economic activity as late as 1820. Even the lines of trade to Montreal continued pretty much as they had been when Cadillac founded the city. One of the few symbols of commercial change was in the Indian trade, where American whiskey began to replace British rum, just as it had earlier replaced French brandy. In short, Detroit's first American decade was not a time of transition except in a very narrow institutional and formal sense. The installation of American judges, governors, and other officials was the primary influence of the new regime. Even here the influence was limited, for a majority of Detroiters in 1810 and 1820 still spoke French, which made it necessary to attach interpreters to key civil offices in the territory and city. Although formal institutions were altered to fit the new sovereign, the substance of life continued much as it had.[12]

During this period of slow transition, roughly from 1800 to 1825, the profound influence of a century of French Canadian *seigneurialism* became more apparent. The habits of the seventeenth century, hardened and sustained by long usage, were to exhibit uncommon longevity. *Seigneurialism* as a system of land ownership appeared to have hampered the *habitants'* productive energies from the time of its first implementation in Detroit in 1707. French officials and traders, later their English counterparts, and then American observ-

ers had from the beginning of the eighteenth century commented on the *habitant's* "crude" and "slovenly" methods of
cultivation and his "shiftlessness and lack of consistent industry." Detroit fur concessionaire Louis Gatineau declared
in 1726 that the dependents neglected the soil and that "it is
only to their idleness they can impute the want of grain and
provisions." In 1765, George Croghan, a western traveler,
observed that "all the people here [Detroit] are generally
poor wretches, and consist of three or four hundred French
families, a lazy, idle people, depending chiefly on the savages for their subsistence; though the land, with little labor,
produces plenty of grain, they scarcely raise as much as will
supply their wants."[13]

As late as 1818 the state of agriculture had not improved.
"In the immediate vicinity of Detroit it is deplorable," said
Estwick Evans. "The French have no ambition to excel in
this honourable and profitable calling. There is here, however, everything to encourage an active husbandman. The
soil is fertile and the climate perfectly congenial to the
growth of New England productions. A Yankee farmer, carrying with him to this place his knowledge of agriculture, and
his industry, might soon acquire a very handsome estate."
Thomas L. McKenney, on a tour in 1826 of the French strip-
settlement between Grosse Pointe and Detroit, reported that
the inhabitants "appeared reconciled to let the earth rest and
the houses go to decay around them; and the orchards decline
and die." He looked forward to the day when these "neglected lands" would be placed in more skillful hands and
become bountiful. Senator Isaac P. Christiancy, who worked
as a young man in Detroit's sister French community of Monroe (thirty miles south of Detroit), corroborated the judgment
of earlier observers: until 1828 or 1830 the French of Monroe
"by habit had quite generally come to think there was no
great object in raising a crop much beyond the necessary
annual supply for their own families. And this habit continued, to a considerable extent, till after I came to the
county, but gradually wore away. They were unambitious,
limiting their wants mainly to the real necessities of life,
which were easily supplied; industrious so far as they felt

labor to be necessary, but with none of that disposition to excessive exertion for the sake of gain or rapid accumulation of wealth which generally distinguished the American of New England descent."[14]

The *habitant* was clearly an inefficient subsistence farmer by American standards. The agricultural revolution of the eighteenth century had passed him by. He left much of his acreage uncultivated, continued to use the fallow field system when it was in discard elsewhere, and neglected the soil when its fertility was exhausted. He was also charged by others with dumping his manure on ice-covered rivers to be rid of it, and for employing an inefficient and shallow plow which barely cut the crust of the soil. The result was that Detroit continued to pay high prices for staple foods that had to be "transported across the lake from the upper parts of the states of New York, Pennsylvania, and Ohio" as late as the first quarter of the nineteenth century.[15]

Nor was the *habitant's* ownership of prime river and lake frontage in Detroit to benefit him very much with the great influx of newcomers in the 1830s and 1840s. Although windfall profits were to be made, very few Frenchmen became wealthy by their ownership of real estate when the population of Detroit mushroomed from 2200 in 1830 to 21,000 in 1850. It seemed like Henry George's "unearned increment" seldom fell into French pockets. The most prominent and wealthiest land speculators were newcomer Yankees and Yorkers like Lewis Cass of New Hampshire, who parlayed a $12,000 purchase in 1816 into a $100,000 sale in 1835. When the *habitant* did become a freeholder it seemed almost as if his peasant land-hunger worked against his best interests. He earned an unenviable reputation for his unwillingness to part with his property even when his own profit and the public interest could both be served by such sales. It was often recalled by newcomers that the *habitant's* holdings were a barrier to street openings and the expansion of the city, and that the *habitant* was a prominent opponent of real estate taxes for the support of public schools and internal improvements. The elder Antoine Beaubien forcibly resisted city surveyors when they staked out the city's main

From C. M. Burton, The City of Detroit, I *(Detroit, 1922)*

The ancestral home of Joseph Campau

thoroughfare, Jefferson Avenue, which was to run through his property. Joseph Campau refused to receive a payment due to him for damages incurred when Griswold Street was trenched upon his property.

Furthermore, the *seigneurial* land ownership patterns of long narrow strips leading back from the riverfront muddled the process of platting towns with modern land surveys. The *seigneurial* land measure of *arpents* did not correspond to acres, and the long narrow ribbon farms did not conform to the forty-acre tract by which Easterners packaged land. *Seigneurial* land tenure had not prepared the *habitant* to reap the benefits of Detroit's great land speculation spree of the mid-1830s. When poor agricultural conditions in the East and "Michigan fever" in the West pushed and pulled thousands of Easterners into the region, they and not the old settlers were the beneficiaries of the boom.[16]

Nor was French culture able to withstand the invasion of
the aggressive, literate, and institutionally mature "cultural
imperialism" of the Yankee. The liabilities of few schools,
high illiteracy rates, and no newspapers that could sustain
themselves could not be offset by a rich oral tradition. Even
that, lamented the foremost student of Detroit's *habitant* culture, was left to the "pen of the Englishman."[17] By the time
the French found the "stuff for books, it was English books
that enlisted their attention." Few cultural and intellectual
leaders emerged from the French community. The excessive
space devoted to Father Gabriel Richard in state histories
testifies not only to his greatness but to the fact that he was an
exception. Richard was almost the sole figure concerned with
what might be described as the nonmaterial side of French
existence, and he disapproved of much of what had been
nativized. His clerical successors from the more metropolitan
areas of the United States or Europe were even less
sympathetic.

The *habitant* also complicated the problems of maintaining his cultural integrity by marriage beyond the race and
beyond the faith. The frequent unions between *coureurs de
bois* and Indians were the subject of much comment. Similarly, large numbers of the daughters of restless *habitants*
married British and American soldiers and successful English fur traders, much to the distress of the clergy. There
seemed to be lacking in the Detroit French the ritualistic
barriers to marriage beyond the faith and beyond the tribe
that appeared to be so pronounced upon the part of later
Catholic immigrants. Endogamy was not a weapon of cultural
defense for a people who had been practicing miscegenation
with the Indians for more than a century.

Finally, the forces of demography began to work against
the French after 1825. Their majority position of the preceding one hundred twenty-five years would be threatened by
new immigration. Relatively static population figures had favored the French. During the eighteenth century Detroit had
failed to grow significantly in population: some estimates
credit the city with 2,000 people in the mid-1700s, yet the
city had not exceeded that figure by 1820. The reasons for the

apparent lack of or slow growth were many. The town's resident population, which remained around 600 for much of the
eighteenth century, was probably in equilibrium with social,
economic, and military conditions that obtained in the region. Furthermore, the French were not anxious to colonize
the area and permitted no independent colonization schemes
like those emanating from New England, such as the Western
Reserve or the Ohio Land Company. Settlement would have
been disruptive to the fur trade and Indian relations, and
American frontiersmen had earned an unenviable reputation
for being able to provoke even reasonably friendly Indians
into war. The British, after the conquest in 1763, accepted the
logic of the French system and tried to restrict American colonial settlement to the East coast with their famous Proclamation Line, which ran down the spine of the Appalachian
Range and banned settlement in trans-Appalachian America.
Thus, in the center of this sparsely populated fur preserve,
Detroit's population of 600 was sufficient to support the fur
traffic, supply and service the military, and provide a large
enough physical presence to control the Indians most of the
time. In addition, surplus population was constantly being
drained off to the voyageur system and the expansion of other
way stations and fur rendezvous points. Detroit's precipitous
drop in population during the conquest (1760-63) from 2,000
to perhaps 600 is explained by the rapid dispersal of French
habitants to the Illinois country and St. Louis. This average
of about 600 appeared to be Detroit's natural equilibrium for
the remainder of the century.[18]

Detroit's predominantly French population, which varied
from 500 to 770 people between 1760 and 1810, managed to
reach only 2,200 by 1830. However, the next four years saw
the population double, and then double again in the four
years after that, so that by 1838 the city had about 9,000
people. Very little of this new growth came from the French.
Although most estimates list the proportion of the French
population at about one-half in 1830, they had shrunk to
about one-sixth by 1834. Their share of the civic and political
offices — never proportionate to their numbers in population
— declined markedly after 1835. Even when they had com-

From C. M. Burton, The City of Detroit, I (Detroit, 1922)

St. Anne's Street, now Jefferson Avenue, Detroit, **1800**

prised a majority of the city's population in the 1820s, they had never held political office commensurate to their numbers. *Habitant* political power peaked before 1825, when Father Richard, the incumbent, was turned down by the voters as territorial delegate to the United States Congress. The Detroit *Gazette* had warned Frenchmen in 1817 that they would never gain a grip on public office without public education and that high illiteracy would cause them to lose their birthright. The next two decades proved the prophecy. The *habitants* quietly faded from the social and political scene after 1835, and by 1850 they were the forgotten element in Detroit politics, noticeable only for their occasional opposition to free public schools, antislavery, and temperance movements.[19]

Joseph Campau, one of the wealthiest and most illustrious of the old French generation, captures much of the essence of the *habitant* lifestyle. Campau, who was descended from one of the original Detroit settlers, was born there in 1769 and sent to Montreal at the age of ten for five years of schooling. He returned to the Detroit region something of a gentleman, judged by the rude frontier standards of the time, and began

Courtesy of The Detroit Institute of Arts: Frederick E. Cohen, artist

Joseph Campau, *grand seigneur*

clerking in a store connected with the fur trade. After an unsuccessful venture in private contracting, which left him penniless, he went back to his old clerking job and soon thereafter began to make his way successfully as a provisioner and fur trader. Linking up with John Jacob Astor's North West Fur Company proved profitable, and soon his mercantile business was one of the most prosperous in the territory.

In Campau's *seigneurial* world of station and rank, slavery was a part of the natural order of things. Like the other *habitants* of the Great Lakes, he accepted slavery as normally as they did a good beaver harvest or an empty whitefish seine. Some such as Joseph Droillard's lucky daughters were given away in marriage with two slaves apiece as dowries. Negro slaves were bought from marauding Indians who raided white-owned plantations and exchanged their booty for guns, traps, and brandy with traders such as Detroit's Campau. Campau was known to own as many as ten slaves at one time and was thought to be a kindly master. One of his favorites was a Negro named Crow, whom Campau converted into a kind of court jester. Campau often dressed Crow in scarlet and sent the supple and winsome black clambering up St. Anne's church steeple, where he performed aerial gymnastics for his master's divertissement and the town's amusement.[20]

Slavery, of course, was a stench in the nostrils of newcomer Yankees and placed them and Frenchmen in opposing camps. And if slavery was not enough, the Yankee pietists from the "burned over" districts also brought with them the issue of temperance to inflame the political passions of the area. On February 19, 1830, the newcomers planted among the incredulous *habitants* the Detroit Association for the Suppression of Intemperance, Michigan's first temperance society. Campau, like most of his confreres, was puzzled by this passion for abstinence; he knew that the good Catholic fathers and missionaries had railed against the traffic in firewater to the Indians for more than a century — to no avail. So ineffective were they and so profitable was the liquor trade that Campau had erected his own distillery in 1809 to supply his ten fur factors in the Lakes country.

The fur trade, mercantile business, and related activities raised Campau to such great wealth and comfort that by his death in 1863 he was one of the wealthiest men in the state, reportedly worth $3,000,000. He lived like a Spanish grandee with his horses, dogs, farms, and "plantations." He was the largest "Norman" horse fancier in the Midwest, at one time holding some five hundred of these French equines under bridle. Despite his great opulence he never lost the common *habitant* touch; he reportedly slept on a bearskin rug until his death. His *rentier* fashion and his *seigneurial* love of the land led Campau to develop estates and maintain some seventy-four tenant farms in an age when freehold proprietorship was the ideal of every Yankee farmer. Campau knew his tenants personally, visited with them in prosperity and adversity, and developed a genuine old-world paternalistic solicitude toward those who worked his acres. According to one source, his books once showed that accounts due him and in arrears were in excess of two million dollars. Money was not always his first consideration, for he often supported many slow or nonpaying renters.[21] That was the benign side of the old-world *seigneurial* tradition.

The Yankee commercial style seemed much more exacting, demanding, and less solicitous and understanding of crop failures and adversity. Yankees foreclosed and collected. One exemplary merchant spared himself the personal pain of shaking down his debtors by conveniently arranging buying trips to the East while his clerks dunned the patrons for past due bills. Debts were held in high obligation; the entrepreneurs staked out their moral reputations on prompt and exact payment. They celebrated material and economic progress.[22] They looked upon the French *habitants'* ability to coexist with nature and to cohabit with the Indians as an atavism of heathen times.

The newcomers, who were irreverently called by one observer "strict sobersides from the land of Jonathan Edwards," appeared humorless, dour, and often intolerant of the easygoing French-Canadian mannerisms and the casual moral torpor of Indian fur-trading posts. Sabbatarians, prohibitionists, and abolitionists sought blue laws and public legislation to reform the human frailties and the untrammeled lusts of the frontier past. The newcomers ridiculed those who lived in marshy areas with the name "muskrat Frenchmen." This opprobrious slur seems to have derived not only from the unwholesome location of their huts but also from their habit of eating the flesh of the marshy creatures they trapped. This practice apparently began in the eighteenth century, when the Pope — like many zoologists of the period — classified the beaver among the fishes and permissible to eat on fast days and Fridays. Thus the beaver "dispensation" permitted the eating of the pungent black meat of this aquatic fur-bearer when fish were in short supply. When the beaver ran out, the *habitant* turned to eating the humbler and more abundant muskrat, a tradition which did not commend itself to fastidious Yankees.[23]

Detroit's historic mission as a fur-trading post and a voyageur way station was over by the 1830s. The last of the large fur roundups, to which Indians clustered from distances of hundreds of miles, occurred in the mid-1820s. These events saw hundreds of Great Lakes Indians gather downriver from Detroit on the Canadian side to receive gifts from the British governor general; this was a century-old goodwill offering to win favor and lubricate the flow of peltries.

The new migrants who came in increasing numbers during the 1830s altered the town's cultural life, unleashed a spectacular real estate boom, and began rebuilding the old French town so that its Gallic character was almost unrecognizable to oldtimers by the 1850s. A dramatic shift in folkways occurred between 1830 and 1840: the old Detroit of easy social relations, swaggering bucks and blanketed squaws, frank-mannered voyageurs and *coureurs de bois* with their aromatic fur packs, and stores filled with Indian goods was disappearing. Steamboats plied a regular trade after 1825; steam mills sawed lumber and ground grain; ploughs, pitchforks, and scythes were the working tools of the new residents. Traps, guns, shot, and Indian goods, the implements of the French, receded to the back shelves of provisioning stores. Bela Hubbard celebrated this material progress with a lament:

I listen in vain for the melodies which were once the prelude to many joyous hours of early manhood. But, instead, my ear is larumed by the shriek of the steam-whistle and the laborious snort of the propeller. All announce that on these shores and waters the age of the practical, hard-working, money-getting Yankee is upon us, and that the careless, laughter-loving Frenchman's day is over.[24]

How does one account for the missed opportunities, the failure to capitalize on natural advantages, and the fact that the French left so weak an imprint on the political, social, and economic life of the Detroit region? How does one explain the rapid vanishing of a culture that had founded, nourished, and shaped the history of the Detroit region for more than a century?

Michigan Governor Lewis Cass believed that a sharply constricted economic experience had stunted the entire French lifestyle, particularly its habits of industry. Economic specialization took its toll. "The fatal mistake of educating a whole community for a single and temporary business is now deeply felt and acknowledged," Cass wrote in 1816. "The spinning-wheel and the loom are unknown in the country," he said, noting that in the past the "wool of sheep was thrown away, and even now, I presume a pound of wool is not manufactured in the Territory by any person of Canadian descent. . . ."[25] As late as 1821 the Detroit *Gazette* noted that "there are not three families that manufacture their wearing apparel . . . not five looms in the territory . . . not a carding machine or fulling mill within, perhaps, a hundred miles of Detroit." Undoubtedly, the intense concentration and diversion of almost all human effort to harvesting one crop — furs — had crippled the potential range of industry and dimmed the *habitants'* vision of enterprise.

Yet it was more than a problem of a one-crop economy and premature specialization. Other social groups, such as the Boston Yankees, had specialized early but adjusted satisfactorily to economic change. It seems more likely that the social and economic behavior of the French was in large measure the result of the social system of *seigneurialism. Seigneurialism* was clearly more than a mode of land tenure: it

Courtesy of Michigan Department of State, State Archives

Lewis Cass, Yankee modernizer, whom the Indians slyly called "Big Guts"

was a complicated and intricate economic lifestyle that was "intimately blended with their laws and customs," and a web of social usages that penetrated every nook and cranny in the social strata. Sanctioned by the Church, prescribed by the government, and overseen by the *seigneur* and fur factors, it was a straitjacket that left little room for maneuvering. A system so honeycombed with regulations, restrictions, bans, licenses, monopolies, and social deference was not calculated to instill in the *habitant* the business spirit of the new age.

Seigneurial and *rôture* tenure took the profit out of land speculation and prevented the private sale of timber rights, minerals, and stone. Land held in such encumbered form was not a free instrument for enrichment by speculation, nor was it likely to become the site of manufactories or the development of the tenants' mechanical skills. Limited markets encouraged precommercial subsistence farming, and the peltry and fur trade monopolies cut severely into freelance selling. No ingenious Yankee peddlers, like Sam Slick of Slickville, emerged from the Detroit *habitant* culture. The *habitant* met his *corvée* obligations by work, and in this pre-money culture he generally paid other debts with capons, minots of wheat, beaverskins, buckskins, and the like. The *habitant* was not allowed general commerce with the Indians or traffic for profit in any form. Although not all of the precommercial behavior that characterized the French communities of North America may be attributed to *seigneurialism*, the institution was unquestionably part of a general scheme of paternalism which retarded the advance to material prosperity.[26]

Seigneurialism brought to the communities it touched a premodern character and all of the identifying features of tradition-bound and undeveloped societies: low literacy rates, high birth rates, and a tightly suppressed consumer base. Its economy was immobilized at the extractive level, and it failed to develop a homespun industry or to generate a native technology; its business and occupational structure was hampered by precapitalistic hangovers. The *seigneurial* system injected into the economic process irrationalities that were aimed at upholding a status society and a feudal ruling order. Its rigid social structure was defined by usage and the custom of Paris, and it had a warrior-priest — in the Northwest a soldier-fur-factor and missionary — class at the top of a narrow social pyramid. In the Detroit region there was no intermediary bourgeoisie present that was capable of transmitting new ideas about social and economic organization. This folk society had no representative political institutions until outsiders forced the issue. The mode of land-holding not only failed to draw from its tenants high productivity but seemed more often, as a notable English traveler to Detroit observed in 1837, to produce the "symptoms of apathy, indolence, mistrust, hopelessness" in a "supine and ignorant peasantry." It may be, as Professor Eugene Genovese has argued, that *seigneurial* societies tended to elicit from their working classes a "lack of industrial initiative" of the kind that "produced the famous Lazy Nigger, who under Russian serfdom and elsewhere was white." Whatever the cause, social types of this description abound in the literature and documents of New France and the Detroit region.[27]

The point should again be made that both French and English observers, travelers, and officials, both sympathetic and unsympathetic, made almost identical observations on the enterprise and work style of Detroit's French *habitant*. The most plausible explanation is that Detroit was colonized by a time-bound and archaic social system — *seigneurialism* — that failed to evolve from its transplanted form, and, as Louis Hartz suggested for Canada, lapsed into a tradition-bound and historic form of immobility. *Seigneurialism* worked very well as a military system for conquering the wilderness and for exploiting a primitive, extractive industry such as fur-gathering. But because of its many archaic features, its heavy emphasis on status, and its pre-market and feudal values, it was not a suitable instrument for equipping Detroit's French *habitants* to achieve mastery in the modernizing Yankee society of nineteenth-century Detroit.[28]

Chapter III

HUGO P. LEAMING

The Ben Ishmael Tribe:
A Fugitive "Nation" of the
Old Northwest

The air, the water and the ground are free gifts to man, and no one has the power to portion them out in parcels.

— Ishmael, in James
Fenimore Cooper's
The Prairie

I reckon ours is the oldest family in the world.
— George Ishmael, of the Ben
Ishmael Tribe

THE TRIBE OF ISHMAEL, OR ISHMAEL-ites, was a tightly knit nomadic community of African, Native American, and "poor white" descent, estimated to number about 10,000. Fugitives from the South, they arrived in the central part of the Old Northwest at the beginning of the nineteenth century, preceding the other pioneers. After a century of fierce culture conflict with the majority society, the tribe was forcibly dispersed. Camp sites became nuclei of present-day black communities, and Ishmaelites of the diaspora participated in the rise of black nationalism, perhaps even contributing memories of African Islam to the new Black Muslim movements. Though utilized fictionally for local color in nineteen-century American literature, as by James Fenimore Cooper, the Ishmaelites have not previously been identified as an historic people.[1]

Origin and Settlement

The first known appearance of the organized tribe occurred between 1785 and 1790 in the hills, or "Refuse land," of Bourbon (then Noble) County, Kentucky. Those who became Ishmaelites had gathered from Tennessee, the Carolinas, Virginia, and Maryland, in a region still largely wilderness and at a time still turmoiled by the Native American wars and mass slave escapes of the American Revolution. That the Ishmaelites were fugitives is shown by their double removal, first from the Southeast to frontier Kentucky, then on to the unexplored Old Northwest; and by their ethnic composition, the three subject peoples of the South's slavery society: chattel slaves or "free" blacks, remnants of destroyed Native American nations, and European indentured servants or their landless, despised children.[2]

The first patriarch of the Ishmaelites, Ben Ishmael, was revered as its charismatic founder as long as the tribe endured, and his wife, the first queen, Jennie Ishmael, as a warrioress of mighty physique. Tradition, perhaps related to the tribe's nomadism, averred that in advanced age, between 1802 and 1810, Patriarch Ishmael and Queen Jennie set forth into the unknown, toward the setting sun, never to be seen again by their people.[3]

Soon after their passing, and with the rapid settlement of Kentucky as a slave state, their eldest son John, the second patriarch, led the tribe across the Ohio River into the Old Northwest. At first, the Ishmaelites moved into the Ohio interior north of Cincinnati. But anticipating white farmer settlement of this new state, they moved on again, west into what was still "Indian territory." By 1819 the tribe established its capital in the deep woods of the White River, where now stands the city of Indianapolis. The late-nineteenth-century state summary of Ishmaelite materials reports: "John Ishmael, then, arrived in this city while yet the Indian was here." The principal Ishmaelite settlements, on opposite banks of the river, were the points from which, much later, grew the two oldest and still existing black neighborhoods of Indianapolis.[4]

Regarding the relationship between Patriarch John and his Native American hosts, "he found most of his associates among them." The western Native American nations had set aside this country between the Ohio River and the Great Lakes as a refuge for defeated brother-nations of the east; the most prominent of the latter, the Delawares, had in turn opened the White River valley, unusually rich in game, to all fugitives, without need for the usual special application.* Hither, therefore, came the recently founded nation of black and poor white as well as Native American membership.[5]

---

*The Tribe of Ishmael was not the only new nation — in the Native American sense — founded during the eighteenth century with an ethnically plural membership. The Seminoles were a union of African-Americans (escaped slaves) and Native Americans.

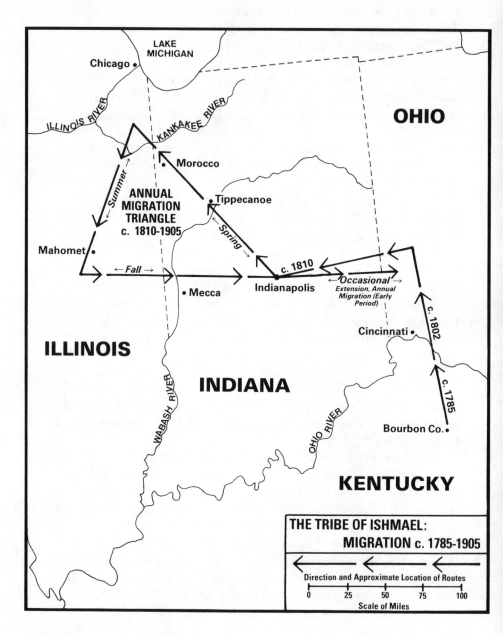

Migrations of the Tribe of Ishmael

After the defeat of Tecumseh's alliance and the end of Native American jurisdiction over this region, the new state of Indiana decreed the establishment of its capital in 1821 at the central point of the state, on the White River. When the surveyors and first officials arrived at the spot, they found the Tribe of Ishmael — and the Ishmaelites did not budge. Thus Indianapolis grew up into a great city around the Ishmaelite settlement, and this strange arrangement continued into the twentieth century.[6]

The earlier migrations of the tribe had been involuntary, but they now pursued a nomadic way of life as a central feature of their distinctive culture. Their annual migratory route was northwest from Indianapolis to the Kankakee River south of Lake Michigan, from there south through eastern Illinois to the vicinity of Champaign-Urbana and Decatur, and finally due east, back to Indianapolis. This triangular route is about 350 miles as the crow flies. Every spring many hundreds of small carts set off, filled with children and the elderly, drawn by donkeys or horses (usually scrawny in latter years), the Ishmaelite men and women walking alongside them. In the late spring (until "Indian removal" in the north in the 1830s) there was joyful reunion with the Native Americans of the Kankakee. During the summer the tribe moved south, and when fall came they turned again to winter quarters. The migration was repeated every year for nearly a century. It was during one of the beloved yearly journeys, on a summer day in about 1846, that Patriarch John Ishmael died, an aged man still traveling like his father before him.[7]

There was great trouble ahead for his people. Indianapolis, which had been a village "Capital in the Woods," was becoming a populous commercial depot and political center, large buildings and congested blocks hemming in the Ishmaelite shantytowns. Across the frontier Midwest, land was cleared, paths became policed roads, and towns were established. A unified network of social order and authority was emerging.

The Ishmaelites had earned a sufficient livelihood from the ample game and the kitchen gardens of their settlements. But now the beasts were dying, or branded, and proprietary eyes gazed jealously at each plot of land. Difficulties in travel and hardships in winter quarters steadily increased.[8] Extraordinarily conservative and stubbornly loyal to their way of life, however, the tribe refused to adjust, to accept the validity of title deeds, fences, brands, to give up their migratory custom, to enter the majority social system as farm laborers or common wage-laborers in the city. The Ishmaelites chose to suffer terribly from loss of livelihood rather than forsake the tribe.

By the late nineteenth century (exclusive of surgical, acute, and out-of-town cases) three-quarters of the patients at Indianapolis City Hospital were from the Tribe of Ishmael. An average of six Ishmaelite children a week were stillborn, from scarcely more than two thousand women of child-bearing age. And the average height of Ishmaelites had shrunk incredibly. Once known for their unusual tallness for those days, often six feet or more, the Ishmaelites were now characteristically as short as children, often five feet and less.[9] The transformation of the rural frontier, with its venison and cooking herbs, into the town slum, with its stale bread and rotten potatoes, was turning giants into dwarfs.

But the tribe continued.

The Culture of the Tribe of Ishmael

The hostility toward the Ishmaelites found in almost every source for their history is so intense that scandalous value judgments may be readily identified and with reasonable confidence separated from the attempts to report events. A greater problem for the reconstruction of Ishmaelite social history is one which the historian of ethnic minorities often encounters: they were in no position to maintain archives. It is thus necessary to extrapolate a good deal from little evidence, to fit bits and pieces together. The history is then threatened by distortion from the value judgments of the historian. However, though the history of privileged peoples with abundant sources may be more objective, the threat of subjectivity must be risked if there are to be any histories of mankind's majority of less fortunate peoples.

The culture of the Tribe of Ishmael was clearly not normative "Anglo-Saxon" or European-American. Contemporaries
stressed the difference by comparing the Ishmaelites to Native Americans: the "brood were so like the Indians in their
habits of life . . . so primitive in their habits, that they were
readily admitted to the reservations. . . ."[10] Some forms of
Ishmaelite culture no doubt descended from the ancestral
groups — Native American, African-American, and British
rural labor. But it appears that the dynamic of the culture was
in large part a product of the tribe's origin in escape from
slavery, and that much of the substance and function was a
response to the physical environment of the western wilderness. This new synthesis, developed with such surprising
speed, is here analyzed in terms of economy, economic system, nomadism, family and tribal structure, religion, arts and
recreation, hierarchy, and other notable features.

The Tribe's economy in Kentucky was based primarily on
hunting.

> They lived in the hills, and hunting was their chief occupation.
> The bill of fare would be the result of the hunt . . . .If a raccoon,
> a bear, a deer, were brought, it served the purpose.[11]

In the Old Northwest this economy was maintained until the
new settlers occupied the land.

> . . . they were readily admitted to the [Native American] reser-
> vations, with liberty to hunt and fish, which was refused the
> genuine sportsmen and professional hunters and trappers.[12]

As the hunting and fishing economy grew more difficult,
the Ishmaelites refused to enter into the new wage-labor
available to the poor in farm or town. Their ways of obtaining
a livelihood to replace hunting reflected values of the lost
vocation: they sought forms of self-employment and outdoor
work; they avoided hiring others for wages and eschewed the
accumulation of capital; when wage-labor was necessary,
they chose temporary, marginal jobs that they might easily
leave when the spring migration called. These requirements
were narrow and led to work that was often "dirty," often
"shady," and usually near the lower limit of the subsistence

level. Ishmaelites sacrificed health and comfort to avoid majority patterns of labor and to hew to the tribal values. Perpetuation of hunting values may have been reinforced by an association of wage-labor with slavery.

Ishmaelite ingenuity tried many means to meet their criteria for obtaining a livelihood. One Ishmaelite worked as a horse-tender. Another repaired umbrellas from door to door. Another made a literal but criminal adjustment from frontier trapping: he poisoned watchdogs (the natural enemies of nomads), returned and solicited the chore of removing the remains (for a quarter), skinned the carcass, and sold the pelt for a dollar to those who made skin rugs. Fred Ishmael, a son of Patriarch John, followed the seasonal trade of floating river ice to the icehouse chutes, a task requiring outdoor stamina and skills and offering the challenge of danger.[13] For a time the tribe sought to solve the problem of its economy with home laundries. But the development of laundry plants by the majority society, with capital equipment and hired labor, was a competitive challenge the tribe could not meet and at the same time preserve its values.[14]

Prostitution fulfills the requirement of self-employment without capital, and there may have been some, amid the great welter of dubious charges.[15] Petty pilfering does appear to have been common, perhaps justified by the Ishmaelite belief that the land was rightfully theirs.

> The disposition to steal was only from a desire to get some corn for the horses or bacon for the family use. There never known [sic] a case of this family [the Ishmaelites] committing theft except in a small way.[16]

In latter days there seems to have been a considerable number of beggars among the Ishmaelites. The regular practitioners of this vocation dropped "bluestone water" (blue vitriol) into their eyes to feign blindness, a practice of medieval British origin.[17]

The most widespread occupation of the Ishmaelites, a tribal identification by the late nineteenth century, was scavenging. Public rubbish removal had not yet been established, and the majority community considered the work too "dirty" or "dishonorable" to compete for. The tribe used its migratory carts and draft animals to pick up and dispose of trash, ashes, and junk for a fee. At the disposal end, reusable scrap was sold or used in the Ishmaelite settlements. It is said that the carts of the Ishmaelites were a familiar sight every winter day in the streets of the city.[18] This occupation met every Ishmaelite requirement: self-employment, outdoor work, and the use of their only legitimate capital, the caravans. Perhaps even the search for usable scrap took on some of the zest once attached to the hunt.

The economic system of the Tribe of Ishmael is suggested by the observation, "the Ishmaels never seem to try to accumulate property to any extent."[19] This value, so different from the majority society's, would seem to have been an outgrowth of their hunting economy, like the search for self-employment. Hunting cultures often view the land and its animals as common property, or nobody's, or God's. This wealth is privately owned only when in use. Only the insane hunt beyond their hunger, for accumulated venison rots. This cultural value may have been reinforced by Native American and African traditions of community ownership or an economy of use. Cultural differences in this respect were central to the conflict between the tribe and the majority society. Fences and title deeds were as immoral to Ishmaelites as was their "thieving" to the majority. Highly verbal Ishmaelites (some of whom are discussed below) stated as ideology what was reported for Ishmaelite practice: the tribe had been wrongfully dispossessed from the land; majority institutions were criminal as well as inhumane.

The nomadism of the Tribe of Ishmael was its most distinctive institution,[20] but its origin and meaning to the tribe are a mystery.* Migrations so regular and of such distance are not necessary or characteristic for hunting economies. Most Native American nations were not nomadic. There is no hint of Gypsy contact with the Tribe of Ishmael, nor in its forma-

---

*The notion of the migration as a pilgrimage to burial grounds or other shrines is raised by the progressive change of the eastern terminus from the vicinity of Cincinnati to that of Columbus and then Indianapolis. The idea can be extended to the western terminus by relating it to the disappearance of Ben and Jennie Ishmael in the West, the most charismatic known legend of the tribe.

tive period, historical likelihood. The migrations of fugitives
are occasional and one-way, not annual. The records are silent on any early cattle herding. And none of the three points
of the Ishmaelite migratory triangle is known as a fur-trade
depot, since the triangle falls short of the Great Lakes and
the great rivers.

Another possibility, for lack of any indication of a prag-
matic or social function for the migration, is that the founders
who gathered the tribe (Ben Ishmael and his family) were of a
nomadic heritage and impressed the custom on the others
through their charisma. Each component ethnic group of the
tribe, though sedentary, had included as an exception a
nomadic and charismatic tribe: among Native Americans the
Shawnee nation was migratory and held a legendary position
of leadership; among West Africans the Fulani were a
nomadic tribe who during the eighteenth and early
nineteenth centuries overthrew traditional forms of rule and
presented their conquests as social revolutions as well as
Muslim holy wars; and among the dispossessed and homeless rural folk of the British Isles, who became the indentured
servants, there had been and still is a tightly knit, gypsy-like
tribe of Scots, Welsh, and Irish — the Tinkers — who engaged
in ceaseless hostilities with the English establishment. The
presence at the right time and place of a kingly family of any
of these three groups could have committed the imaginations
of the new Ishmaelites to a persistent nomadism. But so remote are the time, place, and peoples that the question of the
origin and meaning of the Ishmaelite annual migration is not
likely to be answered.

The family and tribal structure of the Tribe of Ishmael was
complex. Each nuclear family belonged to a recognized and
defined clan, or extended family. There were thirteen clans,
of which the clan of Ishmael was paramount. Within the clan
of Ishmael, the Ishmael family was paramount, and within
each of the other clans a paramount family lent its name to the
entire clan. Within each clan there were many family names,
derived from the husbands of women of the paramount fam-

ily. Except for Ishmael, the clan and family names, as reported to the outside authorities, were unremarkable European names, mainly British.[21] It may be assumed that the twelve clans were descended from twelve families which joined the Ishmael family in the founding of the tribe. New members joined the tribe by birth, marriage, or adoption into a nuclear family. In normative Anglo-Saxon-American society (outside the southern states) most families do not know or feel any relationship with distant kin and in-laws. It is said that many southern rural black and Appalachian white families do maintain such a relationship. The clan structure of the Tribe of Ishmael differed in being more formalized and official.

The clan and the tribe joined the nuclear family in providing livelihood, affection, and child care. The charges of child neglect that could not be legally sustained may reflect the

Each nuclear family belonged to a defined clan, or extended family.

Courtesy of the Indiana University School of Medicine and the Indiana State Board of Health

difficulty of the majority society in understanding the sharing of parental care by wider kinship groups. The tribe also had its own laws or customs for marriage and divorce, surely a major source for the charges of immorality and licentiousness.[22] The mode of the wedding ceremony, with an officiant stepping forward who was not known to be a "minister" by outsiders,[23] illustrates the tribe's close-mouthed policy regarding customs. Divorce, to the scandal of the majority community, was easily obtained — by mutual consent or on the demand of either partner. The Ishmaelites lacked the shame taboo on divorce. Yet divorce was not common: "One of the strange things in the history of the Ishmaels is that separations and divorce are not so common as would be expected among such people."[24]

Most Ishmaelite nuclear families were monogamous. When polygamy occurred, it was practiced openly, without shame, and perhaps with pride. There are indications that it was the prerogative of leaders, or nobility. A spiritual leader of the tribe raised fourteen children, each said to have been the offspring of a different wife. A secular leader (and a great one) was married to fifteen wives at the same time, all living in the same home without any observable friction.[25]

In contrast to the majority society, Ishmaelite women played important public roles in activities requiring physical strength and courage, as spiritual leaders, and as leaders of clan and tribe. More female than male nobles or notables of the clans appear in the case studies. The queens of the tribe were not merely the consorts of the patriarchs but important personages in their own right.

The spiritual system of the Tribe of Ishmael, not known in detail to outsiders, was not orthodox Christian. Not a single Ishmaelite was ever known to belong to any of the churches of the majority society.[26] In the 1830s, when the majority society was organizing its first churches, Ishmaelites briefly attended Methodist meetings. A favorite message of the preacher was that "all good things will come to Christians." After a few weeks an elderly Ishmaelite woman arose when testimonies were invited and declared:

Courtesy of the Indiana University School of Medicine and the Indiana State Board of Health

A typical Ishmaelite home

> We all joined and we ben waitin' fur good things. We ain't got none yit. I h'ain't had a speck of good butter in my house sence that day.

Whereupon, she turned around and marched from the church, the other Ishmaelites following her out — permanently.[27]

The tribe wanted a practical religion, one that would help in hunting, health, or making the stubborn butter come in the churning. Over the generations Ishmaelites answered inquiries about the state of their soul with the emphatic declaration that their tribe did not believe in life beyond the grave.[28] Though oriented toward this world rather than a world to come, the Ishmaelites were mystics. Indeed, it is reported that a greater proportion of this tribe was spiritually gifted than in those churches of the majority community which had a special inclination toward visions and prophecy:

... all (are) firm believers in omens for good and evil; all are
sure that they have seen ghosts, demons, witches, 'sperrets' and
all the rest of the uncanny and intangible brood that troop
about.[29]

It was with this dimension of Ishmaelite mysticism that the
bound girl, Riley's "Little Orphant Annie," frightened her
master's children, whispering to them: "The goblins will get
you if you don't watch out!" If among the "sperrets" there
were benign and higher spiritual beings, the Ishmaelites
were not prepared to discuss them with members of the
majority society; nor were the latter, with their Christian
orientation, inclined to distinguish between higher and lower
spirits.

The arts and recreations of the tribe of Ishmael were a
wonder of the region. Architecture and music were the tribe's
specialties. Appropriately for nomads, the usual Ishmaelite
dwellings were simple: one-night lean-tos during the annual
migration, small cabins for winter quarters. The scrap wood
of which the cabins were built in the late nineteenth century
was selected, worked over, and assembled with care and
skill. The cabins were sturdy and well proportioned, with
tightly crafted windows and doors.*

Ingenuity and originality were Ishmaelite hallmarks.
Flooding was a problem for the tribe. The winter settlements
were on the mud flats of the White River and its creeks (land
not required by the majority society), and this river frequently overflowed. They solved the problem by constructing wooden skids under the cabins. When the floods came,
the homes floated until they could be pulled up the mud
banks by the tribe's donkeys and horses.[30] Even the permanent homes were mobile!

---

*Identifiable cabins still stood in 1970, now used as sheds behind more recent
homes. Also in that year, at the Ishmaelite or river end of the oldest black neighborhood of Indianapolis, there stood sizable wooden "Gothic" houses, apparently not
designed by professional architects, with unusual decorations across their fronts:
stars, circles, triangles, and other geometrical shapes cut out of flat pieces of un-
painted wood and attached in regular order to the structure. That these might relate
to the Ishmaelites is suggested by a similar but larger cutout of the sun, with rays
attached, across the upper front of one of the still existing Ishmaelite cabins. Journals
of architecture sometimes publish illustrations of "American bad taste," old rural
and small-town houses usually Midwestern, which they assign to individual eccen-
tricity rather than a subculture.

Courtesy of the Indiana University School of Medicine and the Indiana State Board of Health

Ishmaelite homes were built on skids so that they could be pulled or floated when the mud flats were flooded.

The tribe sometimes built in monumental dimensions.[31] The winter home of Tom Ishmael, son of Patriarch John and grandson of Ben Ishmael, located in the northern sector of the migration route, was a vast log mansion, three-cornered and in other unspecified ways of a most curious design. In the majority community it was famed as the most unusually shaped structure in the state of Indiana.[32] Within the tribe the size and striking design may have been related to the ancestral prestige of its occupant.

Another monumental building of the tribe was its central communal dance hall on the west bank of the White River, across from downtown Indianapolis. Its great size, its posts sunk twenty feet into the muddy ground, and materials obtained entirely from Ishmaelite scavenging, excited the pride of Ishmaelites and the grudging admiration of outsiders.[33] There was a smaller dance hall in each Ishmaelite neighborhood. The dance was the tribe's passionate recreation. In these centers the Ishmaelites, cramped into winter quarters, passed the time dancing, singing, listening to their musicians, talking, flirting, eating, but not drinking alcohol, a habit they eschewed.[34]

Music played a greater part in the culture of the tribe of Ishmael than in that of the majority society, and it has been reported as a distinctive kind of music. The tribe was well known for its large and frequent gatherings to sing. The voices could be heard far away, singing the "jollyest, noisiest songs." These were not the songs of the majority community; they are described as "quaint," with "some jingle of words" and "some music." There were many instrumentalists, some sought after by the majority community for its social events, such as a highly esteemed harpist and "the blind fiddler," who was reported to have been one of the finest musicians of the Midwest.[35]

Reports frequently mention nobility and other notable members of the tribe of Ishmael, persons of striking character who were especially esteemed by the Ishmaelites. The reports are silent on the tribe's system of government, its assemblies, whether there was a council of clan elders, and the relationship between leaders and members in decision-making. However, there was clearly a social hierarchy; and the reverence for paramount families, the character ascribed to notables, and the general pride of Ishmaelites in their tribe indicate the existence of a leadership and prestige group that warrants the term nobility. Polly H., director of an important dance hall center, is said to have held "rank." Susan S., daughter of Jehu S., is described as a remarkable character in the tribe, a superior being to whom homage was paid. Her funeral procession was marked by the rushing of the hearse and tribal carts at breakneck speed through a torrential downpour; it was referred to long after by the majority community as the day Susan "Ishmael" was buried. Another enigmatic leader, Sarah Ishmael, tall and "rawboned" like so many of the early Ishmaelites, is said to have been "very prominent." Perhaps a spiritual leader, she was called "the Ishmael woman who walks like a man and talks bass." She had had four husbands, and it was she who was first to leave and last to return on each annual migration. Her people had many oral legends about her.[36]

A latter-day Ishmaelite who verbalized the tribe's economic value system into an ideology was George W. One observer says of George:

> He is an anarchist of course, and he has the instinctive, envious dislike, so characteristic of his people, of anyone in a better condition than himself.

He quotes George W. as follows: "The law is against us. . . . It is meant to crush the poor." The observer continues: "He abused the law, the courts, the rich, factories — everything." He wished to see commercial laundries burned and the laundry given out to the poor to wash. He stated that the police should be hanged. And he condemned the underemployment of women laborers while men were unemployed. He was ready, he said, to burn the institutions of society. "I am better than any man that wears store clothes." And the observer adds:

> After his last vicious remark George stepped in front of me and assured me that he did not want me to be scared; that people were always afraid of him when he got earnest like and made speeches . . . . [37]

The report indicates that George's wife, Maggie Ishmael, was present and describes her as large-boned, tall, spare, and handsome.

> She did not say much, but the manner in which she folded her arms and strode too [sic] and fro in the room was a [sic] unconscious piece of posing on her part that impressed me greatly and made the others in the room seem insignificant in comparison. I don't think the woman regarded society except as her enemy.[38]

The largely illiterate Ishmaelite culture produced authors whose works were printed and sold. One was the poet Pamelia H., a tiny, "very slender" woman who weighed less than seventy-five pounds, described as a "queer character" whose "curious looking face was not easily forgotten once seen." When the authorities remonstrated with her for her begging, which was so successful that she banked the proceeds, she snapped back: "That's all right; I'll leave my fortune to the Public Charities!" She had her poems printed as each was completed and sold them on the streets or on the annual migration. If her poetry was anything like the characterization of her conversation, it was indeed "strange" and "interesting."[39]

The other Ishmaelite author was Robert Chism. Born a slave in Virginia about 1808, he had worked the Mississippi and Ohio as roustabout, sailor, and gambler before joining the Tribe of Ishmael. He was a brown-skinned man and his wife Milly Brown was dark black in complexion. At the White River wintering grounds they built a large three-story house with the unusual design that may have been characteristic of the homes of Ishmaelite leaders. The access system was particularly strange and — it would appear — difficult to describe: the second and third floors were entered by a small stairway, and by a "half stairs" and "half ladder" arrangement in the rear, apparently over the roof of a detached kitchen shed. The mansion was a refuge, with a dozen places for hiding and escape. In particular, Chism gave sanctuary to the poor who were sought for imprisonment in the poor houses or for sale as bound servants. He exacted rent when a fugitive had resources; but he did not turn away those who had none. The majority community said that he was also a fence for stolen goods. But Ishmaelites and others who were poor or hunted called him "Papa" or "Grandpa."

Robert Chism wrote two books. One was published in 1885, when he was in his seventies, and contained a description of the wickedness of Indianapolis and its leading citizens; in it he charged that the region had been stolen from its original and rightful owners. He called on the state to indemnify those it had wronged. His other book, *The Dark Lights of Indiana,* purported to be an exposé of criminals. The persons so characterized and attacked were the leading lights of the majority community. Both books created wide if whispered interest in the Midwest.[40]

If the tribe maintained the office of patriarch after the death of John Ishmael in 1846, but kept the identity of the incumbent secret for his protection from the mounting attacks on the tribe, then the most likely Ishmaelites to have been the third and fourth patriarchs were John's son, Tom Ishmael, of the triangular log mansion, and Robert Chism. Certainly "Papa" Chism fulfilled the functions of that office as protector and spokesman of the Tribe of Ishmael.

Some groups of mixed ethnic ancestry and some other ethnic minorities may have been marginal to the majority society and culture in this country's history; the Ishmaelites were not. In the tenacity of their struggle, the distinctiveness of their culture, and their pride of identity, there was nothing marginal about the Tribe of Ishmael.[41] A member of the tribe, George Ishmael, expressed that pride, the symbolic associations of the tribal name, and the literal truth regarding the world between the Ohio River Valley and the Great Lakes shore, when he said:

"I reckon ours is the oldest family in the world."[42]

The Tribe of Ishmael in James Fenimore Cooper's The Prairie

Traces of the Ishmaelites are found in nineteenth-century Midwestern regional literature, where they provided local color, and because they were fictional did not disturb the social fabric. Already mentioned was James Whitcomb Riley's "Little Orphant Annie," who came to stay as a bound girl and terrorized her master's children with supernatural lore. That she was Ishmaelite is supported by her characterization as a "little gypsy" and "from a wild country settlement" in Riley's essay which amplifies the poem.[43] Edward Eggleston's The Hoosier Schoolmaster, the best known of the regional novels, uses the bound servant theme and describes a rough and quaint population. In the 1892 preface, this people is identified as a subculture distinct from the majority of settlers and the descendants of indentured servants who led a seminomadic life in little one-horse wagons.[44] Booth Tarkington's regional novel The Conquest of Canaan recounts a fierce struggle between respectable society and a large population of paupers and petty criminals, not European immigrants, not factory workers, but others well known to the Negro community. Their headquarters — where their leader holds court — is a huge ramshackle dance hall patched with scrap, built over the mud bank of the river.[45]

A much more significant use of the Tribe of Ishmael in literature is not a regional work but a classic of the national literature, James Fenimore Cooper's novel *The Prairie*. The tribe, identified by name, is the center of action and theme. Moreover, Cooper's unknown source for the tribe dates from the first decade of the settlement on the White River or earlier: the novel was written in 1826.[46] Cooper scholars have identified sources for other elements of *The Prairie*; but finding nothing on the Ishmaelites, they have assumed that these were a fictional construct of Cooper's imagination.

This is the last of "The Leatherstocking Tales," an epic of westward pioneering. The hero of the series, Natty Bumppo, is a benevolent representative of the frontiersman whose ways and values are free of the deceits and other artifices of civilization. Cooper presents the Tribe of Ishmael as a similar type, but sinister rather than heroic. It is a tribute to literary scholarship that Orm Överland, a Norwegian authority on Cooper, without benefit of knowledge of the historicity of the Ishmaelites, nevertheless reaches many of the same conclusions that arise from the analysis of the sources for the historic tribe: its patriarchal quality, the issues of tribal or natural law against the law of civilization or the majority society, and the conflict over possession of the land. Överland interprets the novel as a social conflict between normative American society and the frontier anarchy of the tribe. He summarizes: "*The Prairie* remains a disturbing work because it embodies tensions that America as a nation has not been able to resolve."[47]

Independently, a similar significance of the fictional Ishmaelites for American history was seen by the distinguished American scholar Perry Miller, in his last and posthumous work, *The Life of the Mind in America: From the Revolution to the Civil War* (1965). According to Miller, Cooper's hero and his Ishmaelites are the innocent and the

THE PRAIRIE

BY

JAMES FENIMORE COOPER

LEATHER-STOCKING EDITION

NEW YORK ·
G. P. PUTNAM'S SONS
The Knickerbocker Press

The Prairie—fiction based on history

destructive sides of the other America on the western frontier. He adds: "It was a creature from the wilderness, like
them, but one who had tutored himself in the laws of the
majority, who emerged during the greatest crisis of the
United States, the principal agent in preserving the nation —
Abraham Lincoln."[48]

Cooper's fictional Ishmaelites and the historic Tribe of
Ishmael coincide in most particulars. Cooper calls his tribal
chief Ishmael Bush, the latter name a reference to the wilderness he rules. The tribe is called variously "the sons of
skirting Ishmael" (i.e., skirting the settlements), "the sons of
Ishmael," and "the tribe of wandering Ishmael."[49] Its way of
life is nomadic:

> Contrary to the usual practices . . . this party . . . had found its
> way . . . to a point far beyond the usual limits of civilized habita-
> tions . . . .
>
> [Their] personal effects [were such] as might be supposed to
> belong to one ready at any moment to change his abode without
> reference to season or distance.
>
> Ishmael Bush had passed the whole of a life of more than fifty
> years on the skirts of society. He boasted that he had never
> dwelt where he might not safely fell every tree he could view
> from his own threshold, that the law had rarely been known to
> enter his clearing, and that his ears had never willingly admit-
> ted the sound of a church bell.

Says Ishmael:

> It may do for you people, who live in settlements, to hasten on
> to their houses; but thank heaven, my farm is too big for its
> owner ever to want a resting-place.[50]

The time assigned by Cooper for the tribe's initial migration across the West is 1805;[51] the actual historical time was
between 1802 and 1810. The place of origin is also the same:
Kentucky. If Cooper's account is accurate about the reason for their departure from Kentucky, a missing piece of the
history is provided. The Ishmaelite hills were claimed by
others under a United States land grant, and a posse sought to
evict the tribe. During the fight that ensued the sheriff's
officer was killed, and a reward was posted for the apprehension of the Ishmaelites. But Ishmael in the novel proudly

defends the principle for which his people suffered outlawry:

> . . . you have said hard things ag'in me and my family. If the hounds of the law have put their bills on the trees and stumps of the clearings, it was for no act of dishonesty, as you know, but because we maintain the rule that 'arth (earth) is common property.[52]

Cooper did not choose to present his Ishmaelites as other than white.[53] But there are condemnatory references to their ancestry. They are "the offcasts of all honest people." And an Anglo-Saxon character says, "I know the vagabond would gladly cross his breed with a little honest blood . . . . "[54] At one point there is a statement that seems to have slipped by Cooper's decision not to mention the ethnic pluralism of the tribe. The young children are described as "white-haired, olive-skinned." This striking combination is also reported in the sources for the historic Ishmaelites.[55]

The historic first queen of the tribe, Jennie Ishmael, is called a warrioress of renown. Esther, the wife of Cooper's Ishmael Bush, is an "Amazon" and says, " . . . if your . . . friend can be counted as a man, I beg you will set me down as two." During a scouting expedition, "the advance was led by Esther in person, who, attired in a dress half masculine and bearing a weapon like the rest, seemed no unfit leader for the group of wildly clad frontiersmen that followed in her rear." "Follow me," she cries, "I am leader today and I *will* be followed."[56]

The Ishmael of the novel is governor of the tribe and the charismatic father. He officiates at the funeral of a son:

> "He died as a son of mine should die," said the squatter, ". . . a dread to his enemy to the last, and without help from the law! Come, children, we have the grave to make, and then to hunt his murderer."
>
> The sons of the squatter set about their melancholy office in silence and in sadness . . . .
>
> Ishmael stood, with folded arms . . . and when the whole was completed, he lifted his cap to his sons, to thank them for their services, with a dignity that would have become one much better nurtured. Throughout the whole . . . ceremony . . . the squatter had maintained a grave and serious deportment. . . . Taking his wife by the arm, he raised her to her feet . . . saying in a voice that was perfectly steady, though . . . kinder than

usual — "Eester, we have now done all that man and woman
can do. We raised the boy, and made him such as few others
were like, on the frontiers of America; and we have given him
a grave. Let us go on our way."[57]

The denouement of the novel is a tribal court presided
over by the patriarch. In this session he frees two captives
who are young sweethearts, grants permission to an Ishmaelite to leave the tribe with her lover from outside, finds one
person innocent of the charge of murder, judges another
guilty of the crime and executes him on the spot.

> Grave in exterior, saturnine by temperament, formidable by his
> physical means, and dangerous from his lawless obstinacy, his
> self-constituted tribunal excited a degree of awe . . . .
> "I am called upon this day to fill the office which in the settle-
> ments you give unto judges, who are set apart to decide on
> matters that arise between man and man. I have but little
> knowledge of the ways of the courts, though there is a rule that
> is known unto all and which teaches that an 'eye must be re-
> turned for an eye' and 'a tooth for a tooth.' I am no troubler of
> county houses, and least of all do I like living on a plantation
> that the sheriff has surveyed; yet there is a reason in such a law
> that makes it a safe rule to journey by, and therefore it are a
> solemn fact that this day shall I abide by it and give unto all and
> each that which is his due and no more."[58]

The social philosophy which Cooper puts into the mouth
of Ishmael is very similar to the values of the historic
Ishmaelites: an opposition to the accumulation of wealth, de-
testation of the laws of the majority society, and advocacy of
the free use of the land (the last of particular interest to
Cooper).[59] Ishmael says:

> "I have come . . . into these districts because I found the law
> sitting too tight upon me and am not overfond of neighbors who
> can't settle a dispute without troubling a justice and twelve
> men . . . . I am as rightful an owner of the land I stand on as any
> governor of the States! Can you tell me, stranger, where the law
> or the reason is to be found which says that one man shall have a
> section, or a town, or perhaps a county to his use and another
> have to beg for earth to make his grave in? This is not nature,
> and I deny that it is law . . . .[60]
> "The air, the water and the ground are free gifts to man, and
> no one has the power to portion them out in parcels. Man must
> drink, and breathe, and walk, and therefore each has a right to

his share of 'arth. Why do not the surveyors of the States set their compasses and run their lines over our heads as well as beneath our feet? Why do they not cover their shining sheepskins with big words, giving to the landholder, or perhaps he should be called airholder, so many rods of heaven, with the use of such a star for a boundary mark... ?"[61]

The conclusion of *The Prairie* states what is also reported of the historic Tribe of Ishmael: the tribe did not continue west indefinitely; it waxed large in numbers; some Ishmaelites passed into the majority society; others remained true to the tribe; and Patriarch Ishmael and the first queen were never again seen after the westernmost point of their travels.

> On the following morning the teams and herds of the squatter were seen pursuing their course towards the settlements. As they approached the confines of society the train was blended among a thousand others. Though some of the numerous descendants of this peculiar pair were reclaimed from their lawless and semi-barbarous lives, the principals of the family themselves were never heard of more.[62]

Thus Cooper's unknown source reinforces the reconstruction of the history of the Tribe of Ishmael, and provides glimpses of the development of Ishmaelite culture and traditions in the mid-1820s and earlier.

The War upon the Ishmaelites

Besides the impersonal disasters of radically changing social and physical environment, the Tribe of Ishmael faced growing hostility from the "Anglo-Saxon" (or European-origin) farm and town settlers. This antagonism took on a remorseless ferocity beyond the objective conflict of needs and ways of life. The excess can only be explained by racism. The tribe incorporated all three ethnic groups most despised by the majority society of the day.[63] Moreover, their amalgamation into one community flaunted the violation of a most powerful taboo.

One component of the Tribe of Ishmael, southern poor whites, though European in ancestry, received some of the stigma of caste as a people partly separated from the rest of white society and forever at the bottom.[64] A poor white is not merely a white who is poor, says the old Southern proverb.

A second component of the Tribe of Ishmael and a major target of racism, the Native Americans, were identified among the Ishmaelite population in general, in the persons of two clan mothers or female leaders of tribal subdivisions, and above all in the second queen of the Tribe, Betsy Harbet, wife of Patriarch John Ishmael. Betsy was of predominantly Native American descent and spoke little English. A grandchild recalled: "She was a curious critter . . . talked such lingo as I never heard anyone talk." The best friends of the tribe had been the Native American nations, and even in the late nineteenth century the Ishmaelite way of life was seen as more Native American than white.[65]

The third component of the Tribe of Ishmael, the blacks, were equally unmistakable. The Ishmaelites were described as persons most often of tan or olive complexion and of mixed or indeterminate features, but also of European or African appearance. Numerous specific Ishmaelites were identified as "Negro." Moreover, there was no evidence of color hierarchy within the tribe. One Ishmaelite identified as "Negro" was Mrs. Tom Ishmael, wife of the most honored son of Patriarch John and grandson of Patriarch Ben Ishmael. Another was the last-known leader of the entire tribe, Robert Chism.[66]

The three ethnic components were united in a tightly knit society, and many Ishmaelites were descended from two or all three. In Latin America the Tribe of Ishmael would have been considered a mulatto or mestizo caste, intermediate between whites and blacks or Native Americans. Under the normative polarized definition of race in the United States, the Tribe of Ishmael could only be categorized as "colored," therefore "Negro" or African-American (but including others, by marriage or adoption). The unusual composition of the tribe intensified rather than mitigated racist reactions.[67] Here was an exceptional concentration of racial symbols to excite the majority society. An Ishmaelite could be seen at one time as a childish but lascivious "Negro," a violent and savage "Indian," a shiftless and feeble-minded poor-white, and — most unspeakable — a mongrel product of the defilement of racial purity. This was the deadly mix that conjured up the nightmarish events of the war upon the Ishmaelites.

The irrational element of racism lent inordinate fury to the conflict, but the causes of conflict were objective. It was not a social class struggle, for the Ishmaelites and the others did not even belong to the same social structure. It was a *culture conflict* between a migratory hunting and fishing society and a stationary agricultural and commercial society, with attendant opposition of institutions, customs, and values. As the environment changed, the Ishmaelites became more desperate and stubborn, the majority more impatient. The Ishmaelites' anger mounted as their woods, fields, beasts, and pathways receded from them; with equal honesty, the majority could only see Ishmaelite efforts to maintain their economy and culture as criminal trespass and theft, and their refusal to enter the wage-labor economy as degenerate. The question was: shall this land remain as it has been, or shall it change to suit the new order? It could not be both ways.[68]

The conflict between majority society and Ishmaelites occurred in four stages, each one fiercer and more intense.[69] The first stage, from the founding of the tiny state capital to the completion of the pioneer period in the 1840s (coinciding with the death of John Ishmael), was a time of suspicious encounter. There was still room for both peoples: sufficient wilderness remained. Lack of contact was likely and avoidance easily arranged. But in time mutual visibility increased, and each became a nuisance to the other. To the majority people the shantytowns became a scandal, the annual migration an invasion by the "Grasshopper Gypsies," as they called them, and both were a cause of trouble for the authorities and alarm for the citizenry. In the eyes of the majority, the Ishmaelites were transformed from possibly harmless if most peculiar backswoodsmen into n'er-do-well paupers, lower than the lowest laborer. Ishmaelites responded with equal enmity, quite likely coming to identify the Midwestern majority society with the slavery society of the South. Cautious wonder turned to distaste, then to hostility.

In the second stage of the conflict, from the 1840s to the 1880s, the new local governments acted to force the Ishmaelites to abandon their tribe and its ways. Poor laws were enacted which provided for the arrest of "permanent paupers" and their sale to the highest bidder as "bound servants," and for the separation of the children of paupers from their parents, to be sold into involuntary servitude until they reached their majority. Ishmaelites were frequently seized under these laws.[70] The expense of public charity was avoided, and a source of labor was provided for the farms. The children and grandchildren of slaves were thus back in bondage — in the North.* The "bound boy" and "bound girl" became fixtures in Midwestern regional literature. Indiana's foremost poet, James Whitcomb Riley, in the opening line of his best-known poem, sang significantly:

> "Little Orphant Annie's come to our house to *stay*." [Italics mine]

Ishmaelites may have made unsatisfactory bound servants. For after the middle of the century "correctional" institutions burgeoned in the Midwest. Now Ishmaelites in large numbers were sentenced to the new penitentiaries, women's reformatories, poor houses, and "orphan" asylums.[71] However, though Ishmaelites were often incarcerated, there is evidence that they committed few serious crimes. In 291 individual case studies, collected as a representative sample to demonstrate the criminal degeneracy of the tribe, there are no charges of murder or other violent crimes against persons, and only six crimes that can be considered major, committed by five individuals. Major theft is explicitly ruled out.[72] Tribal cohesiveness may have made the Ishmaelites less prone to violence than other slum-dwellers of the industrial revolution.

---

*During the Civil War, an extraordinary proportion of Ishmaelites enlisted in the Union Army. The majority community was puzzled, considering Ishmaelite hatred of regimentation from outside, but could come up with no explanation except that it had become a "fad," without rational motive. There was no suggestion that fugitives from the South might volunteer to fight slavery.

The reports express equal condemnation and revulsion for the six major — but nonviolent — crimes,* the minor crimes, behavior that would not be considered criminal a generation later, noncriminal sins, and deviations from the customs of the majority. In the same horrified manner are reported petty theft, prostitution, begging, "immorality," unemployment, vagrancy, chewing tobacco, smoking cigarettes, drinking "a little," dirt on the face, dirt on the hands, illegitimacy, and the tears of a widow weeping for her husband who "did not appear to realize that he was a bad man."[73]

Prostitution is constantly alleged against the tribe but impossible to assess, so mingled is it with more frequent and vaguer accusations of the sins of "immorality" and "licentiousness."[74] The reports assume depravity because the person under consideration was Ishmaelite. A woman without record of a "vicious life" was still suspect because she lived with her sister who *was* "bad." Another Ishmaelite was given the testimonial, "He was not a criminal so far as was known."[75] Other reports reveal the same logic:

> I have never doubted that she was unchaste after her marriage . . . probably was unchaste, but this is not definitely established, however, that was her reputation.
> It has never been charged that she was a prostitute, but it was a life she knew all about.
> She may not have been unchaste; she certainly was very dirty, coarse, ignorant . . . .
> I don't know that she was unchaste; it was a general rule that all Ishmaels were.[76]

Aside from the multitude of allegations and accusations not brought to trial, the usual court charges against the Ishmaelites were pauperism (chronic unemployment), vagrancy, begging, prostitution, and petty theft.[77] It is difficult not to conclude that the crime of the Ishmaelites was their culture — a nuisance to the majority society and an especial abomination to the Midwestern pious of the Victorian Age.

The Ishmaelites were often defeated in their struggle to maintain the integrity of the tribe. One such defeat was the

---

*The six major crimes charged were a highway robbery, two horse thefts, a burglary, counterfeiting, and receiving stolen goods.

withdrawal from the tribe of an early adolescent Ishmaelite girl, who had entered the majority social system to work for wages in the rag factories. She was one who had complied with the majority's demands of the tribe. At nineteen she lay dying of industrial tuberculosis back in her Ishmaelite cabin. At the deathbed, an official representative of the community reprimanded the mother for having urged her child to return to the tribe and take up begging rather than continue work amid the rag dust. He added to his report, as a touch of humor, that the weeping mother referred to her dying daughter, who was a large young woman, as "my little girl."[78]

Another defeat for the tribe was the seizure of another little Ishmaelite girl and her incarceration in an "orphan" asylum, where she began to suffer convulsions. The parents prepared to sue; the authorities, without proof of child neglect, changed the charge to incorrigibility and sent the child to a reformatory. Her convulsions grew worse, the authorities declared her feeble-minded, and she was treated as such. She soon died; the cause of death was not stated. Incredibly, her younger sister was next seized and sentenced to the reformatory, again for lack of a child-neglect case. The sister contracted an unspecified disease, and she too died behind bars without family or tribe.

The philosophy behind such actions is stated in the reports: Ishmaelites must pay the price of imprisonment until they settle down to steady work; otherwise, the detestable ways of the tribe would be perpetuated. The case studies conclude that though the decisions to sentence to the reformatory may have been incorrect, the fate of the two children was still better than a life of beggary in the Tribe of Ishmael.[79]

Far from being paralyzed by their grief and rage, the Ishmaelites fought back with characteristic stubbornness. An Ishmaelite family sued the state and regained custody of their child; as usual, child neglect could not be established. Another Ishmaelite, who had been imprisoned, sued the authorities for the unsanitary condition of the jail and won considerable damages. An aged Ishmaelite, totally blind, escaped from the poor house and successfully maintained herself, hidden in the abandoned cellar of a demolished house.

Inside, she had constructed basic furnishings, including a stove, from junk. Her entrance was a declivity in the ground, down which she slid, and up which she clambered.[80]

The third stage of the war on the Tribe of Ishmael, between 1880 and 1907, was the creation of an ideology, system, and unity for the crusade. The social engineer was the Reverend Oscar C. McCulloch, minister of the Congregational Church of Indianapolis, a pioneering Modernist, or Liberal, Protestant, who placed social reform ahead of doctrinal orthodoxy. And in his parish the most pressing social problem was the Tribe of Ishmael.[81] In his then nationally known manifesto "The Tribe of Ishmael," he announced the solution to the Ishmaelite problem, an extension of the direction already taken by local authorities: 1) the end of all public assistance to Ishmaelites, except incarceration in correctional institutions; 2) the end of all help to Ishmaelites by private citizens; and 3) the legal separation of Ishmaelite children from their parents. With the men in penitentiaries, the women in reformatories, and the children in asylums, the tribe would be destroyed.[82]

To insure the first two steps, lobby for the third, and unify the war on the tribe, McCulloch organized one of the first councils of social agencies, the Marion County Charity Organization Society, a pilot project and model for the nation. Thus he became a respected advisor to local government, a famous and powerful leader in the Midwestern charity field, and a nationally honored mentor of the new profession of social work.[83]

Now only the ideology was required. The scientific-minded minister asked: how can it be that 10,000 persons and five generations of their ancestors have clung together with such adhesiveness, so uniformly holding to the same immoral practices, such as nomadism and the avoidance of wage-labor? The answer was heredity. The tribe was biologically degenerate, the Ishmaelites hereditary misfits; they could not be reformed or re-educated. The adults must be placed where they could no longer propagate. Some children might

The Tribe of Ishmael:

A Study in Social Degradation.

By Oscar C. McCulloch.

·◁ ∴ ▷·

The studies of Ray Lankaster into " Degeneration " are not only interesting to the student of physical science, but suggestive to the student of social science.

He takes a minute organism which is found attached to the body of the hermit crab. It has a kidney-bean-shaped body, with a bunch of root-like processes through which it sucks the living tissues of the crab. It is known as the Sacculina. It is a crustacean which has left the free, independent life common to its family, and is living as a parisite, or pauper. The young have the Nauplius form belonging to all crustacea : it is a free swimmer. But very soon after birth a change comes over it. It attaches itself to the crab, loses the characteristics of the higher class, and becomes degraded in form and function. An irresistible heriditary tendency siezes upon it, and it succumbs. A hereditary tendency I say, because some remote ancestor left its independent, self-helpful life, and begau a parasitic, or pauper, life. Not using its organs for self-help, they one by one have disappeared,—legs and other members,—until there is left a shapeless mass, with only the stomach and organs of reproduction left. This tendency to parasitism was transmitted to its descendants, until there is set up an irresistible hereditary tendency ; and the Sacculina stands in nature as a type of degradation through parasitism, or pauperism.

From McCulloch, "The Tribe of Ishmael . . . ," National Conference of Charities and Correction, Proceedings *(1888)*

Reverend McCulloch's "scientific" degradation theory

be saved if reared away from the reinforcement of parental influence.[84]

The study of heredity and genetics was a new science; eugenics, its application to the improvement of a species, was even newer. Again McCulloch was a pioneer. His study, published in 1880, was only the second in the United States to apply genetic theory and eugenic proposals to a specific human population. This work on the Tribe of Ishmael was to retain a respected place in the growing literature of eugenics for sixty years, until the movement's collapse.[85] At its high point, during the second and third decades of the twentieth century, McCulloch's warnings and the example of the Tribe of Ishmael were continued and extended throughout the nation and the world by the Eugenics Record Office of the Carnegie Institution. Its director, and the principal founder of the International Eugenics Congress, Charles B. Davenport, incorporated the ugly portrait of the Ishmaelites in his standard eugenics textbook. The field worker of the Eugenics Record Office, Arthur H. Estabrook, famed for his publicizing of "The Jukes," a scorned East Coast community, and for his support of sterilization in the South, borrowed the summary compilation on the Ishmaelites from the state of Indiana and published a sequel to McCulloch's study for the new generation.[86]

Eugenics was intimately related to the rise of "scientific" racism. Proponents of the biological superiority of the white race selected elements from eugenic thought, with the cooperation of some eugenicists, and this full development of racist ideology was widely taught into the fourth decade of the twentieth century. It provided a rationale for the subjugation of African-Americans, as well as for European colonial rule in Africa, Asia, and elsewhere. The Nazis developed their own version of this ideology for the persecution of European ethnic groups.[87] It is appropriate — and not coincidental — that what came to take on world significance, a battery of genetic theories and eugenic proposals in the service of "scientific" racism, can be historically traced to the war on the Ishmaelites as one of its earliest sources. What had been deemed useful in a small and regional ethnic confrontation was seen as useful on a worldwide scale.

The Ishmaelites had shrugged off the early hostility of the newcomers to their land. They had fought back against the efforts of local governments to harass, separate, and imprison them. Their response to the third stage of the war on their tribe, a majority community effort ideologically armed, unified, and systematized, was to organize the tribe's methods of escape. As the twentieth century began, the annual migration continued, the tribal structure remained intact, and 10,000 Ishmaelites stood firm in their loyalty and way of life. But within several years the annual migration had ended, the tribal structure was dissolved, and the Ishmaelites had dispersed from their countryside, scattering beyond the reach of regional authorities.[88] Few again admitted to the tribal name they had so proudly borne. The fourth stage of the war on the tribe was the "final solution" to the Ishmaelite problem. It was compulsory sterilization.

Inspired by their understanding of genetics, criminologists, physicians, and eugenicists had for years discussed the possibilities of castrating chronic offenders, the feeble-minded, and other social undesirables, to prevent the hereditary transmission of their flaws. Illegal castrations had already been performed in "correctional" institutions. Then, as a substitute for castration, sterilization was introduced in the United States by the surgeon of the Indiana State Reformatory, an institution central to the history of the war on the Ishmaelites. In the heritage of McCulloch, this surgeon and the superintendent of the reformatory aroused support for a compulsory sterilization law, while a segment of eugenicists, rallied by the Eugenics Record Office, joined other civic leaders in agitation for enactment of such laws throughout the country. In 1905 a bill was introduced in the Indiana Legislature, and in 1907 the first compulsory sterilization law in the world was enacted by the state of Indiana.

The proposal in other states was justly called the "Indiana Plan." Adherents of the Progressive movement lent their support to what they considered another social reform, and the law spread to twenty-nine other states between 1907 and 1931. European eugenicists watched America pioneer in this

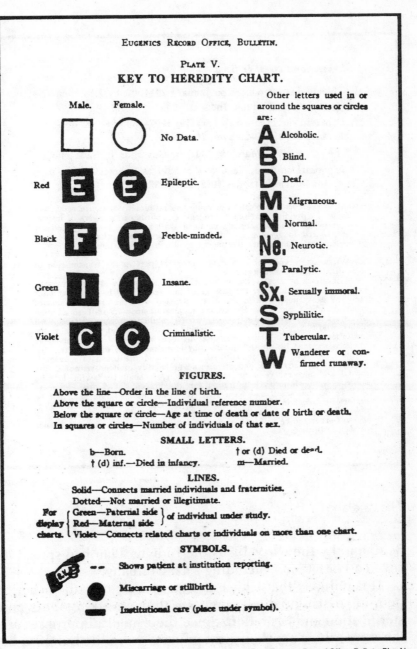

A key to "degenerate peoples" — Eugenics Record Office

1. *Sterilization Law of Indiana.*

The bill was introduced on January 29, 1907. by Representative Horace D. Read, of Tipton, Ind.

It passed the House February 19, 1907—59 ayes, 22 noes; the Senate March 6, 1907—28 ayes, 16 noes.

It was approved March 9, 1907, by Governor J. Frank Hanley.

It appears on the Indiana laws of 1907 as Chapter 215, on page 377; Burns' Indiana Statutes 1908, sec. 2232.

AN ACT to prevent procreation of confirmed criminals, idiots, imbeciles, and rapists; Providing that superintendents or boards of managers of institutions where such persons are confined shall have the authority and are empowered to appoint a committee of experts, consisting of two physicians, to examine into the mental condition of such inmates.

WHEREAS, heredity plays a most important part in the transmission of crime, idiocy, and imbecility:
. THEREFORE, BE IT ENACTED BY THE GENERAL ASSEMBLY OF THE STATE OF INDIANA, that on and after the passage of this act it shall be compulsory for each and every institution in the state, entrusted with the care of confirmed criminals, idiots, rapists, and imbeciles, to appoint upon its staff, in addition to the regular institutional physician, two (2) skilled surgeons of recognized ability, whose duty it shall be, in conjunction with the chief physician of the institution, to examine the mental and physical condition of such inmates as are recommended by the institutional physician and board of managers. If, in the judgment of this committee of experts and the board of managers, procreation is inadvisable, and there is no probability of improvement of the mental and physical condition of the inmate, it shall be lawful for the surgeons to perform such operation for the prevention of procreation as shall be decided safest and most effective. But this operation shall not be performed except in cases that have been pronounced unimproveable: *Provided*, That in no case shall the consultation fee be more than three dollars to each expert, to be paid out of the funds appropriated for the maintenance of such institution.

From Eugenics Record Office, Bulletin No. 10B

The "Indiana Plan"

field, and by the early 1930s the Indiana Plan had spread to seven other nations, including Nazi Germany.[89]

It is unlikely that Ishmaelites, any more than the majority people, distinguished much in their thinking between sterilization and castration. Since their medical purposes are the same, their psychological impacts were likely felt to be similar. It was at this time — between 1900 and 1910, during the learned public discussions of castration and sterilization for misfits, the agitation for a law, the introduction of a bill, the public political debate, the enactment of the law, and the setting up of administrative machinery — that the Ishmaelites gave up their struggle and moved away. In escaping with at least their persons intact, they were more aware of the precariousness of their situation, better organized socially and individually, and more fortunate than some European minority ethnic groups a generation later.

In 1933, Nazi Germany enacted the last of the sterilization laws that had begun in 1907: 200,000 German subjects were sterilized. In 1939 this sterilization law was supplemented by its logical extension, a provision for euthanasia, under which 50,000 "incurably insane," "feeble-minded," and deformed persons were exterminated. In 1941, with the sterilization-euthanasia laws as administrative foundation, the edict was promulgated ordering the genocide of ethnic groups deemed inferior and obnoxious.[90] The trail runs straight, from the war on the Tribe of Ishmael, through the Indiana Plan, to the extermination of the Gypsy peoples of Central Europe, the murder of six million Slavs, and the pogrom against at least six million Jews.

Was the Tribe of Ishmael Islamic?

Following the Indiana Plan and the dispersal of the Tribe of Ishmael during the first decade of this century, Ishmaelites in exile made an impact on the development of black nationalism during the time of this movement's greatest vitality, the 1920s. It is in this context that the Ishmaelite diaspora is still remembered in the African-American communities of the cities of the Great Lakes region. It is understandable that flight would have been northward and into urban anonymity. The geographic line from Chicago to Detroit, with the then new or newly industrialized cities of the Calumet River between, parallels the old east-west Ishmaelite migration route and is the nearest metropolitan region. And fugitives from racism were obviously less likely to flee south at that time.

A contemporary black Chicago professional community

leader in the field of African-American history testifies that he remembers "long ago" — perhaps around World War II — that a Midwestern Tribe of Ishmael or Ishmaelites were sometimes a topic of discussion among black nationalists or militant black civil rights activists. But he cannot remember what was said about the tribe.[91]

Another testimony is from a Black Muslim who was an official of one of the African-American mosques in Chicago which followed the "orthodox" Muslim form of worship in the 1960s (whose leadership, however, had been influenced by black nationalism). He had formerly been a member of a congregation of Black Hebrews (also usually black nationalist) and remembers conversations among them in which a Midwestern Tribe of Ishmael or Ishmaelites were identified as pioneers for black identity and self-determination, national or religious. The references were to the earlier black nationalist period of the 1920s. He cannot remember whether the Ishmaelites were described as Black Hebrews, Black Muslims, or secular nationalists.[92]

Another active Black Muslim, describing himself as a Sufi (mystic) and associated with the "Orthodox" African-American mosque in Detroit, states that in the 1950s or early 1960s he encountered persons who referred to themselves as Ishmaelites by descent and identified with the heritage of a Midwestern Tribe of Ishmael. They were still nomadic, travelling by car between Detroit and Philadelphia. They were definitely black nationalists and also had their own dietary laws; but he was never able to determine whether they considered theirs to be a religious or political movement.[93]

The most valuable testimony to a relationship between the dispersed Ishmaelites and the rise of twentieth-century black nationalism is from an African-American wholesale grocer of Chicago, whose work takes him into rural Illinois and Indiana. He has been a devoted student of African-American history all his life, but his first loyalty is to Moorish Science, of which he has been a member for some forty-five years. Moorish Science, which was politically associated with the largest black nationalist organization, the Universal

Negro Improvement Association (UNIA) led by Marcus Garvey in the 1920s, is a religious denomination organized in New Jersey in 1913, and is the earliest known Islamic organization of the black community in the United States. Thus Moorish Science has been both a proponent of black nationalism and an advocate of the Muslim faith. The well-known and larger Nation of Islam, established in 1930, has recognized that Moorish Science was a forerunner of its movement. This adherent of Moorish Science states that when he joined the movement in about 1930, five years after its arrival in Chicago, he met a Mrs. Gallivant, who had joined Moorish Science at Detroit around 1920, when it was first introduced to the Midwest. She had come from downstate Indiana or Illinois and called herself an Ishmaelite. She spoke of the Tribe of Ishmael as a people who had dwelled downstate, and who after moving north were among the first to assist in the establishment of Moorish Science in the Midwest.[94]

It is clear that the Tribe of Ben Ishmael meant something — and something important — in Midwestern black nationalist circles early in the twentieth century. It is not surprising that there should have been significant dialogue between those who had once been an independent nation in North America and those who sought the self-determination of the entire African-American people.

From these oral sources an additional but less certain meaning may be extracted. The province of Ishmaelite influence appears to have been the non-Christian religious nationalist movements, the small Black Hebrew and large Black Muslim groups, rather than the secular nationalist organizations. When this impression, and in particular the reported relationship between Ishmaelites and Moorish Science, are considered together with certain aspects of old Ishmaelite culture, the question arises: Were there Islamic influences within the Tribe of Ishmael from the beginning? That the tribe kept itself apart from the Christian churches has been established. Ishmaelite abstinence from alcohol and the polygamy its tribal leaders practiced are also customs held by Islamic communities of the Old World. A less striking parallel is the nomadism of the Ishmaelites and of the Fulani, one of the few migratory peoples of West Africa and at the same time the most militant missionaries of Islam in that region during the eighteenth and early nineteenth centuries, the period when the Tribe of Ishmael was gathering and developing its culture in North America. African Muslims did get to the Americas as slaves: in Jamaica they planned a slave insurrection; and in Brazil they led a number of such revolts aimed at establishing an Islamic Emirate of Bahía, with a Fulani noblewoman who had been brought to Brazil as a slave as their monarch. The eminent Africanist Ivor Wilks has raised the question whether these New World events were related to the Fulani holy wars occurring in Africa at the same time.[95] The intention of the present speculations is to extend this question to the Tribe of Ishmael.

In this context the most striking element of Ishmaelite culture is the name "Ben Ishmael." An Ishmaelite tradition, given without explanation, was that the "Ben" in this name "was not exactly a name."[96] If, then, "Ben" was something like a title, an honorific or other tribal symbol, in conjunction with the Semitic name Ishmael it strongly suggests the Hebrew phrase *Ben Ishmael*, son of Ishmael, or the nineteenth-century rendering of "Ben" in the Arabic phrase *I'bn Ismail*, which also means son of Ishmael. In the sacred scriptures of Islam, the holy Koran, Ishmael is a revered and patriotic figure, father and founder of the Arab people. By extension the name has come to mean not only Bedouin or Arab but also any Muslim nomad, any nomad, or any Muslim. (It might also be noted that the plural form of the Arabic phrase, *Beni Ismail* — with the accent of the first word on the first syllable — sounds very much like Ben Ishmael and is translated either Sons of Ishmael or Tribe of Ishmael.)

The accumulation of the tribal traits of shunning Christian churches, abstinence from alcohol, polygamy, nomadism, and the symbolic name with its resemblance to Arabic proves nothing conclusive. But they are sufficient to raise the question of Islamic influences on the old culture of the Tribe of Ishmael, in light of its established relationship with black nationalism after the diaspora, and the report of its participation in the Midwestern founding of Moorish Science. One of the sayings of Noble Drew Ali, founder, prophet, and Divine Imam of Moorish Science, was that the National Temple was moved from New Jersey to the Midwest because Islam is closer to the latter region. This saying has been taken as spiritual, but a leading Moorish Science theologian states that there is no reason why the saying may not also be taken historically.[97] A phrase long favored by the Nation of Islam, referring in a spiritual or psychological sense to the African-American people, may also be pondered for possible additional historical meaning: "The lost-found Nation in the wilderness of North America."

There are also curious aspects of old Midwest communities located on the Ishmaelite annual migration route. At the northern end is Morocco, Indiana, at the southern end Mahomet, Illinois, and on the last segment, on the way back to Indianapolis, Mecca, Indiana. That three Islamic names appear in Indiana and Illinois is of no great significance in itself, for there are Islamic, ancient Egyptian, Greek, Roman, Hindu, and Chinese place names scattered across the maps of all the American states. American settlers seem to have favored exotic names. But when a community lies on the Ishmaelite route, has an Islamic name and additional historical characteristics that may be related, it is worthy of comment.

There is nothing more to say of Mecca, Indiana, unless one choose to consider that this location, named for the Muslim goal of pilgrimage, was near the last place where the Tribe of Ishmael could celebrate the completion of another annual migration, before arrival at winter quarters in unfriendly Indianapolis.

Morocco, a few miles south of the Kankakee River near the Illinois border, is distinguished by small, long round-roofed cabins shaped like Quonset huts (or Hobbit houses) but older, sturdily constructed of rounded boards, now old and weathered, apparently designed by country carpenters. Most of them now stand in the yards of newer, conventional houses, but the largest is still a residence. They are constructed as if the builders had heard of Moorish architecture but had not seen a picture, and not realizing that the dome rises from a squared base, constructed elongated roofs that are all dome. Across the Illinois line, a few miles northwest of Morocco, is the all-black rural community of Pembroke. In this old and isolated village there is a Moorish Science Temple, though the movement nationally is very small today and at its height was usually concentrated in large cities. Several miles northwest of Pembroke is Kankakee; it is the smallest town in America to have a Temple of the Nation of Islam.[98]

Mahomet is the oldest settlement of Champaign County and one of the oldest in this part of Illinois. The origin of the name is unknown and rather enigmatic, considering the negative image of Muhammad in nineteenth-century America. Suggestions to explain the name in local histories have included distinctiveness and ease of spelling, imposition by the Post Office Department without local consultation, adoption from the name of the local Masonic lodge (which would extend the mystery), and commemoration of a local Indian chief. The last is the most interesting in context of this inquiry.[99]

In 1870, ten percent of the settlers of Mahomet Township and adjoining townships bore very unusual family names which are difficult to identify as to national origin. Half of these, or five percent of the population, have an "oriental" flavor. Variant spellings of British, French, or German names may be represented, which others will identify. But it is the cumulative effect that lends possible significance to the list:

Aimen	Fayant	Manser	Pusha
Babb	Gamel	Mardin	Shafty
Barlain	Ham	Mathena	Sherfy
Basore	Hamella	Melamne	Swarty
Bensyl	Hayar	Menealla	Tapop
Booromer	Hissany	Morry	Tobaka
Chadden	Kasheur	Nebeker	Tomany
Churry	Lahmon	Omey	Turk[100]
Dalama	Lumen	Osman	
Fardy	Maben	Pankar	

Osman, Booromer, and Nebeker are reminiscent of the early and still revered Caliphs of Islam, Osman, Omar and Abu-Bekr. (Osman, a name given to the leader of the Fulani holy

war referred to, is also the name of a village near Mahomet.)
Sherfy suggests Sharrieff, an Islamic holy name; Pusha is
close to Pasha; Gamel is an Islamic name, and Manser suggests the Islamic Mansour. Fardy recalls the name of the
founder of the Nation of Islam, Master Wallace Fard
Muhammad, or Mr. W. Fard. Basore calls to mind the seaport
of Iraq, Basorah or Basra; Babb is an Arabic word meaning
"gate" (used spiritually by Bahais); and Hamella and
Menealla are constructed like the numerous Islamic names
compounded from the word for God, Allah, such as Nasrallah.

The 1860s are too early for immigrant settlers from eastern
Europe and the Near East. Moreover, in a 1906 Indianapolis
rural directory, Babb, Besore, Fur, and omer [sic], along with
similar sounding names, are identified as old American,
rather than any of the other numerous nationality identifica-
tions used.[101] An historical geography of Champaign County
confirms this identification by singling out Mahomet and one
adjoining township as having been originally settled by persons of "Mixed American Southern Extraction." Whatever
the phrase is intended to convey, it is an admirable description of the composition of the Tribe of Ishmael.[102]

By 1883 (thirteen years after their listing) almost all of
these unusual names had disappeared from the Champaign
County directory.[103] Nor do they appear today in the tele-
phone books of that county or of Chicago.

It should be remembered that, except for Ishmael, the
family names of the Tribe of Ishmael found in the state compilation of case studies were common European names. If
then the unusual names around Mahomet were Ishmaelite,
the tribe must have used two sets of names, one European for
the Indiana authorities, the other for home use — and also
used publicly in the vicinity of Mahomet into the 1870s. If
these uncommon names were not Ishmaelite, there must
have been a second unusual community living along the
Ishmaelite route.

About 1885 an early settler wrote the following statement
in an historical sketch of Mahomet Township. It is an odd
little statement even for the kind of personalized material
found in county histories. It seems to establish that there had

been an earlier settlement, now entirely gone, those who had given the name Mahomet to the place. It could refer to the families with unusual names. At any rate it was published only a few years after their disappearance.

> The first settlers of any community are not always the most permanent. . . . I am unable to tell much about the early settlers of the town . . . but I never had the least idea that I should be called upon to tell of their virtues, for I am sure they had but few if any faults, but had I known of it I might have asked many questions that would have brought out interesting answers.[104]

The enigmas of Mahomet and Morocco, the parallels between Ishmaelite and Islamic culture, and the contemporary testimonies converge to form not proof, but a pattern of circumstantial evidence weighty enough to advance the hypothesis that there was an Islamic cultural element of African origin within the Tribe of Ishmael.

In 1938 a remarkable philosopher of the history of Islam in the African-American community offered a framework for research and analysis that is prophetic as well as historical.

> The story of the Nation of Islam cannot be considered as complete in itself. Militant and cultist movements among migrant Negroes in the cities of the North have formed a sort of tree. After one branch has grown, flourished, and begun to decay, another shoots up to begin over again the same cycle . . . .
>
> Out of the wreck of the Marcus Garvey movement, there sprang Phoenix-like the Moorish-American cult of which the prophet was Noble Drew Ali. After this prophet's disappearance and the stabilization of the movement as a formally organized denomination, there sprang up the Nation of Islam . . . . From among the larger groups of Moslems there has sprung recently an even more militant branch . . . (which) identifies the prophet Mr. W. D. Fard with the god Allah . . . (and raises) to the rank of prophet the former Minister of Islam, Elijah Muhammad . . . .
>
> Thus continues the chain of these movements, each running through its cycle of growth and decay, and all of them interweaving as strands of a web.[105]

The hypothesis now offered seeks to identify an older branch of this tree of African-American Islam. It is suggested that behind the millions of African-Americans who have been affected by Islam in recent years, the affiliated and the un-affiliated, behind the aborted Organization for African-American Unity led by the sainted Malek Shabazz (Malcolm X) and the movements which arose from that example, behind the Nation of Islam founded by the Divine Imam Master Wallace Fard Muhammad and led so long by the Honorable Elijah Muhammad, behind the Moorish Science of the Divine Imam Noble Drew Ali, behind the Islamic elements of the Universal Negro Improvement Association led by the Honorable Marcus Garvey, there stands one more earlier Islamic saint or Imam, Ben Ishmael, and one more earlier Islamic community, the Tribe of Ishmael, a bridge between African and American Islam, a lost-found nation in the wilderness of North America.

Chapter IV

VICTOR GREENE

"Becoming American":
The Role of Ethnic Leaders —
Swedes, Poles, Italians, and Jews

> *We do not want to form a state within a state;
> but we want the Swedes to be a salt in America
> that has a savor.*
>
> — Vilhelm Lundström (1922)

> *Mother:*
> *"You shall speak Italian and nothing else. . . ."*
>
> *Daughter:*
> *"Aw, gwan! Youse tink I'm goin' to talk dago
> 'n' be called a guinea! . . . I'm 'n American."*
>
> — Reported conflict of generations (1903)

LIKE THE HYDRA OF GREEK MYTHOLOGY, American ethnic pluralism is an enigma that has fascinated intellectuals who every so often in our past have tried to explain the phenomenon; just when they have appeared to put the matter to rest, it intrudes itself once again on the scene as puzzling as ever. Now, as at other times in our history, popular critics are again wondering how to explain what appears to be persistent ethnic group identity. The current popular debate is whether cultural diversity really does exist, whether it is artificial or manufactured, and whether the feeling should be encouraged, condemned, or simply ignored.[1]

Academic historians still wonder how ethnic community began here in the first place, how factional it was and is, and whether it was/is a rejection or reaffirmation of majority values. While an early observer of American society, the eighteenth-century French diplomat Crèvecoeur, referred confidently to its ability to assimilate differences, writers in this century have been less certain of those powers of homogenization. With people recently coming from ever more foreign and exotic ethnic sources — southeastern Europe, Asia, and Latin America — the nagging question that kept cropping up was whether that increasingly polyglot mass of arrivals, producing a complex of people with African, Swedish, Sikh, Basque, Armenian, Polish, and other ancestries, do or ever did share any commonly held American principles. This chapter suggests that in the light of the formation of group institutions in the United States, and especially of the people who built them, ethnic values were more complementary than antagonistic.

In general the chapter seeks to illuminate a part of that

144

still little-known process of "becoming American" by focusing on the formal establishment of certain ethnic communities, more particularly on the intentions of their organizers. These group founders are extremely important since they, as pioneers, helped to shape the groups' superstructures, clarify goals, and set up local churches, fraternal associations, newspapers, and voluntary collectives of various kinds. These individuals played a dual and seemingly contradictory function, as preservers of tradition and agents for change: on the one hand, by their organizing effort they assisted the maintenance of their group's ethnic culture, language, religion, and folk life; on the other, they promoted their people's participation in the new American society. I designate these leaders "traditional progressives," mediating brokers who placed themselves advantageously between their own constituents and the dominant society.[2] Whatever personal benefits they derived from their placement — and all did profit from their position — and whether they had any conscious understanding of their influence on adjustment — most did, some did not — the important consequence is the result of their influence. These leaders helped to construct an open-ended ethnic community which, while providing its members with the continuity of tradition, also encouraged their involvement and participation in the larger world.

The methodology of demonstrating an essentially accommodationist leadership among immigrant groups is highly problematical. One major difficulty is defining "leadership" precisely. I would like to designate its meaning as something more than simple prominence: actually, it was *distinction* which rests on the loyalty and support of group members. As such, these leaders had influence on and were representative of rank and file sentiment. A few years ago the sociologist Paul Lazarsfeld and his colleagues referred to this kind of community influence in a well-known study of voter preference in elections.[3] Lazarsfeld cites "opinion leaders" who had gained the confidence of their followers and thereby influenced — though did not determine — their electoral decisions.

Oddly, American social historians have ignored the com-

munity leaders of the sort that the Lazarsfeld group desig-
nates, despite the high visibility of such figures in historical
sources. Whether the recorders of our past have become
overly concerned with inarticulate and anonymous folk
through quantitative methods, or whether the difficulty of
choosing the *most* influential ethnic leaders deters them, the
neglect of these opinion-makers is regrettable. Lionized by
their own immigrant generation at their death, the ethnic
notables are virtually unknown outside their own group and
often little known within it. They are resurrected here not as
heroes to whom to pay homage but as vital agents of continuity and change, people who fashioned their communities
by revealing adjustment devices for the foreign-born.

Besides the problem of specifying the kind of elite to investigate, the task of naming the specific immigrant leaders is
hazardous in another way. The researcher realizes on closer
inspection of foreign life in America that ethnic group life
was hardly monolithic. Each community had a number of
vigorously competing factions, and many groups had a proliferation of leaders: nationalist, socialist, and clerical were
normally the major types. In addition to these differences the
timing and level of leadership further complicate the choice
of person worthy of historical study. Was the major opinion
leader the one who actually initiated a voluntary association
or the person who grouped together several bodies into a
local, regional, or national federation?

Fortunately, the problem of leadership selection is resolved upon a scrutiny of the groups' immigrant history. One
or at most a handful of notable figures do emerge as heads of
the communities in the first generation. These were people
whom we can cite as the group's opinion leaders, architects of
the immigrant societies. While naming the single most significant founder may be debatable, everyone I cite possessed
a remarkably similar philosophy. Each sought to insure that
his constituency worked toward essentially forward-looking
and accommodationist goals. His plan was not innovative but
synthetic, drawing upon the group's past as well as preparing
his followers for a new life in a new land.

To provide some minimal breadth of coverage, I refer to

builders of four of the larger immigrant communities, the Swedes, Poles, Italians, and East European Jews. The leaders I have designated were all well known to most of the incoming group members — if not prior to their coming, then certainly soon after they landed. This elite held occupational roles of supreme status: they were a Swedish minister, a Polish priest, four Italian *padrone*-bankers, and two Jewish Yiddish newspaper editors. Thus their influence rested not only on their personal qualities but also on the title or office they held with the group. They were: the Reverends Tufve Nilsson Hasselquist of Rock Island, Illinois and Wincenty Barzynski of Chicago; Antonio Maggio and Cavalier Luigi Fugazy of New York; Paul Russo of New Haven; Salvatore Pelletieri of Utica; and Kasriel Sarasohn and Abraham Cahan of New York.

The achievement of these men came not merely from the group sanction of their occupations as cleric, labor recruiter, and journalist but from the remarkable insight they had in supplying their constituents with a score of needed social services as group advisors. These "leaders" were also servants of their ethnic group and therefore ideal mechanisms to reveal how the community adjusted group tradition with group future. The people sought group mediators to help in their adjustment to American life; again, these "leaders" were also "followers" who through their unusual talent for group mobilization and organization provided the desired harmonization of old and new, the organizational means for necessary cultural and traditional continuity as well as the institutions to enable them to prosper in a new environment. They were indeed traditional progressives. A view of group needs and how the leaders conducted themselves in fulfilling them requires background in European as well as American conditions.

Since religious institutions constituted the most important framework in the building of Swedish and Polish America, we must examine the principle upon which the ethnic church was established and particularly the most important clerics who performed the task of reconstruction in America, the Reverends Hasselquist and Barzynski.[4] The aim of these powerful group pastors was to maintain the religious tradition of their people, not as a precise replica of their group's Old World institution nor as a rejection of Americanization pressures, but as an integral part of the new American environment.

The Swedish-American case is more obviously and basically assimilative than the others. Most of the first Swedish-American immigrants who left Northern Europe before the 1850s came here as members of a variety of dissenting sects totally committed to rejecting their "homeland." They had crossed the Atlantic largely because of their dissatisfaction with the official state Lutheran church. Even those Swedish arrivals who had held to traditional Lutheranism were also dissatisfied with the "old country" for religious as well as economic reasons. As farmers who had heard of cheap land, they came to settle permanently in the recently opened American Midwest. Thus, early arriving members of dissenting sects, the Jansonites, or recently converted Baptist Mormons or Quakers considered their new land as home, retaining little affection for and certainly no loyalty to the Swedish governmental authority. Even the bulk of later-arriving Swedes after midcentury, nominally faithful Swedish Lutherans, sought rapid assimilation in America. They quickly rejected their traditional church, dropped their language, and became nearly indistinguishable from Anglo-American Protestants.[5]

While many colonies had been started earlier, a separate and distinct Swedish America did not exist until after the Reverend Tufve Hasselquist arrived and organized the Augustana Synod of the American Lutheran Church in 1862. From the mid-1700s until that point, Swedes had either joined mixed Norwegian and/or German Lutheran centers or remained isolated in their own particular pietistic colonies.

The first separate Swedish settlement began in 1841 at Pine Lake, Wisconsin under the direction of Gustav Unonius, later an Episcopal minister who helped begin a combined Swedish-Norwegian church in Chicago in 1849. A Swedish Jansonite sect had settled at the Bishop Hill site in Illinois in 1845; thus a number of isolated group plantings had begun during that decade. Even some Lutherans arrived at this time, led by ministers who were sympathetic to the popular dissatisfaction with the austere and unresponsive state church. Still these clerics sought to minimize leakage of the group away from the traditional Lutheran faith.

The first notable Swedish liberal clergyman in America, the Reverend Lars Paul Esbjorn, came to New York in 1849 to minister to the increasing number of Swedes in Illinois. Even if they disliked being known by that nationality, he labored to keep them within the fold.[6] Esbjorn rallied his people not because of any dissatisfaction with American society in general but rather because of his suspicions of the older, more Germanized American Lutherans. He sought to conserve what one might call the Scandinavian character of doctrine and worship, that is, to keep the Augsburg Confession as the basis of the church. He was certainly not interested in re-establishing Swedish Lutheranism *per se* on this side of the Atlantic. Esbjorn's efforts produced a joint Norwegian-Swedish religious organization known as the Evangelical Lutheran Synod of Northern Illinois in 1851. In addition, he sent an earnest request to his liberal colleagues in Sweden, especially Hasselquist, to help him keep Swedish Americans from leaving their traditional religious persuasion. Hasselquist's position was very similar to Esbjorn's: he shared a distaste for the distant and uninspiring state church and clergy. He differed with his colleague, however, in his more enthusiastic support of the fundamental American principle of church-state separation. Hasselquist endorsed the wide distance between religion and government because he felt that that would make for a more vital low church and produce a freer environment for greater piety.[7] In addition, Hasselquist grew apart from Esbjorn personally. He soon outdistanced the latter as the major Swedish-American cleric because of his greater popularity. Ordinary immigrants were attracted to this large, powerful minister with a "winning personality" who "won [much] respect and admiration."[8] His biographer described him as "the most versatile and ablest leader in the annals of Swedish American Lutheranism," in fact, "in all affairs which concerned the welfare of the

Swedish people." He was a man who "knew the inmost thoughts of his people as perhaps few churchmen have known them."[9]

Hasselquist's pre-eminent influence was evident in the very early years of his arrival in America. He had traveled to Galesburg, Illinois with his wife in 1852, on a petition signed by Swedish parishioners in America and forwarded by Esbjorn. In a short time he attracted church members by his unpretentious carriage, his willingness to live in their homes, his informal manner, and his simple but moving sermons.[10]

It was during the period before 1870 that Hasselquist expanded his influence widely among his ethnic group. By 1870 he, more than any single individual, had contributed to the organization of major Swedish-American institutions on an accommodationist basis. He thus became his people's leading broker, mediating between the Swedish-American community and American society at large. His sponsor Esbjorn, much less committed to American principles, soon became his rival, and a competition for power grew. The rivalry developed chiefly because the earlier pioneer disliked what he considered Hasselquist's excessively liberal and progressive affirmation of American religious practice. Esbjorn especially disliked the lack of piety and the widespread secularism he found in Americanized churches. Lacking Hasselquist's large and growing base of popular support, however, Esbjorn's influence in the 1860s — never strong — continued to wane. This personal struggle took place in the formative phases of the emergence of Swedish America. So the bulk of the Swedish Lutheran arrivals who came after 1870 found Hasselquist clearly pre-eminent and in command. Esbjorn retired to Sweden just before that date.[11]

Hasselquist's objectives are important. He achieved his position as *the* Swedish-American opinion leader, the major intermediary, with a mixed traditional and progressive outlook. He held that his Swedes must retain their adherence to the tenets of the Lutheran Augustana Confession yet at the same time maintain good relations with other American Lutherans and even play a politically active role as American citizens. In short, he urged his followers to select what was spiritually beneficial from the past but also provide for the future.

Further evidence of Hasselquist's organizing and mediating talent and his rise to influence can be seen in some of his other achievements: he established the Swedish-American press in 1853 and edited what was to be the group's most influential journal, *Hemlandet*, through which he broadcast his views; he headed the newly formed Scandinavian Evangelical Lutheran Augustana Synod in 1861 (really *the* Swedish-American church body after the amicable Norwegian and Danish departure in 1870); he became a popular professor of theology at the Synod's seminary and college after Esbjorn's return to Sweden; and he assumed the educational leadership by becoming the head of Augustana College

The Reverend Tufve Nilsson Hasselquist, who "knew the inmost thoughts of his people as perhaps few churchmen have known them"

Courtesy of Lutheran School of Theology, Chicago

in 1875, a post he held until his death in 1891. Most Swedish immigrants came after Hasselquist had achieved his pre-eminence (especially as the major student advisor at Augustana College), so he was able to mold a sizable generation of new Swedish-American leaders.[12]

Hasselquist was certainly a "traditional progressive," for whom the enduring legacy of the past had to be the immutable moral and denominational principles that constituted his people's valuable ethnic inheritance. At the same time he provided for their material and political future in America even at the cost of abandoning the Swedish language — a measure which he favored.[13] This prescription of blending old and new he felt would create a New World community that would be a far better one than that which they left in the Old.[14]

Hasselquist had a Polish-American counterpart who was as conspicuous, as clerical, and as significant a mediating influence in Chicago's Polish community. The Reverend Wincenty Barzynski would not have consciously considered himself in any way related to his Swedish contemporary as an assimilative agent. And in some ways the differences were well founded. On the surface Barzynski was less assimilative, advocating a more cohesive ethnic group in America; he was much less anxious for his people to join in American public issues.[15] Nevertheless, Barzynski's impact was modern too, as it enabled his followers to prepare for an integrated role in their adopted country.

The opinion leader among these East European arrivals, just as among Swedish newcomers, would have to be a cleric, although religion functioned differently in Poland. The Swedish masses were nominal churchgoers; though some were members of splintered pietistic sects, many were generally apathetic to religion.[16] Though Lutheranism was the state church, no specific religious denomination was a prerequisite to being a Swede in the eyes of group members. For most Poles, however, Roman Catholicism was an essential element of Polish identity. Jews and the variety of Protestants who had claim to being Polish by virtue of language or other cultural marks might consider themselves ethnic members; but in America as well as Europe even some of the liberal Poles denied that Jews were Poles, and felt that the Universal

The Reverend Wincenty Barzynski, the leading Polish-American patriarch in an ethnic group that venerated the clerical office

Faith and the Polish identity were synonymous.[17]

If Catholicism and Polishness (*Polskość*) were identical, then the office of priest commanded high esteem among the group in the Old World and the New. The ordinary peasant family considered itself blessed to have a man of the cloth as a member.[18] The position held that very high status and respect among Polish immigrants, more exalted, say, than among Swedes or Italians. As a cleric, Barzynski did have a built-in advantage in exerting influence over his "flock."

While possessing a more substantial cultural sanction than Hasselquist, Barzynski did resemble his Swedish colleague's role in terms of time. Barzynski was not the initial organizer or the earliest pioneer of Polish group worship in America; Esbjorn had been that for the Swedes and a Franciscan, Rev. Leopold Mocaygeba, for the Poles. Polish parishes (in Polish "parish" is synonymous with "settlement") already had begun in Texas, Wisconsin, and Michigan before Barzynski arrived, and elsewhere without his involvement. However, Barzynski did affect an entire immigrant generation by winning his pre-eminent position in the formative era of the evolving Polish-American community. The growth of his influence took place between 1870 and 1900, over three decades preceding the arrival of the majority of his countrymen in America.[19] During the last quarter of the nineteenth century Barzynski was clearly the leading Polish-American patriarch in an ethnic group that venerated the clerical office.

Barzynski's rise was somewhat less self-made than Hasselquist's. He had the good fortune not only of being a Polish man of the cloth but also of being a regular priest. As a member of the wealthy Resurrectionist Order, a European Polish Catholic brotherhood, he possessed resources which he used to advantage. He had personal qualities favorable to leadership, an aggressive personality, and a remarkable self-assured determination. One authority referred to him as a man of an "iron will."[20] There was no question of his unique understanding of and impact on his people.

Barzynski's tangible organizational credits outshone Hasselquist's as a leader, although the Polish priest did stimulate more internal opposition. Having fled the abortive Polish

Insurrection of 1863 and joined the Resurrectionist Order in Europe, he went first to Texas to lead several needy parishes there in 1866, and then proceeded on to Chicago in 1874 to head a burgeoning Polish church there.[21] That parish, St. Stanislaw, was the parent Polish institution for the rest of the mighty *Polonia* there. In his quarter-century as pastor and provincial leader of the American Resurrectionist Order, Barzynski, more than any other individual, personified this major Polish community in America. His Roman Catholic parish grew to be the largest in the country — and probably the world — accommodating between 30,000 and 40,000 souls by the 1890s.[22] Further, for his own benefit as well as a service to incoming group members and parishioners, he set up a bank which received, held, and lent moneys. Although he managed it poorly in his later years, the Polish bank was a resource that financed the score of other Polish parishes in the area, many of which were staffed by priests of his own order. Most of the group's neighborhood churches in this Polish-American capital were established with his help. Barzynski's other organizational achievements show his unrivaled impact: he rebuilt and redirected the group's second largest fraternal association, the Polish Roman Catholic Union; he started a publishing company which put out the Poles' leading daily, *Dziennik Chicagoski;* he established the group's first secondary school, constructed an orphanage, and brought into the area two orders of Polish teaching nuns; and he helped form numerous parish societies in Chicago.

Such an active and strong-willed cleric stimulated devoted followers as well as determined opponents, and thus drew the ire of some critics. But he won the respect of virtually every Polish-American leader, whether friend or foe, as reaction to his passing proved.[23] As the most prominent Polish-American of his day, Barzynski determined ideals for his people which, as with Hasselquist, made him an agent of both cultural preservation and New World adjustment, and which qualify him as a traditional modernist. His major objective was to maintain the historic Polish adherence to Roman Catholic dogma and authority in the group's transition to America. Throughout his long tenure in Chicago, as he reorganized the PRCU, helped organize new parishes, and established all the other ethnic cultural, educational, journalistic, and welfare institutions, he insisted that above all his people must keep the faith. Clearly unlike Hasselquist in this respect, he was suspicious of the outside world, fearing Poles might "drown in the Anglo-Saxon Protestant sea," as group clerics put it. But for Barzynski the hostile environment for Polish-Americans were the non-Catholic evangelists of any group, even his own, whom he felt sought to turn his people from the one true and historic path. In fact, for him Polish "masons," "saloonkeepers," and "atheists" were far greater menaces to his flock than Protestant Anglo-Americans some distance away.

Such unquestioning loyalty to the Church and its leaders got Barzynski into difficulty with emerging Polish nationalists, who increasingly accused him and his clerical supporters of group betrayal, subordinating *Polskość* to Roman Catholicism. Some of his opponents were so antagonized that they joined an Independent (later the Polish National) Catholic Church. In a sense Barzynski was guilty of not being a complete ethnic patriot, but only because he believed that Catholicism was the only true religious identity for Poles. The others, he insisted, those who did not make Polishness and Catholicism synonymous, were simply people "without God." They simply were not Poles, no matter what language they used or what the beliefs of their forebears.[24]

While not consciously aware of his assimilationist influence, Barzynski's impact was actually "modernist" or "progressive" as well as conservative. He was forward-looking in the way he sought to integrate his people into a long-established institution that was Americanist in theory, the American Catholic Church. Ever since it had been established in the late 1700s, the Catholic Church in the United States had labored to demonstrate its compatibility with this nation's laws and culture and its loyalty to American constitutional principles.[25] By insisting on Polish-American submission to American Catholic authority, Barzynski was in fact reaffirming the Church's founding, assimilationist goals in the New World. His position was based not simply on his theological convictions but also on political necessity. The Resurrectionist Order had made an agreement with the Chicago Bishop just prior to Barzynski's arrival that it would supply priests to the emerging Polish parishes for ninety-nine years. The fathers thus became the diocesan advisors on group matters; and the next prelate, the Reverend Patrick Feehan, depended heavily on Barzynski for counsel on all Polish activities and disputes in the area as they mounted during the 1890s.[26] And thus the St. Stanislaw pastor became the formally sanctioned intermediary between the Polish immigrant community he organized and the American Catholic world.

This induced process of integration into an American religious institution did not mean that Barzynski did not express and seek ethnic interests. He firmly did believe in and work for American Catholic recognition of its Polish communicants, fostering group associations within the Church, fraternal bodies and the like. In fact, from the 1870s he urged the German and Anglo-American superiors to appoint a Polish bishop in America and, looking forward to the resurrection of the Polish state, he sponsored and commended demonstrations of nationalist feeling. But such partisan displays of group feeling were less important than the fact that Poles were Roman Catholics, willing to follow religious strictures and diocesan authority, whoever exerted it — Irish, German, or Anglo-American prelates.[27]

This essentially assimilative position was not an idiosyncratic one of Barzynski alone but the conventional view held by Polish-American clerics generally in the late nineteenth century. His counterparts in America, like Rev. John Pitass of Buffalo, Rev. Benvento Gramliewicz of Scranton, and others elsewhere were as tenacious in their reverence for and loyalty to American Catholic authority. The decisive restatements of obedience to diocesan rule at the three Polish Catholic Congresses around 1900 are evidence of the essentially assimilative position.[28] Even the minority of highly critical ethnic priests, Independents who later became National Catholics and broke from diocesan obedience, insisted that they were still loyal to the faith, though not to their specific bishops.[29]

Obviously, not all the major leaders of American immigrant communities were clerics, as was the case with Swedish- and Polish-Americans. Determining notable persons among the Italian newcomers is exceptionally difficult for a number of reasons that have to do with the character and composition of the group. These people from southern Europe were more segmented regionally, economically, and socially. While all were of one faith, Roman Catholicism, the attachment of most was nominal, and while they fervently did observe religious ritual, few honored the clerical office with the esteem of the Poles. Italian immigrants' local origins were intensely felt, which, along with deeply felt family ties, tended to keep them divided. Also, social classes were significant, highly stratified, and distant if not hostile.[30]

With this pervasive social fragmentation, a common condition of Italian life in the Old World, it is a wonder that any individuals at all emerged as persons of substantial influence in America, figures whom a large colony rather than just a few related families could respect. However, such organizers and opinion leaders did appear, and they were designated by the same title by which their immigrant constituents identified them, the community "papa." To understand the rise of these "papas" and the deference paid to them in America's "Little Italies," we must recognize Italian social classifications and the labels and meanings of certain occupations in the group which both members and outsiders used. All the titles lack precision in definition, and some roles were the source of heated controversy.

The earliest Italian arrivals in America came largely from northern Italy. These "northerners" would constitute most of the early group elite in America. The small peasant farmers from the South, the *contadini*, arrived mostly after 1880. The men of some education and skills in Italy and America, more likely "northerners" than "southerners," became the *artigiani* — shopkeepers, fruit merchants, clerks, tradesmen, and artisans. Few of the wealthy gentry, the *dons*, or the poorest day laborers, the *giornalieri*, wished to or could cross the Atlantic. The petty bourgeoisie, named *prominenti* in both Europe and America, deferred to the self-made men, often *artigiani*, who acquired notable wealth and property. *Notabili* were leading officials in Old World villages and esteemed men of distinction in the New.[31]

The major means by which the *artigiani* and other group pioneers achieved their American status as *prominenti* was through rising to better socio-economic and occupational positions, particularly as labor bosses (*padrones*) or bankers (*banchieri*). Authorities disagree widely as to the exact function of these two occupations. Their activities and effectiveness became a well-publicized issue especially in the 1880s and 1890s, as outsiders — especially reformers — bitterly assailed the bosses and bankers for the way they abused and exploited their compatriots, particularly the more defenseless women and children.[32] The agitation of these keepers of the public conscience was helpful in encouraging federal regulation in the mid-1880s of the labor practices the *padrones* employed.[33]

The institution of the *padrone* seems to have originated in the agricultural districts of Italy rather than in the New World, but this role and that of banker developed to fit American urban and industrial needs.[34] According to the imprecise claims of contemporary critics, the two agencies served two specific functions: the banker allegedly imported workers, especially women and children, on contract from Europe to work for him or for someone he designated. The *padrone* was commissioned by an employer, a railroad or large corporation, to supply a certain number of workers for a specific task. It was the *bossatura*, or commission that the workers had to pay their labor agent, that provoked the major outcry from reformers. *Padrones* took a certain amount from the salaries of everyone, even women and children, in return for which workers received substandard food, supplies, and clothing.

This is not the place for an extended assessment of *padrones* and bankers. Recent authorities have tended to see them in less moralistic terms. While abuses of innocent and unprotected workers were common, the present estimate regards the agents as a necessary evil, providing an economic service to both employer and employee. The former needed willing hands, while the latter were fearful in these early years of applying individually for work on their own, outside their ethnic community. In any event, the two institutions became less important after 1905, when other social mechanisms such as families and unions were formed to make laborers less dependent on other countrymen.[35]

It is important to note how *padrones* and bankers acquired community status, for all the "papas" and probably most leaders in the group provided a wide array of needed services. To understand more clearly how these men acquired and wielded their power in this pioneer period requires a review of the concept of chain migration advanced by John and Leatrice MacDonald, Robert Harney, and other recent scholars of Italian migration.[36] The leading Italian pioneers, the *artigiani,* and the rest of the enterprising vanguard from both North and South must be considered not simply as individual migrants but also as continuing members of an extended Old World village or locality. Realizing the urgent and unfilled labor needs in America, these early entrepreneurs saw their personal advantage in encouraging their *paesani* (countrymen, but really local, regional countrymen) to come to the New World. "Bankers" constructed or utilized social networks and encouraged relatives and friends to leave. They also appointed subagents in those localities to persuade villagers through their *notabili* to come under their guidance (but not under labor contract). Spurred by worsening economic conditions at home, the discontented, children and adults, decided to leave Italy, and when they arrived became heavily dependent on the rising American *prominenti.* Thus "bankers" emerged offering the early arrivals — often without family — a host of services from their "office," usually a saloon or shop, as employment agent, travel bureau, currency exchange, and letter writer.[37]

The "papas" were the individuals who developed from particular *padrone*-bankers into influential community leaders. They were traditional progressives in that while keeping family continuity they could discern the future of their people in a new society. They became conscious of their constituents as Italian-Americans and assumed the role of group intermediary. Of course, some did it to further their own power outside as well as inside the group, but many mobilized their clients for the latter's good as well.

The traditional progressives selected here include two from the major Italian-American center, New York City, Antonio Maggio and Luigi Fugazy; the New Haven, Connecticut "papa" Paul Russo; and Salvatore Pelletieri of Utica. They were chosen on the availability of evidence; similar opinion leaders existed in most if not all Italian-American colonies. These men are outstanding representatives of a type.

Just as Chicago had become the Polish cultural capital, New York City became the major Italian-American settlement, if only because of numbers. The group's largest neighborhood was the well-known — and to some infamous — Mulberry Bend district on the Lower East Side. That "cesspool" of crime and vice was the foundation for the success of both Maggio and Fugazy.[38]

Antonio Maggio was not quite the "papa" that his colleague was. He was less popular than Fugazy, for his position of *padrone*-banker led him to an actively partisan political career, first as a Democrat and later a Republican. But despite their differing appeal, it is clear that the impact of both was generally assimilative and certainly influential. Maggio was determined to fashion his group into a formidable bloc in American politics. His early life in America manifested his close acquaintance with and understanding of Anglo-American society. Arriving in New York in 1873 at 13, he left the city soon after to find employment in upper New York state as an apprentice to a craftsman. By 1876 an American milkman had given him a job in Lowville, New York, where he received an American education. To give himself an assimilative advantage in this basically non-Italian community, he changed his name to James March, and just after 1880 the Erie Railroad employed him to recruit workers in New York City. While a *padrone* for thousands of *paesani* he was able to construct a political machine by 1890, known as the James E. March Association. From this position he emerged as the major Italian political leader of the Lower East Side.[39] While Maggio may have had mixed success in rallying all Italian-Americans to vote Republican by the turn of the century — his district was overwhelmingly Democrat — his efforts to politicize his people instructed many to the opportunities in the wider American society. He personally had taken a number of assimilative steps himself: for example, he changed his name, obtained an American education, and married an English-speaking wife.[40] However, though he was a modernist model, Maggio was also well known and even well liked by many for being an ethnic group organizer. He led ethnic societies on group occasions, particularly on Columbus Day, and was known for being generous with his constituents.[41]

The more revered and beloved Italian-American "papa" and group founder in New York was clearly Cavalier Luigi Fugazy.[42] His rise in America was based partially on his heroic military exploits in the Risorgimento; at the least, his participation in that struggle gave him a better sense of Italian feeling — *Italianita*. After his involvement, he went to New York in 1871 and opened a "banker's" office in the then embryonic Italian community. After having acquired some personal influence in that role, he devoted himself to improving his people's welfare by encouraging the formation of mutual aid societies. Such social coalescing did occur naturally, as MacDonald has suggested, but Fugazy clearly facilitated their formal establishment because he saw that voluntary associations could provide necessary services and advancement. In a sense, he was preparing his group's lessened dependence on *padrones* and bankers.

Fugazy expressed his philosophy of social organization and his assimilationist viewpoint in a long, revealing interview in the *New York Times* in 1896. To benefit themselves as a group, to help in their adjustment to the new land, and to contribute to American society, Italian immigrants, Fugazy advised, had to consider becoming American citizens. He suggested that the most convenient way to integrate them-

Courtesy of The University of Wisconsin — Milwaukee

Cavalier Luigi Fugazy, the revered and beloved Italian-American "papa"

selves into the civic life of the United States was to first join
ethnic self-help bodies. It seems paradoxical that Fugazy, a
committed Italian nationalist, would at the same time encourage the locally oriented, fragmented self-help bodies;
but he personally led 50 of them in 1900 and spoke for 145,
with a membership of 30,000. The incongruity is resolved by
the realization that he promoted a fraternalism which was
both traditional and modern. It insured and maintained contact with the life, family, and culture the Italians had left
behind, while at the same time it provided a means for them
to gain an income, an education, and new homes here. In that
material and intellectual achievement Italian-Americans
would make a significant New World contribution.[43] Thus,
again, in fostering the many small fraternal bodies, Fugazy
saw them not as further causes of group disorganization and
social segregation, but rather as a process of American integration.[44]

Such backward- and forward-looking aims were held by
other important Italian-American figures, including "papas"
Paul Russo of New Haven and Salvatore Pelletieri of Utica.
Russo was one of those rare southerners who arrived early in
America, coming to New York in 1869. Like Maggio, he had to
leave the big city quickly with his family to earn money in
outlying towns by playing the harp (organ). He settled finally
in New Haven. There, at the tender age of thirteen, Russo began a grocery business in the mid-1870s, when the community
still consisted of a handful of families.[45] Papa Russo's rise as the
leading pioneer by 1885 was rapid. By then he had become
the colony's first banker, organized the group's first self-help
association, graduated from Yale Law School as its first Italian
alumnus, and founded many other group institutions: its first
church, the Columbus Day observance, the Discoverer's
statue, and the local newspaper. His dual modern-traditional
rationale for his work, similar to Fugazy's, was quoted in a
1930 interview: "We organized for the purpose of promoting
our American citizenship and preserving at the same time a
love for the motherland."[46]

"Pop" Salvatore Pelletieri, whose family's saloon was the
early Italian immigrant reception center in Utica, New York,

was the chief pioneer architect for the group there. Part of his popular appeal, like Maggio's and Russo's, was his musicianship. With all his formative efforts in molding the group's social institutions, he did so as an American. His knowledge of, reverence for, and devotion to the nation's Constitution and Declaration of Independence were widely known; he referred to them as nearly divinely inspired.[47]

Designating particular Jewish-American opinion leaders appears almost as difficult as locating the important Italian-Americans. Having no Jewish homeland until the foundation of Israel, they were for centuries one of the world's most dispersed peoples. American Jewry represented those wide geographic origins. Sephardic colonies began in the seventeenth century, Ashkenazic (German and East European) in the nineteenth and twentieth, and a few African and Middle Eastern arrivals more recently. But closer scrutiny reveals considerable homogeneity, as was the case with the Italians. Most came between 1870 and 1920 from the cities and small villages (*shtetls*) of the Slavic lands. They brought with them the more conservative Orthodox faith; they were generally poor, or ranked in the lower middle- or working-class levels; and they were occupied either in entrepreneurial activities or the needle trades.

The Jewish masses here had another, and more significantly uniform, trait — their Yiddish culture. The immigrants used Yiddish as a spoken vernacular, but it was also the matrix of a rich folklife as well. Hebrew had been the classical language of prayer and religion, but Yiddish emerged, particularly in Eastern Europe, as the living essence of the people's daily life, their speech, and folk customs. The evolving creative and artistic sophistication of Yiddish on the Lower East Side that was evident around 1900 became well known after 1902, when Hutchins Hapgood discovered for Gentiles the writers, dramatists, and poets who inhabited the "ghetto."[48] But the literary and cultural achievements he and others heralded took place at least two decades after the Jewish masses had entered the area following the pogroms of 1881. From then until the end of the century, the pioneer period, is still either little known or casually referred to as an era of insecurity, disorganization, and intellectual and material impoverishment.[49]

Certainly the cultural golden age of the Lower East Side did begin with the twentieth century, but its structural, intellectual, and assimilative foundations had started two decades earlier. Two important Jewish community organizers and opinion leaders of this era, in the tradition of Hasselquist, Barzynski, and Fugazy, should be considered: they were the two leading journalists of the time, Kasriel Sarasohn of the *Yidishes Tageblatt,* and the better-known Abraham Cahan of the *Jewish Daily Forward.*

Of course, these were only two of a host of Jewish notables who lived in the group's largest city over the long span of its immigrant years. New York Jewish history dates as far back as the time of Dutch control in the mid-1600s. It continued through two centuries when wealthy and conspicuous German Jews of New York sought to mold their "poor relations" from Eastern Europe into their own assimilationist image. Historians have already cited the prominent elite Jews who set up welfare agencies, such as the Educational Alliance, to instruct the East European newcomers — called "Orientals" — in American culture.[50] But these dignitaries like Jacob Schiff, Louis Marshall, Nathan Straus, and other "uptowners" had little direct influence on late nineteenth-century Jewish arrivals. One who did win the respect of the Yiddish-speaking masses was Joseph Barondess, a beloved labor leader and popular head of the cloakmakers union. However, his status as the people's hero was short-lived, hollow, and lacked substance: Barondess was convicted of extortion soon after his rise, and he had really had few ideas about assimilation or group persistence in any event.[51] The two leading architects of East European Jewry in New York between 1880 and 1900 were its leading journalists, Sarasohn and Cahan.[52]

Most observers of these early decades of the community stress the potency of the Yiddish press as a major influence on the colony since the 1890s. They refer particularly to the bitter exchanges between its Orthodox and Socialist camps, and Sarasohn and Cahan provided the voice for those factions. Sarasohn came first, establishing his *Tageblatt* in 1885, the world's first Yiddish daily, and upholding the principles of Jewish Orthodoxy. He railed against the assimilationist Reform Jews as well as the "godless" Socialist and left-wing radicals.[53] Cahan, on the other hand, edited several labor-oriented newspapers, first *Noye Tsayt* in the 1870s, *Arbeiter Zeitung*, and finally the *Forward* in the 1890s. A war of words — often *ad hominem* — was fought between the two men, based on differing, indeed opposing orientations. Nevertheless, in their ideas of the best way for the Jewish community to develop, the antagonists were more alike than different. Both held progressive principles, that is, they wished to improve the conditions of their Yiddish audience through education and an American assimilationist process. But both were also traditional: Sarasohn upheld the primacy of the Orthodox faith, and Cahan honored and enriched American Yiddish culture. Their only real dispute was over the importance of religion in Jewish-American progress.

Sarasohn's influence may seem to have been much inferior to Cahan's when one compares their respective newspapers. The *Tageblatt* of the 1890s was a relatively smaller journal compared to the later and immensely popular *Forward*. However, before the turn of the century the more conservative paper was the more popular, and even afterward it was regarded as the organ of the Orthodox wing of the community and its most pious members. Sarasohn's stature among New York Jewry has been obscured by the more recent attention historians have paid to his antagonist.[54] The Lower East Side demonstrated its respect for the Orthodox journalist at his well-attended funeral in 1905; the event was a massive spectacle with widespread outpouring of public grief. As the *New York Times* described the enthusiastic response, it was a "surprisingly large turnout of 75,000 to 100,000 people, recalling the huge crowds who appeared at Chief Rabbi Joseph's passing two years before."[55]

While Sarasohn was the leading Orthodox layman, conservative in social philosophy and Cahan's major opponent on the Lower East Side, he did not worship the *status quo* unequivocally. His ideals for the immigrant were progressive

Kasriel Sarasohn, the leading Orthodox layman, was traditional in matters of the Jewish faith and conservative in social philosophy.

and thus similar to Cahan's. In particular, both men considered their papers instruments of enlightenment through their dissemination of the news. They were guiding their Jewish audience to adjust to the "new and complex American environment."[56]

Even before coming to America, Sarasohn indicated his interest in social change. The son of a rabbi, Kasriel was exposed in his early years to the reform ideas of the *Haskalah*, the Jewish enlightenment, which sought to modernize religious practice. He became a follower of Moses Mendelssohn, the leader of the movement that urged Jews to learn the language of the country they lived in, but to continue to study the Torah and know Hebrew, not cultivate Yiddish. A Mendelssohnian and a *maskil* in Eastern Europe, Sarasohn accepted all the movement's principles, although he insisted that printed Yiddish was justifiable to instruct the people.[57] Going to America as a Yiddish pioneer early in 1869, he became a rabbi in Syracuse and later settled in New York City in 1874 to begin his weekly *Yidishes Gazetten*. His family arrived later, and with them he began the world's first Yiddish daily, *Yidishes Tageblatt*, in 1885.[58]

Sarasohn did insist in his paper that all Jews should retain their Orthodoxy, but he also sought to uplift the masses, offering practical help and showing his readers that they should appreciate their adopted land. He was thus mobilizing them to attain sufficient intellectual and political power to win a secure place in America.[59] Like Hasselquist, his Swedish counterpart, he fostered a number of formal organizations and institutions for their welfare. In particular, this "conservative" layman personally initiated the Hebrew Immigrant Aid Society as well as the Hebrew Shelter Home.[60]

The better-known Jewish figure is of course Abraham Cahan, who had less personal appeal among the masses but who better perceived their needs and instructed them more generally on how to prosper in America. As a socialist, Cahan fought bitterly with Orthodox leaders, particularly Sarasohn, condemning their spiritual hypocrisy and their insensitivity to the "capitalist exploitation" of the people. He cared little for the religious tradition of Orthodoxy — or Judaism in general — although he did utilize and therefore perpetuate certain distinctive Jewish cultural marks, particularly the Yiddish language. Cahan would have insisted, though, that his ultimate aim was not ethnic preservation but enlightenment and adjustment, even if he was something of a traditionalist in the process. Certainly he always regarded himself a teacher of a persecuted proletariat, rarely as a Jew.[61] Even his commitment to socialism gave way to his desire to fit his audience into the new American context. As a journalist, even while his Marxist colleagues excoriated him for avoiding revolutionary

rhetoric, he insisted that American education, both practical
and intellectual, came first.

Cahan's teaching and assimilationist ideals, like
Sarasohn's, were apparent early. Although Cahan was raised
near the major Jewish religious center at Vilna, the proximity
had no effect on him. Cahan quickly eschewed group traditions and became a Russian instructor in a state school for
Jews.[62] While converting to socialism and departing Europe
in 1882 to found a utopian colony in America, his deeper
desire to uplift his countrymen began to move him away from

Abraham Cahan, assimilationist who synthesized past and future for
the more progressive Jews' successful adjustment

From The Critic (January 1905)

his earlier radicalism.[63] As editor of the small labor paper *Arbeiter Zeitung* in 1890, Cahan realized the enormous power of Yiddish journalism to reach, instruct, and motivate the Jewish masses to participate in the new society. He rejected the kind of formal German Yiddish that Sarasohn employed in his paper (called *Daitchmersh*) because it was not the vernacular of the people and was thus ineffective. As editor of a newly formed left-wing daily later in the decade, the *Forward*, he wrote in the Americanized Yiddish tongue. He accepted the use of English expressions so that he could realize his goal of reaching his readers. As he put it in a somewhat paternalistic metaphor, "If you want to lift a child from the ground, you must bend over him."[64]

Already by the first years of the new century Cahan's achievement was astounding. Even before he initiated his famous *Bintel Brief* in 1906, a column of practical advice to readers, the *Forward* was the Jews' major intermediary agency with American life. For hundreds of thousands — if not millions — of New York Jews it served as the group's leading tutor in learning, its guide to family problems, and its advisor on the host of everyday difficulties the ordinary worker and his family encountered in America. Cahan's constant goal was his reader's social advancement.

Cahan, then, was a cultural broker who, while consciously criticizing certain Jewish traditions, actually synthesized both past and future — as did Sarasohn — for his group's successful adjustment. He honored tradition by dignifying the popular speech; in fact, he enhanced Yiddish as a literary form by giving newspaper space to fine fiction writers and poets. Yet he was assimilationist at the same time, urging his readers to master English, learn the great English-language classics, use American political institutions, and work toward personal fulfillment in America.[65] He saw no contradiction, for example, in upholding the value of the Yiddish theatre to his people, yet also authoring the well-known *Forward* editorial, "Has Your Child a Handkerchief in his Pocket?"[66] To Cahan traditonal culture was a means to promote individual Jewish success in America.

The leaders identified here were unusual and yet representative individuals whose life and goals illuminate some of the workings of American pluralistic society. They were exceptional and merit recognition because of the unrivaled influence they wielded and the organizational talent they possessed in their ethnic communities. Yet they were also typical of other lesser leaders who were traditional modernists and cultural brokers, mobilizing their people on both a past and future foundation. They were in a way also typical of the rank and file people they served. New York Jewry, the New Haven, New York, and Utica Italians, Chicago Poles and Midwest Swedes all have honored these men as ethnic group architects. This is as it should be; but their accomplishment was also an American one. The source of their achievement came not from supplying a European foundation here, since the society they helped build was not simply a precise reconstruction of the Old World setting they had known. Such a total replanting was a structural impossibility. Both leaders and followers knew that, or they would never have left Europe even temporarily in the first place. Neither was their community design a total rejection of Anglo-American society. Whether these immigrant architects realized their aim or not, they were seeking to provide their followers with a new and more advanced community structure, to assure them a better material life, a better education, and more effective involvement in American institutions. Their only reservation was that preferably, but not necessarily, all these positive progressive ends should be worked for within the ethnic community being built under their tutelage.

Thus ethnic institutions in America were mechanisms for group accommodation, enabling immigrants and their children to better realize and accept the American values of success and social advancement. These institutions, immigrant and ethnic voluntary associations, remain little known and neglected and have a poor reputation as vestigial remains of an alien culture. Through this century outside observers have decried the proliferation and persistence of ethnic fraternal associations because they were thought to maintain social segregation, inhibit foreign adjustment, and prevent ethnic individuals from acquiring American values. A representative criticism was voiced in about 1920 by a close student of the foreign-born, Robert Park. He conveyed the timeless, troublesome concern about American pluralism which many Americans felt immigrant institutions caused:

> The nationalist tendencies of the immigrants find their natural expression and strongest stimulus in the national societies, the Church, the foreign language press — the institutions most closely connected with the preservation of the [ethnic] languages. In these the immigrant feels the home ties most strongly; they keep him in touch with the political struggle at home and even give him opportunities to take part in it. Both consciously and unconsciously they might be expected to center the immigrants' interest and activities in Europe and so keep him apart from American life.[67]

A critical and indeed pejorative term used here is "home." For many — perhaps most — immigrants who had gone to America voluntarily, their residence was now the New World rather than the Old, as the above statement would assume.

The contention in this study is not that *all* group institutions were assimilative or progressive; but the conclusion supports the suggestion of sociologist Milton Gordon and the seminal research of anthropologist Frederik Barth outside America, that assimilation can occur *across* ethnic boundaries without eradicating the structural framework of minority communities or their social networks.[68]

This preliminary investigation has stressed the forward-looking orientation of ethnic organizers. But another question arises concerning how representative these "builders" were of the rank and file itself. Did ethnic leaders influence their constituents to prepare for the future against their will, or did they simply apply their administrative talents to tasks and aims that the masses were already committed to but unable to realize individually and personally? In other words, how eager for assimilation or "progress" were the rank and file themselves? No conclusive answer is yet possible. Immigrants did not choose their leaders in democratic elections; the elite held their positions in part because of their religious, journalistic, or economic function as priest, editor, or *padrone*-

banker. They were emblematic as well as popularly selected leaders.

Nevertheless all, even the most paternalistic, like Barzynski and Cahan, did have a large and loyal following for their philosophy, if not for their person. The outpouring of grief at the funerals of several was a surprisingly broad affirmation of their status, especially in the cases of Barzynski, Sarasohn, Maggio, and Fugazy, despite the fact that the latter two lived long after the era of their greatest influence. While all obviously did have enemies, they also had devoted friends and willing listeners among the rank and file for whom they provided badly needed services — lodging, food, and a cultural continuity that nonethnic social services could not offer. Just how much ethnic members agreed with their leaders' progressive rationale for their institutions is difficult to measure; but little evidence exists of any significant opposition to their modernizing objectives. It seems clear that these major figures possessed unusual sensitivity toward and insight into the aspirations of their followers, what they were, and how they as leaders could benefit personally from their realization.

A final implication of this examination of immigrant leadership is the bearing their ideals have on our current view of American pluralism. Speaking for a growing number of intellectuals and scholars considering the matter, John Higham has pointed out: "The essential dilemma of our multi-ethnic nation is the opposition between a strategy of integration and one of pluralism."[69] The current debate has been to assess the implications of cultural diversity. The liberal hope for our national growth since the Enlightenment has been to realize a sustained process from traditional and varied ethnic roots to one of a homogeneous, enlightened, and progressive people, one idealizing individualism and personal freedom. But the twentieth century has not shown that we have attained that goal; in fact, it has revealed social disorganization and disorder. The historian Robert Wiebe has seen the course of American development as one of growing segmentation. Our subdivisions based on kinship ties, occupation, locality, and ethnicity have led us to more clearly distinguished differences. In fact, "the most enduring measures of difference in American society," he discerns, "were in a broad sense ethnic."[70]

These differences, however, from the view of immigrant leaders and organizers, the architects of those "segments," were neither substantial nor general. Obviously, community builders did act to segregate their people physically from the general society and place them in separate enclaves. Even Cahan wanted to set aside his Yiddish-speaking fellows in order to educate them in his way; Barzynski did the same with the Poles. But to these leaders the segments they were forming were certainly not to be self-sufficient fortresses prohibiting ethnic members from taking some role in American national life. Not one of them argued for total ethnic segregation. Indeed the objective they sought was the opposite: to prepare their constituents in a limited area of activity for a more substantial contribution intellectually, economically, and professionally to the nation as a whole.[71]

The history of these traditional progressives, these cultural brokers, suggests that organized ethnic communities were — and probably still are for many — sanctuaries in which individuals can find cultural comfort, but which also encourage them to use their abilities in the wider society. As it began and as it has evolved, American ethnic pluralism has meant not enclosed alternative communities but open-ended subcultures with easily traversed boundaries.

THE URBAN FRONTIER:
CHICAGO

Chapter V

EDWARD R. KANTOWICZ

Polish Chicago:
Survival Through Solidarity

> *A nation . . . is part of nature. A nation is of*
> *Divine origin, not human invention.*
> — Fr. Waclaw Kruszka (complaining to
> His Holiness, Pope Pius XI, 1923)

WHAT PRECISELY IS A POLISH-AMERICAN? The question is not as thorny as that perpetual puzzler, what is a Jew? But it occasionally causes confusion. At the first Chicago Consultation on Ethnicity in 1969, a noted urbanologist, expounding on a series of census maps and tables, concluded that the most heavily Polish neighborhood in Chicago was Rogers Park. But this far north side neighborhood is populated largely by Polish and other Eastern European *Jews* and is never considered a "Polish neighborhood" by Chicagoans. A meaningful definition of Polish-Americans includes only Polish Christians.[1]

It is true that the Polish Commonwealth during its heyday in the late Middle Ages was a multinational state, remarkably tolerant of the many Jews who fled from persecution in Western Europe. But when, after the decline and partition of the Polish state, Polish nationalism arose in the nineteenth century, it was linked very closely with traditional Roman Catholicism. Romantic nationalist writers like Adam Mickiewicz made a mystic, messianic fusion between God and Nation.

In the United States, Polish-American historians have occasionally beefed up their filiopietistic lists of great Poles in America with the names of Polish Jews, like Haym Salomon, a financier of the American Revolution.[2] But for the most part, though Poles and Polish Jews often lived close by in American cities, their community histories were separate. No anti-Semitism, simply analytical precision, is intended in excluding Jews from the definition of Polish-Americans.

Counting Polish-Americans is excruciatingly difficult and imprecise. The United States Census Bureau changed its method of enumerating immigrants nearly every ten years, sometimes counting only the foreign-born, at other times including the second generation, "native-born of foreign parentage." No census data includes the third or subsequent generations of Poles in America. Furthermore, many of the tables in the 1900 and 1910 censuses, when immigration was at its peak, contain no listing at all for Poles, counting them instead by their origin in the partitioning countries of Germany, Austria, and Russia. Yet by supplementing the federal censuses with other sources, such as school censuses, it is possible to produce the following population estimates.

Table I
Polish-Americans (1st and 2nd generations)

	United States	Chicago
1890	250,000	40,000
1910	1,663,808	210,000
1930	3,342,198	401,316

The 400,000 Poles in Chicago in 1930 formed 12 percent of the city's population of 3,376,438. Contemporary guesses for the 1970s place Chicago's Polish population at about 600,000, or roughly 20 percent of Chicagoans. Since at least 1930, Polish-Americans have been Chicago's largest white ethnic group, but they have never approached a majority in the city.[3]

Settlement Patterns: Ethnic Clustering

Polish peasants left the land in the late nineteenth and early twentieth centuries and journeyed to cities in Poland, Germany, and the United States in a search "for bread" (za chlebem, in the words of the novelist Sienkiewicz). Their settlement patterns in the United States were largely determined by that search. Most Poles and other turn-of-the-century immigrants settled in the northeastern quarter of the United States, where industry was crying for manpower. But Carol Ann Golab has shown in a survey of fifteen cities from 1870 to 1920 that Polish immigrants, who had only their peasant strength to offer industry, were very selective even within this quadrant. Poles avoided semi-southern cities like Baltimore, Cincinnati, and St. Louis, where large black populations took up the unskilled jobs; they settled sparsely in other cities like Boston and Philadelphia, where light industry demanded mainly skilled labor; but they poured into new, raw cities of heavy industry like Buffalo, Chicago, and the numerous mine and mill towns of Pennsylvania.[4]

Within the city of Chicago, both the search for bread and a desire to find relatively familiar neighbors determined the sites of Polish neighborhoods. By 1890 five large Polish colonies had been settled in Chicago. Each was in an area of heavy industry: Polish Downtown on the northwest side, just west of the Goose Island industrial complex; the Lower West Side, adjacent to many factories along the Burlington Railroad and the ship canal; Bridgeport and Back of the Yards, circling the Union Stock Yards; and South Chicago, hard against the steel mills. In at least three of these areas the Poles settled among Germans and Bohemians, with whom they were familiar in the old country.[5]

It has been a truism that Poles and other immigrants lived in ethnic clusters or "ghettoes" in American cities; but the term "ghetto" is imprecise and merits a closer look. The Polish settlement pattern was both segregated and decentralized. The segregation can be indicated by a statistical measure, the index of dissimilarity. This index measures the general unevenness of a group's distribution throughout a city. For instance, if Poles were thirty percent of a city's population, a perfectly even distribution would find them forming thirty percent of the population of every ward. This situation would produce an index of zero (0). At the opposite extreme, if all the Poles resided in one ward with no non-Poles present, this situation of perfect segregation would produce an index of 100. The intervening values of the index from 0 to 100, which are the only ones found in reality, give a rough indication of the extent of segregation. In 1898 the Polish index of dissimilarity by wards was fifty-nine; as late as 1930 that index still stood at fifty-five. By way of comparison, the following table gives the index of dissimilarity for most of Chicago's ethnic groups in 1898.

TABLE II

Indexes of Dissimilarity, by Wards, 1898[6]

Russian (Jews)	67	Norwegian	55
Bohemian	64	Danish	43
Italian	61	Swedish	34
"Colored"	60	German	29
Polish	59	Irish	27

Two of the major Polish settlements were overwhelmingly Polish in population. Polish Downtown, near Division and Ashland Avenues, was a classic ghetto. In 1898 eleven precincts in this neighborhood formed a contiguous area, about three-quarters of a mile long and a half mile wide, which was 86.3 percent Polish. One precinct in the heart of this area was 99.9 percent Polish, with only one non-Pole among 2,500 inhabitants. A total of 24,374 Poles — 25 percent of all the Poles in the city — lived in just these eleven precincts. Two of the largest Catholic parishes in the world, St. Stanislaw Kostka and Holy Trinity, served the Poles of this neighborhood. Headquarters for three Polish-language daily papers and the two largest Polish fraternal organizations were located here. Polish Downtown was to Chicago Poles what the Lower East Side was to New York's Jews. The Polish area near the steel mills of South Chicago also had a high Polish population dominance: four precincts forming an arc around the gates of the mills were 72.4 percent Polish in 1898. The other three Polish clusters were not as heavily dominated by Poles; each was less than 50 percent Polish.[7]

But if Poles were segregated in clusters, the clusters themselves were decentralized and scattered. Slightly less than half the Poles lived on the northwest side of Chicago; the rest resided in the four other large colonies on the west and south sides, or in several smaller clusters which formed along railroad lines near industries.[8]

Other immigrant groups at the turn of the century showed similar settlement patterns. Each ethnic group settled in at least one classic ghetto and a series of smaller, less dominated clusters. All were highly segregated, but some groups were not as decentralized as the Poles; for instance, 78 percent of the Bohemians lived in a narrow corridor on the west side.

The two largest Bohemian neighborhoods, Pilsen and Cęske Kalifornia, were each about 77 percent Bohemian.[9] Three wards of the near west side contained over three-quarters of all Russian Jews in the city in 1898. Four precincts at the heart of the area had a Russian Jewish dominance of nearly 75 percent. The area around Hull House contained about a third of all Italians in the city. An L-shaped area of five contiguous precincts near Hull House had 63 percent Italian dominance.

Poles, then, clearly shared a common experience with other immigrants. Demographic mixing, where it took place, did not generally lead to social mixing. The process of community-building in Polish neighborhoods produced a social and cultural ghetto.[10]

Building a Polish Community

The process of community-building is probably the best-known aspect of Polish-American history, thanks to the monumental sociological work by William I. Thomas and Florian Znaniecki in *The Polish Peasant in Europe and America.* Polish immigrants built a complex of community institutions at the neighborhood level, re-creating in part the milieu of the peasant village they had left behind. The Polish communities in Chicago approached very closely what one sociologist has called "institutional completeness."[11] This meant that the Polish ethnic group supported such a wide range of institutions that it could perform nearly all the services its members required — religious, educational, political, recreational, economic — without recourse to the host society.

The process of community-building generally began, ironically, with thoughts of death. The Polish peasant who was uprooted to Chicago, far from the village churchyard where his ancestors lay, worried about his own final resting-place. The first mutual aid societies formed by Polish immigrants were mainly death-benefit societies. A tiny yearly payment of a dollar or two ensured that when an industrial worker succumbed to disease or occupational hazard, his wife would receive a payment sufficient to bury him properly.

These local mutual-aid societies, often composed of individuals from the same village in Poland, quickly proliferated and took on additional functions. They provided social life for the immigrants, many had religious overtones, and others formed to promote specific activities like community singing or needlework. A particularly important form of mutual aid was provided by the building and loan associations. Land-hunger, a prime motive force in Polish peasant communities, was translated into the urge to buy one's own home in Chicago. While the Bohemians made the most extensive use of building and loan associations, these cooperative institutions were significant in the Polish communities as well. An association member made regular payments of fifty cents or a dollar per week for a number of years to build up a down payment, and the association supplemented this accumulation with a low interest loan when the member actually purchased his home. By 1900, Polish building and loan societies held assets approaching one million dollars.[12]

A local society usually took the next step in the community-building process by founding a Catholic parish. The Catholic Poles worshipped at first in Bohemian or German churches, like St. Wenceslaus on the west side, or St. Michael's on the north; but before long the Poles organized churches of their own. A society of laymen formed under the patronage of some Polish saint obtained contributions from their countrymen in the neighborhood, purchased a piece of property, and then asked the bishop to help them find a Polish-speaking priest. Thus the first Polish community in Chicago, which had been pioneered by Anton Smarzewski-Schermann in 1851, organized the St. Stanislaw Kostka Society in 1864 under the leadership of Smarzewski-Schermann and Peter Kiolbassa. They formally petitioned the bishop for a priest in 1867, and St. Stanislaw Kostka parish built a small frame church and received a resident pastor in 1869. This process of lay initiative and episcopal approval was repeated in every settlement of Poles; but after this pioneering effort

Przez Oszczędność do Dobrobytu, Siły i Wpływu
— Oto hasło Polaków w Ameryce.

Odpowiedniem miejscem do składania waszych oszczędności na 3 procent jest dobrze znany i zaufania godny

BANK POLSKI
1201 Milwaukee Ave. róg Division ul.

Dostaniecie książeczkę Kasy Oszczędności bez jakichkolwiek kosztów składając 1 dolara lub więcej.

Bank Polski wysyła pieniądze do starego kraju i wszystkich części świata.

Sprzedaje pierwsze złotem płatne hypoteki w sumach od 300 do 5000 dol. przynoszące 5½ do 6 dolarów procentu.

Skrzynki ogniotrwałe do przechowania rzeczy wartościowych kosztują 3 dol. rocznie.

Zasoby Banku Polskiego wynoszą już przeszło 4,000,000,00.

JAN F. SMULSKI, Prezes.
JAN PRZYBYSZ i WM. H. SCHMIDT, Wice Prezesi.
T. M. HELINSKI, Kasyer.
M. FOERSTER, Sekretarz.
A. J. KOWALSKI i WINC. JOŹWIAKOWSKI, Ass. Kas.

Courtesy of the Polish Museum, Chicago

Community-building: Polish thrift encouraged in bank ads

the time lag between the founding of a church-building society and the actual foundation of a parish was generally only a
year or two. Eventually, forty-three Polish Catholic churches
were founded in the city of Chicago and eighteen more in the
suburbs and outlying cities included in the Archdiocese of
Chicago.[13]

Local societies were both the cause and effect of the
parish-building process. Once a Polish church arose in a
neighborhood, some pre-existing societies affiliated with it
and numerous others organized. Thomas and Znaniecki
counted seventy-four parish societies at St. Stanislaw Kostka
in 1919, ranging from the Needlework Club of St. Rose of
Lima to the Court of Frederic Chopin.

The most important adjunct of a Polish parish was the
parochial school. At the Third Plenary Council of Baltimore
in 1884, the American bishops had decreed that every church
should be accompanied by a school. In Chicago, under Archbishops Feehan, Quigley, and Mundelein, the school was
often built first, with church services held in the basement
until a more suitable house of worship could be built later.
Yet not every parish responded to the Church's call for parochial education. In particular, Italian Catholics saw little reason not to utilize the free public schools. In 1910 only one of
the ten Italian parishes in Chicago had a school. But the Poles
responded more enthusiastically than most. The Resurrectionist Fathers, who administered St. Stanislaw and several
other Polish parishes, not only built large elementary schools
but also founded St. Stanislaw College in 1890 as a collegiate
preparatory school. By the 1920s every Polish parish in the
city and suburbs had its accompanying school. Attendance at
Polish parochial schools in 1920 was 35,862, roughly 60 percent of Polish youth between the ages of seven and seventeen. No other Catholic ethnic group in Chicago equaled this
percentage of parochial school attendance.[14]

The Polish Catholic Church in Chicago attained a remarkable institutional completeness. Of the estimated
213,000 Poles in Chicago in 1910, 140,000 were members of
Polish Catholic churches. The criterion of membership used
by the various Polish pastors was generally more than bap-

tism but less than regular Sunday attendance. Probably anyone who at least performed his Easter Duty and made some financial contribution to the parish was counted as a member. Thus about two-thirds of Chicago's Poles were part of the Polish Catholic complex, with the remainder not church members, members of the schismatic Polish National Church, or communicants in non-Polish Catholic parishes. In 1930 the proportion of Chicago Poles attending Polish parishes was still nearly 60 percent.[15] In addition to churches, elementary schools, and St. Stanislaw College, Chicago Poles also supported St. Hedwig's Orphanage and Industrial School, Holy Family Academy for girls, four cemeteries, two day nurseries, an old-age home, and a hospital.

Historians have often noted the tangible evidence of Polish financial support for the Church, particularly the cathedral-like churches in Polish neighborhoods, and have speculated on the sacrifices involved for immigrant laborers earning low wages. Actually, though Polish church support was consistent and substantial, it was not as crushing a burden as sometimes supposed. In the year 1908, Polish parishioners in the Chicago area contributed $3.51 per capita to their local churches. For a family of five, this amounted to $17.55 a year. This amount was about one and a half week's wages for an unskilled laborer at that time. Viewed another way, it was equal to two months' rent in a tenement or the amount an ambitious laborer might put away yearly in a savings and loan association.[16]

This level of church support was probably higher, relative to income, than most Chicago Catholics maintain today; but other ethnic groups at the time contributed more. The Immigration Commission in 1911 found that a foreign-born Pole made about one-third less in wages than a foreign-born German.[17] As the following table shows, the territorial (mainly Irish) and German parishes received higher per capita contributions, reflecting the higher economic levels of the Irish and German communities.

The per capita totals fluctuated considerably over the next forty years with the ups and downs of the economic cycle, but

TABLE III

Catholic Parish Support, 1908

Type of Parish	No. of Parishioners	Total Contributions	Per Capita Contribution
Territorial	208,500	$1,197,400	$5.74
German	69,300	$434,800	$6.27
Slovak	7,300	$28,400	$3.89
Polish	151,400	$532,000	$3.51
Lithuanian	17,800	$55,500	$3.12
Bohemian	32,800	$59,500	$1.81
Italian	39,000	$14,800	.38

the respective positions of the various parish groups stayed largely the same.[18] All in all, it seems that Polish Catholics gave a respectable amount of financial support to their churches, according to their economic means; but they certainly did not drain their family budgets to do so. Yet the evidence of the "Polish cathedrals" is not totally misleading. Both in 1926 and 1947, Polish parish buildings had a higher median valuation than the parish buildings of any other nationality in Chicago. Polish parishes, apparently, channeled more of their resources into bricks and mortar than did others.

After the creation of local societies and parishes, the final step in the building of a mature Polish-American community was the federation of many local societies into a number of national, superterritorial Polish fraternal organizations. National fraternals emerged in the late nineteenth century, such as the Polish Falcons (a gymnastic union on the order of the German Turners), the Polish Alma Mater (which specialized in youth work), and the Alliance of Polish Socialists (not really very socialist, but rather a nationalist organization linked to Pilsudski's party in Poland). But the two most important Polish-American fraternals, both of which had their headquarters in Chicago after 1880, were the Polish National Alliance and the Polish Roman Catholic Union.

An individual immigrant did not belong to one of these fraternals directly but rather as a member of some local society affiliated with it. The key to each society's mass membership was its ability to provide greater insurance benefits through large organization. But in addition to providing practical advantages, both the PNA and the PRCU pursued definite ideological goals. The PNA was a nationalist organization, directed by political *emigrés* from Poland who worked as a sort of Polish "Zionist" force for the liberation of the motherland from the partitioning powers. PNA leaders considered the American Polish colonies to be a "fourth province of Poland." The Alliance's leaders were laymen, its policies at least mildly anticlerical, and its membership open to Polish Jews, schismatics, and nonbelievers as well as Catholics. The PRCU, as its name implied, was a religious organization, open only to Catholics, dominated by the clergy, and dedicated primarily to the strengthening of Catholicism among the immigrant Poles.

The two organizations were bitter rivals for membership and influence. PNA leaders considered the PRCU insufficiently nationalistic, whereas the PRCU leaders thought the PNA godless. Yet this polarization can be exaggerated. The rank and file members of both organizations were overwhelmingly Catholic; they joined primarily for social and economic benefits, and because they usually belonged to several local societies, they often found themselves affiliated with both PNA and PRCU. The two organizations worked closely together during World War I. Once Poland was liberated, no ideological issue separated the two fraternals.

The national fraternals published Polish-language newspapers and other literature. Each had an association organ that appeared weekly. The PNA's *Zgoda* (Harmony) was started in 1880; the PRCU began publication even earlier, went through several titles, and finally in 1897 settled on *Naród Polski* (Polish Nation) as its main propaganda arm. Both papers are still published in Chicago today. The two organizations later moved into the daily newspaper field in Chicago, the PNA with *Dziennik Zwiazkowy* (Alliance Daily News) in 1908, and the PRCU with *Dziennik Zjednoczenia* (Union Daily News) from 1923 to 1939. The Alliance's *Zwiazkowy* remains today as the last of Chicago's Polish-language dailies.[19]

The PNA-PRCU rivalry reflects an important division in the leadership class of Polish-Americans, a division into two camps which Victor Greene has termed "nationalists" (PNA) and "religionists" (PRCU).[20] Division into two ideological groupings was a common experience for all the East European immigrants. The nationalist-religionist dichotomy that troubled the Polish community actually split the Bohemians into two mutually exclusive groups. Bohemian nationalism harks back to the Protestant followers of Jan Hus in the fifteenth century, who were ruthlessly suppressed by the Catholic Austrian Emperor. When it re-emerged in the nineteenth century, Bohemian nationalism was not only anti-Catholic but secularist. Though Bohemia was a nominally Catholic country, the leading nationalist intellectuals were self-styled atheists and "free-thinkers." In the United States the free-thought movement broadened its base and embraced a large number of uprooted Bohemian peasants and workers as well. Free-thought had all the trappings of a secular church and engaged in its own drive for institutional completeness. The largest Bohemian fraternal organization, the Czech-Slovak Protective Society, identified itself with free-thought; the *Slovenska Lipa* organized as a national cultural center on Chicago's west side; nineteen free-thought schools taught Bohemian language and the principles of free-thought outside regular school hours; and the Bohemian National Cemetery became the final resting-place of those who disdained consecrated ground.

Though Bohemian religionists, led by the Benedictines of St. Procopius Abbey, counter-organized with a full panoply of eleven national parishes, parochial schools, an orphanage, and a Catholic cemetery (shared with Polish Catholics), the free-thinkers greatly outnumbered Bohemian Catholics in Chicago. An estimated seventy percent of the Bohemians in Chicago avoided religion altogether. Compared with this Bohemian split into two completely separate cultural communities, the religionist-nationalist rivalry among Poles was mild. Nationalists and religionists formed two tendencies within one community of Polish-Americans, rather than two separate communities.[21]

Midway between the Bohemian and the Polish experiences was that of the Lithuanians. Though the majority of

Lithuanians in Chicago remained Roman Catholics, a vigorous free-thought movement did appeal to some, under the name of Liberalism. During the 1920s and 1930s, an increasing number of Lithuanians chose to be buried in the Lithuanian National Cemetery rather than the Catholic St. Casimir's. Yet in 1934 the burial statistics still ran roughly three to one in favor of the Catholics. Among Slovaks the nationalist-religionist split was complicated by the issue of union with the Czechs in Europe. The free-thinking, secularist element among Slovaks tended to support the Czech-Slovak experiment, but the majority of American Slovaks remained Roman Catholics and Slovak nationalists.[22]

Unlike Bohemian free-thinkers, Lithuanian Liberals, or Slovak Czechophiles, Polish nationalists were not antireligious. The only permanent schism within the Polish-American community produced another religious denomination, the Polish National Church. Most nationalists remained fervent Catholics, and secularism made few inroads. The mutual aid societies, the parishes, the fraternal organizations, and the Polish-language press made Polish Chicago more institutionally complete as a Polish-Catholic community. This interpretation of the community-building process may seem too monolithic to those who lived through the fierce internal quarrels in Polish Chicago. Just how fierce the quarrels were is illustrated in the next section. Yet those divisions remained for the most part within the Polish family, which prayed together and stayed together.

Polish-Catholic Factions

The main theme of Polish-Catholic history in Chicago was the community-building drive for institutional completeness. But as this drive unfolded, three stages of fierce controversy ensued. The first stage, which began as soon as the first Polish parish was organized in 1869 and continued until about 1900, was a struggle for control of the finances and administration of the parishes. The second stage witnessed a campaign, running from about 1900 to 1920, to obtain Polish bishops in America. The final stage was a holding action, to preserve the institutional separateness of Polish Catholics and prevent absorption by the rest of the Church in Chicago. This stage began with the arrival of Cardinal Mundelein in 1916 and still continues today.

The first phase of controversy surrounding the Polish parish dealt not with dogma or belief but rather with church polity, the structure of church government. In the late nineteenth century, Poles, Slovaks, Lithuanians, and other recent Catholic immigrants reopened a fundamental question that had troubled the American Church from the beginning: who held legal title to Catholic Church property? The hierarchy had always maintained that legal title to all parish property must rest with the local bishop. Ultimate authority over parish finance would then be vested in him or in his direct representative, the pastor. But in the early years of the American republic, a more democratic polity, akin to American congregationalism, appealed to many lay leaders. In such a system, repeatedly condemned by the bishops as "lay trusteeism," a board of lay trustees would hold title to parish property, administer the parish finances, and hire and fire the pastor.[23]

The Polish nationalist faction in America revived the demands for lay trustee control, for they viewed the Irish bishops in Chicago and elsewhere as foreigners. Furthermore, the European church custom of *jus patronatus* (right of patronage) seemed to support their position. In Europe a noble patron often founded a local church, retained title to the property, and hired the pastor — all with Vatican approval. Polish lay leaders in America tried to transform this custom into a collective right of patronage by the whole local congregation, expressed through the board of trustees. In order to get a parish founded, the Poles usually surrendered title initially to the bishop; but if a particular pastor's personality or financial management later displeased them, they reasserted demands for lay, nationalist control.[24]

In Chicago the nationalist dissenters were opposed by the Resurrectionist Fathers, and especially by Rev. Wincenty Barzynski, C.R., pastor of St. Stanislaw Kostka from 1874 to 1899.

In 1871, Bishop Thomas Foley made an agreement with the Resurrectionists whereby legal title to all church property would be vested in the bishop, but the Resurrectionists would exercise administrative supervision over all Polish parishes in Chicago as the bishop's representatives. The nationalists resented the Resurrectionists' "sellout" to the Irish bishop and chafed under their authoritarian control of church affairs. In 1873, when overcrowding at St. Stanislaw necessitated the building of another church, a lay society founded Holy Trinity church three blocks away and tried to retain title and find a pastor more to their liking. The bishop and the Resurrectionists wanted the church to be merely a mission of St. Stanislaw. This Holy Trinity-St. Stanislaw dispute dragged on for twenty years. Several persons were excommunicated, and Holy Trinity was closed by the bishop for long periods of time. Finally, in 1893 a papal representative, Monsignor Francis Satolli, visited Chicago and personally ended the dispute. The dissidents had to yield the formal question of legal title, which was finally ceded to the bishop. But Satolli also ended the special relationship of the Archdiocese of Chicago with the Resurrectionist Order and brought in Rev. Casimir Sztuczko, a Holy Cross Father from South Bend, Indiana and a strong nationalist priest, as pastor of Holy Trinity. This was a compromise solution which worked. Fr. Sztuczko was the pastor at Holy Trinity for the next sixty years.[25]

Controversy broke out again a year later in a new location. A few miles to the northwest of St. Stanislaw, the Resurrectionists had founded a new parish, St. Hedwig. Fr. Wincenty Barzynski unwisely gave ammunition to his opponents by appointing his brother, Joseph Barzynski, to be pastor of St. Hedwig's. When Fr. Anthony Kozlowski came to St. Hedwig as an assistant priest in 1894, he formed an anti-Barzynski faction of parishioners. Noisy disturbances broke out whenever the pastor said mass. On a cold February day in 1895, a mob of dissatisfied parishioners stormed the rectory and had to be driven back by the police. Though the bishop quickly brought in a new pastor, the dissidents would not settle for less than total control. So in June 1895, Fr. Kozlowski and about one thousand families seceded from St. Hedwig and formed a new parish of All Saints.[26]

Over twenty years of nationalist battles with the Resurrectionists and the presence of a willing leader in Fr. Kozlowski had heightened the intensity of the St. Hedwig's conflict. Unlike the Holy Trinity affair, no reconciliation occurred. The dissident parishioners still considered themselves Roman Catholics at first; but when Kozlowski was consecrated a bishop in 1897 by the schismatic Old Catholic Church in Switzerland, and subsequently excommunicated by the Pope, they found themselves outside the Roman Church.[27]

These two church quarrels should not be viewed as freak

St. Stanislaw Kostka, one of the largest Polish parishes in the world

Courtesy of University of Illinois Library at Chicago Circle, Manuscripts Division

Kościół, Hala, Dom Sióstr i Szkoła

occurrences, caused only by personality conflicts or the special position of the Resurrectionist Order in Chicago. Trustee quarrels with bishops and pastors broke out in numerous Polish, Slovak, and Lithuanian communities throughout the United States in the late nineteenth century. Among Poles they resulted in three separate federations of independent, non-Roman parishes, headed by Kozlowski in Chicago, Fr. Stephan Kaminski in Buffalo, and Fr. Francis Hodur in Scranton, Pennsylvania. After Kozlowski's death in 1907 and Kaminski's in 1911, Fr. Hodur obtained Old Catholic consecration as a bishop and consolidated all the schismatic churches into one denomination, the Polish National Church. This church maintains nine parishes in Chicago and embraces an estimated 5 percent of Polish-Americans in the United States.[28]

The first stage of Polish-Catholic controversy had many causes. High-handed pastors, financial mismanagement, the release of pent-up emotions in the free air of America — all contributed to the turbulence; but fundamentally the rebelliousness of the Polish parishioners was rooted in a desire for national autonomy within the American Catholic Church. The majority of Polish Catholics remained within the Roman church, and title to church property was ceded to the Irish bishops; but the struggle for the greatest possible national independence continued at a higher level with the launching of a drive for Polish bishops after the turn of the century.

During the second stage of Polish-Catholic controversy, initiative shifted from laymen to the clergy. This shift has been little noted and never studied in detail, but it is significant. It was part of a general damping down of lay activity in the American Catholic church as bishops and clergy slowly consolidated their administrative control in the twentieth century. What probably happened among the Poles was that the most outspoken lay leaders departed into the Polish National Church, leaving the Roman Catholic clergy in firmer control. It is also significant that at this stage the conflict was purely between Poles and outsiders. Though many Polish priests held aloof from the campaign for Polish bishops, none actually opposed it. Unlike the first stage of controversy, the new campaign united Polish-Americans.

The primary leader in the drive for Polish bishops was Rev. Waclaw Kruszka, a priest of the Milwaukee archdiocese stationed in Ripon, Wisconsin. Fr. Kruszka, one of the first historians of Polish America, was a journalist and publicist of great talent. His brother, Michael Kruszka, edited an influential Polish-Catholic newspaper in Milwaukee. Fr. Kruszka opened the campaign with an article entitled "Polyglot Bishops for Polyglot Dioceses" in the July 1901 issue of the New York *Freeman's Journal.* He carried on the fight at two Polish-Catholic Congresses in 1901 and 1903 and made two trips to Rome. In Chicago he was supported by most of the diocesan Polish clergy, though the Resurrectionists remained aloof.[29]

The watchwords of the new campaign were equality and recognition. The appointment of Polish bishops would recognize both the numerical importance and the special cultural needs of Polish Catholics, which were neglected by the Irish, German, and Anglo-American bishops who ruled virtually all American dioceses in 1900. Ideally, the Polish clergy would have liked a reorganization of the American church completely along ethnic lines. Instead of the existing territorial dioceses, where all Catholics in a given area were subject to one bishop, they desired the creation of purely Polish, Lithuanian, German, and Irish dioceses irrespective of territorial location. Ukrainian Catholics in the United States actually obtained this goal in 1913, over the protests of the American bishops. Since Ukrainians worshipped in a separate rite and utilized Old Slavonic as their liturgical language, Rome removed them completely from the jurisdiction of American bishops and established a separate exarchy, or diocese. But Rome held firm against any jurisdictional separation within the Latin rite.[30]

Failing to obtain separate dioceses, Poles tried to secure the appointment of a fair share of Polish bishops to rule over American dioceses. At the very least, they wanted Rome to appoint Polish auxiliary bishops in dioceses like Chicago, where Poles were numerous. This would give symbolic recognition to Polish Catholics and insure that the ruling bishop had a Polish advisor. The result of the Kruszka campaign was Rome's concession to the minimum demand, the appointment of a Polish auxiliary in Chicago in 1908 and in Milwaukee in 1914. Paul Rhode, the pastor of St. Michael's Polish church in South Chicago, was chosen auxiliary bishop of Chicago by the Polish priests of the archdiocese in a special election called by Archbishop Quigley. When Rome ratified his selection, he became the first bishop of Polish ancestry in the United States.[31]

Bishop Rhode proved a popular, energetic, and diplomatic leader of Chicago's Polish clergy. As Archbishop Quigley's Polish lieutenant, he had more influence than an auxiliary bishop usually does. Besides making the rounds of Polish parishes for confirmations and ordinations, he determined the assignments of Polish priests in the archdiocese. As the only Polish-American bishop until 1914 and an organizer of the Association of Polish Priests in the United States, his influence extended outside Chicago as well. Yet his appointment was essentially a form of tokenism. Without jurisdiction over a diocese, an auxiliary bishop's importance is largely symbolic. Rhode was not even a member of the diocesan consultors, the bishop's financial council. But the Polish clergy were satisfied for the moment.[32]

The recognition drive heated up again after Rhode was transferred from Chicago in 1915 to become Bishop of Green Bay, Wisconsin. In a sense this was a promotion, for Rhode now became the first Polish Ordinary, or ruling bishop, of a diocese in America. But Green Bay was a very small see, and the Poles were deprived of their symbolic leader in Chicago. When George Mundelein, a German-American, was appointed Archbishop of Chicago shortly after Rhode's departure and he failed to appoint a Polish auxiliary, the Polish clergy suspected a conspiracy. In the overheated atmosphere of World War I, friction developed between the Poles and their German bishop.

The campaign for Polish bishops climaxed in 1920, when the Polish clergy in the United States joined the newly formed Polish legation at the Vatican in drawing up a thirteen-page memorial. All the Polish nationalist rage

Paul P. Rhode, the first bishop of Polish ancestry in America

against the neglect and insensitivity of "Americanizing" bishops — Archbishop Mundelein in particular — came out in this memorial. Specifically, the Polish priests requested that Bishop Rhode be transferred to a more important see, that Polish auxiliaries be appointed in a number of cities, and that the Poles be allowed a largely separate development of their Catholicism in the United States. The American hierarchy, in their annual meeting of September 1920, formed a three-bishop committee, including Archbishop Mundelein, to draft a strong rebuttal to the Polish memorial. Cardinal Gibbons of Baltimore forwarded the committee's reply to the Vatican, and Rome apparently accepted the American bishops' explanation. No action was taken on the Polish memorial.[33]

Waclaw Kruszka in Wisconsin had still not given up. In 1923 he wrote to Pope Pius XI:

> A nation . . . is part of nature. A nation is of divine origin, not human invention. . . . As a rule, even in the fourth and fifth generation . . . families are purely Polish in America. . . . Parishes of mixed nationalities in America are generally considered a necessary evil. . . . Therefore, as both families and parishes are regularly purely Polish . . . consequently dioceses also should be purely Polish. . . .[34]

Despite the token victories and many defeats of the previous twenty years, Kruszka was reiterating the maximum demand, purely Polish dioceses. But this issue was dead, and even the lesser demands of the Polish recognition drive were ignored. Chicago remained without a Polish auxiliary until 1960; few Polish bishops were appointed elsewhere in the United States.

Previous studies of Polish-Catholic controversies in Chicago have not given adequate attention to the third stage of the struggle. Victor Greene ends his book on a note of triumph with Rhode's appointment in 1908; Joseph Parot and Charles Shanabruch end their studies in the early 1920s on a note of defeat for the Poles. Since none of them explores fully the successful holding action of the third stage, they miss much of the significance of the struggles.

By the second decade of the twentieth century, Polish

Catholics had suffered notable defeats in their movement for a purely ethnic Catholicism. The right of parish councils to hold church property in their own name had been denied; the desire for purely Polish dioceses had been rejected; and the demand for Polish ordinaries and auxiliaries in existing dioceses had been met with tokenism. Yet Polish Catholics in Chicago retained a remarkably complete complex of churches, schools, and welfare institutions, which, though technically part of the archdiocese of Chicago, were quite separate. Polish language predominated in the churches and schools, Polish priests served exclusively in their own churches and institutions, and a lively Catholic press was printed in Polish. Furthermore, the existence of an alternative church in the schismatic Polish National denomination gave the Roman Catholic Poles a secret weapon against any Americanizing bishop who might try to break down this institutional complex. If the Polish clergy yelled loud enough, a bishop's hand could be stayed by the fear of further defections. This secret weapon did not prove sufficient to make further gains, such as the appointment of Polish bishops; but it helped the Poles protect what they already had.

The coming of Archbishop George William Mundelein (Cardinal Mundelein after 1924) to Chicago in 1916 made necessary a Polish holding action to preserve their institutional complex. Mundelein ruled the Chicago archdiocese like a Renaissance prince from 1916 to 1939. He was a vigorous centralizer, a consolidating bishop in the mold of Cardinal O'Connell in Boston, Cardinal Dougherty in Philadelphia, and Cardinal Spellman in New York. Furthermore, he prided himself on his fourth-generation Americanism and was determined to break down the ethnic separatisms within the Church in Chicago. Besides opposing the wishes of Poles, Slovaks, and Lithuanians for auxiliary bishops of their own nationalities, he initiated three policies in the first years of his reign which seemed to threaten the institutional completeness of Polish Catholics: he declared a moratorium on the building of purely national parishes; he initiated a standardization of the curriculum in the parochial schools and a policy of English only for teaching most school subjects; and he began to assign newly ordained priests of Polish and other East European ancestry to Irish or mixed parishes. By vigorous protests and a tacit use of their secret weapon, the Polish clergy deflected the impact of the first two policies and completely defeated the third.[35]

As Polish-Americans and other ethnic groups moved out of their original neighborhoods into more middle-class areas on the southwest and northwest sides, Mundelein was reluctant to establish new national parishes for them, preferring territorial parishes open to all. The revision of canon law in 1918, which required Vatican permission for any new national parishes, supported his position; but he acted largely from his own motives. The expense and inefficiency of building many separate parishes in new areas bothered him; besides, he wished to expose the younger generation of Poles to a more mixed environment. The Poles were numerous and cohesive enough to defeat his purposes. Mundelein founded new parishes that were technically territorial, but in many cases he assigned only Polish priests to them. Parishes like St. Bruno, St. Camillus, and St. Turibius on the southwest side and St. Constance on the north side were just as Polish as any technically national parish.

Mundelein's establishment of the first diocesan school board in 1916, to coordinate the heretofore independent parochial schools, to standardize the curriculum, and to mandate English-language instruction, evoked much favorable comment in the Chicago daily papers and a storm of protest from the Poles, Lithuanians, and even the French-Canadian Catholics. But the centralization implied in this policy extended only to choice of textbooks, and languages other than English were still permitted for the teaching of catechism and reading. In what was perhaps an overreaction to Polish protests, Mundelein made sure that both the school board chairman and one of the two superintendents were always Polish priests throughout the whole of his administration. Through the teaching of the Felician Sisters and other Polish orders of nuns in the elementary schools, and that of the Resurrectionist Fathers, who expanded St. Stanislaw College into two modern high schools, Weber High and Gordon Tech,

Polish leaders insured a distinctively Polish education for most of their youth.

Finally, when Mundelein assigned three newly ordained Polish priests to non-Polish parishes in 1917, sixty-eight Polish priests signed a letter of protest against this attempt to denationalize the Polish clergy.[36] Mundelein fumed and wrote testy letters in response. He later fired one of the protest leaders, Fr. Louis Grudzinski, from his post on the board of diocesan consultors, replacing him with one of the few Polish pastors who had not signed the letter, Rev. Thomas Bona. But despite this retaliation, the incident was one of Mundelein's most stinging defeats. Within two years the newly ordained priests in question were back in Polish parishes; and for the rest of his jurisdiction, Mundelein never assigned a single Polish priest to a non-Polish parish, even though he continued to assign priests of other ethnic groups to territorial parishes when the supply of priests permitted. The Polish clergy had succeeded in their holding action against one of the most authoritarian of archbishops.

Despite the losses at the first two stages of Polish-Catholic controversy, the underlying process of community-building and the holding action against Archbishop Mundelein were so successful that the "Polish League" has remained a largely separate component of the Catholic Church in Chicago. Polish pastors acted like feudal barons throughout much of the twentieth century, answerable only to the Polish "boss," Monsignor Thomas Bona, whom Mundelein and his successor left in nearly complete control of Polish clerical affairs. When Mundelein built his new major seminary of St. Mary of the Lake, one of its purposes was to unify the clergy and instill *esprit de corps*. Accordingly, ethnic divisions were slight at the seminary; but after ordination, young Polish priests were assigned to the Polish League, indoctrinated by the pastor, and often forbidden to attend class reunions or to go on vacations with Irish priests. In 1934, Cardinal Mundelein organized a mission band of diocesan priests to preach missions of spiritual renewal in the parishes of the archdiocese; but he had to arrange for a separate Polish mission band since the Polish pastors would not accept the ministrations of outsiders. As late as 1960 students of Polish descent at the minor seminary were required to study the Polish language whereas all other seminarians could choose any modern language.

This victory of the Polish League was a Pyrrhic one in several ways. For the priests themselves, assignment only to Polish parishes meant a longer than average wait to become a pastor. A Polish priest ordained in Chicago in 1926 or 1927 waited an average of twenty-four years until a pastorate in the Polish League opened up, whereas the average waiting time for an Irish priest was sixteen years, and the average for all priests in the diocese was eighteen years.[37]

More important, the Polish commitment to separate Catholic development meant a lack of influence in the affairs of the archdiocese as a whole. Polish priests had influence on the school board, and Monsignor Bona and one other Polish pastor sat on the board of consultors. But none of the newer archdiocesan agencies established by Mundelein and his successors, such as Catholic Charities or the Society for the Propagation of the Faith, had Polish directors. The crucial positions in the chancery office were completely devoid of Polish names. Even today, a glance at the Chicago clergy directory shows very few Polish priests in influential church positions.

Polish Catholics today often decry this lack of influence as discrimination, and discrimination there may have been. But the choice of separate development largely predestined this result. Polish Catholics could not have it both ways — separate development and influence in wider circles. Confined to their own community, Polish priests did not develop the contacts, the political skills, or the diversity of experiences necessary to forge ahead in internal church politics. Cardinal Mundelein offered the Polish clergy a beginning on the road to greater influence in Chicago Catholicism, but the Polish priests chose to stay with the path of separate development. Their choice was thoroughly consistent with the process of community-building that had been going on for half a century in Polish Chicago, but it closed off new options in church politics. Polish leaders made a similar choice in secular politics.

Polish-American Politics

The voting record of Chicago Poles in American politics can be summarized briefly: Poles voted Democratic from the beginning. In eighteen mayoral elections from 1889 to 1935, the identifiably Polish voting precincts gave a majority of their votes to the Democratic candidate in every instance. In thirteen Presidential elections from 1888 to 1936, the Polish precincts produced a Democratic majority in all but two cases. This political allegiance was rooted in a perception of the Democrats as the party of average workingmen and of broad-minded toleration for the Poles' religion and customs. The Republicans, on the other hand, were perceived as puritanical, aloof, and plutocratic. These perceptions and their attendant voting patterns were not a product of Franklin Roosevelt's New Deal, as is sometimes supposed, but of the nineteenth century.[38]

More significant, perhaps, than the voting record is the political strategy pursued by Polish Democratic leaders, a strategy of solidarity politics. Polish politicians organized their bloc vote around in-group concerns, constantly tried to perfect the unity and solidarity of the bloc, and neglected the building of coalitions with other political blocs. The high point of this solidarity strategy came in the 1930s, with the organization of the Polish American Democratic Organization (PADO) as a political service agency and an ethnic lobby within the Democratic party. This strategy parallels the separate development of Poles within the Catholic Church during the same period.

Polish leaders were misled by the fact of their large numbers into thinking that political power would fall to them like a ripe fruit if only they could perfect the solidarity of their group. Since Polish voters never formed a majority of the electorate in Chicago, however, such a strategy was doomed to failure. Despite their large numbers, Polish-Americans never elected a Polish mayor of Chicago and they remained weak in the councils of the Democratic central committee until the late 1970s. With the death of Mayor Richard Daley in the winter of 1976, a special post of vice-mayor was created specifically to represent Poles.

Polish solidarity extends to the business world.

Anton Cermak, the Bohemian political boss, rose to power in Chicago politics in the 1920s by pursuing a different strategy. Through such organizations as the United Societies for Local Self Government, an antiprohibition lobby, Cermak allied a great number of ethnic blocs behind him. Polish leaders, on the other hand, organized around specifically in-group concerns, like having the name of Crawford Avenue changed to Pulaski Road. This won them no allies. At the time of Mayor Cermak's death, the influential *Dziennik Chicagoski* seemed to understand the lesson of his political career:

> A Pole will be mayor of Chicago, only if we continue the poli-tics of the dead mayor Cermak, i.e., if we make alliances with other groups . . . . Unfortunately, the majority among us is now playing at Pan-Slavism and forgetting that Mayor Cermak practiced a different kind of politics. In his organization were found next to the Czechs, Jews; next to the Poles, Irish; next to the Germans, Swedes.[39]

However, neither the *Chicagoski* nor other Polish spokes-men took this advice to heart. As in the Roman Catholic Church so in the Democratic party, Polish leaders continued to nurture separate development and internal solidarity. They did not engage in bridge-building, coalitions, or broker politics.

The Polish In-group

Through their numbers and the success of their community-building process, Poles in Chicago attained a large measure of institutional completeness. Within the Catholic Church and the Democratic party they achieved a cohesive, largely separate existence. This solidarity led to considerable success in preserving a Polish-American sub-culture, in attaining symbolic victories like Paul Rhode's ap-pointment as auxiliary bishop and the renaming of Pulaski Road, and in opposing external threats such as the unfavor-able school legislation of the 1890s, the Ku Klux Klan in the 1920s, and Cardinal Mundelein's Americanizing policies.

But such success has been purchased at the expense of wider influence in Chicago Catholicism and city politics.

One important area of Polish-American life, economic development, has been left out of consideration. This aspect of the Polish-American experience has not yet received detailed historical treatment, and reliable data is scarce. Such neglect is unfortunate, for the primary goals of Polish immigrants were economic ones. Furthermore, economic life is the one realm which escaped the institutional completeness of community-building. From the very beginning the majority of Poles were salaried workers in large industries not controlled by other Poles. One study counted about 30,000 persons employed in businesses owned by Polish-Americans in the 1920s. But since there were at least 80,000 Polish heads of households in Chicago at that time, the majority of workers still earned their livelihood outside the Polish institutional complex.[40] It is likely, then, that the most significant contact of Polish-Americans with members of other ethnic groups occurred not in the Church or in politics but in factories, trade unions, and businesses.

Yet even in the economic realm it appears, from very fragmentary evidence so far, that Polish-Americans in Chicago were slow to attain prestige or influence. A study by the National Center for Urban Ethnic Affairs revealed a very small number of Polish names on the roster of board members controlling Chicago-based corporations. A National Opinion Research Center study similarly shows few Poles in prestigious economic positions — though it also indicates that Polish workers make more money than most.[41] This latter finding, if it is solidly based, may provide a clue to the economic history of Poles in Chicago. Polish workers appear to have opted for monetary success in unionized jobs and for economic and psychological security in home-owning rather than for more prestigious occupations in business and the professions. Even though Poles did not achieve separate development in the economic realm, a process similar to the trend in the Church and politics seems to have been at work. Poles attained one kind of success at the expense of wider influence and prestige.

If Polish immigrants came to Chicago seeking primarily bread and a home, it appears that they got what they wanted. Yet Polish-Americans of the 1970s seem to be wondering, Is that all there is? Repeatedly Polish leaders now decry their lack of influence in the archdiocese of Chicago, in city politics, and in business and the professions. However, under the banner of the so-called "new ethnicity," these Polish leaders are still often repeating the patterns of the past, calling for progress through ethnic solidarity, quota systems, and group pride. The historical record indicates the limitations of this approach. The present generation of Polish-Americans should notice that many champions of the new ethnicity are spokesmen of the old institutional complex. They may need to look elsewhere if they wish to pursue new goals in politics, religion, and economic life in America.

Chapter VI

CHARLES BRANHAM

Black Chicago: Accommodationist Politics Before the Great Migration

> The Negro vote alone would of course affect
> but little. It must make combination with the
> controlling forces in the party . . . . Social, in-
> tellectual, or other admirable qualities count
> for nothing if you cannot "deliver the goods."
>
> — Edward E. Wilson
> (black leader, 1907)

> The growing good of the world is partly de-
> pendent on unhistoric acts; and that things are
> not so ill with you and me as they might have
> been, is half owing to the number who lived
> faithfully a hidden life, and rest in unvisited
> tombs.
>
> — George Eliot,
> Middlemarch

NO GOLDEN LADY STANDS ASTRIDE THE Chicago harbor, bidding welcome to the refugees from Southern tyranny and offering solace to the oppressed. Perhaps it is just as well, for those first black migrants who came to Chicago in the 1890s and the early 1900s found themselves entering a city where the lines of racial restrictiveness were being more and more tightly drawn. The idea had preceded the experience; the pattern of ethnic politics, already firmly entrenched, would draw the energetic and ambitious among them into the tangled web of organizational and personal linkages which would in time come to characterize black politics in Chicago. Equally important, the city which came to symbolize the possibilities for black political advancement in America had already begun to etch out the limits to those possibilities.

The essential features of black politics in Chicago, then, were clearly evident before the Great Migration. Most of the leading figures who were to dominate the politics of Black Metropolis for the first third of this century had arrived during the 1890s.[1] And while personal and political fortunes rose and fell, the network of private and public relationships and political obligations between black and white leaders had been forged before 1900.

According to tradition, the city of Chicago was founded in 1779 by Jean Baptiste Point du Sable, a French-speaking Negro from Santo Domingo.[2] Although the city's black population remained small throughout the 1800s, the relations between the races had been a persistent if not prominent theme in the history of Illinois politics. In 1818, when Illinois became a state, its constitution was regarded as fairly liberal.

From Intercollegian Wonder Book *(Chicago, 1927)*

Jean Baptiste Point du Sable, a French-speaking Negro from Santo Domingo, who according to tradition founded the city of Chicago

Slavery was forbidden, although provision was made for the continuance of indentured servitude. Illinois did, however, have a black code, which required every Negro in the state to post a thousand-dollar bond and carry a certificate of freedom. A state law passed in 1853 forbade blacks from entering the state. Illinois blacks had no rights which white men were bound to respect. They could not vote or serve on juries; they could not serve in the militia; and they could not testify against a white man in court. Racial intermarriage was expressly forbidden. Although the laws were often ignored, especially after the passage of the Fugitive Slave Law of 1850, black residents were essentially invisible before the law.[3]

Nevertheless, Chicago became a mecca for refugees from Southern bondage — some remaining, others passing through to Canada and points east. Despite the Fugitive Slave Laws of 1793 and 1850, several homes and churches served as "stations" on the Underground Railroad. Planters in the lower Mississippi Valley dubbed Chicago a "nigger-lovin'" town, and an editor in southern Illinois contemptuously dismissed Chicago as a "sink hole of abolition."[4]

The city's black population grew quickly in the last half of the nineteenth century. The number of blacks tripled in the 1850s, almost quadrupled in the 1860s, and nearly doubled itself each decade between 1870 and 1900. Yet blacks were only 1.8 percent of the population in 1900. Most were employed in some form of domestic or personal service, the vast majority in white establishments or white households. By 1900 the black minority were dependent on the white

Chicago, dubbed "nigger-lovin'," a "sink hole of abolition," became a mecca for refugees from Southern bondage.

From "Negroes in Chicago" (Chicago: Mayor's Committee on Race Relations, 1944)

majority for their jobs and their livelihood. The black populace was uncomfortably situated near the lowest rung of the economic ladder in the most menial and unskilled trades.

Although blacks were only 1.3 percent of the population in 1890, they provided 37.7 percent of all the male and 43.3 percent of all the female servants in the city. The servant class claimed 53.7 percent of all Negro workers, 47.3 percent of the males and 77.1 percent of the females.[5] Foreign-born whites still supplied the bulk of the servant population, but black men were viewed as the rightful holders of positions as butlers and coachmen to wealthy whites. "The Negro footman and horseman," writes historian Estelle Hill Scott, "were expected figures around the mansions of the moneyed class."[6] As early as 1878, a contemporary observed, "Negroes were waiters, coachmen and janitors. All the big buildings had colored janitors and a few had colored clerks." Another old resident recalled that all of the fashionable downtown restaurants and hotels employed black waiters and porters, except the Sherman House.[7]

Black Chicagoans were not a significant factor in the city's basic skilled trades before the 1890s. The better jobs in construction, transportation, and industry were already reserved for whites. When blacks did enter local industries in the 1890s, it was as strikebreakers, incurring the hostility of white workers and the enmity of unions. When strikes were settled, whites were usually rehired and blacks fired, leaving the blacks unemployed and facing a legacy of racial hostility. Scant attention was paid to the fact that blacks were merely following in the footsteps of the Poles and Lithuanians, who had often been employed as strikebreakers in the 1880s.[8]

The presence of nonunion black workers at the 39th Street intercepting sewer was the cause of a minor riot in 1899 on the city's South Side. Newspapers spoke of a "reign of terror" which gripped South Side merchants and residents after three hundred and fifty whites struck over a salary dispute. The hostility had been inflamed by white threats to blow up the sewer machinery — and the remaining workers. Tensions within the plant had also resulted from the refusal of two white workers to take orders from "Big Sam," a Negro.

The refusal, followed by an exchange of words, led to a fight between several of the black and white workers. When five of the whites took the matter to the work's contractor, he sided with the blacks; the white workers were dismissed. Several blacks were attacked on the way home from the plant and tempers were brought to the flash point when seven dynamite cartridges were found in different parts of the plant machinery used in constructing the sewer.

The actual riot occurred when between 50 and 60 blacks were leaving work and were met by a crowd of 100 to 150 white strikers. A pitched battle took place on 39th Street between Indiana and Michigan Avenues. More than a hundred shots were fired and nine men, including a policeman, were injured; twenty-seven blacks — but no whites — were arrested. The riot received extensive newspaper coverage and, coupled with black strike-breaking activities in the stockyards strike and the 1905 teamster's strike, heightened antiblack feeling in the city. The teamster's strike was especially bitter: hostilities spread far beyond the strikebreakers to threaten the entire black community. The strike, according to one historian, "brought Chicago to the brink of race riot."[9]

Modern black politics emerged during this period of increased racial antipathy in the 1890s. Local businessmen often drew the color line between black and white customers. Numerous community meetings, including the interracial public discussion at the Central Music Hall in February 1890, attested to public concern over the widespread denial of public accommodations in the city. Blacks were often forced to resort to legal action to protest the discriminatory practices of local merchants.[10]

Residential segregation was also beginning to appear after 1890. By 1900 several predominantly Negro enclaves merged to form the beginnings of a South Side Black Belt. Historian Thomas Philpott has argued that the residential segregation of blacks was nearly complete by the turn of the century. By 1900 sixteen wards were 99.5 to 100 percent white. Over half of the city's black population lived in three contiguous South Side wards. While various ethnic groups continued to be identified with specific communities, no single Chicago neighborhood was ever ethnically "pure," and a majority of kinsmen lived outside any one particular enclave. Immigrants often clustered, but they were rarely segregated. "All groups which had the choice," Philpott points out, "opted for mild clustering and dispersion."[11] On the eve of the twentieth century black Chicagoans had become acutely aware that they no longer had this choice.

For black Americans the last quarter of the nineteenth century was, in Rayford Logan's words, "the nadir, the Dark Ages of Recent American History," when the second-class citizenship and indeed the inherent inferiority of black Americans was accepted by the vast majority of white Americans. Southern blacks had been systematically stripped of the franchise. Jim Crow, the jocular prewar minstrel figure, had come to symbolize institutional white supremacy.[12]

It was an era of social Darwinism and the "white man's burden." In the decades after 1885, Richard Hofstadter points out, the racist myth of Anglo-Saxon superiority "was the dominant abstract rationale of American imperialism." It was a period of unprecedented violence directed against blacks. Race riots increased in number and severity. Whites attacked blacks in Wilmington, North Carolina in 1898, in New York City in 1900, in Atlanta in 1906, in Springfield in 1908. The new century offered no respite and little hope for a race at bay: in the first year of the new century more than one hundred blacks were lynched. Before the outbreak of World War I, the number had risen to eleven hundred.[13]

Black leadership — locally and nationally — was divided and unsure of its response to this era of racist dementia. Many counseled accommodation and retrenchment; others accused conservative leaders like Booker T. Washington of acquiescence if not complicity in fostering notions of white supremacy. Edward H. Morris, a prominent Chicago attorney and politician, charged that Washington believed in Negro inferiority and that his statements encouraged racial segregation. The man from Tuskegee, he contended, was "largely responsible for the lynching in this country." Washington encouraged black docility in the face of white violence, Morris argued, and taught "that Negroes are fit only for menial positions. . . . I prefer a radical like Senator Tillman of South Carolina to Booker T. Washington. . . . The colored people think it doesn't matter so much what he says . . . [but they] believe and do what [Washington] tells them. Then they don't insist upon being treated the equals of whites."[14]

Other Chicagoans were not so sure. They admired Washington and encouraged their neighbors to view racial segregation as an opportunity for community uplift and race advancement though group solidarity. They were not happy about increased segregation, they merely accepted its inevitability. Some even held other blacks at least partially responsible for the unfortunate turn of events. Fannie Barrier Williams, prominent club woman, a member of the pre-Migration black elite and a Washington partisan, blamed the increase of the black population for the social and economic plight of the black middle class. "Prevented from mingling easily and generally with the rest of the city's population, according to their needs and deservings, but with no preparation made for segregation, their life in a great city has been irregular and shifting, with the result that they have been subject to more special ills than any other nationality amongst us." Mrs. Williams was particularly concerned about the "huddling together of the good and bad, compelling the decent element of the colored people to witness the brazen display of vice of all kinds in front of their homes and in the faces of their children." For some, the inconvenience of racial segregation was compounded by the fact that it obscured class distinctions within the black community.[15]

Whatever the divisions among black Chicagoans, the black community that emerged in the last quarter of the nineteenth century was an extremely self-conscious community, aware and increasingly anxious about the emerging pattern of social, economic, and residential proscription. Labor conflict had heightened interracial antipathy. Employment patterns reflected the general dependence of the community on white society. Denials of public accommodation, though illegal, reflected the secondary position of black Americans in the general society. Out of this context came black politics.

* * * * *

The pattern of interracial cooperation that dominated black politics before 1914 had its origins during the Civil War period. In Chicago — as was the case nationally — early black political debate revolved around questions of freedom and enslavement.[16] In the summer of 1862 blacks in Chicago and other Midwestern cities were the victims of violent confrontations with white laborers. In the state constitutional convention of that year, the outnumbered Republicans failed to keep an exclusion article out of the proposed new constitution, and in 1863 the lower house adopted a series of resolutions condemning the Emancipation Proclamation, the "unconstitutional" prosecution of the war, and the transportation of Negroes into the state.*

For Chicago blacks, organized protest activity began as early as 1864 with campaigns to repeal the Illinois Black Code and to challenge the segregationist policies of the city Board of Education. In 1865 the Illinois Black Codes were repealed, and four years later blacks throughout the state met in convention to challenge all racial distinctions in state laws. The Colored Convention, held in 1869, drew up a list of grievances and announced its intention to "devise ways and means whereby a healthy opinion may be created . . . to secure every recognition by the laws of our state and to demand equal school privileges throughout the state." By 1870, Illinois blacks were granted the right to vote, and in 1874 segregation in the public school system was abolished. In 1885 the state passed a comprehensive civil rights law "designed to protect the liberties of Negroes in the less advanced counties of southern Illinois."[18]

The spearhead behind the repeal of the black laws and other antiblack prohibitions was John Jones, the first black man to hold public office in Illinois. Jones was born November 3, 1816 on a plantation in Greene County, North Carolina. His father was a German named Bromfield, his mother a free woman of color. Fearful that his father's rela-

---

*By 1861, Illinois and six other Midwestern states barred blacks from suffrage and the state militia. In Illinois no provision was made for black education, and exclusion laws were passed, with severe penalties, to prevent blacks from settling in the state. Indiana and Iowa had similar laws.[17]

John Jones, the first black man to hold public office in Illinois

tives might attempt to reduce him to slavery, his mother apprenticed him to a man named Sheppard, who took him to Tennessee, where he was "bound over" to a tailor who taught him the trade. Jones lived as a tailor in Memphis, where he met and married Mary Richardson, the daughter of a blacksmith. He left Memphis for Alton, Illinois and eventually came to Chicago on March 11, 1845, only twelve years after its incorporation.[19]

From the 1850s until his death in 1879, Jones was the unquestioned leader of black Chicago. An ardent abolitionist who frequently played host to such luminaries as John Brown and Frederick Douglass, Jones was active in the state convention of 1856, called by blacks to petition for legal rights in Illinois. Jones was also a member of the prewar Vigilance Committee, and in 1853 was elected vice-president of the Colored National Convention held in Rochester and named a member of that convention's National Council. Throughout his life he continued to campaign for full and unequivocal manhood rights. "We must have our civil rights; they must not be withheld from us any longer; they are essential to our complete freedom."[20]

Before the war Jones had been instrumental in sending hundreds of fugitives to Canada. In fact, on the day after President Millard Fillmore signed the fugitive slave law, Jones recorded, ten carloads of blacks were sent across state lines to safety. But the "most satisfaction in life" came to Jones from his unremitting "warfare upon Black Laws." In the course of this campaign he had gained some powerful white allies. Joseph Medill, editor of the *Chicago Tribune*, was a former Free Soil newspaper staff writer and an early opponent of the black codes. Many prominent local and state Republican leaders, including Governor Yates and Cook County Senator Francis Eastman, were enlisted in the cause.[21]

From the beginning, the issue of partisan political self-interest intruded. For example, when the Repeal Association sponsored a dance and concert attended by approximately 500 Negroes on November 22, 1864, the pro-Democratic Chicago *Times* suggested that the event had been staged to raise money to buy votes for the Republicans. The entire campaign was marked by partisan as well as sectional self-interest, and when the black laws were finally repealed, the vote was cast along strict party lines.[22]

The repeal campaign highlights the sensitive position in which Illinois blacks found themselves. Jones, in his pamphlet *The Black Laws of Illinois and a Few Reasons Why They Should Be Repealed,* stressed white self-interest as well as humanitarian reasons for the abrogation of the black laws. These laws, he argued, had had a damaging impact on normal interracial business relations. In an open letter to the *Tribune,* dated December 9, 1864, Jones argued that "the great advantage to be gained by the repeal will not only benefit the colored man . . . the great benefit will be to the white for reasons that white men employ us and not we them. We hold their property and not they ours. We ask you to repeal these laws and give us the right to testify that you may protect your property."[23]

The repeal campaign set the pattern for early black political activity. Pre-twentieth-century black politics began as an amalgam of the black protest tradition, local and national Republican politics, and the personal, social, and political relationships that had developed among white and black Chicagoans. When Jones was proposed by Republicans — and accepted by Democrats — as one of the fifteen candidates for the county board on the bipartisan "Fire Proof" ticket after the Great Fire of 1871, it was not to secure the votes of the city's approximately 5,000 blacks; most of them were already in the Republican camp. Jones was selected because he had through the repeal controversy established himself as a distinguished member of the larger Chicago community with important and powerful Republican contacts. Jones' election in 1871, then, was not the opening gun for the emergence of black politics in Chicago. Rather, it was part of the legacy of the abolitionist-Republican tradition of the city.[24]

Jones served for one year and was re-elected for a three-year term in 1872; but he was defeated along with other Republicans in 1875. A year later, he and several of his fellow commissioners were indicted for an "alleged conspiracy," but he was acquitted "without difficulty, there being no evidence against him."[25]

After Jones' death no single individual emerged to assume the mantle of leadership among black Chicagoans. The last few decades of the century presented an increasingly diversified leadership. Civic direction passed to such individuals as Dr. Daniel Hale Williams, the best-known black physician in the country and founder of Provident Hospital; Dr. Williams' colleague at Provident, Dr. Charles E. Bentley, a dentist; lawyer and journalist Ferdinand L. Barnett, who published the city's first black newspaper, and his activist wife, Ida B. Wells-Barnett; and the distinguished attorney and fraternal leader Edward H. Morris. The new elite included men and women who were primarily business people and lawyers, clergymen and journalists — individuals who viewed politics primarily as a sideline, an avocation rather than a basic source of income.

Such men and women were community leaders who saw politics as an extension of their various civic activities. They were important, however, as a bridge between the activist tradition of John Jones and the emerging political professionalism of Ed Wright and Oscar DePriest. They were the bearers of the heritage of genteel civic protest and of the post-Civil War abolitionist tradition.[26]

This civil rights and protest tradition is central to our understanding of black politics from the mid-1870s to the eve of the Great Migration. In 1876, when the black population was only one percent of the city's total, John W. E. Thomas, a black Republican, was sent to Springfield as a representative from the second senatorial district. His election margin indicated that a large proportion of his supporters was white.[27] Thomas, a native Alabaman, was born in 1847 and came to Chicago at the age of twenty-six. His first enterprise, a grocery business, was destroyed by fire in 1873. He later turned to teaching and opened a private school near the center of the city.

Thomas established the tradition of black representation in the Illinois legislature and is often cited as one of the earliest black politicians of the postwar period. However, he

From College of Life *(Chicago, ca. 1920)*

Dr. Daniel Hale Williams, the best-known black physician in the country, and the founder of Provident Hospital

is best remembered as the author of the Civil Rights Bill of 1885. The bill provided for equal access to public accommodations in "inns, restaurants, eating houses, barber shops, public conveyances on land or water, theaters, and all other places," and provided for a fine of between $25 and $500, or a maximum of one year imprisonment, for any person guilty of violating the statute. No other interest or activity of the earliest black legislators was as important as the defense and expansion of the basic provisions of the bill Thomas introduced.[28]

Thomas was not re-elected in 1878, but he served another two terms in 1882 and 1884, and the Civil Rights Bill was passed at the end of his last term. He was succeeded by George F. Ecton, a former Kentuckian, one-time waiter, and later the owner of an all-black baseball team. Ecton's legislative career also reflected black concern for the protection of basic civil liberties. He introduced a bill to fix a penalty for

From College of Life *(Chicago, ca. 1920)*

Dr. Charles E. Bentley, a dentist and Williams' colleague at Provident

abduction, perhaps in response to black fears of being kidnapped and illegally transported out of the state to stand trial
in Southern courts. Ecton also framed a bill fixing greater
responsibilities on constables and judges, those who were
specifically charged with protecting black prisoners from
being kidnapped by white lynch mobs. Ecton was re-elected
in 1888, and in 1890 was succeeded by a fellow black Kentuckian, Edward H. Morris.[29]

In the career of Edward H. Morris we can see the fully
realized amalgam of civic protest, community leadership, the
national black protest tradition, and increasing local political
savvy. Born a slave in Flemingsburg, Kentucky in 1858, Morris
had been a practicing attorney since 1879 and was regarded
as one of the leading black lawyers in the country. He had
also gained something of a national reputation as a sharp critic
of Booker T. Washington. An uncompromising foe of racial
discrimination, Edward Morris was one of the founders and

the chairman of the executive committee of the Equal Rights League of Illinois, an organization created to protest the attempt to segregate black school children in the state's public schools.[30]

Morris' first term, however, was legislatively undistinguished, and he was defeated for re-election by James E. Bish, known as Adjutant Bish because of his rank in the Eighth Regiment, an all-black military outfit. Bish alone among pre-twentieth-century black legislators left no record at all of legislative accomplishment, and contemporaries de-

Edward Morris, Illinois legislator and civil rights activist

From College of Life *(Chicago, ca. 1920)*

scribed him as a man of less than sterling character. His election in 1892 was contested, and at least one paper hinted that he won through trickery and corruption.[31]

Morris' second term, in 1902, reflected his main legislative concerns. He introduced an amendment to strengthen the Civil Rights Bill of 1885, and an act to suppress mob violence. He also offered a bill to "investigate the most humane and improved method of carrying into effect the sentence of death" and another to regulate the traffic in "deadly weapons" and to prevent their sale to minors.[32] However, his second term was not without controversy. The *Chicago Tribune* accused him of tampering with an election bill provision that would have allowed a candidate for public office to appear more than once on a ballot. The idea of allowing a candidate's name to appear more than once was seen as an aid to independent and fusion candidates, and Morris was accused of deleting the provision in behalf of vested party interests. He was also criticized in some quarters of the black community for proposing a bill to legalize some form of gambling in Chicago. Ironically, the measure antagonized not only middle-class black reformers but alienated one of Morris' chief political allies, Robert T. Motts, a black saloonkeeper and South Side gambler who had gradually become a power in Morris' district. Motts had no intention of encouraging legal competition to his illicit but highly successful enterprise, and his defection brought Morris' legislative career to an end.[33]

Probably the most politically active of the pre-twentieth-century black legislators was John C. Buckner, who was elected to the state legislature in 1894. Buckner was a former headwaiter for fashionable parties, and what he lacked in formal education he made up for in presence and style; he had "the polish of the cultured class."[34] Buckner was born in Kendall County, Illinois. He entered the catering business in 1877 and after 1890 held a succession of management jobs with caterers until 1890, when he was appointed Deputy Collector of Internal Revenue for the First District of Illinois.[35]

Upon his arrival in Springfield, Representative Buckner found himself almost immediately embroiled in controversy with the state leadership. First he quarreled with Democratic Governor John P. Altgeld "over patronage and preference," and later with Altgeld's Republican successor, John R. Tanner. After his re-election in 1896, however, Buckner turned his attention to the state Military Affairs Committee, which he chaired, and to his pet project, the Eighth Regiment.[36]

With John Marshall and B.G. Johnson, Buckner had been a founder of the all-black Ninth Battalion, a resurrection of the "Old Sixteenth," a black veterans organization that had ceased to exist because of inadequate aid from the state. With the assistance of his white political mentor, Martin B. Madden, Buckner maneuvered the passage of a bill to make room for the Ninth Battalion as a part of the state's National Guard. He also had himself named the unit's first commanding officer.[37]

Buckner's two terms in the legislature were not completely taken up by this campaign on behalf of the Eighth Regiment. Like his contemporaries, Buckner's career reveals a concern for welfare legislation and the protection of black rights. He offered a bill designed to limit the time young boys and girls could be kept in training and industrial schools. He also proposed legislation dealing with child abandonment and the welfare of paupers.[38]

Buckner was widely praised for his activities during the Spring Valley riots of 1895. When native white miners protested poor working conditions and a recent cut in pay, the absentee mine owners closed the mines and brought in Italian, French, and Belgian immigrants. These new miners learned English, and in 1894 they too struck. This time the mine owners imported black workers from the South, many of whom were soon murdered by protesting immigrant strikers in what came to be known as the "Spring Valley Massacre." Buckner arrived on the scene and demanded justice on behalf of the beleaguered black workers. Other blacks joined in to protest police indifference — as did the Italian consul, who protested the mistreatment of Italian nationals forced to riot to protect their jobs.[39]

Three years later, John Buckner was succeeded by William L. Martin, a Missouri-born lawyer. Martin was described

as a man of "ability and courage," and his legislative record in
Springfield reveals a man of widely varied reform interests.
He introduced bills to suppress mob violence and to prevent
discrimination by life insurance companies against "persons
of color."[40] Martin also pushed legislation to grant tax-paying
women the right to vote for presidential electors and for candidates for certain specified offices. He sponsored legislation
designed to expand the social service responsibilities of government and to protect the rights of poor and working-class
citizens.[41]

One of Martin's measures would have provided attorney's
fees for a mechanic, artisan, or laborer who was forced to sue
for back wages. Another sought to exempt personal property
in certain specified categories from sale due to judgments
against debt or rent. Still another would have provided attorney's fees for the defendant in a suit brought for money due
or debts incurred for rent, meals, and costs in boarding-
houses. Martin also wanted to prohibit exorbitant interest
charges on small loans of not more than two hundred dollars.[42]

Martin's successor was John G. "Indignation" Jones, an
old settler who made a career of consistently opposing any
effort or program designed to segregate or disfranchise black
Chicagoans. Jones earned the epithet "Indignation" for his
habit of calling "indignation" rallies whenever he felt Negro
rights were under attack. He protested both the establishment of an all-black Y.M.C.A. in 1887 and the creation of
Provident Hospital in 1891. When Daniel Hale Williams told
an interviewer that black Chicagoans were fond of secret
societies, Jones called an indignation meeting to protest Williams' "slander" of the Negro race. When a coroner's jury
handed down a verdict critical of integrated employment in
the city, Jones called another rally and announced that the
coroner — and his entire jury — should be tarred and feath-
ered.[43]

Jones, like his predecessor, showed an interest in a wide
range of legislative reforms. And, like Martin, Jones' bills
often involved the expansion of government to safeguard the
rights of the underdog. Following the example of his two
predecessors, Jones fought to suppress mob violence in the

state as well as to punish law officers if a person in their charge was beaten, struck, or assaulted.[44] He sponsored acts to prohibit false advertisement by doctors; to pay the attorney's fees when a lawyer was appointed by the court of record for indigent clients; to prevent unlicensed lawyers from becoming judges; and to combat vote fraud by having all ballots printed at public expense.[45]

Jones wanted to expand the rights of accused persons in court. One of his bills would require that a grand jury hear witnesses for the defense as well as for the prosecution. Another would protect any person charged with the commission of a crime from making self-incriminating statements by stipulating that no agreement, statement, or confession could be made without the presence of the defendant's lawyer. It was not until sixty years later that the Supreme Court ruled in *Gideon v. Wainwright* (1963) and *Douglas v. California* (1963) that the states were required to guarantee counsel in all criminal trials. And in *Escobedo v. Illinois* (1964) the Court ruled inadmissible a confession extracted through police interrogation during which the accused had been denied the right to consult with an attorney.[46] "Indignation" Jones was thus belatedly vindicated.

These black legislators, from Thomas to Jones, saw themselves as champions of Negro rights and defenders of black civil liberties. Little is known about their political activities and even less about their personal lives; but it is clear from their speeches, legislative records, and contemporary news accounts that they were active in the protection of black rights and in the extension of the social service function of state government. As vigorous — if genteel — opponents of any attempt to curtail black rights or impose segregation by race, they were clearly in the earlier John Jones tradition of black protest. To the extent that they were capable of marshaling community support for their programs, as for the Eighth Regiment, their successes reflect the convergence of civic activity, practical politics, interracial cooperation (and sometimes sponsorship), and the black protest tradition.

What then was the legacy of pre-Great Migration black legislators for black Chicagoans and urban politics in the twentieth century? They are to be praised, if faintly, for their commendable attempts to extend local services and legal protections to disadvantaged citizenry. However, their essential significance lay in another direction: the true legacy of turn-of-the-century black politics was in the extensive and intricate series of personal obligations and practical limitations placed on black politics in the city.

Early black politicians were the often willing — but sometimes petulant — captives of the power fights, patronage deals, petty squabbles, and financial machinations that characterized Chicago politics. Nothing is more obvious in the history of early Chicago politics than the essentially passive and generally subordinate role of black political leadership to white interests. The essential relationship between black and white politicians was a patron-client nexus. Black politics was from its inception inescapably entangled in the web of dominant white political interests.

Ed Morris was elected to his second term with the support of a prominent white politician named Elbridge Hanecy, a "tough South Side judge." Hanecy was himself a protégé of Republican Senator William Lorimer, the "blond boss," a ruthless North Side faction leader who was later unseated by the U.S. Senate in 1912 following two investigations of bribery charges in connection with his election.

Judge Hanecy had been actively building influence with black politicians like Morris and Ed Wright and was a minor force in South Side politics until 1904, when he was forced into premature political retirement after losing a tilt for Republican leadership — and patronage — in the Third Ward with Congressman Martin B. Madden.[47] Madden himself had also been assiduously cultivating young black politicians and indeed maintained himself in the 1920s largely through the support of black politicians and voters.

John Buckner, the "Father of the Eighth Regiment," was Madden's most trusted black lieutenant. Madden had made many contacts with blacks from 1889 to 1897, first as an alderman and later as a congressman for the first congressional district on the near South Side. Buckner was Madden's chief liaison with his black constituents.

Martin Madden had been instrumental in securing Buckner's nomination for the legislature in 1894 and aided him in the creation of the all-black regiment in the National Guard. Buckner, for his part, was particularly effective in organizing the black community. He established the first Negro Bureau of the Republican State Central Committee and was chairman of that bureau during the national campaign of 1898. He held a number of political posts, including membership on the State Central Committee from 1894 to 1896. When Madden sought the Republican nomination for United States Senator in 1897, Buckner got petitions for him from South Side blacks. Buckner also gave Madden his proxy so that Madden could attend the party caucus in Springfield in 1897.[48]

Perhaps Buckner's most significant contribution to Madden's continuing political influence was as a successful recruiter of young political talent in the congressman's behalf. Buckner was an influential "godfather" in the political careers of several young black and white politicians. One of his most successful recruits was Madden's successor, Oscar DePriest, the first black U.S. congressman since Reconstruction, as well as DePriest's secretary, Morris Lewis.[49]

DePriest had begun his political career by going door-to-door in behalf of party candidates. He was so successful as a political organizer that in 1904 the still relatively obscure DePriest was influential enough to demand and receive slating by the Madden organization for the county board. After two terms on the board, DePriest entered into a disastrous alliance with Samuel Ettelson, state senator and later corporation counsel under William Hale Thompson against the Madden forces. Ettelson was defeated, and DePriest was out, forced to wander the political wastelands for five years until he was re-established in Madden's good graces. Paradoxically, Ettelson, a protégé of utilities magnate Samuel Insull, had also been a political client of John Buckner.[50]

It is significant that Buckner's most important accomplishment — and the lone institutional creation of these

From Intercollegian Wonder Book *(Chicago, 1927)*

Oscar DePriest, the first black U.S. congressman since Reconstruction

early black politicians — was the Eighth Regiment. When President McKinley requested 175,000 troops for the Spanish-American War, a group of prominent black civic leaders met with Governor Tanner to ask why no blacks had been included in the call. Black service in the Spanish-American War became a source of signal pride for black Chicagoans, and while the regiment was never a base for black political power, it was viewed as an important symbol of black patriotism and state recognition of the contributions of its black population.[51]

Beyond its symbolic significance, the Eighth was an inherently limited avenue for the advancement of group political aspirations. It was far too dependent on white patronage for both personal and military advancement. Buckner himself found that out when he was suspended and finally forced to resign over differences with the governor. While the entire community could rally around the issue of race heroism in the military and the creation of a black regiment as a proper institutional recognition of Negro military contribution, it would always be little more than a source of status and prestige for men who officered it. Many black politicians combined military prestige and political activism. At least two assistant corporation counsels, six state representatives, one state senator, three aldermen, and one congressmen came out of the Eighth or the all-black Giles Post of the American Legion. But regimental politics was not a significant force in the fuller integration of blacks into state and city politics. A source of prestige and important political contacts, perhaps — but not an avenue to political power.[52]

Fannie Barrier Williams had noted as early as 1905 this general dependence of the black population on white Chicagoans. Certainly, in politics the web of political influence and obligation extended throughout the black middle class. President Grover Cleveland appointed Dr. Daniel Hale Williams surgeon-in-chief of Washington's Freedman's Hospital, though Williams was a prominent Chicago Republican. But such appointments on merit, regardless of political affiliation, were rare. S. Laing Williams, a Booker T. Washington informant in Chicago, struggled diligently in beseeching Washington and prominent white politicians for political appointments. In 1910, President Taft made him the first black assistant district attorney in Chicago.[53]

If they were clever, black politicians could play both sides against each other. This was risky business, but it could work if one had a semi-independent power base such as a black church. Rev. Archibald Carey, a minister and later bishop of the African Methodist Episcopal Church, was a close friend of Boss William Lorimer. In 1900, when William Hale Thompson, scion of a wealthy family, ran for alderman of the

Second Ward, Carey was his main black supporter. Carey took the political novice door-to-door and advised him on the liberal but well-placed expenditure of money in black saloons. Thompson credited Carey with his election and rewarded the clergymen by introducing an ordinance for Chicago's first public playground, constructed across the street from Carey's own Institutional Church.[54]

But Carey, who remained a trusted Thompson ally, also aided Democrats when it served his interests. He supported Carter Harrison II for re-election in 1911, and Harrison appointed him to the Motion Picture Censor Board, where he led the protest against the showing of *Birth of a Nation*. In 1912, Carey successfully supported Edward Dunne, the Democratic candidate for Governor, and Dunne subsequently appointed him to head a committee to celebrate the fiftieth anniversary of the Thirteenth Amendment. It was a lucrative as well as prestigious appointment: the legislature appropriated $25,000 for the event, and Carey's church was selected as the committee's headquarters.[55]

The Reverend E.J. Fisher liked to think that he was above the common political fray. He was not, his son and biographer observed, a "hat-in-hand" profiteering politician, as by inference other religious leaders were. He accepted no "filthy lucre"; there was no "office-seeking": "The jobs sought him."[56] If Fisher was less politically active than Carey, he was also less politically prominent. But he *was* active. Almost immediately after arriving in Chicago in 1903 to serve the Olivet Baptist Church, Fisher began to participate in politics. He supported Republican Charles Deneen for governor in 1904, but also worked for Edward Dunne, then mayor of the city. Deneen appointed him a delegate to the National Negro Educational Congress in 1912, and a year later Dunne appointed him a delegate to the celebration of the fiftieth anniversary of the Emancipation Proclamation in Atlantic City. Fisher and Carey may have acted from principle rather than the desire for power and financial reward, but their activities did not go unrewarded. Miles Mark Fisher's biography of his father begins with an "appreciation" from Congressman Martin B. Madden.[57]

From Intercollegian Wonder Book *(Chicago, 1927)*

The Reverend Archibald Carey, bishop of the African Methodist
Episcopal Church

The close interrelationship between black institutions
and party politics may also be seen in a brief overview of the
pre-Migration black press. In a 1973 study, Albert Kreiling
uncovered eighty-nine magazines, newspapers, and newslet-
ters published in Chicago between 1878 and 1929. Among
the most prominent were the *Chicago Conservator*, Chicago
Appeal, Illinois *Idea*, and Chicago *Broad Ax*.[58] The Chicago
Appeal was begun in 1885 in Saint Paul, Minnesota, but by
1888 had become a joint St. Paul-Chicago publication with a
sizable black readership throughout the Midwest in the
eighties and nineties. Its founders, Cyrus Field Adams and

his brother, John Quincy Adams, were both active Republicans and supporters of Booker T. Washington. Cyrus Adams was prominent in the work of the first Negro Bureau in Chicago, a race organization connected with the national Republican campaign; between 1900 and 1912 he also served on various Republican advisory committees during presidential campaigns. In 1901, President McKinley appointed Adams assistant registrar of the Treasury, a traditional "Negro" post; and in 1912, President Taft appointed him to a position in New York City "protected" — from the incoming Democratic president — by civil service.[59]

The Illinois *Idea* was a Republican newspaper edited by

The Olivet Baptist Church

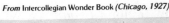

From Intercollegian Wonder Book *(Chicago, 1927)*

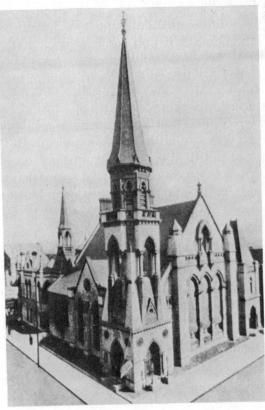

Sheadrick B. Turner, an active Republican politician who served in the Illinois House of Representatives from 1913 to 1917 and from 1919 to 1927. The *Idea* was used to promote Turner's personal political ambitions and the interests of the Republican party among blacks. It had no national news service of its own, and most out-of-town news was garnered through personal exchanges or "appropriated" from other newspapers. The *Idea* carried a good deal of news of local churches and many personal items (such as deaths, illnesses, and accidents), as well as information on the "race problem"; but much of its revenue came from political advertisements and propaganda during election periods. White politicians were placed on the *Idea's* mailing list, and advertisements from white firms contributed substantially to the paper's coffers.[60]

Julius F. Taylor's *Broad Ax*, which started in Chicago in 1899, attacked the traditional Republican affiliation of Chicago blacks and supported the candidates of the Democratic party. It was suggested that Taylor's Democratic loyalties were based, at least in part, on political opportunism. Taylor arrived in Chicago during the regime of five-term Democratic mayor Carter H. Harrison, and at least one contemporary contended that Taylor found the "Democratic field for the Negro was a relatively fertile and unexplored field."[61] This charge of political opportunism is bolstered by the fact that the *Broad Ax* in Salt Lake City was conspicuously less political; and Taylor's first Chicago edition featured a particularly revealing letter of commendation from Mayor Carter Harrison II:

> To Whom It May Concern:
> Julius F. Taylor, who comes to this city well recommended, has begun the publication of the *Broad Ax*, which I am informed will disseminate Democratic principles and contend for the higher intellectual development of the Afro-American Race and mankind in general. *While he is thus engaged* [italics mine] I bespeak for him the hearty support of all loyal and true friends of the Democracy.
>
> Respectfully,
> Carter H. Harrison

The paper also boasted the "endorsement" of the Democratic State Central Committee of Illinois.[62]

Taylor was born in Virginia and migrated to Salt Lake City, where he founded the original *Broad Ax* in about 1895. Four years later he moved the paper to Chicago. He was an anomaly at the turn of the century, a western Democrat when most black Chicagoans were Republican; he was also an admirer of William Jennings Bryan and an economic radical in sharp contrast to the generally conservative ideas of the black community's leadership.

Broad Ax was literally a one-man operation, characterized by a type of personal journalism that often veered toward idiosyncratic interpretations of news stories and blatant character assassination. His enemies were generally characterized as drunks, adulterers, and thieves, and his news stories were often indistinguishable from his editorials.[63]

Among the early black Chicago newspapers, the *Chicago Conservator* alone escaped the fate of becoming a vehicle for clearly partisan, patron-client political interests. Founded in 1878, the city's first black newspaper appeared at a time when blacks were not yet fully integrated into South Side political affairs. Yet even here partisan politics intruded. The paper's founder and first editor was Ferdinand L. Barnett, a member of the Deneen faction within the Republican party and a minor officeholder through the sponsorship of both black and white politicians.[64]

Fisher, Carey, DePriest, Morris, Buckner, and the various black editors — these were all articulate and intelligent men. They were not "Uncle Toms"; indeed they saw themselves as champions of Negro rights. But they chose to define black political advancement within the narrow confines of established urban political orthodoxy. They did not see themselves subordinating black advancement to white political interests. They were simply "playing the game." Influence was garnered through party loyalty, votes delivered, services rendered; they did not seek to create separate and independent political organizations. When Buckner formed voters' groups, they were in the service of his patron Madden, or an adjunct to national or local political campaigns. They tended to be the children of whatever campaign was in process. When the election was over, so were the organizations.

The prominent black lawyer and political leader Edward E. Wilson noted the transience of black political organizations — and of some of their members:

> From campaign to campaign some loiter about county buildings, living heaven knows how. Others seem to hibernate like a bear. When a campaign comes on they are in their glory. They attend political meetings and shout "hear, hear"; they hold forth from corners with pot-eloquent fervor, they show mysterious letters from a senator or representative calling on them to come to his district and help him out. These gentlemen go about rather shabby, having refused, as they will tell you, a job paying a thousand dollars a year. A marked characteristic of this kind of statesman is that he is always armed with a number of newspapers — literally weighted down with them — and refers to them on every occasion to prove his prophetic vision and the infallibility of his stand on this or that question. It is gentry of this kind that have given the Negro a bad name in politics; for not a few of these, though burning with patriotism, have a burning palm also, and are not seldom found refusing to vote without being persuaded thereto by some other than patriotic influences.[65]

Black politics was shaped by the aggressive and often vituperative interparty and internecine struggles for place and power which characterized city politics in general. Black leadership was molded in the crucible of white politics. As early as 1892, a group of Second Ward black Republicans held a caucus at 1823 State Street to organize a vigorous campaign for the Republican ticket. James E. Bish, who was elected to the state legislature that year, was selected president. The club made clear its intention of organizing and incorporating a permanent black political organization that would not evaporate after the fall election. In 1893 the newly formed Second Ward Colored Republican Club announced its unanimous endorsement of Republican Mayor Swift for renomination and "took steps to gain recognition for the colored people in the distribution of patronage by the county board." Specific requests for more patronage were made to the president of the County Board, and Bish himself asked to be made custodian of the County Building.[66]

In 1894, Bish's name was again mentioned, this time as a possible candidate for county commissioner; but another group of newly organized black politicians were sponsoring a prominent black political organizer for the post — Edward H. Wright.[67]

John Jones represented the postwar, postabolitionist tradition of civic protest and civil rights. Black legislators from Thomas to William Martin and "Indignation" Jones reflect the role of the black legislator as a vigilant defender of existing black rights and supporter of the social service role of government. Buckner, Bish, and Morris reveal the relationship between politics and legislation and the importance of white sponsorship in black political careers.

Wright represents something new. In many ways he was the father of twentieth-century black politics in Chicago. This nineteenth-century black legislator was the bridge between civic protest and white clientage politics. Wright illustrated the emergent orientation of black politics toward ward and precinct organization on the city's South Side, and, more important, he pioneered in the establishment of an independent political organization designed to increase black influence in Republican councils and give black politicians a coequal role in the political leadership of the black community.

Edward H. Wright was born in New York City in 1864, attended the city's public schools, and at seventeen graduated from the College of the City of New York. He taught school in New Jersey for three years and came to Chicago in 1884, working his way across the country as a Pullman porter's assistant. Wright held a series of minor posts, but it was politics that landed him a job in the county clerk's office. As a result of his work as delegate to the Republican State Convention in 1888, political service again garnered him a position as bookkeeper and railroad inspection clerk in the secretary of state's office in Springfield, the first clerical position in state government held by a black. When the term of his patron ended, Wright became employed in the city clerk's office in Chicago.[68]

From Intercollegian Wonder Book *(Chicago, 1927)*

Edward Wright, father of twentieth-century black politics in Chicago

In 1893, Wright emerged as president of a group called the Afro-American League, and a year later he represented one of the two black factions seeking to nominate a "Race Man" to the county board. Since there was no chance that two blacks would be nominated, Wright rose in the county convention and asked that his name be withdrawn from contention. He called on all of his supporters to support the leader of the other faction, Theodore Jones, who was nominated and elected. Jones became the first black member of the county board in almost twenty years. Two years later Wright replaced Jones as the sole black county commissioner.[69]

As county commissioner, Wright was described as "shrewd, forceful and highly race-conscious." "Through sheer ability," wrote the *Chicago Defender*, "he became a power on the county board." Wright and Daniel Healy, a Democrat, led opposing political factions on the board, a feat all the more impressive because Wright was the sole black member.[70]

Perhaps the best example of Wright's political tenacity came in a well-publicized battle with Charles Deneen, later governor and U.S. Senator from Illinois. Deneen had at that time just served a term as a state representative and was seeking the Republican nomination for state's attorney. He made a deal with Wright for the latter's support in the county convention by promising to name a Negro as one of his assistants. Deneen was nominated and elected, but no black assistant state's attorney was nominated. Wright called on Deneen to remind him of their previous agreement and to find out when his nominee, Ferdinand L. Barnett, would be appointed. Deneen said that he would get around to it soon but refused to be committed to a specific date. The nomination "continued to hang fire," and Wright decided to act. When the county board met to appropriate money for various offices, Wright deliberately held up the appropriations for the state's attorney's office.

Deneen inquired among the members of the board about the delay and was told that Commissioner Wright "was sitting on the lid." He called on Wright and is reported to have said: "Ed, what's the idea of you holding up the appropriations for my office?" Wright replied, "You had an understanding with me that in the event of your election you would appoint F.L. Barnett assistant state's attorney and you have failed to keep your word; until that is done I shall continue to prevent the passage of your appropriation." Deneen declared, "I am state's attorney of Cook County and you can't dictate to me!" Wright replied, "Yes, and I am county commissioner." A few days later Barnett became the first black assistant state's attorney for Cook County, and Deneen's appropriations were soon passed.[71]

Wright was re-elected in 1898 and briefly, in 1900, was elected president pro tempore of the county board when the president was away for a short time. Wright accomplished this feat by going around to all the members of the board individually, telling them that he did not expect to be elected but that he would appreciate one or two votes as a sign of recognition for his race. There were two other prominent contenders for the post, but when the votes were counted Wright had received all but two of the fourteen votes cast.[72]

Wright's term as commissioner was not without controversy. This was the era of boodlers, fixed conventions, and frequent utility scandals. In the 1896 Cook County Convention, for example, many of the delegates had criminal records; over one-third of them were saloonkeepers and one-fifth political employees. City and county government were both in the throes of political corruption. Money oiled the wheels of government and soothed discordant political interests.[73]

The problems of local government were exacerbated by the rapid expansion in the city's population. Between 1890 and 1900, Chicago's population grew to 1,698,575 — an increase of 595,725, or over 52 percent. Newly annexed territories, many of them villages and expanses of prairies, required large expenditures for normal city improvements and often for the assumption of their former debts. These townships, "vestiges of frontier Chicago," continued to retain their own taxing power and entered, in Ellen Beckman's words, "an era of graft and pillage which frightened the politicians themselves."[74]

Edward Wright's reputation was blemished with more

than one charge of corruption. When civic leaders protested the attempts of townships to secure funds for filing fake or padded expense accounts, Wright, acting as attorney for the county board, maintained that the board's president had no legal right to deny funds to the townships. He was also criticized for supporting a measure that granted a blanket franchise without compensation to the Metropolitan Traction Company. The franchise gave the company a monopoly in building street railways over the principal highways outside the Chicago city limits not already occupied by streetcar tracks.[75]

Wright failed to secure nomination in 1900 and for a period moved out of the district that had been his base of political support. He had not been able to work in harmony with Congressman Madden or George F. Harding, Madden's chief lieutenant. Although he was chosen state central committeeman as a reward for his services to Second Ward Committeeman Chauncy Dewey, Wright did not acquire any real political power for another two decades. Dan Jackson, an undertaker and big-time gambler, was slated to replace Wright in 1900. However, Jackson, who ran one of his gambling joints in his funeral home, was defeated when several newspapers, for the first time, drew attention to his color.[76]

In 1904, Oscar DePriest, a Buckner and Madden protégé, was elected to the board. DePriest was born in Florence, Alabama in 1871 and had come to Chicago in 1889 "to grow with the Metropolis of the West."[77] No two men could have been more different — or had more in common. Wright was big (about six-feet-four) and black, an intelligent, intense behind-the-scenes organizer — "the iron master." DePriest was equally tall, but so fair that he successfully passed for white when he first arrived. He was gregarious, sometimes overbearingly so. But he was also an organizer and a skilled politician.

Before the 1904 county convention, DePriest had collected the support of a majority of the black precinct captains. Madden had only just begun his congressional career, and DePriest demanded that he be named to the ticket and that the county convention be held before the state convention.

Madden wanted to be sure of united local support, and so he put the still relatively obscure DePriest, seven years Wright's junior at thirty-three, on the ticket. Like Wright, DePriest knew when to be intransigent as well as cooperative.[78]

DePriest was re-elected in 1906. As commissioner he chaired a committee on education and industrial schools and was a member of the committee on outdoor relief. He took part in the planning of the new five-million-dollar courthouse and was praised for his energy in educating blacks to the relief services offered by the county. DePriest benefited from the ambiguous morality of the period. At fifteen DePriest had been apprenticed to a painter and began his career "carrying a ladder up and down State Street" painting and plastering. He now used his position as commissioner to advance his business. His specialty was salvaging old buildings. He also had a keen sense of the value of a dollar: in 1903, for example, he sued Olivet Baptist Church for an unpaid bill.[79]

By 1905 the *Broad Ax* boasted that DePriest had the "largest painting and decorating contracting business conducted by any member of the Negro race in the Northwest." Between 1903 and 1905 he was awarded contracts for an estimated $25,000 from the Chicago Board of Education. After siding with the losing faction in the Ettelson-Madden tilt, however, DePriest was momentarily consigned to political oblivion. He used the time to invest heavily in real estate. He opened an office on State Street, on the edge of the "black belt," and engaged in "block-busting," buying property, renting it to a black family, and when neighboring whites fled, buying their property and renting it at inflated prices to incoming blacks. Before the Depression, DePriest was reputed to have been a millionaire.[80]

While DePriest made money, Wright was casting about for the appropriate vehicle for black political expression. In 1898, Wright played a leading role in organizing the Sumner Club, designed to hold "much the same position as the Hamilton Club does in the ranks of the white Republican residents."

> While there are social features in the Sumner club, its main object is almost entirely political, and while it neither asked nor

received official aid or recognition it has become an influential means for the advancement of Republican politics in Cook County. Being now thoroughly organized and in effective working shape, the members are shaping a program with this end in view.[81]

Wright was also one of the organizers and the first president of the Cook County Bar Association, a black lawyers' organization; but the Sumner Club, and the creation of a viable, independent black political organization were central to Wright's long-range political aspirations. In 1900 the Sumner Club was succeeded by the Appomattox Club, Wright's "one major avocational interest" and a "rendezvous for Negro Republican politicians."[82]

The Appomattox Club, however, never developed into an effective vehicle for the exercise of independent political leadership. From time to time it would be called on to act as the representative spokesman for the Negro community. In 1900, for example, the *Defender*, arguing that "concerted action is better than individual [action]," called on the club "with its representative men" to protest the blatantly racist advertisement that the all-white Hope Cemetery had placed in another paper.[83] But for the most part the Appomattox Club was a place of good comradeship for a group of socially and sometimes politically compatible men.

It is clear from an overview of Edward Wright's entire career that he had sought to create an effective and independent black political organization. In the early 1900s, Wright was wandering in the political wilderness; between 1910 and 1915 he was engaged in a running battle with the white leadership of the Second Ward, in an often bitter campaign to have a black slated as alderman for this increasingly black ward. In 1910, with blacks an estimated 25 percent of the population of the ward, Wright ran as one of four candidates for the post. The *Chicago Defender* made an impassioned plea for racial unity. "We must have a colored alderman not because others were not friendly, but because we should be represented just the same as the Irish, Jews, and Italians." But Wright finished third, capturing only 18 percent of the votes.[84]

Wright tried again in 1912, and the *Defender* again trumpeted race unity and argued that blacks comprised half of the Republican voters in the ward and were entitled to at least one alderman. Again he was defeated, and in 1914 he supported William R. Cowan, a prominent black real estate dealer. Even though he lost, Cowan garnered a very impressive 45 percent of the vote. The white organization was visibly shaken. Madden assured blacks that although he was obligated to support the present white incumbent, as soon as an opening occurred he would support a black candidate.

The chance came the next year when Madden's chief lieutenant was elected to the state senate, thus vacating an aldermanic post. The nomination and subsequent election went to a black, but one who had supported the organization throughout the Wright-Cowan insurgency. Much to Ed Wright's displeasure, the plum went to Oscar DePriest.[85]

Wright was simply unable to mold the Appomattox Club into a strong independent political force. Even Appomattox leaders like Louis B. Anderson, who owed their early political careers to Wright, were unable to withstand the blandishments and ready rewards of the organization. The club's membership was simply too divergent in private ambitions and factional allegiances to coalesce on all but the most basic — and trivial — political concerns.[86]

A brief overview of some of the more prominent members of the Appomattox Club reveals the inherent difficulties of creating a truly independent coalition of black political leaders. Dr. George Cleveland Hall, for example, was an active Republican partisan as well as a widely respected civic leader. In 1895 he had served as treasurer of the Young Colored Men's Republican League of Cook County, but his interests in politics were, for the most part, an adjunct to his civic activities in the NAACP or as president of the Chicago Urban League. Men like Wright, DePriest, and Anderson, by contrast, were earnest if not intense in their quest for political advancement. Anderson, DePriest, and R.R. Jackson, all future South Side aldermen, had become allied with Martin B. Madden and later with William Hale Thompson and Fred Lundin, prominent white politicians and major shapers of black politics in the first third of the twentieth century. Ferdinand L. Barnett and his wife, Ida B. Wells-Barnett, on the other hand, were allied with the opposition camp of Charles E. Deneen, whom they believed had "higher principles than the regular organization."[87]

Beauregard F. Moseley and R.R. Jackson co-founded the *Leland Giants*, the first successful "race" baseball team on the South Side. Mosely was an active Republican and a past president of the Appomattox Club, but in 1912 he supported the Progressive party of Theodore Roosevelt and became president of an organization called the Progressive Negro League.[88]

Dr. Hall tended to ally himself with "good government" organizations and candidates. He was on the "Merriam for Mayor Committee" in 1911 and was a member of the Executive Committee of the Municipal Voters League, a "good government" organization. DePriest, Anderson, and — to a lesser degree — Jackson were routinely criticized by the MVL, which condemned their voting records and opposed their re-election to the city council.[89]

A critical factor in the early history of the Appomattox Club was the intense rivalry among the members themselves. "It was such a small area," one long-time Chicago resident observed, "that there was always competition among politically inclined Negroes."[90] Equally important, many of the club's leaders and most of its successful politicians had, before 1900, contracted alliances or acquired patrons from one or more of the many factions and subfactions within the city's Republican party. The difficulty of creating a community political consensus amid individual ambitions was evident almost from the organization's inception.

But perhaps the most complex and definitive explanation lay in the inherent limitations of black middle-class politics in Chicago. Pre-Migration black politics was formed from the confluence of post-Civil War black middle-class ideology and black acceptance of established conventions of urban ethnic politics. That the middle class should have effectively maintained political hegemony is not unusual or peculiar to black Chicagoans. The political scientists Heinz Eulau and Kenneth Prewitt have observed:

> To this day, elected legislatures, in the established democracies
> of the Western world, are overwhelmingly chosen from the mid-
> dle and upper-middle strata of society. This is the case whether
> the basic political organization of the society is along vertical or
> horizontal lines. If politics is vertically organized, as is true
> where ethnicity, religion, or geography is politically salient,
> political groups include members of the various social strata in
> the society, but tend nevertheless to be led by their middle and
> upper-middle-class members. These leaders provide the pool
> from which most political officeholders are selected. If politics
> is horizontally organized, as is true where class is politically
> salient, the membership of political groups is more homogene-
> ous and the leaders may be of the same social origin as the
> members. But even under these conditions, the bourgeoisie
> supplies the large majority of political leaders. . . .[91]

Chicago politics was organized vertically, along ethnic,
racial, and — to a lesser extent — geographic and religious
lines. Black political leadership, in terms of income, education, social position, and self-perception, was conspicuously
middle class. They were conscious of their position as
pioneers, and they saw in their own personal advancement
the broader advancement of the race.[92]

Several political scientists (but interestingly, no historians) have offered possible explanations for the particular
character of black political life in Chicago. Ira Katznelson
argues that black politicians had the potential to mobilize the
black masses and demand solutions to black problems, but
instead they opted for individual rewards for a select few.
Black politics, he argues, was inherently and necessarily conservative because any agitation for change that challenged
the racial status quo would endanger "structured relationships" with powerful and influential whites and "place the
[rewarding] alliance in jeopardy."[93] Black politics was limited, Katznelson strongly implies, because avaricious and
status-seeking black politicians entered into narrowly self-
serving alliances with corrupt white political machines.
Black politics was "co-opted"; black political organizations
became "buffers" between the elite and the masses. The
"system" offered access only to a "nonrepresentative" black
elite while "defusing social conflict" and "leaving the dis-

tribution of political power largely intact."[94]

James Q. Wilson's approach is more empirical and less critical. Although his area of concentration is post-World War II and 1950s Chicago politics, his perspective is informing. For Wilson, black politics is dominated by the physical fact of racial segregation. Emerging from this reality is a multi-faceted conflict within black leadership groups over the function of politics. The conflict is between those who believe politics should provide material services to individuals or to the masses — "welfare ends" — and those who seek the less concrete goals of racial integration, civil rights, greater black visibility in public offices — goals generally defined by Wilson as "status ends."[95]

Martin Kilson presents the most clearly defined ideological explanation for the shape of black politics in Chicago. For Kilson, the pattern of "political adaptation" to American cities or political "modernization" begins with clientage or patron-client relationships between black and white politicians, most widespread throughout the period 1900-1920. Clientage, Kilson argues, "was almost exclusively the political method of the Negro middle class," where the black bourgeoisie sought to mask their search for political, social, and economic advantage as "race politics."[96]

In Kilson's conceptual framework, urban black politics advances in stages from clientage politics to interest-group articulation, in which established groups or influential cliques seek to institutionalize black demands. Groups like the NAACP, Urban League, and Marcus Garvey's UNIA took on parapolitical functions, articulating black discontent, making demands on local or national power elites, and exerting pressure or using persuasion on community leaders. The growth of interest-group articulation did not at first replace clientage politics but supplemented it. However, the failure of traditional clientage relations to serve wider segments of the black community and to create its own black political "sub-system" meant that interest-group articulation would eventually "encroach upon" and ultimately supersede clientage politics.[97]

The final stage, the period 1920-1940, showed the rise of

black machine politics. In its formative stage whites entered into a "neoclientage" relationship with a hand-picked black "influential," who handed out patronage and was primarily responsible to the "machine." As black machine politics matured, the goal of neutralizing or limiting black political "clout" was replaced by the institutional inclusion of the black sub-machine into "the dominant pattern of machine or boss rule in a given city." Kilson points out that such inclusion was "extremely rare . . . the notable exception being Chicago from 1915 onward."[98]

What these three analysts share is a keen perception of the pre-eminence of the relationship between black and white politicians in the shaping of black politics in Chicago; of the tendency of black middle-class politics to seek individual or status rewards from politics; and of the generally conservative nature of black politics in the city.

While I have no essential argument with such observations — and am in particular agreement with the Kilson-Katznelson emphasis on the patron-client nature of early Chicago politics — I must add an historian's additional observation about the particular character of pre-Migration black politics. What is missing in these generally admirable observations is the particular historical context of black political development. Morris, Wright, and DePriest did not spring full-blown from the head of Zeus. The generally conservative and essentially individualistic pattern of black politics emerged from a specific tradition of black and Chicago politics.

Returning to John Jones, we can observe two dominant features of the politics of black Chicago: a general faith in the efficacy of American political parties and the essentially defensive nature of black politics. Jones' political ideas had been forged in the anti-black-laws campaign of the 1860s, a campaign which would not have succeeded without powerful white allies and the Republican party. "My colored countrymen," Jones once declared in a speech, "the republican [sic] party has lifted us up from the degradation of slavery and put us upon an equal platform with themselves."[99] Jones' diary contains numerous references to the importance of voting.

Jones preserved the full text of a speech entitled "The Importance of a Single Vote," and he counseled the importance of blacks' exercising the franchise. Jones was not unaware of the obstacles that lay ahead for his people, but he seemed genuinely optimistic about the race's future. A quote from Goethe was prominently displayed in his diary: "In imminent danger the faintest hope should be taken into account."[100]

Black Chicagoans clung to Jones' Republican party, the one that offered them protection and some modicum of political advancement. Many black politicians opposed the entire spate of progressive electoral innovations, including the direct primary, initiative, referendum, and recall. When Governor Deneen's administration was considering instituting the direct primary in 1907, Rev. Archibald Carey and other prominent black leaders sent a resolution to each state senator:

> We the undersigned citizens ask in our own behalf and at the special insistence and request of the colored citizens do hereby protest against the passage of the so-called Primary Election Law Bill being House No. 895. We feel that the passage of this bill will completely eliminate from the politics of the state the colored voters and take from them all opportunity of any member of their race being nominated to office and we respectfully ask that you vote against the passage of this bill.[101]

However, the bill was made law. Five years later a *Defender* editorial criticized another set of Progressive reforms.

> The Initiative, Referendum, and Recall is simply a dose of disfranchisement, sugar coated, albeit with high sounding and illusive verbiage for the consumption of the northern Negro, but nevertheless an emetic which will sooner or later force him to disgorge every right that he possesses under the law and the constitution.
>
> Out in the broad light of day and in the courts where publicity obtains, the Negro has a chance for justice, but under the Initiative, Referendum, and Recall the civil rights of the Negro will be decided in the silence and seclusion of the voting booth, where his enemies may stab him in the back and none be the wiser; because they will be swallowed up in the great concrete majority that Roosevelt likes to call "the people."[102]

The *Defender* was magniloquent — but not entirely honest. The "broad light of day" which they and prominent black politicians sought was the machine anonymity that would allow blacks to seek city-wide or county-wide elective office on the Republican ticket and not be "cut" by regular party voters because of their race. However, their fears were justified. Before the bill was made law in 1910, several blacks had been successfully elected to the Cook County Board of Commissioners. After 1910 no black was elected until 1938.[103]

These black machine politicians were not unthinking loyalists. Carey, DePriest, and Wright would often play faction against faction and would even abandon particular party nominees when it served their interests. But they saw in a certain political consistency the quickest and safest avenue for their own — and by extension — the race's political advancement.

The era from John Jones to "Indignation" Jones must have seemed a period of impressive progress. One state representative and a county commissioner had become the expected reward for black party fealty. By 1900 there were black policemen, black school teachers, black assistant corporation counsels — all gained through black political influence. Blacks were still economically disadvantaged, and they were still discriminated against; but from the perspective of middle-class black politics it was an era of adequate if not exceptional progress for a people little more than a generation removed from slavery.

The task, then, was to preserve and insure their — and the race's — advancement amid crumbling race relations. If this was to be achieved, caution, in the tradition of Booker T. Washington, suggested that it be done within the established tradition of Chicago ethnic politics. They were painfully aware of the limits of adventurism. Washington had implied that Reconstruction and the Populist period had offered a naive race the illusion of political advancement while robbing them of economic security and the necessary good will of the wealthier classes of the white South.[104] When Ferdinand Barnett ran for the municipal court in 1906 on the

Republican ticket, blacks were again reminded of their vulnerability. Barnett faced substantial and, apparently to many blacks, surprising white hostility. With one exception, every white newspaper urged that he be defeated, and the Chicago *Chronicle* wrote: "The bench is a position of absolute authority and white people will never willingly submit to receiving the law from a negro." While the rest of the Republican ticket swept to victory, Barnett was defeated, amid charges of election fraud.[105]

What I am suggesting is the convenient convergence of the essentially reactive nature of early black politics and the pre-existent tradition of Chicago ethnic politics that offered certain — if limited — political rewards to a receptive black elite. These rewards were themselves small: financial backing for campaigns, some patronage, a few minor appointive posts, status within their own community, and eventually limited and usually shared power within a narrowly proscribed geographical area with a majority black population. The rewards were perhaps paltry, but they were substantial enough to convince the black political elite, and through them the voters, of the benefits of machine politics and the dangers of political independence.

My reading of the evidence suggests that more than avarice or political cupidity shaped pre-Migration black politics in Chicago. The black political elite was predisposed by the dominant political conservatism of the times toward the relative safety of the ethnic political machine. Booker T. Washington, perhaps the most powerful Republican — black or white — in the South, lunched with President Roosevelt and counseled against radicalism, class antagonism, and political independence. John Jones was certainly radical in his opposition to slavery. But in a speech before a workingman's union, he was careful to delineate his political aims: "We are not demanding what is known as social rights," he said. "The social relations lie entirely outside the domain of legislation and politics. They are simply matters of taste, and thus I leave them."[106]

Jones' rise to wealth and social prominence was the archetypal Horatio Alger story. An ardent advocate of the mid-nineteenth-century capitalist ethic, his vision of the future was entirely conventional and somewhat optimistic. "I expect," he said, "to see the day myself when the colored men of the South will be the cotton lords and bankers of that favored section of the country. We are making rapid strides in acquiring education and wealth. Our children are going to school. We are buying real estate and paying for it, both North and South, and these, my friends, constitute the true road to success." Jones even emulated the upper-class pattern of entertaining, complete with quadrille orchestra to provide "inspiring music" for the "terpsichorean pleasure" of the evening.[107]

DePriest was widely praised throughout his lifetime as a "Race Man," someone firmly committed to black advancement. Yet he was an economic conservative who made a fortune in "block-busting," helped organize the Chicago branch of Booker T. Washington's Negro Business League and later, as a congressman, voted *against* Democratic New Deal relief measures. Carey was critical of the radicalism of labor leader A. Phillip Randolph and was equally conservative: "I believe that the interest of my people lies with the wealth of the nation and with the class of white people who control it. Labor and capital cannot adjust themselves by rival organizations; they must work together."[108]

Perhaps most instructive of the convergence of political and economic conservatism was an incident involving black Chicago postal employees. The Phalanx Forum, a social organization for black postal workers, had been formed in 1911 by members of the Appomattox Club. Black workers in the post office qualified for middle-class status in the early twentieth-century community, and a former postal worker, R.R. Jackson, was the community's state representative in 1912. With the election of Woodrow Wilson, the postal service was segregated and many black workers fired. Instead of joining the National Alliance of Postal Employees, which fought to protect black jobs through trade unionism, the workers opted instead to pursue the more individualistic but safer approach of using the political influence of the Appomattox Club to protect their jobs.[109]

This approach was not unique to black Chicagoans. As Robert Factor makes clear from an overview of the post-Civil War career of Frederick Douglass and black labor organizations in the 1870s, even groups ostensibly formed to deal with the problems of black labor tended to focus attention away from economic and class grievances and toward conventional political demands for equal rights and resolutions of support for the Republican party.[110] Black leaders from Douglass to Washington, from John Jones to Ed Wright, regarded economics as a matter of individual concern, eschewed class antagonism and labor militancy, and entombed black political ideology within the relatively safe and conventional limitations of American partisan orthodoxy.

Black Republicanism, of course, brought with it the heritage of Lincoln and Sumner, with images of abolitionism and emancipation. Negro Democracy, on the other hand, bore the burden of Southern white redemption, the Klan, and lynching. In 1888, when the Cook County Democratic Club opened its headquarters, one old Negro is reported to have wept "to think that Colored men should be Democrats."[111] Yet, whereas suspicion of Democrats was never fully assuaged, many blacks were attracted to Carter Harrison I, the Democratic mayor from 1879 to 1887 and briefly again in 1893 (he was assassinated at the end of the Chicago World's Fair); and his son, Carter II, mayor from 1897 to 1903 and from 1911 to 1915. In 1885, Carter I received an estimated 50 percent of the black vote, and twelve years later his son was elected mayor with 65 percent of the black vote.[112]

The first organized unit of black Democrats is perhaps lost in antiquity, but the Logan Hall Democrats, the Thirteenth Ward Democrats, and the Colored Tammany were among the earliest black Democratic clubs formed in Chicago. By the 1890s the Colored Democratic League, led by Enos Bond, had apparently attained a degree of political permanence unusual for Chicago politics, where most political groups, Republican or Democrat, black or white, tended to be creatures of whatever campaign was at hand.[113]

The most impressive of the early black leaders of the Chicago Democracy was Lawrence Arthur Newby. Newby was born in Pauli, Indiana and spent his early years in Indianapolis, where he served briefly as owner and editor of the black newspaper *Indianapolis Courier*. He came to Chicago in 1895 and became active in the presidential campaign of William Jennings Bryan. In 1898 he was elected president of the Colored Democratic League.[114] While Newby was considered an effective and widely respected political organizer, the nascent Democratic party was racked with petty jealousies and factional discord. Party unity was hampered by the emergence of rival organizations such as the Thomas Jefferson Club. In 1901 the sable Democracy was further splintered with the emergence of the Cook County Colored Democracy under the leadership of Captain H.C. Carter.[115]

For Julius Taylor, the black editor of *Broad Ax*, Captain Carter represented the lowest form of political opportunism. Carter was accused of surrounding himself with the "worst class of Negroes," and failing to recruit new members to the party. *Broad Ax* was also highly critical of Carter's morals. Respectable Democrats, Taylor wrote, "have not forgotten the fact that for years Captain Carter lived with Mrs. Fanny Brown in open violation of all the laws of decency and morality. . . ." Carter responded by having Taylor arrested for libel.[116] Despite Taylor's continued carping, Carter appears to have retained the favor and the financial backing of the Democratic powers.

It is difficult to explain the popularity of the two Carter Harrisons within the black community. They did appoint a few blacks to minor municipal offices, and — equally important — they maintained the pattern of black municipal employment inherited from Republican mayors. Their success, however, seems more a matter of style and personal attractiveness than any general movement of blacks to the Democratic party. With the exception of the Harrisons, *père* and *fils*, black Chicagoans demonstrated an understandable fidelity to the Republican banner. For black Chicagoans, the Harrison periods were glorious exceptions, incongruous eras capped by the election of 1911, when Carter II, running for his last term, carried the black vote against the Republican reformer, Charles E. Merriam, and became the first Democrat to capture the Second Ward. Black Republican loyalty persisted, despite the fact that in twenty mayoralty contests between 1871 and 1915, ten were won by a Carter Harrison.[117]

The failure of the Chicago Democrats to build on the Harrison popularity and to attract a larger black constituency is one of the interesting "might-have-beens" of black history. Traditional Republican loyalty cannot serve as the only answer, for blacks in Boston were attracted to the Democratic machine of Mayor Curley, and certainly the successes of the Harrisons indicated that blacks could be induced to vote for Democratic candidates. Furthermore, many prominent blacks had been critical of Theodore Roosevelt's handling of the Brownsville Incident and of Republican overtures to conservative white Southerners. Prominent black leaders like William Monroe Trotter and W.E.B. DuBois were counseling increased political independence, and Edward E. Wilson argued that Chicago blacks could be induced to support "liberal-leaning" Democrats.

> While the great majority of Chicago Negroes are Republicans there is a respectable and growing element that has allied itself with the Democratic Party. There is but little difference — save in name — between a white Chicago Democrat and a white Chicago Republican. Because of tradition and of the support given it, the Republican party has granted the Negro most of his political recognition, but this party shows manifest restlessness at Negro demands. A Democrat of liberal leanings always commands some Negro votes in city elections and it is a good guess to say that henceforth there will be fewer Negroes of the unalterable Republican faith in local contests.[118]

Wilson failed to recognize the impact of what August Meier has called the migration of the Talented Tenth. Chicago's black population increased by more than 30 percent between 1900 and 1910; already by 1900 over 80 percent of the city's black population had been born outside Illinois, the majority of them coming from the border states and the upper South. As the historian Allan H. Spear has pointed out: "As migration from the South swelled the population of the black belt, it brought with it voters who regarded the

Democrats as the natural enemies of the Negro people and whose previous experiences committed them to the Republican Party."[119]

But Wilson's own words reveal an additional element. The Republican party gave the Negro "most of his political recognition." The Chicago Democracy was unable to shake the racial conservatism that dominated that party throughout the first third of the century. They ignored the requests of their few black supporters and never nominated a single black for even the most minor elective office. Blacks were being asked to support a party largely composed of the more overtly antiblack "new immigrants" and identified with working and lower-class whites. It was an unlikely adventure for a largely conservative and essentially cautious black leadership.

* * * * *

The transformation from the civic-protest tradition to organizational politics, the emergence of a small cadre of full-time black professional politicians, and the conflict between race politics and the patron-client relationships contracted between black and white politicians characterized black politics in Chicago before the Great Migration. The emerging Negro elite attempted, through politics, to translate intra-racial status into political influence and to manipulate its personal and occupational prestige within the black community into service as a buffer between white leadership and the black masses. The institutional and social circumscription peculiar to the black urban experience, plus the pre-existing tradition of ethnic representation and group politics, combined to aid this new elite in translating credibility with black voters and contacts with white politicians into limited political influence.

Chicago's black politicians recognized their roles as "pioneers" in black political development. They also perceived, perhaps indirectly, the tenuousness of their political leadership roles. They were, to paraphrase Martin Kilson, attempting to assert their eligibility — in concert as an elite or in competition as individuals — to assume a leadership role in the necessary political change that would occur with the introduction of the black voter as a new constituent into the existing political system, an introduction that might well generate friction with existing claimants to political authority.

Thus they were faced with a dual obligation: they had to assure their constitutents that their interests were identical with group racial interests, and they had to frame race demands in ways and through channels that would be comprehensible and ultimately resolvable within existing urban political procedures. Those black politicians who chafed under the explicit obligations of Chicago ward politics faced personal (i.e., financial) as well as political punishments for their recalcitrance. Ed Wright and Oscar DePriest were both examples of political self-assertiveness that was rewarded with temporary political banishment.[120]

The period from the mid-1870s to the early 1900s may be seen as a transitional era, in which black leaders were acutely aware of the inherent limitations of their group leadership. Edward E. Wilson, writing in 1907, reflected clearly this perception of the limits of black political possibilities:

> The Negro vote alone would of course affect but little. It must make combination with the controlling forces in the party. He who gets closest to the powers that be is for the time being the biggest leader. Negro political leaders like those among the white rise and fall as their faction is up and down, and he that is so situated as to pass through a desert of official and political obscurity is in the long run the most successful politician. One must necessarily have the ability to bring in delegates to nominating conventions, or greatly influence bringing them in, in order to get any serious consideration from the big leaders or "bosses" as they are sometimes called. In this matter, social, intellectual or other admirable qualities count for nothing if you cannot "deliver the goods."[121]

Black politics was fashioned within the limits of existing Chicago ethnic politics. Black leaders were willing, even eager, to "play by the rules." They were acclimated to the security — and to the rewards — of conventional party loyalty.

A certain consistency pervades this period. Black politicians would continue their vigilance in defense of black civil rights and their opposition to any blatant attempts to segregate or discriminate on the basis of race. Black legislators would remain important political leaders, but by 1910 the thrust was toward building political power bases within the city itself. When hundreds of thousands of blacks migrated to Chicago during and after World War I, their power and their demands for political rewards increased. But black demands, and indeed black aspirations, were limited by a black political tradition molded in pre-Migration experiences.

The politics of Black Metropolis, then, were forged before the ghetto, before the Great Migration, the mayoralty of "Big Bill" Thompson, or the political sub-machines of Ed Wright and Oscar DePriest. This is the legacy — and perhaps the tragedy — of the pre-Migration period.

Chapter VII

EDWARD MAZUR

Jewish Chicago: From Diversity to Community

> Upon entering the Yiddish theater, one left America.
>
> — Ghetto resident (Chicago)

> I left the Old Country because you couldn't be a Jew over there and still live; but I would rather be dead than be the kind of German Jew that brings the Jewish name into disgrace by being a Goy.
>
> — Ghetto resident (Chicago)

FROM A MERE HANDFUL IN 1836, Chicago's Jewish population increased in a century to more than 270,000 persons by 1940. To many outsiders, the Jews of Chicago appeared to be a monolithic group. Upon closer examination, however, philosophical, economic, religious, geographical, psychological, and linguistic differences delineate two district Jewish communities. Each group, in varying degrees, re-created in America a somewhat altered version of its familiar European environment.

The German-speaking Bavarian, Prussian, Bohemian, Polish, and Austrian Jews who came to America before 1880 found a country that was warmly receptive to their participation, and avenues for success appeared limitless. To the two million Eastern European Jews who came to America between 1880 and 1914, the city's "Little Israels" and "Jewtowns" were districts bordered by frequently hostile neighbors and institutions. In addition, the newcomers were regarded by German Jews as unnecessary public charges, an embarrassment, a backward, superstitious, theologically conservative, and Yiddish-speaking people. Not only did they threaten the German-Jewish position in the Gentile community, but some observers called for Eastern European exclusion, declaring that "many of these East European Jews, as reared in their native land, are not desirable in our American communities; however much of these may be mixed ... it would indeed be desirable if they would stay away altogether."[1]

The German-Jewish movement to this country, prior to the 1830s, was one in which each individual, for a variety of reasons, had made his own decision to immigrate. The philosophy of the Enlightenment, the French Revolution, and the spread of the Napoleonic Empire had expanded the dimensions of intellectual, political, and economic equality for Western European Jewry, in marked contrast to the previously familiar lifestyle of recurring massacres, persecution, restricted opportunities, and social ostracism. Following the 1815 Congress of Vienna, however, Jewish emancipation efforts were thwarted and sabotaged by general reaction in the post-Napoleonic era, renewed xenophobia, and increased emphasis on nationality instead of the universality inherent in the philosophy of the Enlightenment.

The failure of emancipation to provide lasting benefits after 1815, the spreading industrial revolution and the economic dislocation of the 1830s, and the political revolutions of 1830 and 1848 provided the impetus to turn the minds of many poor, small-town Jews from the western and southwestern German states toward America. After tasting greater freedom, these Jews could not settle for less. The combination of restrictions and a slump in trade led to the first "mass migration to America." Between 1815 and 1880, the American Jewish population increased from 15,000 to 250,000 and was almost entirely a German-speaking people.[2]

Though the majority of the German-Jewish arrivals settled on the East Coast, some ventured into the Midwest and settled in Chicago. Jacob Gottlieb, the city's first known Jewish resident, was a peddler who arrived in 1838. Within seven years, he was joined by the Benedict Shubarts, the Philip Newburgs, the Isaac Zeiglers, the Henry Horners, and other Jewish families.[3] All but Horner, a Bohemian, were from Bavaria. These families settled near the center of the expanding city in the vicinity of Lake and Wells streets, establishing their residences on one or two-story frame dwellings near or above their aspiring businesses.[4]

Between 1850 and 1860 the Jewish community grew, as arrivals from Bavaria, Posen, and German Poland swelled the Jewish population from 100 to 1500 and expanded their initial boundaries. Jews settled on Randolph, Clark, and LaSalle streets, and some moved north of the Chicago River. The more prosperous and entrenched members of this community resided on the southern rim of the central business district.

For the first decades of its existence, the community was a tightly integrated entity related by country of origin, religious practice, vocational enterprise, and intermarriage. The tobacco dealer Philip Newburg married Ernestina Shubart, sister of the prosperous merchant tailor and dry goods entrepreneur Benedict Shubart. Business partners Levi Rosenfeld and Jacob Rosenberg married sisters in the Reese family. Of the dozen Lake Street Jewish-owned businesses in 1847, six were clothing stores and the remainder dry goods establishments.[5]

Throughout the nineteenth century the German-Jewish community underwent rapid economic and social achievement and upward mobility. One observer, reminiscing about the evolution of the community, commented that "there were no millionaires among the Jews, but all felt independent." This independence characterized the active involvement of German-Jewish bankers and merchants in the city's financial affairs and the successes of firms such as clothiers Hart, Schaffner, and Marx; B. Kuppenheimer and Company; the Florsheim Shoe Company; and department stores such as Mandel Brothers; Siegel, Cooper, and Company; and Maurice L. Rothschild.[6]

The first communal decision facing the group was the necessity of providing formal religious services and a burial ground. In 1845 the Jewish Burial Ground Society was established and cemetery lots were purchased in what is today Lincoln Park. Later that year two dry goods merchants, Levi Rosenfeld and Jacob Rosenberg, provided facilities for the first formal religious services. Shortly after the Yom Kippur observances in 1846, less than twenty Jews formed Kehillath Anshei Maariv (Men of the West) Congregation. Fourteen men signed the initial constitution, and the unity of the community continued when the fledgling Jewish Burial Ground Society ceded its property to the new congregation and ceased its independent existence. In 1849, K.A.M. leased a lot on Clark Street between Adams and Quincy Streets and erected a frame house of worship.[7]

Before the Civil War the extrareligious concerns of the community members were also being addressed. Bankers and merchants Moses and Elias Greenebaum, Mayer Klein, Levi Klein, Isaac Wolf, and Moses Rubel founded the Hebrew Benevolent Society in 1851 to provide sick and burial benefits for its members. The group purchased three acres in suburban Lake View for a cemetery and held monthly meetings to discuss the problems of the organization and the greater community. The organization was soon absorbed by the United Hebrew Relief Association (UHRA). This was the first central Jewish relief organization to provide aid for "immediate cases" and maintain a reserve fund to provide for a "hospital in which poor coreligionists shall be attended to when sick and for an asylum to receive Jewish widows and orphans without means."[8]

The UHRA was the result of the unification of the Bavarian and Polish segments of the community into one common organization. The synthesis was facilitated by the development of the first of many B'nai B'rith Lodges, Ramah Number 33 on June 15, 1857. Founded in New York in 1843, B'nai B'rith combined mutual aid functions with purely fraternal features. The charter of the organization promised to "banish from its deliberations all doctrinal and dogmatic discussions . . . and by the practice of moral and benevolent precepts bring about union and harmony" among Jews. The Chicago organizers, led by Henry Greenebaum, optimistically hoped the group would lead to the eradication of "the miserable provincial boundaries existing in Chicago."

In succeeding years other B'nai B'rith chapters, some with distinctly Teutonic names like Germania No. 83 and Teutonia No. 95, were chartered. The use of Germanic names among social, charitable, and fraternal associations was commonplace in the German-Jewish community; and many members identified primarily with the general German population. Morris Gutstein, an historian of the nineteenth-century Jewish community, has written that "the German-speaking Jew considered German his vernacular . . . attended the German theater, preferred German music, read the German newspapers, shaped his social life on the German pattern, sponsored German organizations, and belonged to German clubs."[9]

Perhaps the most important and ambitious undertaking for this community during the nineteenth century was the building of a Jewish hospital. In 1865 the UHRA purchased a site on LaSalle Street between Schiller and Goethe streets for seven thousand dollars. Mass fund-raising meetings were held and pledges made to admit all cases "irrespective of creed or race." Open scarcely a year, the hospital was completely destroyed during the Chicago Fire of 1871. For the next decade the Jewish community was without "their own hospital." In 1881 the new Michael Reese Hospital, located at Twenty-ninth Street and the Lake, began admitting patients. Named after Michael Reese, whose six sisters were pioneer members of the Jewish community, its first officials, staff physicians, and surgeons — with the exception of Dr. Michael Mannheimer — were non-Jews.[10]

The hospital was not the only loss suffered by the Jewish community. The Jewish area in and around the central business district was completely destroyed, rendering over five hundred Jews destitute and homeless. The disaster forced Chicago's Jews to move both north and south of the city's center. Scarcely had the community regained its footing, when another fire raced across the near South Side in 1874, inflicting great damage to the embryonic Russian-Polish settlement located south of the area leveled by the earlier blaze.

Until 1874 there was no definite demarcation between the German-Jewish "Golden Ghetto" of the South and near North Sides and the "West Side Ghetto" of the Russo-Polish Jews. After the second fire a sizable number of East Europeans crossed the Chicago River and relocated on the West Side, thus marking the beginning of Chicago's real ghetto district.[11] The more prosperous members of the German-speaking Jewish community continued drifting south into the Prairie Avenue district, where resided such noteworthy neighbors as the Armours, Fields, Pullmans, and Kimballs, and the Kenwood and Hyde Park areas. By 1900 the area south of 22nd Street attracted the majority of Chicago's

German-Jewish population. The near South Side residences
were not abandoned because of an "invasion of people of a
lower economic status nor the settlement of another racial
group. . . ." Rather, the movement of the community's first
families and the relocation of community institutions
heralded the movement into the Grand Boulevard, Kenwood,
and Hyde Park areas.[12]

Despite the apparently ongoing dispersal of Jewish population, the synagogue remained the primary focal point of the
Jewish community. It not only provided spiritual sustenance,
but also administered the sacrificial slaughter of animals and
the baking of matzoth, educated the children, and responded
to the needs of the aged and sick. On the Sabbath and other
holidays, businesses in both the retail and wholesale district
were closed for the day. The windows and doors of every
Jewish business house had a placard reading "closed on account of Jewish holiday."[13] However, by the 1850s the successful growth of Jewish business establishments and the desire to become "Americanized" led to public violation of the
Sabbath. Many no longer attended religious services, or
otherwise arrived late and departed early.

In 1852, Old World distinctions and intragroup differences resulted in the initial divisions of the community. A
group of German-Polish Jews, upset by the clannishness of
the Bavarian Jews and their *Bayerische Shul* (KAM), established the B'nai Shalom (Men of Peace) Congregation. The
drama of superior and inferior class and caste, of personal,
factional, and programmatic differences that resulted in se-
cession and erection of new organizations, would become
one of the most familiar characteristics of the Chicago Jewish
community.

Declaring that its purpose was "to awaken and cultivate a
truer conception of Judaism and a higher realization of
Jewish religious life," the *Juedischer Reformverein* society
was formed by such notables as real estate investor Mayer
Klein, banker Elias Greenebaum, and schoolteacher Bernard
Felsenthal. The introduction of Reform Judaism was concurrent with German-Jewish communal growth and synagogue
relocation. Imported from Germany, where Jews of high so-

cial status decided to dignify and modernize their religious services, Reform Judaism emphasized the progressive nature of Jewish law and called for the preaching of sermons in the vernacular, the use of organs, and questioning the divinity of the Bible.

Reform Judaism was readily embraced in this country because American Judaism had no overall community leadership or structure. Furthermore, there were so many different synagogues and unaffiliated social, fraternal, and service institutions and organizations concerned with varying aspects of Jewish life. By the 1880s, German-Jewish congregations instituted preaching in both English and German. With the use of the vernacular in the liturgy, the demand for making Sunday the Sabbath increasingly gained momentum. In 1885, Rabbi Emil G. Hirsch of Temple Sinai (formerly the *Juedischer Reformverein* Society) reported that "no services were held on Saturdays for the last four weeks because there was no audience."[14] By the turn of the century German-Jewish temples generally agreed on the substitution of Sunday for the Sabbath. Hirsch's explanation of the change indicates the decline not only of the synagogue as the focus of the community, but of the success of Jewish citizenry within the larger Gentile community and the pressure of the larger community on the minority group. Rabbi Hirsch observed: "It is our opinion that in this hustling and busy country where everyone is compelled to toil six days every week for a living, and where Sunday is a legal day of rest . . . the Jew cannot afford to rest for two days and compete with his neighbors. . . . Speaking for the vast number of Jews here it is safe to say that most of them do not regard Saturday as a holiday. With very rare exception, all Jewish business houses are open. . . . Which would be wiser, to lose all our religion or simply to change our Sabbath day?"[15]

Concerned individuals and religious leaders continually sought to stimulate Jewish intellect and dialogue through the establishment of literary societies, newspapers, journals, and club affiliations. The first literary group, the Clay Literary Society, was established as early as 1859 by Henry Hart, an immigrant from Eppelsheim, Germany who later became a partner in the Hart, Schaffner and Marx clothing firm. He announced that the purpose of the society was to cultivate "literary interests and speaking and debating ability among the Jewish youth of Chicago."[16] Community leaders hoped that the establishment of Jewish publications would facilitate the aims of the group in addition to providing the community with general information, original essays, smatterings of political information, and commentary on Jewish spiritual and religious problems. By 1891 there were at least five publications serving the German-Jewish community. Despite claims of objectivity, the journals became the personal vehicles of editors who were products of Jewish emancipation and advocates of Reform Judaism.

The more prosperous members of the community held their ethnic-oriented meetings and social functions at the *Concordia Club,* located at Dearborn and Monroe streets.

Upper-class German Jews at a charity show

Courtesy of University of Illinois Library at Chicago Circle, Manuscripts Division

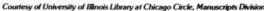

The organization was "the rendezvous for leading personalities in Jewish community life." However, by 1869 the membership became bitterly divided over political questions. Sixty-nine Concordians, including the most important members of Chicago's German-Jewish financial and political community, met and established the Standard Club. This event signaled an increasing affluence and security of commercial interests that allowed leisure time for social activities. Several additional social clubs and a country club were added: North Side German-Jewry established the Ideal Club; South Side Jews organized the Lakeside Club; and German-speaking Bohemian Jews who resided on the near West Side founded the West Chicago Club.

When the increasingly affluent German-Jewish community organized the Ravisloe Country Club in south suburban Homewood, Illinois in 1901, it was "the foremost, as it was the first, Jewish organization of its kind in the city." Urbanologist Louis Wirth has written that by 1901 the country club and the Standard Club, "even more than the separate religious institutions that characterized the Jewish community and divided off the various strata from one another . . . was indicative of the great chasm which separated the Bavarians from the . . . latest arrivals, the Russians."[17]

While Chicago's 20,000 German-Jews were undergoing rapid acculturation, showing upward economic, social, and residential mobility, two million Jews from Russia, Romania, Poland, and Austria-Hungary were preparing to come to America. The East European Jews who began to come to America in the 1880s dramatically and indelibly altered the character of the Jewish-American community. They emigrated for a variety of political, religious, social, and economic reasons. During one period, between 1815 and 1914, Russia issued more than one thousand decrees regulating Jewish religious and communal life, economic activities, military service, educational opportunities, and property rights. Between 1882 and 1914 these restrictions culminated in officially sanctioned and frequently ferocious pogroms that resulted in mass emigration. The hardships of Jews from Romania, Austria-Hungary, and Poland differed only in degree from the sufferings of their Russian coreligionists.

Vast numbers of newly arriving immigrants were disappointed in the Chicago that greeted them. Unlike the legends, the streets were not paved with gold — they were not broad and beautiful or even paved at all. Life was not as gay and bright as many had fantasized. They crowded into the near West Side, an area bounded by Canal, Halsted, Polk, and 15th streets. Within a few years the near West Side encompassed both a large and small ghetto. The former was bounded by Polk Street on the north, Blue Island on the west, 15th Street on the south, and Stewart on the east, and had a population of 70,000, of whom 20,000 were Jews. The smaller ghetto, bounded by 12th, Halsted, 15th, and Stewart avenues, had a population of 15,000-16,000 of which 90 percent

The other Jews: life and trade near Maxwell Street

Courtesy of Chicago Historical Society

were Jews. Bohemian Jews were the first to enter the West
Side ghetto; in short order they were followed by Russians,
Poles, and Hungarians. Though the coreligionists were resi-
dentially intermingled, there was a tendency to settle into
separate little colonies. Hull House resident Charles Zeub-
lein observed in 1895 that the Russian and Polish Jews clustered between Polk and 12th streets, while the Bohemians
resided in the better zone south and west of Halsted and 12th
streets.[18]

The near West Side was convenient and commodious to
East European Jews because it was close to the train depots,
rentals were cheap, and landlords were not finicky about nationality. Furthermore, reminiscences of the European *shtetl*
abounded — including bearded males, frock coats, wide-
brimmed hats, shawled women, and *landsleute* (people from
the same town or area). Employment with no Saturday work
was frequently available.[19] The ghetto's focal point was the
intersection of Halsted and Maxwell streets. Radiating from it
was a conglomeration of houses, stores, shops, open stalls,
stables, peddlers' carts, kosher butcher shops, dry goods em-
poriums, matzoh bakeries, synagogues, sweatshops, tailor
and seamstress shops, pawnshops, secondhand stores, Hebrew schools, lawyers' and doctors' offices, marriage arrangement bureaus, and approved circumcisers. From early morning to late in the evening the streets were filled with people
coming and going to their places of employment, socializing,
or seeking everyday necessities.

The tall tenements characteristic of New York's lower East
Side were uncommon in Chicago. As the population density
of the West Side increased, frame houses and warehouses
were converted and partitioned to hold the newcomers. The
ghetto-dwelling Jews lived in small, low, one- or two-story
wooden shanties built before the streets were elevated and
graded, three- or four-story brick tenements, or in buildings
erected at the rear of a lot, with no light in front and the
ever-present aromas of a squalid alley. Frequently, these accommodations served double duty — as living and working
quarters for the sweatshop industry. Single people rented
furnished rooms or boarded with already overcrowded

Jewish families. Rentals began at one dollar a week and included coffee and tea in the morning. The overcrowding and the poverty taxed even the legendary capabilities of Jewish housekeepers.[20]

Bathtubs were conspicuously absent in the ghetto. One study recorded that almost 97 percent of the people had "no opportunity in their own homes to bathe." The area supported at least six bathing establishments that charged fifteen to twenty-five cents per bath. On the other hand, the area also contained only twenty-four saloons in 1900, the lowest ratio of bars to people of any immigrant quarter in Chicago.

Overcrowding often drove the residents into the streets for relief. At night adults and children slept on the sidewalks and roofs of the ghetto buildings. Disease was a frequent visitor to area residents, and even when preventive measures like the smallpox vaccination became available, many in the Jewish quarter resisted. It was not until the shopowners found their businesses empty during the busy season that they reluctantly consented to vaccination for themselves and their employees. The rapid opening and shuttering of sweatshops inhibited efficient inspection. Smallpox and tuberculosis were concealed because of the fear of financial ruin and the evils — real or imaginary — of the pesthouse.[21]

In contrast to the experience of German-Jews, these East Europeans had entered a Chicago that was in the full bloom of its industrialization. For at least a decade their immediate economic future was to serve that machine economy as a fluid and inexpensive labor supply. Many found employment in the garment trades, not because of any inherent affinity for the needle and thread, but because of the constant demand for cheap labor. The majority were "Columbus tailors" who became wedded to the sewing machine *(Katrinka)* only after they reached America.[22]

Starting in the 1880s, the United Hebrew Charities found jobs for the new arrivals in the burgeoning German-Jewish clothing firms. Critics described the areas on 12th Street between Canal and Jefferson streets as "pools of sweat and blood" where "human lives are sacrificed on the altar of profit." Prior to the workers' organization and unionization, they were lined up "in rows like soldiers seated at their machines. . . . They cannot speak to one another, they cannot sing at their work . . . they must do only what their machine commands. . . . When the workers come home . . . they have not sufficient strength left . . . to think or read . . . and for that reason hundreds of workers . . . are considered slaves. . . ."[23] Employment was seasonal, and wages, low enough during the peak season, became poor or nonexistent in the off-season. Workers received between five and twenty-five dollars per week, but wages varied according to the individual branch of the garment industry and the degree of skill required. Necessity led to the use of child labor in many of the factories and sweatshops. Frequently, fathers had to compete with their own wives and children for survival.[24]

Despite taxing working conditions and inadequate salaries, the clothing trades offered a future; they were part of the "coming business." Shops were often small enterprises run on a shoestring. If a worker could accumulate a few dollars, he was able to enter the circle of bosses. Those who could not find success in the garment industry tried their luck at peddling or trades like tobacco merchandising.

Although small numbers of ghetto residents were employed as store clerks, stockkeepers, office clerks, mail carriers, post-office clerks, government employees, and even as teachers, lawyers, dentists, and physicians, peddling was nonetheless the easiest avenue to entrepreneurial success. The ghetto teemed with a multitude of peddlers. Some rang doorbells, others were customer peddlers who visited a regular clientele. Others owned horses and wagons and collected rags, old bottles, papers, and odds and ends. Some positioned their pushcarts, crammed with wares, at fixed locations, while others plied their carts up and down the streets searching for prospective customers. These pushcarts, boxes, wheelbarrows, and wagons served as mobile department stores, but the peddlers were often the target of well-aimed missiles and physical attacks.[25]

Institutions developed among East European Jews to implement, preserve, and enhance economic, social, and religious practices and traditions. The first permanent Jewish labor organizations appeared after the 1886 Haymarket Riot. Early attempts at unionization were only mildly successful, primarily because of divided ideologies and seemingly utopian demands. The United Hebrew Trades was founded in 1888 by Jewish socialists and labor organizers, and the United German Trades was formed to guide the unionization of Jewish workers and coordinate labor, fraternal, and cultural groups in the Jewish community. At first, the UHT was divorced from the general labor movement, but eventually they sent delegates to conventions of international unions and meetings of central labor federations to protect and enhance "Jewish interests." The UHT became the trade union *modus vivendi* since "there was a need for a separate Jewish trade union movement because of differences in psychology, language, and the general mode of living between Jewish and other workers."[26]

Yiddish *Volkstheaters,* the Metropolitan Hall, Irwin's, and later Glickman's became the dramatic and musical centers of the neighborhood. A resident noted that "upon entering the Yiddish theater, one left America." A similar but unsympathetic sentiment was articulated by a reviewer for the German-Jewish newspaper, *The Occident,* who complained that "the play was decidedly unethical while the culture of the gallery-gods appeared more like cossacklike fiendishness; there was stamping, yelling, whistling, smoking, spitting, and hooting in the manner of the lowest of Arabs."[27]

For those who possessed the inclination and strength, there were night schools dispensing lessons in "American." Social worker Grace Abbott observed that "they attend night school more regularly than . . . any other nationality, and in a year they usually make rapid progress if they are strong enough to keep up the day and evening work." Numerous social and service agencies appeared with increasing rapidity in the ghetto. The Chicago Hebrew Institute, Maxwell Street Settlement, and Hull House aided the newcomers in adjusting to urban living and offered protection against the multifarious forms of exploitation. Esther Kohn, a Jewish social worker, commented that "cultural and recreational needs were met in classes in literature, art, music, and handicrafts which relieved the monotony of the only jobs offered to newcomers. They also found appreciation of their worth as human beings."[28]

For others, the Yiddish newspapers served as classroom and socialization agency. These newspapers enabled both the learned and the uneducated to follow local, national, and world affairs in a familiar language while giving the newcomers an elementary education in the process of Americanization. Between 1877 and 1914 at least twelve Yiddish newspapers and periodicals were published in Chicago. Unlike the German-Jewish press, the editors of the Yiddish press were not religious leaders. Rather, they were a varied mixture of printers, journalists, businessmen, and trade union officials. While the German-Jewish press concerned itself with ethical and philosophical questions, the Yiddish press addressed itself more to the problems of adaptation to and dissemination of information relative to surviving in what was often a baffling and puzzling America.

In the struggle for existence and advancement the East European Jew was, however, sustained by his religion. Though religion was assuming a secondary role with the German-Jewish community, it was growing and strengthening itself among the newest arrivals. By 1910 more than forty orthodox synagogues were established in the city's East European Jewish neighborhoods. Some congregations were located in imposing structures, others in modest and unpretentious surroundings. For at least one immigrant generation, religious orthodoxy was clearly interwoven with daily life. Although attendance was not and could not be compulsory as it had been in the *shtetls,* these synagogues, both simple and magnificent, were open most of the day and evening. Services began early so that workers could pray before going to work. Hebrew liturgy was used even though a majority of the congregants probably could not understand it. Men and women sat separately, and there were no organs or mixed choirs. Sermons were frequently delivered in Yiddish.

Within the confines of the synagogue, Jews of varying degrees of piety could for a time forget their struggles for existence and advancement in America.

For those who drifted from Orthodoxy but found Reform Judaism distasteful and foreign, the Conservative movement offered an alternative that claimed to retain "the best of the traditional form and spirit of our heritage, in as thorough an American and modern setting as possible." Nevertheless, the majority of East European Jews clung tenaciously to Orthodox Judaism. They were horrified and dismayed by the lack of religiosity, the desecration of tradition, heterogamy, and lack of knowledge of Yiddish of the German-Jews.

If the assimilated German-Jews were rudely jolted by their Eastern cousins, Russian-Jews often felt as distant from their coreligionists as they did from the gentile community. One ghetto dweller summed up the general feeling of the community when he proclaimed: "When I first put my feet on the soil of Chicago, I was so disgusted that I wished I had stayed . . . in Russia. I left the Old Country because you couldn't be a Jew over there and still live, but I would rather be dead than be the kind of German Jew that brings the Jewish name into disgrace by being a Goy. That's what hurts: They parade around as Jews, and down deep in their hearts they are worse than Goyim, they are *meshumeds* [apostates]."[29]

Such feelings were reciprocated within the German-Jewish community, resulting in less than harmonious relationships between the coreligionists. Many German-Jews decried the conspicuousness and "antiquarian" religious practices of the Russians, claiming that they were "not a part of the Jewish religion" and placed the immigrants in "a light which is anything but commendable." Ghetto residents were referred to as a "collection of nihilists" who were singled out for praise during one High Holiday season for being peaceable and remaining at home.

Having "arrived" socially and economically, the German-Jews were embarrassed and fearful that association with *Ostjuden* would endanger their marginal acceptance by Gentile society. As 1886 drew to a close, *The Occident* lamented: "Twenty-six thousand Polish Jews in a single year! That is certainly an overdose for our American national economy.... Why should we be deceived? These Polish Jews are indigestible for the American stomach as are the Chinese.... As they are here, they must be put to some use.... It is to be assumed that ... the first, if not the second generations, may become sufficiently Americanized to be tolerable.... It would indeed be desirable if they would stay away altogether. We have enough and sufficient Polish Jews ... and will thank the powers that be in Europe, to not send us any more."[30]

At times the German-Jewish community urgently sought to exclude East Europeans from the United States by suggesting that they immigrate to South America because Russian-Jews were a "burden upon the well-to-do of their race and religion." One observer falsely claimed that "they are assisted to cross the ocean; but a few are self-sustaining; as a body they are paupers; many are diseased and many are criminals." This German-Jewish observer piously claimed that "this is the judgment of the most intelligent American Jews . . . . "[31]

Lest the East Europeans become embarrassingly visible public charges, German-Jewish organizations somewhat reluctantly voted moneys to aid the Russian refugees. Relief stations providing temporary shelter facilities and hot meals were provided for the needy. The Jewish Training School was established on the near West Side to teach the East Europeans wage-earning skills, while the Society to Aid the Russian Refugees and the Hebrew Immigrant Aid Society attempted to relocate ghetto residents in *rural* areas.

Demands by both the German and East European communities led to the founding of an orphans' home, a residence for aged Jews, and a settlement house. Recognizing that many of the services available to the Jewish communities were overlapping, leaders in the German-Jewish community in 1900 created the Associated Jewish Charities, an umbrella organization responsible for the central collection and distribution of aid and information.

Nevertheless, Russian Jewry believed that the German-

Jewish "scientific" approach to charity, complete with documents, inquests, and other forms of 'snooping," corrupted the religious obligation of charity — that it be an act of pure loving-kindness. Thus, by 1915 both communities had highly organized charitable groups offering duplicate services. The German-Jews were represented by the Associated Jewish Charities and the East Europeans by the Federated Orthodox Jewish Charities, which supported Maimonides Hospital, the Consumptive Relief Society, the Marks Nathan Orphan Home, and other institutions. The parochialism of Chicago's Jewish communities at the organizational level was at last formally eclipsed in 1922, when the AJC and the FOJC merged to form the Jewish Charities of Chicago.

By 1900 the German-Jewish community, despite the appearance of uniformity, was in reality a diverse amalgam with forebears from Bavaria, Prussia, Western Poland, Bohemia, Austria, and the Netherlands. German Jewry no longer lived "in the bonds of one family circle." Unlike during the founding years, they did not worship "harmoniously in one temple" if they worshipped at all. The sharing of common satisfactions and concerns had become increasingly bothersome, and intracommunity relations were maintained with great effort. Such an evolution had been prophesied as early as 1870 by Dr. Liebman Adler, spiritual leader of KAM. He observed that the Jewish community was composed of "thousands scattered over a space of nearly thirty miles ... divided by pecuniary, intellectual and social distinctions, provincial jealousies and even religious distinctions and differences." Adler decried the process of acculturation, noting that "we are losing the consciousness of homogeneity and the strength gained for each individual by concerted action."[32]

Early in the first decade of the twentieth century the area south of 22nd Street had increasingly become the residential district for the majority of Chicago's German-Jewish population. By World War I, South Side German-Jewry was located in the Kenwood, Hyde Park, and Grand Boulevard areas. The more affluent and assimilated residents, however, were increasingly attracted to the northern suburbs of Wilmette,

Winnetka, and Glencoe. By the middle of that decade the original West Side ghetto of the Eastern Europeans had become a largely non-Jewish area; the Jews had moved to the new "Israels" — Lawndale, Humboldt Park, Columbus Park, Albany Park, Rogers Park, Hyde Park, and South Shore. Those who came earliest were now farthest removed from the original ghetto.

The remaining ghetto residents referred derisively to Lawndale as "Deutschland" and to its residents as "Deitchuks." Those who remained behind viewed the migrations as a desertion of old customs and religious beliefs in an attempt to emulate the non-Jewish ways of the highly assimilated German-Jews. Actually, East European Jews were only demonstrating a new-found socio-economic mobility as they moved westward to areas not yet overcrowded or substandard, but with spacious streets, yards, parks, and substantial duplex apartments. With the Jewish influx, the two-family, two-story buildings were supplanted by large apartment houses with no fewer than ten dwelling units, to accommodate an increased population. By 1930, Lawndale contained a population of 112,000, of whom an estimated 75,000 were Jewish.[33] Once ensconced, the Jews organized a far-flung network of secular and religious institutions throughout Lawndale.

Another secondary area of settlement for East European Jewry was Humboldt Park, located on Chicago's northwest side. In 1906 this area contained approximately one-quarter of Chicago's Jewish population. By the 1930s, Humboldt Park had a Jewish population of almost 25,000, and the area of settlement was expanding. During the 1920s the northside Albany Park community attracted Jewish families striving for rapid secularization and economic advancement. In 1923 an estimated 4,700 Jews resided there; by 1930, Jews made up an estimated 23,000 of the community's population of 55,577.[34]

In the city's far northeast corner, East Rogers Park, two congregations had been established by 1930. Temple Mizpah, founded in 1919 by residents interested in Reform Judaism, had grown to a congregation of 500 families by 1926. The memberships of Mizpah and of B'nai Zion, a nearby

Conservative synagogue founded in 1918, were composed primarily of second- or third-generation Jewish-Americans who had moved from the West, Northwest, and South sides.[35] Following World War I, East European Jews began moving into the German-Jewish bastion of Kenwood-Hyde Park. There they joined Reform or Conservative temples and gave up orthodoxy "as they changed their residence." Wirth observes that "even the aristocratic German-Jewish clubs are beginning to open their doors to the more successful and desirable members of the Russian group." In 1930 these areas contained about 12 percent, or 11,000, of Chicago's 270,000 Jews.[36]

By 1930 the Jewish settlements of Chicago included approximately ninety Orthodox synagogues, thirteen Reform temples, and ten Conservative congregations. There were three rabbinical associations, two synagogue federations, a theological seminary, a board of Jewish education, the Jewish People's Institute with an annual total attendance of one million, and a multitude of social, benevolent, fraternal, and charitable organizations.[37] Nonetheless, tangible and intangible boundaries continued to separate and divide the ranks of Chicago Jewry. Tangible differences included location and type of residence, areas and concentrations of employment, religious postures, synagogue and temple affiliations, clubs, lodges, and union or business association memberships. Less discernible to many observers, but of signal importance, were national and ancestral origin, degree of identification with the lifestyles of the larger Anglo-Saxon society, and the expressed political attitudes and voting patterns of Chicago Jews.

The American political milieu acted as a transmitter of economic and psychological succor, individual advancement, and group recognition. Jewish political figures composed a diverse group, including classic boss types who emphasized personalized politics, reformers, and middle-grounders who used machine tactics to achieve beneficial and constructive socio-political ends. Neither the German or East European Jewish communities had a monopoly on any one type. The most successful municipal leaders combined the efficiency and personalization of the machine with the ideology of good government and reform, in order to appeal to the widest possible electorate.

In local affairs the German-Jewish quest for security, status, and acceptability by the larger American community led them to support measures, policies, and candidates advanced by "Protestant Puritans" who found their major supporters in the do-good reformist wing of the Republican party. Increasingly, they called for nonpartisan operation of municipal government as a means of curbing the excesses of urbanization. Favorable Jewish support for Republican commercial and industrial policies, first established in the 1860s, coalesced to forge a strong tradition of voting Republican in state and national contests that remained unchanged until the 1930s.

East European Jews cut their political teeth on issues other than those that attracted the German-Jews to the local and national Republican standards. Faced with the challenge of individual, family, and cultural survival in a strange environment, the East Europeans responded to matters of immediate and pressing concern. These included personal liberty and Sunday closing laws, sensitivity to and recognition of Jewish-Americans, and generous immigration policies. They quickly established a rapport not only with Republican bosses like William Lorimer but also with Democratic chieftains like the Carter Harrisons.[38] Shortly thereafter, individual Jewish political figures like Adolf Kraus, William Loeffler, and Adolph Sabath became trusted lieutenants and confidants of their party leaders. German-Jewish entreaties and blandishments for reform were rejected by the East Europeans in favor of a more comprehensible, traditional, conservative, and trusted approach. However, when reformist policies were advanced by a trusted Democratic leader like a Harrison, Sabath, or Jacob Arvey, they responded positively.

In national and state affairs before World War I, the Eastern European Jewish response was mixed. Regardless of party, they supported those candidates who manifested concern for their socio-economic positions, displayed ethnic sensitivity, and fought to keep a free and open immigration policy. One man, however, was able successfully to unite these diverse propensities and produce a unified "Jewish vote." He was Henry Horner, five-time probate court judge and a favorite of both the German and Eastern European Jewish electorates because he satisfied the ever-present desire for ethnic recognition.

Born in Chicago on November 30, 1878, Henry was the third son of Dilah Horner and Solomon Levy. The relationship of his parents was anything but harmonious, and in 1883 they were divorced. The children moved in with Hannah Dernberg Horner, their maternal grandmother, and assumed the family name. Henry grew up in a decidedly political atmosphere. His uncle Isaac was a veteran member of Hinky Dink Kenna's and "Bathhouse" John Coughlin's First Ward forces. As a law student, too young to vote, Henry received his political baptism campaigning for Carter Harrison II in 1897.

In 1899, Horner graduated from Kent College of Law, was admitted to the bar, began specializing in real estate and probate law, and cultivated Harrison leaders and members of the Jewish community. By 1900 he had joined the prestigious German-Jewish Standard Club, where his maternal grandfather, Henry Horner I, had been one of the club's charter members in 1869. Between 1906 and 1912 the enterprising lawyer-politician was serving on the club's board of directors.

In 1902, the Harrison organization slated young Horner as the party's nominee for collector of South Chicago. However, at the same election a referendum was held on the question of abolishing the seven "towns" existing within Chicago. Although Horner defeated his opponent, the elimination of town government also carried; Horner's triumph was meaningless. Significantly, the German-Jewish community began their tradition of rallying to his side. He was, according to the *Reform Advocate*, a "young man, eminently fitted for the responsible position he seeks."[39]

Following the 1902 campaign Horner expanded his law practice, strengthened his political relationships, and furthered his social and business associations with German-

Jewish leaders. Between 1907 and 1911, Horner was appointed attorney for the Cook County Board of Assessors. In 1911, Mayor Harrison appointed him delegate to the city charter convention for Chicago. In the succeeding three years he developed an intimate political association with the assistant county treasurer, Jacob Lindheimer. Supported by Lindheimer and Harrison, Horner was elected to the probate court in 1914.

Thereafter — every four years through 1930 — he was returned to office by progressively larger margins. In 1926 he had no Democratic primary opposition, and the Republicans encountered difficulty in finding a "strong candidate to oppose him." In 1930 he led the county ticket, a "distinction that carries a great deal of significance among politicians."[40] Judge Horner developed a reputation as one of Cook County's outstanding jurists; he was an efficient and personable judge of impeccable integrity.

Although the jurist belonged to both Sinai and KAM congregations, he was not a devout Jew. He observed the High Holidays but did not practice other Jewish rituals. He enjoyed the social obligations of political life and established working relationships with such Eastern European Jewish political figures as Michael and Moe Rosenberg, Jacob Arvey, Harry Fisher, and Adolph Sabath.[41] Politically, Horner had the ability to relate successfully to Democrats, Republicans, reformers, and organization types. Although friendly with German-Jewish reformers like Emil G. Hirsch and Julius Rosenwald, Horner resisted political involvement with individuals and groups that wanted to function outside the framework of the Democratic and Republican parties, because he believed that it was suicidal to step beyond the working structure of organized politics.

Before a 24th Ward gathering in 1932, Horner paid homage to Mayor Anton Cermak, the Rosenbergs, Alderman Arvey, and other political regulars who were responsible for his gubernatorial candidacy. He realized that political patronage and favors were the mortar that held the organization together. Horner promised to utilize his patronage powers, if he was elected governor, to reward the party faithful.

Courtesy of Chicago Historical Society

The winning Governor Henry Horner, shown with Mayor Anton Cermak, Mrs. Floyd Finley, and Tom Courtney

The 1932 gubernatorial campaign theme declared: "With Horner we'll turn the corner." Horner was depicted as sincerely interested in the welfare of all Illinoisans. The electorate was warned that the 1932 primary contests were of the utmost importance. Precinct workers and newspapers in Jewish areas emphasized the necessity of registering to vote. The Jewish press reported Horner's appearance at any Jewish-oriented event. Voters were reminded that if Horner were victorious, the Democrats would triumph in November at the local and national levels and a deathblow would be dealt the growing economic depression. The *Daily Jewish Courier* proclaimed that Chicago's Jews had a dual duty:

"They must express their appreciation of Judge Horner and confirm the choice of the Democratic party."[42]

Horner's two major opponents in the primary, State Representative Michael Igoe and Democratic State Chairman Bruce Campbell, ran well downstate and succeeded in cancelling each other out. The city's Jewish electorate, regardless of area of residence, degree of assimilation, socio-economic position, national origin, or religious philosophy, overwhelmingly supported their coreligionist.[43]

With precinct work in the able hands of regulars such as Arvey and the Lindheimer family, Horner was at liberty to stump the state; he emphasized the themes of economic dislocation, the ills of Prohibition, and the influence of corrupt politicians, especially his opponent, former Governor Len Small.

The totals in the November general election mirrored the results of the spring primary. Chicago's Jewish voters provided Horner with handsome majorities. In North Lawndale's 24th Ward, he bested Small by a ten-to-one margin. Nevertheless, so far as the national presidential election was concerned, many already Republican German-Jewish voters also fostered the idea that "with Hoover we'll turn the corner." In Hyde Park's 5th Ward, a "2H Club" for Horner and Hoover was active. Republican precinct captains lamented that the "Jewish vote is not controllable." In one precinct there were only fifteen registered Democrats, but 137 votes were cast for Horner. A distraught captain observed that "this shows that many Jews switched for Horner and then voted a straight Republican ticket." Horner aide and Fifth Ward Committeeman Horace Lindheimer, recognizing the ethnic attraction, indicated that Horner's triumph was more than a "question of turning the ins out and the outs in."[44]

On February, 15, 1933, Mayor Cermak was fatally wounded by an assassin's bullet intended for President Roosevelt, and his death on March 6 germinated the seeds for conflict as well as cooperation. Newly elected Governor Horner bypassed the opportunity to become party leader, perhaps naively believing that fellow Democrats would happily endorse his policies and programs solely on merit. The City Council, authorized to select a new mayor, chose Ed Kelly, party loyalist and chief engineer of the Sanitary District — and a resident of Horner's own 4th Ward.

When Prohibition ended in 1933, Kelly wanted sole control of the licensing and regulation of Chicago's saloons. However, Governor Horner was diametrically opposed to Kelly's plan, believing that the state should have sole control. Mayor Kelly became increasingly agitated over Horner's independence and constantly derided the governor to his associates. By mid-1933 the relationship had deteriorated severely, threatening the unity of the Democratic party. Horner's independent style and executive actions even alienated some of his Jewish allies.

During the 1936 primary campaign, the Democratic organization, led by Mayor Kelly, dedicated itself to prove to Jewish voters that the decision not to endorse Horner's quest for re-election was not based on the issue of religion or ethnicity, but rather was related to the success or failure of the New Deal. Many of the submerged antagonisms between the German and Eastern European Jews surfaced as they became opposing forces.

In the primary, Jewish voters responded to Horner in direct proportion to their degree of assimilation, area of residence, and position on the economic scale. In those areas primarily inhabited by Eastern European Jews, the voter was more likely to be dependent on the favors and gratuities which the regular organization was capable of dispensing. Here these voters gave less weight to ethnic considerations. Horner carried eight Chicago wards, including the 5th, 6th, and 7th. These were South Side districts with large German-Jewish populations. His victories in the 39th, 40th, 48th, and 49th wards in North Side districts can be credited to the large numbers of middle- and upper-class Jewish residents in these areas. The only inner-city ward carried by Horner was Al Horan's 29th. There voters were free to vote their convictions because Committeeman Horan had been the beneficiary of Horner's state bonding patronage and remained loyal to the governor.

West Side Jews were trapped between the practicalities of everyday life and their affection for coreligionist Horner. Although many chose to follow the advice of men like 24th Ward Chief Jacob Arvey, who distributed jobs, obtained aid, and predicted that a Horner victory would threaten Roosevelt's position, they were not happy. "You did a terrible thing to me today...," shouted one elderly man to Arvey. "You made me vote against Henry Horner, our Henry Horner."[45]

Nevertheless, Horner beat Chicago Health Commissioner Herman C. Bundesen, choice of the supposedly invincible machine of Mayor Kelly and county chairman Patrick Nash, and carried every downstate county, amassing a plurality of 317,105 votes outside Cook County.

Preparing for the November election, Horner set about shoring up his ethnic support in Chicago, and the Jewish communities girded up for the general election. On Tuesday, November 4, 1936, Horner was swept to re-election in the great Democratic landslide that engulfed Chicago, Illinois, and the nation. In defeating Republican gubernatorial hopeful C. Wayland Brooks, he received a plurality of 385,176 votes in the state and carried Chicago by a 319,690-vote margin. Jews who were organization Democrats and the Hornerites had ignored past differences, economic and social distinctions, national origins, areas of residence, and religious postures in order to secure the re-election of their coreligionist.[46] Unity reigned throughout the city's Jewish communities as the aspirations of both the Democratic organization and Chicago Jewry were satisfied. The covenant linking "Abraham's descendants" was reaffirmed and made lasting for future generations.

Henry Horner acted as a catalyst, uniting the traditionally Republican German-Jewish community with the Eastern European Jewish masses. Although he suffered a serious stroke following the 1938 elections, and died within twenty-four months, his candidacies and elections represented the apex of the Chicago Jewish electorate's drive for recognition.

The bridge formed by Henry Horner and those who slated him for office provided a solid foundation for a lasting rapprochement among the Jewish communities of Chicago.

The ending of mass European immigration and the establishment of national origin quotas in the 1920s accelerated the interweaving of Eastern European and American lifestyles. The Depression, the New Deal, the onset of Nazism, World War II, and, above all, the birth and development of Israel, have dramatically affected and changed not only Chicago's but America's Jewish communities. During the war they knew that the Nazis did not distinguish between areas of origin and national ancestry when they selected victims for the gas chambers and crematoria. Furthermore, intermarriage between members of the Jewish communities and a common concern for the survival of Israel have forged a community consciousness and solidarity that was decidedly absent or ineffectual until relatively recent times.

Chapter VIII

LOUISE AÑO NUEVO KERR

Mexican Chicago:
Chicano Assimilation Aborted, 1939-1954

> *The Mexican is here and in considerable numbers. He is here to stay. We have welcomed him because he works well and cheaply. We have used him to do the tasks which Anglo-Saxons do not care to do. We have used little or no intelligence in helping him to a decent housing situation. We have given him the back alleys of our cities. We have called him 'greaser' and left him to fight his own way as best he can. We have wondered that he does not show more enthusiasm for becoming Americanized.*

> — Hubert Herring (1931)

Large-scale Mexican immigration to Chicago began in 1916 with the recruitment of 206 railroad track laborers from the Texas-Mexican border. The 1920 census counted 1200 Mexicans in Chicago, most of whom worked for the railroads, the steel plants, and the packing houses. Expanding steadily through the twenties, the Chicano community (Mexican and Mexican-American) reached 20,000 by 1930, establishing Chicago as a major center of Mexican settlement in the United States. Like the European ethnics who preceded them, they gathered in neighborhoods adjacent to the industries which recruited them: the Hull House area of the near West Side (railroads); South Chicago (steel plants); and Back of the Yards (packing houses). As ethnic newcomers they suffered the traditional hardships of limited and unstable employment along with cultural prejudice; as Mexicans they also suffered from racial prejudice. Although family formation was increasing, most of the Mexicans at the end of the decade were still young, male, and unskilled. Hoping to return eventually to their homeland, they remained Mexican rather than "American" in cultural as well as legal nationality.[1]

The Depression years of the thirties markedly reshaped the Chicano community. Immigration halted, back-and-forth journeys to Mexico dwindled, and repatriation — both voluntary and involuntary — reduced the number of Chicago's Mexicans to 16,000 by 1940. Despite Depression rigors, the settlements firmly established their identities, and Mexicans began to play a new — if still limited — role in interethnic union and community activities in all three neighborhoods. While the proportion of Mexican immigrants in the Chicano

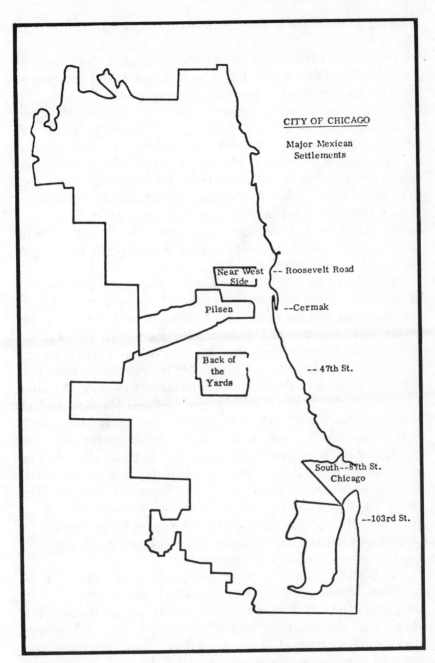

CITY OF CHICAGO

Major Mexican
Settlements

Near West
Side -- Roosevelt Road

Pilsen --Cermak

Back of
the
Yards -- 47th St.

South--87th St.
Chicago

--103rd St.

Major settlement areas of Mexican Chicago, 1945

population decreased, their American-born children grew in number.

By 1940 a relatively large second generation, for the most part born or raised in Chicago, was beginning to reach maturity. On the verge of assuming leadership and defining the direction of community activities, these young people were Americans with little interest in Mexico. Guided by past experience, observers presumed that within a decade, given a normal course of events, Mexicans would find it easier to obtain skilled jobs, move freely throughout the city, and enter the mainstream of life in Chicago. Chicago's 1940 Chicano population showed every sign of becoming Mexican-American instead of Mexican in culture as well as in citizenship, and of following the traditional European pattern of settlement and assimilation.[2]

By 1940, however, both the United States and Mexico had begun to prepare for war. When war became a reality, two separate and distant events took place. One influenced the nature and direction of Chicano communities in Chicago for more than a generation; the other evoked anti-Mexican-American attitudes which would later be felt in Chicago. The first, the signing of the International Bracero Contract Labor Agreements in 1942 and 1943, precipitated the renewal of both temporary and permanent Mexican immigration, thus re-establishing Chicago as a major destination for Mexican immigrants.[3] The second, the *pachuco* "zoot-suit" riots in Los Angeles in 1943,[4] in which allegedly riotous second-generation Mexican-American youths were carefully and invidiously distinguished from Mexican immigrants, demonstrated the fate awaiting the American-born leaders of Chicago's Chicano community once the pressing wartime need for Mexican labor had passed.

In short, the renewal of permanent in-migration of Mexicans and Mexican-Americans coincided with an increase in antipathy toward Chicanos and other Spanish-speaking peoples in the United States. Suspended during wartime, discrimination against the "Spanish-speaking" in immigration and employment was revived after the war. In Chicago, Mexican-Americans expecting to be assimilated were eventually outnumbered by new immigrants. By the mid-1950s, moreover, the "Spanish-speaking" included Puerto Ricans, Cubans, a variety of South and Central Americans, and Americans of Mexican descent from other parts of the United States. Non-Chicanos — friends as well as enemies — found it difficult to distinguish among the city's "Spanish-speaking." After a promising beginning, Chicanos found their emergence into the life of the larger Chicago community indefinitely delayed.

In 1940, as it became increasingly necessary to prepare for war, the negotiation of labor agreements with Mexico was of strategic importance to the United States. Requiring first the settlement of long-standing disputes, the process of arriving at those agreements was involved and delicate, and no one could have foretold their future ramifications. Relations between the two nations, historically tumultuous, had been particularly strained during the 1920s and 1930s by arguments over expropriated United States industries in Mexico.[5] But Franklin Roosevelt's Good Neighbor Policy had modified the old semicolonial relationship, and as the thirties came to a close, Lazaro Cardenas, president of Mexico from 1934 to 1940, sped negotiations so that an outline for the resolution of outstanding differences had been agreed upon by both nations before the 1940 elections, opening the way for mutual cooperation.

Immediately after the election of Manuel Avila Camacho in the hotly contested Mexican presidential race of 1940, the Western Hemisphere's foreign ministers agreed at Havana on "schemes of political and economic cooperation in the event of war." It was decided that Mexico would supply raw materials while the United States took direct action against the Axis powers. Gradually, following the United States' lead, Mexico began to restrict Nazi activities within her borders and to act as a belligerent neutral. The petroleum expropriation claims finally settled, Mexico shipped increasing amounts of oil to the United States. But not until six months after the United States had declared war did Mexico formally enter the fray, when, in May 1942, two of her tankers were attacked by German submarines and seven of her citizens killed.[6]

For the first time in decades Mexico was a relatively unified nation, the political left pacified by the alliance with Russia and the leaderless right weakened by repressive government action. Mexico agreed to contribute manpower as well as raw materials to the war effort. In fact, one day after the first oil tanker sinking, 3,000 Mexicans were certified by the Immigration and Naturalization Service for temporary entry into the United States to harvest sugar beets.[7] But cognizant of the difficulties which previous immigrants had encountered and fully aware that Mexicans would probably emigrate despite those difficulties, the Mexican government insisted on an international agreement guaranteeing workers decent housing, employment, and health conditions, and freedom from discrimination.[8] For the first and perhaps only time in the history of diplomatic relations between the two countries, Mexico held a competitive bargaining position from which to force the United States to protect the interests of Mexican immigrants, and she took advantage of the opportunity.

Based on recommendations made fifteen years earlier by Manuel Gamio, the first *bracero* ("worker") agreement was designed to alleviate the United States' agricultural labor shortage, especially in the Southwest. The agreement of August 4, 1942, the model for those that came later, guaranteed workers a specified, mutually agreeable contract period (usually six months), prevailing minimum United States wages and hours, paid transportation to and from their homes, and housing during the period of the contract. United States agencies were to supervise the recruitment of workers in Mexican cities, and Mexican government representatives were given inspection and appeal privileges.[9]

While it helped to satisfy the need for agricultural labor in the Southwest, the August 1942 covenant did nothing to stem the growing shortage of unskilled labor in U.S. transportation and industry. Industrial employers looked to Mexico to fill the void.[10] As late as November 1942, the Mexican government opposed any importation of Mexican labor "outside the present labor agreement."[11] Indeed, citing repeated and flagrant violations, Mexican authorities threatened to suspend further recruitment under the August arrangement unless corrective measures were taken.[12]

To convince Mexico of his intention to abide by the labor agreement and to negotiate nonagricultural compacts, President Roosevelt traveled to Mexico on April 20, 1943 to talk with President Avila — only the second time in history that presidents of the neighboring countries had met face to face (the first was when Presidents Taft and Diaz conferred at the border).[13] Out of this meeting came Avila's commitment to allow the temporary migration of nonagricultural workers under the same terms as agricultural workers. Most of these were destined for track labor on southwestern railroads, but many were recruited directly to the East and Midwest to work in other industries as well as on the railroads.[14]

Chicago's need for additional workers had already been established by the time the negotiations were completed. In the spring of 1943 a government survey of major labor markets reported that without "full use of all minority groups the labor supply [will be] inadequate."[15] In addition, Chicago's industrial diversity proved a handicap to companies dependent on unskilled labor. For as the manpower shortage worsened, the low wages paid for these jobs proved less and less attractive to domestic workers (including blacks). A study of "Unfilled Openings" in the Chicago region predicted that only five percent of track labor jobs would be filled by domestic workers at the prevailing wage of sixty-five cents an hour.[16]

As the headquarters city of the Railroad Retirement Board, the agency charged with supervising the importation of Mexican railroad workers, Chicago had ready access to this new and important souce of war manpower. Between May 1, 1943 and September 30, 1945, more than 15,000 Mexican railroad workers were brought to Chicago — 11 percent of the 135,350 imported to the United States during the war. The number and percentage of workers recruited to Chicago during that period was exceeded only in the San Francisco

Mexican-American camp housing in Rock Island

area. The great majority of workers brought to the Chicago "region" — including Wisconsin and Iowa — were housed in the northern half of Illinois, most of them in the Chicago metropolitan area. Major employers were the Chicago, Burlington, and Quincy; Chicago, Minneapolis, St. Paul, and Pacific; Chicago, Rock Island, and Pacific; Chicago River and Indiana; Chicago and Northwestern; and Chicago's Union Station.[17] These employers alone recruited a total of 15,344 Mexican workers between 1943 and 1945. The Indiana Belt Harbor Railway housed additional workers in Blue Island and Norpaul, two Chicago suburbs which still have Chicano populations.[18]

Of the more than 15,000 workers recruited to Chicago, a substantial but undetermined number renewed their contracts at least once, their average total stay lasting seven and one-half months. In 1944 and 1945, at the peak of labor importation, the Mexican immigrant population in the Chicago area increased by approximately 7,500 — the average number of contracts in effect at any given time.[19] Most of these immigrants, of course, had only temporary status. But while the *bracero* agreements provided employers with temporary labor, they offered many workers an opportunity to familiarize themselves with the city in anticipation of returning — legally or illegally. Some workers broke their contracts and attempted to remain permanently. Special instructions were issued by the Immigration and Naturalization Service for the return of "missing workers."[20] Clearly, Chicago was re-established as a major destination for Mexican immigrants.

Although Chicago railroads benefited substantially from the *bracero* program, imported workers were still not adequate to fill labor needs. Even as late as October 1945, when the program was coming to a close, three railroads that had consistently exceeded their quotas of Mexican workers had a combined total of more than one thousand unfilled jobs.[21] This was true of other Chicago industries as well, some of which had also been made eligible for recruitment of Mexican laborers. In order to reduce their manpower shortages further, some employers sought Mexican-American as well as Mexican workers. Mexican-American agricultural workers found industrial wages and working conditions better than those on farms and thus were attracted by the offers of these employers. Northwestern Wire and Steel, needing "861 workers . . . to take care of their present needs" in 1945, was unable to provide housing that filled the requirements of the international agreements and was therefore ineligible to obtain immigrant workers. Undaunted, the company decided instead to request "50 or more American born Mexicans . . . in the vicinity of Pharr, Victoria, and San Antonio, Texas."[22] For perhaps the same reasons, Sears, Roebuck and Company, in need of "garment markers," asked that a circular be sent to Dallas and Fort Worth, where "the employer feels that persons with these qualifications would probably be available."[23] The qualifications were unspecified. Thus Mexican-Americans as well as Mexican immigrants came to Chicago as a result of the general labor shortage.

While the wartime need for Mexican laborers continued, and it could be assumed that their stay would be short, the increase in the Mexican population posed little threat to the city or its Chicano settlements. Long-time Chicano residents knew of *braceros* in their neighborhoods but initiated little direct contact with them. While the program lasted, however, Chicanos observed the friendly concern of federal and city officials for the well-being of the temporary workers. For example, when the *braceros* complained about the constant diet of meat and potatoes, demanding beans and tortillas instead, Mexican cooks were hired, if they were available.[24] If they were not, American cooks were given the recipes and foodstuffs necessary for the preparation of Mexican dishes.[25] When the *braceros* objected to filthy and unsanitary bathrooms, federal inspectors made sure that new bathrooms were added and old ones thoroughly cleaned. Wage disputes were submitted to arbitration.[26]

Mexican-Americans learning English in adult education classes during the early forties

Courtesy of Chicago Historical Society

City officials were no less solicitous. English classes were provided for the *braceros*, paid for by the Chicago Board of Education; the Chicago Department of Recreation offered facilities for sports and entertainment; and legal assistance was available in case of arrest. In 1944, 1945, and 1946, the Board of Education added a new social studies unit to the public school curriculum to help familiarize all American students with their nearest good neighbor, Mexico. And public school teachers were encouraged to participate in summer institutes in Mexico to perfect their use of the Spanish language and to increase their understanding of Mexican culture.[27]

After the war, *bracero* recruitment was phased out as the need for workers diminished. However, the number of Chicanos in the city kept growing. Along with ex-*braceros* who had broken their contracts in order to remain, there were legal and illegal immigrants arriving without the aid of the War Manpower Commission or the Railroad Retirement Board. Faced with a continuous and permanent increase in the Chicano population, city officials gradually became less tolerant. In Chicago, tensions similar to those which had led to the *pachuco* riots in Los Angeles just a few years before were revived, making it clear that the sources of those tensions had only been suspended, not eliminated.

The nature of those tensions had been delineated in Los Angeles in mid-1943, just as an agreement was being negotiated for the importation of nonagricultural Mexican workers for industrial labor in the United States. The California episode began when zoot-suit-clad Mexican-Americans allegedly sought out and beat sailors dating Chicano girls, as a warning to stay out of Chicano neighborhoods. First in Oakland in May 1943, and then in Los Angeles in June, retaliating sailors and other servicemen cruised unmolested through Chicano neighborhoods in taxicabs, seeking zoot-suiters upon whom to vent their anger. These incidents had been preceded by a barrage of incendiary press reports portraying *pachucos* as delinquent, subversive, and socially unredeemable Mexican as well as Mexican-American youths.[28]

The "zoot-suit riots" — so-called despite the involvement

of servicemen — threatened to disrupt friendly relations between the United States and Mexico. After a flurry of correspondence between Mexican consular officials and the State Department, it was reported in the *New York Times* in late June 1943 that there were "no cases where Mexican *citizens* [italics mine] were involved in recent fights in Los Angeles between service men and youths wearing zoot-suits, but the State Department promised speedy action on claims resulting from such cases if there were any. The announcement followed a visit to Secretary Hull yesterday by Francisco Castillo Najero, the Mexican Ambassador, who expressed his government's concern over the disturbance."[29] *Pachuco* youth, whether involved in the incidents or not, were characterized as socially "marginal" *Mexican-Americans* unable to accept either the majority culture or that of their parents (presumably immigrants), and as conscious or unconscious agents of subversion trying to disrupt the war effort.

Under the press of wartime labor needs, a distinction was thus being drawn between the Mexican-Americans who had allegedly participated in the "riots" and the Mexicans who were being exhorted to work — temporarily — in the United States. The actions of the two governments confirmed a belief long held in the Chicano *barrios:* it was better to be an alien protected by the shield of international diplomacy than to be a second-, third-, or fourth-generation American unacceptable to the majority.*

At the time, there were no such disturbances in Chicago, but Chicanos in the settlements were very much aware of and worried by their occurrence in the West. Reaction to the riots, moreover, showed not only awareness but identification with the plight of Chicanos in California — an ethnic identification relatively new in the Chicago neighborhoods. For example, while decrying the "riots," one local Chicano leader called for unified *nation-wide* celebration by all Chicanos of Mexican Independence Day (September 16, 1943), "in honor of the ideal of democracy and of human rights."[30]

---

*It should be emphasized that the United States-Mexico agreements concerning *braceros* stipulated only that Mexican *nationals* be protected against discrimination.

The Chicago Area Project, a local social service organization attempting to find solutions to the problems of growing
juvenile delinquency, was aware of the potential for similar
outbreaks in Chicago. In 1942 this predominantly professional and non-Chicano group had requisitioned a "Survey of
Resident Latin American Problems" to determine the depths
of deprivation and the potential for "subversion" in Chicago's
Latin-American communities. Concluding that there were
severe problems of illiteracy, poverty, and delinquency, the
survey had strongly suggested that the "depressed and
downtrodden" were particularly susceptible to subversive
influences.[31]

On the basis of that report, the Chicago Area Project ap-
plied for a $45,000 grant from the Office of Inter-American
Affairs, a federal agency headed during the war by Nelson
Rockefeller. The $10,000 eventually granted was authorized
by Rockefeller, perhaps coincidentally, on April 22, 1943,
two days after the meetings between Roosevelt and Avila.[32]
Intended to aid "Latin Americans in Chicago" — inaccu-
rately described as "first and second generation immigrants
from [sic] Chicago" — the grant proposal noted that "it is the
conviction of those making this request that the full integration of the Mexicans into *our national life* [italics mine]
depends upon the development of programs which will build
leadership in the Mexican group and the encouragement of
programs of self-help in which the Mexicans themselves can
play a responsible and active part."[33]

The grant's sponsors believed that Chicanos, like any
other immigrant group whose immigration flow had ceased,
would be easily assimilated into "our national life." They
went ahead with their program for "Latin Americans in
Chicago," declining for whatever reasons to make distinctions between alien and American-born Chicanos and other
"Latin Americans." The program initially met with some success. A social center, reported by the *Chicago Tribune* to be
for "Americans of Mexican descent," was built on the near
West Side.[34] Community organizations were formed; an
American-born leadership emerged, and important segments
of the Chicano community responded.

By the early 1950s, however, the assimilationist policy enunciated in the Chicago Area Project program was cast in doubt as the Chicano population grew and changed in composition. Renewed in-migration, begun as a temporary measure during the period of wartime tolerance, drew fire after the war when it turned into permanent, often illegal, immigration. The antagonisms it fed culminated in 1954 in "Operation Wetback," the roundup and forcible return of "undocumented" aliens and their families.[35] Mexican immigrants thus found that, with the need for their labor ended, they had lost the strong diplomatic support of their government and were at the mercy of American public opinion. And the "Americans of Mexican descent" who had been partially successful in entering "our national life," though profiting at first from the harsh experience of Mexican-Americans in Los Angeles, soon discovered that the favorable treatment of Chicanos in Chicago had been a temporary expedient. Meanwhile, second-generation Chicano leaders who had developed as spokesmen during the war were being challenged by newly arrived immigrants as well as by those in authority.

Between 1943, when the nonagricultural labor agreements were first implemented, and 1954, when anger against "illegal Mexican immigrants" reached its peak, Chicago's Chicano population grew to include not only the first immigrants and their children, but a new generation of immigrants — legal and illegal — along with a substantial number of Mexican-Americans from elsewhere in the United States. The flow into the Chicago area paralleled the general movement of Chicanos to cities in the 1940s: by 1950, 71 percent of all "Mexican Foreign Stock" recorded in the U.S. Census were living in urban areas; 19 percent were in rural nonfarm communities; and only 10 percent were on farms, despite the large-scale recruitment of Chicano agricultural workers during the war.[36] Larger and more widely dispersed than a decade before, the Chicano population of 1950 had undergone other profound demographic changes, the contours of which are only partially revealed by census returns.

We know, for instance, that nationwide there was an extraordinary upsurge in the number of illegal immigrants dur-

Mother and child on the steps of their home in the Hull House neighborhood

ing the late 1940s. A glance at the reports of the Immigration and Naturalization Service shows that between 1946 and 1950, besides the few temporary *braceros* who stayed behind, only 38,000 Mexicans were admitted legally as permanent alien residents. In those same years, however, 1,110,000 undocumented aliens were apprehended by the Immigration and Naturalization Service and returned to Mexico. The agency itself has calculated that, in the absence of extraordinary measures, it has the capacity to "catch" only 20 to 25 percent of the actual illegals in the United States at any given time. In this four-year period, without such measures, by the service's own calculations there were an estimated four million undocumented Mexicans in the United States.[37] As early as 1947 there were reports in the Chicago press of the apprehension of illegal Mexican aliens in the city.[38] Even if INS estimates were reduced by half (that is, to one apprehended illegal for every two in the country), there would still have been an estimated 2,038,000 new immigrants between 1946 and 1950.

In the 1920s, when the first period of Chicano immigration was at its peak, Illinois ranked fourth as the state of intended destination listed by legally admitted Mexican aliens.[39] Though many fewer immigrants journeyed to Illinois than to Texas, California, and Arizona, word-of-mouth news of opportunities in Illinois had been greatly responsible for the rapid increase in its popularity. But for the Depression, the rate of immigration would likely have grown, for since the resumption of immigration in the 1940s, Illinois has maintained its fourth-place position as a state of intended residence. Since 1950, 10 percent or more of all legally admitted Mexican aliens have given Illinois as their destination.[40] Even if only 1 percent of the estimated 2,038,000 illegal Mexican immigrants between 1946 and 1950 (already half the government's estimated figure) had reached Chicago (the only major metropolitan area in Illinois), at least 20,038 new immigrants should have been counted in the city in 1950. It seems surprising, therefore, that the 1950 census showed only 4,200 new Mexican immigrants in the entire Chicago region, half of them in the suburbs rather than in the city. Nor does this figure differentiate among those immigrants who were legally admitted and stated their intended destination, those who were illegal entrants (and may not have been enumerated in any case), and those who migrated to Chicago after living elsewhere in the United States.

Because of clear undercounting of all minorities, occasional miscalculations, and changes in definition over the years, census data must be handled cautiously. Nonetheless, they do give some insight into the nature and extent of the demographic changes that took place among Chicago's Chicanos between 1940 and 1950. First and most obvious was the growth of the population. Despite undercounting, the number of Chicanos in the city grew from 16,000 to 24,000 (50%), and the number of Chicanos in the metropolitan region grew from 21,000 to 35,000 (66%). Half of the 4,200 new immigrants recorded were living outside the city limits in 1950.[41] While the city's Chicano population expanded by 50 percent, its total population increased by only 6 percent — the smallest proportional increase for any previous decade except that of the Depression. Chicanos arriving in metropolitan Chicago were evidently running counter to the general movement of the entire population, for while their numbers grew by more than 14,000, the region as a whole recorded a net out-migration of more than 18,000. Between 1940 and 1950, the city's officially counted foreign-born Mexican population grew by 21 percent, but was still only a little more than one-third of the total Chicano population.[42]

Those recorded in the 1950 census as "new" or additional immigrants were in all likelihood legal entrants who were eligible to remain permanently. They brought with them greater affluence, better work skills, more education, and more contacts in the United States than had the earlier immigrants. Half of these "new" immigrants settled in the suburbs, making use of their skill advantages in the expanding industries of the metropolitan region. Joining the more than 2,000 immigrants in the suburbs were 2,200 Mexican-Americans; together they formed new Chicano settlements which date their beginnings to the war and postwar periods. Some of these Mexican-Americans may have moved from Chicago, but most were new in-migrants recruited by small suburban factories in Aurora, Bensenville, and Arlington Heights. The emergence of these outlying settlements illustrates a new pattern of migration and settlement which began in the 1940s, one which bypassed Chicago entirely and took the more affluent and skilled from Mexico and Texas directly to the suburbs.[43]

Migrants to the older and more established Chicano settlements in the city included more illegal immigrants ineligible to remain permanently than did those going to the suburbs. Whether Mexican or Mexican-American, moreover, migrants to the city were poorer and less skilled, in search of the same kinds of jobs that had drawn the original immigrants of the 1920s. They became laborers, service workers, and "operatives" (semiskilled industrial workers) — occupational groups which the 1950 census indicated were increasing in number in the city. White-collar and professional positions, also expanding in number, were being filled by better-educated workers who apparently were just beginning to use their higher earnings to leave the city.[44]

The 1950 census made no distinctions between old and new Mexican immigrants, or between Chicago-born and Southwest-born Mexican-Americans, so it is difficult to be precise about their proportions. But the census does show that the average age of the total Chicano population rose more than fifteen years between 1940 and 1950, and that the average age of U.S.-born Chicanos rose more than nineteen years in the same period, certainly indicating a substantial in-migration of older Mexican-Americans. Just as significantly, the average age of the Mexican-born rose hardly at all — from 40.3 years in 1940 to 43.1 in 1950 — suggesting that there had been a substantial in-migration of younger Mexican immigrants. Without including either the *braceros* observed by Chicanos in their own neighborhoods, or the undocumented workers complained about by the INS as early as 1947, these figures demonstrate that the recent influx of younger Mexican immigrants and older Mexican-Americans was sufficient to alter the normal aging curve of Chicanos.[45]

Further evidence of major Chicano in-migration was the rising sex ratio, which once again reached the first-generation proportions of the twenties. Reflecting the in-migration of large numbers of young men, the sex ratio for foreign-born over the age of fourteen was 1.926 — almost two men for every woman. For the native-born, the ratio was 1.269, lower than that of the foreign-born, yet still higher than in the thirties, when virtually all of the native-born were second-generation children of Chicago's first immigrant Mexican families. For native-born between the ages of fourteen and forty-four, the sex ratio was 1.870, almost as high as that of the immigrants and much higher than a decade earlier.[46]

Of the four groups of Chicanos living in the Chicago settlements in 1950 — the first immigrants, their children, new immigrants, and Mexican-Americans from elsewhere — the immigrants, old and new, fared better than the Mexican-Americans, and for the first time compared favorably in average income and education to the European foreign-born with whom they most frequently lived, the Poles and Italians. In fact, foreign-born Mexicans had a higher average education than either the Poles or Italians (probably because of the in-migration of better-educated younger Mexicans from urban Mexico), and they were earning more money than Polish foreign-born immigrants, who were by that time much older than Mexicans.

TABLE I

Foreign-born Income, Education, and Age in Chicago, 1950

	Income	Years of Education	Age
Mexican	$2566	5.6	43.1
Italian	$2630	4.8	
Polish	$2374	5.5	58.3

U.S. Bureau of the Census, *U.S. Census of Population: 1950*, Vol. IV, *Special Reports*, Part 3, Chapter A, "Nativity and Parentage" (Washington: U.S. Government Printing Office, 1954), pp. 3A-258, 3A-262, 3A-265.

Midway between what the census calls "whites," whose average income rose from $1100 in 1939 to $3300 in 1951, and "non-whites," whose income rose from an average of $500 in 1939 to $2100 in 1951, all of the foreign-born, including Mexicans, had benefited from the war and postwar prosperity. Though their "real" income had risen very little, their wage increases at least corresponded to those of the general population.[47]

Mexican-Americans, on the other hand, including those from Texas, were receiving lower wages than either the foreign-born or second-generation Italians and Poles, despite the fact that they had more schooling than immigrants and almost as much as other native-born ethnics.

TABLE II

Education and Income: Mexican-Americans, Mexican-born, Italian-American, and Polish-American: Chicago, 1950

	Years of Education	Income
Mexican-American	9.0	$2066
Mexican-born	5.6	$2566
Italian-American	10.2	$2610
Polish-American	9.3	$2701

U.S. Census of Population: 1950, loc. cit.

Mexican-Americans aged fourteen to twenty-four, the group which had received its education most recently, would continue to be at a disadvantage when competing with second-generation European ethnics for jobs because the gap in their years of schooling was growing wider, partly as a result of the in-migration of less-educated Mexican-Americans from Texas (see Table 3).

TABLE III
Education: Second-generation Ethnics, Ages 14 to 24: Chicago, 1950

	Years of Education
Mexican-Americans	9.4
Italian-Americans	11.5
Polish-Americans	11.7

U.S. Census of Population: 1950, loc. cit.

Despite the apparent and growing disparity in education between native-born Mexican-Americans and other second-generation ethnics in Chicago, Mexican-Americans from Texas and other parts of the Southwest continued to come, in part because they were having an even more difficult time in rural areas and in other urban regions of the United States. In Los Angeles, for example, income was much lower for both the foreign-born and the native-born, even though their average education was similar to that of Chicanos in Chicago. *Tejanos* (Texas Chicanos) lagged behind in education and income both in cities and rural areas, with rural *Tejanos* earning the least money of all Chicanos and completing the fewest years of school (see Table 4).

In October 1953, the *Chicago Sun Times* reported that according to the director of the Chicago office of the Immigration and Naturalization Service, there were "nearly 100,000 Mexicans" in the city, including "15,000 wetbacks," even though the census had counted only 24,000 Mexicans three years earlier.[48] Old immigrants, new immigrants, and Mexican-Americans from elsewhere viewed their lives in Chicago through the prism of past experience. The old immigrants, settled into a routine existence, had made great economic strides in the twenty or more years they had been

TABLE IV
Income and Education: Chicanos in the U.S., 1950

	Income	Years of Education
Los Angeles		
Mexican-born	$1931	6.1
Mexican-American	$1731	9.5
Texas Urban		
Mexican-born	$1164	3.1
Mexican-American	$1096	6.0
Texas Rural		
Mexican-born	$ 748	1.4
Mexican-American	$ 803	3.8
Chicago		
Mexican-born	$2566	5.6
Mexican-American	$2066	9.0

U.S. *Census of Population: 1950, op. cit.,* pp. 3A-265, 3A-378; U.S. *Census of Population: 1950,* Vol. IV, *Special Reports,* Part 3, Chapter C, "Persons of Spanish Surname," p. 3C-56.

in the city. Nostalgic for a Mexico which no longer existed, they had little in common with recent arrivals except national origin. New immigrants, from a Mexico almost 50 percent urban,[49] came for industrial jobs that were better paying than the agricultural work some of them had done as *braceros.* Mexican-Americans, especially those from Texas, left behind migrant farm work and a depressed rural economy. Economically at least, for all of them — old and new immigrants and Mexican-Americans from the Southwest — life in Chicago was an improvement over what they had known before.

Chicago-born Chicanos, on the other hand, having grown up in the city, realized that the promises of progress made in the thirties and forties had not been fulfilled. At a time of heightened interest in the needs of various "nationality groups" in the city, a time also of official desire to maintain "good Latin American relations" for the sake of the war effort, they had been encouraged to step forward as community leaders and spokesmen. For a brief period, from 1943 to shortly after 1950, these Chicago natives became the articulate representatives of Chicano interests, recognized as the liaison between the settlements and the larger Chicago community. Intent on entering that community and forcing it to take account of Chicano needs, they failed, however, to recognize that in-migration brought with it conflicting needs and, indeed, conflicting interests which they could no longer fully represent. They were supported initially as a counter force to the potential influence of *pachucos*, delinquents, and subversives, only to be outnumbered and eclipsed by the thousands of new migrants who came partly as a result of their success. In the end, their economic status did not improve. For the foreseeable future, in fact, they would continue to fall behind other ethnic groups in the city.

Neither the eruption of intra-ethnic conflict nor the gradual dissipation of utopian promise could have been predicted as the decade of the 1940s opened. The city's need for workers and the fear of subversion enabled Chicanos to gain the attention of civic leaders and their organizations. One such group, the Pan American Council, issued a report in 1942 noting the need for Chicano workers.[50] Speaking on behalf of Mexican immigrants "not accustomed to organize . . . and not vocal about matters which are of deep concern to them," the director of the Immigrants' Protective League observed that United States citizenship was being "forced upon" Mexican immigrant residents working in defense industries and suggested that the pressure be eased if their labor was to be retained.[51] At the same time the *Chicago Tribune,* in February 1942, applauded "loyal" South American allies for severing relations with the Axis powers and acting "to suppress totalitarian influence, bar war materials to the Axis, halt business relations with the same, and outlaw Fifth Column activities."[52] In general, then, the exigencies of war temporarily created a more positive atmosphere for Chicanos as well as for *braceros.*

The Chicago Area Project, led by Clifford Shaw and Henry McKay (associates of Saul Alinsky at the Institute for Juvenile Research), capitalized on the general feeling of good will when it appealed to the Office of Inter-American Affairs for money to develop "Mexican" leaders who could represent their own communities. Shaw and McKay had long ago concluded in *Delinquency Areas* (1929) that "disorganization [juvenile delinquency] is intensified by the influx of foreign national and racial groups whose old cultural and social controls break down in the new cultural and racial situations in the city."[53] Growing out of the research of Shaw and McKay, the Chicago Area Project had been organized in the early 1930s to find ways in which "nationality groups" and low income populations living in deteriorated city neighborhoods could be "incorporated into our culture and through which they could find their place in the physical and social structure of the city."[54] As we have seen, the Project's 1943 grant request in behalf of the "20,000 Latin Americans in Chicago" was based on these assumptions.

The Chicago Area Project, the Immigrants' Protective League, and the Pan American Council had conflicting ideas about who the "Mexicans" were and what they needed. The Pan American Council and the Immigrants' Protective League saw "Mexicans" as immigrants needing help in combating job discrimination — that is, as permanent immigrants. The Chicago Area Project defined "Latin Americans" as Mexican-Americans and Mexican immigrants raised in the United States who required help in developing community leadership. Each of these civic groups, however, was intent on "Americanizing" the foreign-born through naturalization and the United States-born through social programs.

The Immigrants' Protective League, for example, surveyed "Leading Employers of Mexicans in Chicago" in 1944 and found that most Mexicans "still" worked for the railroads, steel mills, and packing houses. In the "tight" wartime labor market "there were no unemployed Mexicans in South Chicago," the railroads had been forced to import "contract laborers from Mexico under international treaty," and the meatpackers were "seeking more contract laborers."[55] Contract workers, protected by the agreement with Mexico, were guaranteed good working conditions and job security. Permanent Mexican aliens, on the other hand, enjoyed no such protection and were subject, as always, to discriminatory hiring practices.

Defense industries were required to screen out undesirable or potentially subversive elements in the work force, and one means of doing so was to require citizenship. Though Mexico was an ally, Mexican alien residents had almost as much difficulty establishing their loyalty as did Italians and Germans, and throughout the war they were continuously pressured to certify their permanence by becoming citizens. On the basis of the survey of "Leading Employers," the Immigrants' Protective League and the Pan American Council, concerned about the rights of resident aliens, spoke out in behalf of Mexicans. Employers and government agents charged with maintaining security eventually agreed to a compromise proposal presented by the Council and the League: aliens registered in citizenship and naturalization programs would be eligible for employment in defense industries.[56]

Adena Miller Rich of the Immigrants' Protective League pointed out, however, that the educational prerequisites for naturalization worked a particular hardship on those who, previously without educational opportunity, found it difficult to attend night classes. There were not enough child-care facilities to allow women to take advantage of English and civics classes. Many communities simply lacked the teachers and social workers necessary to staff adult education programs, though the Board of Education had attempted to provide English instruction for *braceros*. Arguing that "the solidarity of the United States is best promoted by removing old obstacles, not creating new ones, and by making naturalization possible for the great numbers of foreign-born who have cast in their lot with this country and are so eager to call it their own by legal right," Rich urged that the educational requirements for citizenship be modified. Looking beyond domestic "solidarity," moreover, she warned that "the 'shut-out' effect upon the citizenship applications of certain races and peoples at this time, such as Mexicans and Chinese, might easily reverberate abroad and endanger the avowed 'Good Neighbor Policy' of the United States."[57]

Under Rich's leadership, the Immigrants' Protective League took an active part in creating and staffing adult English and civics classes to prepare Mexican aliens for citizenship. These "Americanization" programs were located in railroad work camps, defense plants, and neighborhood schools as well as in the traditional settlement houses. Permanent aliens who were eligible recognized the advantages of acquiring citizenship. Encarnacion Chico, a long-time resident of Back of the Yards, had entered the country legally in the 1920s and worked in the packing houses throughout the Depression. Fluent in English, Chico was able to become a citizen soon after the war began. For him the coming of the *braceros* meant prosperity and job security. "Many braceros," he has recalled, "came to work in the [stockyards] and for the railroads. They lived in their own areas and stayed away from us. Practically all the Mexicans worked in the yards in those days."[58] Chico's language facility and his long experience in the United States enabled him to mediate between the contracted workers and the foremen, and his eligibility for naturalization quickly made him a valuable employee, a candidate for advancement. He became a meat inspector and after the war bought a home in the neighborhood.

On the other hand, a good many long-time residents found it difficult to establish their permanence and to take advantage of their work experience in Chicago. This was especially true for those who had entered the United States before 1924, when registration was first required of entering Mexican aliens, and for those who — knowingly or unknowingly — had continued to cross the border without legal sanction. The Pan American Council pointed out that Mexicans seeking to be naturalized "are now finding that they must apply for a certificate of registry to legalize their unregistered entry. In effect a Mexican who entered the country in a legal manner [that is, before 1924] now finds himself illegally in the country."[59] Illegal aliens, of course, were subject not only to discriminatory hiring practices but to deportation. Many aliens, unsure whether they could prove legal entry, declined to apply for naturalization, thus limiting their participation in wartime prosperity.

The Americanization plan of the Pan American Council and the Immigrants' Protective League was based less on the desire to see Mexicans naturalized than on the realization that there was an intimate connection between the positive public response to "Mexicans" and the war effort, and that this positive response to Mexicans was dependent on the willingness of Mexicans to be Americanized. In fact, while advocating enlightened revision of naturalization requirements and encouraging the creation of programs to benefit Mexicans along with other foreign-born aliens, the League predicted as early as 1942 that xenophobia against non-naturalized Mexicans would surface during postwar demobilization.[60]

In any case, between 1942 and 1945 many older Mexicans were able to take advantage of the wartime labor need and of the help of the Pan American Council and the Immigrants' Protective League. Long-time residents with jobs, especially in the packing houses of Back of the Yards and the steel mills of South Chicago, were better off than younger Mexican-Americans not in the armed services. The latter possessed relatively little work experience, and were less able than their Spanish-speaking elders to mediate between *braceros* and management.

To aid "Americans of Mexican descent," the Chicago Area Project used its $10,000 grant from the Office of Inter-American Affairs to organize the Mexican Civic Committee in 1943. As an ethnically segregated neighborhood group, the committee was meant to develop political leaders who could articulate and implement social and economic goals for "the community." The organization's English name symbolized its "American" orientation, if not its Mexican-American membership.[61]

Neither the committee nor its leadership generated antagonism during the war. Most permanent residents were too busy working to be concerned about the problems raised by the group. Chicanos, like others in the city, felt unified by their extensive participation in the war. "There is hardly a [Mexican] family," said the *Chicago Tribune,* "that does not have a father, brother or sweetheart in active service."[62] The committee pragmatically cultivated good relations by informing the Chicano community of war news, social news, and current projects through its newsletter, a mimeographed sheet written almost entirely in the American argot of the young.[63] It also capitalized on the general good will fostered by the Pan American Council, the Immigrants' Protective

League, and other sympathetic civic organizations by initiating contact with the larger Chicago community.

One of the Mexican Civic Committee's first projects was to launch yet another "Mexican Social Center" on the near West Side. Late in June 1943, days after the outbreak of the *pachuco* riots in Los Angeles, a meeting was held at Hull House to generate backing for the proposed center; in attendance were not only the Mexican Consul and Father Joaquin De Prada, the priest at St. Francis of Assisi Church, but also Mayor Kelly — a demonstration of the Committee's early success in bringing its efforts to the attention of official Chicago. Unfortunately, Father De Prada, speaking after the mayor had departed, ended his expression of support for the project with the words, "Long live Spain, Franco's Spain!" Reflecting the committee's new-found sense of power, Chairman Frank X. Pax did not let the incident pass unnoticed. He complained directly to Cardinal Stritch (with carbon copies to the Mexican Consul, the Chicago Area Project, and the Office of Inter-American Affairs), reporting that members of the priest's congregation had been dismayed at his remarks. "A great majority of the people," Pax informed Cardinal Stritch, "booed Father De Prada's fascist outburst."[64] No doubt one element in the Civic Committee's fledgling display of muscle was its awareness — and perhaps the awareness of the mayor and the Mexican Consul as well — of what Pax, writing to the local Mexican Patriotic Committee in August 1943, called "unhappy incidents for all the American continent which had taken place recently in Los Angeles" — the *pachuco* riots.[65]

A request for further government funding was denied in 1944,[66] but the Mexican Civic Committee was well enough established by then to continue on its own and to expand its activities, many of which were aimed at overcoming intra-ethnic and neighborhood differences among "Mexican-Americans" in Chicago. The Mexican Social Center was successfully completed in 1945. Ceremonies dedicating the center to the memory of Manuel Perez, a Chicago-born Congressional Medal of Honor winner who had died in Luzon "en defensa de los ideales libertadores de su patria y de su raza" ("in defense of the liberating ideals of his country and of his race"), received city-wide press coverage.[67] The center's director was paid by the Illinois Department of Welfare and the Chicago Area Project, but its staff was "Mexican."[68] Built for all Chicano residents, in point of fact it served the young, almost all of whom were United States-born.

At war's end the Mexican Civic Committee seemed to have fulfilled two of its major goals: providing a platform for the airing of Chicano grievances and giving leadership training to its members. Part of its success came from its near West Side proximity to the Immigrants' Protective League, the Hull House Association, and the Juvenile Protective Institute, all of which took an interest in Chicano problems. As

Mayor Martin Kennelly honors Toribio Tapia, president of the Latin American Fraternal Society, November 16, 1947.

Courtesy of Calumet Industrial and Railroad Photographs

members of the Metropolitan Welfare Council of Chicago, an umbrella organization of social service agencies, these groups were instrumental in aiding the Mexican Civic Committee to find a broader forum. In 1947 the Metropolitan Welfare Council created a subcommittee on Mexican-American interests. Chaired by Frank Pax, the subcommittee laid the groundwork for a city-wide conference held in May 1949. Composed almost entirely of Mexican-American men and women from all three settlements, most of them long-time residents, the subcommittee agreed on a common set of problems and presented a unified front to the conference, which was convened for the sole purpose of learning about "Mexican Americans in the city."[69]

Representatives of twenty-three organizations listened to the report prepared by Pax and his subcommittee. "Due to the absence of an official survey or study of the Mexican American in Chicago," he noted, "there are no exact figures available on this subject." Beginning with a brief history of the Mexican settlements, Pax went on to acknowledge their contemporary differences. But his major emphasis was on their common achievements and problems. Social life, he said, had changed dramatically since the Depression. Pool halls had given way to *cantinas* as meeting places for men. But ownership of the *cantinas* remained in the hands of "Greeks, Italians, Irishmen, and Poles." Entertainment had expanded in the early forties to include two Spanish-language moviehouses, one of them an abandoned Jewish operahouse, neither of them owned by Mexicans. English-speaking Chicanos freely attended downtown and neighborhood moviehouses where general audience films were shown, without fear of segregation. And there were two weekly radio programs of Chicano news and entertainment.[70]

In the eyes of Pax and the subcommittee, however, these were meager improvements. Despite the wholehearted participation of Chicanos in their churches, unions, settlement houses, jobs, and in the war, they were still isolated from the larger community and subject to conditions outside their control. Pax prodded his audience with the information that the only Spanish-language newspaper in existence in Chicago during the war had opposed the participation of Mexicans and Mexican-Americans because of continued discrimination against them. As proof of Chicano efforts in the war, he cited veterans' groups in all three settlements, most of them composed of "American born or Mexicans raised in the United States since childhood." A state-chartered veterans' group had eighty members, but could claim a "potential of 400." Near West Side veterans organized posts of both the American Legion (named in honor of Manuel Perez) and the Veterans of Foreign Wars. Characteristically, in Back of the Yards, where Chicanos were accustomed to interethnic organization, they joined with other ethnics to form neighborhood veterans' clubs.[71]

Their wartime achievements had presumably confirmed the right of Chicanos to claim the perquisites of "Americanness." But Pax asserted that they were still not accepted by either the churches or the unions. Neither Catholic nor Protestant churches served the communities well, said Pax, because they perceived Chicanos as non-Christians still in need of missionary efforts. And though Mexicans had participated enthusiastically in the unions at first, they were now apathetic — and with good reason. He reported, for example, that although an estimated 6,000 Chicanos worked in Chicago's steel industry, after a decade of unionism there was still "no Mexican American on the staff of the union in the entire Calumet region with the exception of a single office girl in Indiana Harbor."[72] Chicanos were doing somewhat better in the packing house unions, but not as well as in the 1930s, when their support had been important to union survival. Historically excluded in Chicago as elsewhere, only a small proportion of Mexican railroad workers were unionists.[73] In all these industries, the postwar recession saw many Chicanos lose their jobs to returning veterans.

Even the settlement houses, always more sympathetic to Chicanos than other Chicago institutions, had failed to respond adequately. As of 1948, said Pax, no Mexican had ever served on the Hull House board of directors, and there was only one Chicano staff worker. The Mary McDowell Center (formerly the University of Chicago Settlement House) had

A Spanish-speaking meeting of the United Packing House Workers

never appointed a Mexican to its board, although there were a few in its community advisory group. South Chicago's Bird Memorial Center did have two Chicanos on its board of directors and several staff members as well, but these latter were clerks, semiprofessionals, and janitors.[74]

In sum, Pax's report was a scathing condemnation of the policies and programs carried on by the very organizations he was addressing. Using his experience as past chairman of the Mexican Civic Committee and hoping to capitalize on the general air of receptivity which had prevailed in the 1940s, Pax deliberately made his report stern and unbending in tone.

As a result of the meeting and of Pax's report, the Met-

ropolitan Welfare Council formed another subcommittee, this
time on "Special Problems of Mexicans in Chicago," with Pax
as coordinator. Citing the lack of Mexican leadership in
unions, civic groups, and social service agencies, this new
subcommittee recommended that a new and expanded
Mexican-American Council be established, along with a
city-wide umbrella organization of various Mexican-
American groups. In the fall of 1949, as a direct result of the
Welfare Council's efforts, the Illinois Federation of Mexican
Americans (ILFOMA) was born.[75]

Funded initially by government money, staffed by
younger Mexican-Americans, and encouraged by receptive
Chicago civic leaders, the Mexican Civic Committee must
have seemed to have fulfilled its original objectives with relative success in 1949. But already nativistic sentiment against
Mexican immigration had begun to rise again. As early as
1948, the number of unwanted illegal aliens in Chicago had
increased to such an extent that the Immigration and
Naturalization Service included Chicago in its national
search for "missing" alien workers.[76]

Still, the attitude toward Mexican immigrants was ambiguous: so long as they did not remain and become a permanent problem, they were acceptable. It was reported, for
example, that while illegal immigrants were being deported,
approximately 800 contract laborers had been "sited" in
Chicago during 1947.[77] That same year, the *Chicago Star*,
according to Frank Pax, had reported a latter-day attempt to
use Chicanos as strikebreakers:

> At Inland Steel last week May 1, 1947, the company imported
> some 250 Mexican workers two days prior to the calling of the
> strike. They were brought up from Texas for the sole purpose of
> scabbing, but the company plans back-fired; not only did the
> Mexicans refuse to scab but they marched into the Inland Steel
> office in a body to demand the company pay their transportation
> back home and to add to the company's chagrin, signed up in
> the union as an indication of their solidarity.[78]

It is not clear whether the "Mexican workers . . . from Texas"
were immigrants or Mexican-Americans. In either case, they
were used as a weapon against steelworkers in general, especially against long-time Chicano steelworkers who were di-

vided from these "scabs" only by claims of longer residence and employment, and perhaps by citizenship.

On the recommendation of the Metropolitan Welfare Council, the Mexican American Council was formed in 1950. Its stated objective, like that of the Mexican Civic Committee of the 1940s, was to "bring about the integration of the Mexican residents of Chicago into the life of the wider community through education and organization among Mexican Americans."[79] At first the Council had some success in defending Chicanos in the courts: two of its cases received national attention. In October 1951, the *Christian Science Monitor* reported that the Council had proved that a Chicago policeman, Michael Moretti, without provocation or sufficient cause, had fatally shot two Chicanos and wounded another. Moretti was fired, charged with manslaughter, and jailed.[80] In the second case, that of Pedro Romero and his family, the Council reported to the police and the city's Commission on Human Relations that the Romero home in South Chicago had been vandalized, and a sign saying "Get Out! We Don't Want Mexicans!" placed in their front yard. The Council noted that Maynard Wisher, Director of the Civil Rights Division of the Commission on Human Relations, was too busy to investigate the charges. The police, on the other hand, assigned a guard to the family's home, effectively curtailing further harassment.[81]

Notwithstanding these minor successes, a 1953 *Chicago Sun-Times* story demonstrated, graphically and depressingly, that with all the efforts made over the previous decade, there were "in all of Chicago ... 7 Mexican nurses, 5 teachers, 1 lawyer, 1 dentist, 1 policeman." School enrollment among Chicano children was shrinking even as the population expanded. Between 1951 and 1952, for instance, the number of high school graduates dropped from eighty-three to sixty-nine.[82]

Meanwhile, new Mexican immigrants attacked the Mexican American Council's leadership and diluted its effectiveness. Angry at a 1953 press report which referred to Martin Ortiz, the Council's chairman, as a representative spokesman of the "community," Salvador Herrera, president of the

newly organized *Comite Patriotico Mexicano*, denounced
Ortiz, stating emphatically that the latter did not represent *La
Colonia Mexicana* at all, and that if he continued to be so
presumptuous as to claim to do so, the *Comite* would consider legal action.[83] The Council and its leadership were
similarly criticized by Jose Chapa, Chicago's most popular
Mexican radio personality.[84] The Council's loss of support
was an ironic blow: Mexican-Americans who had replaced
the leadership of an earlier immigrant generation in the forties now found themselves challenged in the early fifties by a
new, more outspoken, and more numerous generation of
immigrants.

In 1954 the roundup of undocumented workers reached
its peak in "Operation Wetback." Virtually everyone in the
Chicano settlements was affected in one way or another. Recently arrived illegal immigrants, of course, were vulnerable
to apprehension and deportation, as were members of their
families, some of them American-born. In addition, older
immigrants still without proof of legal entry, and — by virtue
of the McCarran-Walters Immigration Acts of 1950 and 1952
— naturalized aliens suspected of subversive activities, were
also subject to deportation.[85] Mexico, no longer of strategic
importance, had lost the diplomatic leverage which had enabled her to support and defend immigrants during the war.

An illustrative if perhaps extreme example of the shifts
that had taken place in ethnic identity within the community,
in the larger community's response to "Mexicans" in the city,
and in the relative position of the two countries, is the case of
Ramon Refugio Martinez, a naturalized American citizen
who had led Mexican popular front organizations in Chicago
during the 1930s and participated in the packinghouse labor
controversies of the 1940s. A former president of the Mexican
Community Committee, Martinez had been defended during
the forties against accusations of subversion and attempted
overthrow of the government on the ground that he was a
United States citizen whose conviction should be resisted
"because the democratic rights of the American people are in
danger." In 1953, still accused of unspecified subversive activities and vulnerable to deportation under the McCarran-

Walters Act, Martinez was both supported and attacked as a *Mexican* rather than as an American. His defenders wanted to "strike a blow to the oppressive mass-scale deportation of *Mexican* [italics mine] people from the United States."[86]

Despite the official 1950 census count of only 24,000 Chicanos in the city, it was obvious that old residents had been outnumbered. Their claims of permanence and longevity no longer sufficed to distinguish them from newly arrived in-migrants. Mexican-Americans, mindful of the strides made during and after the war, felt ambiguous toward continued Mexican immigration, but resigned themselves to the change which that immigration necessitated. In December 1953, the Mexican American Council took note of the change:

Mexican-Americans commemorate the 153rd anniversary of Mexico's independence in 1963.

Courtesy of Chicago Historical Society: James M. Hall, photographer

With the influx of thousands of Puerto Ricans, Mexican nationals and other Spanish-speaking people to the city, particularly during the past five years, the Council has been extending its works and programs to include all Spanish-speaking people. The membership of its board of directors and its city-wide membership list consists of persons from all walks of life and represents many nationalities. . . . The Mexican American Council serves as a means to an end by which Spanish-speaking people may have a representative voice in the affairs of the Chicago community.[87]

But without the ethnic unity that had been encouraged during wartime, Mexican-American leadership receded, representing only a small percentage of the city's Chicanos, and an even smaller percentage of the Spanish-speaking. After a decade of vital participation during which Chicanos had looked beyond the settlements toward one another and toward the larger community, they once again turned inward, divided by neighborhood interest and loyalty as in the past, but also by generation and ethnic identity. The assimilationist vision of Mexican-Americans had been overwhelmed by the Mexican ethnicity of postwar immigrants.

THE STRUGGLE
CONTINUES

Chapter IX

ARNOLD HIRSCH

Race and Housing:
Violence and Communal Protest
in Chicago, 1940-1960

> *Some of those with whom I talked [had] ...
> such thick Bohemian, German, Polish or
> Greek accents that it was not always easy to
> know what they were saying. ... It was appall-
> ing to see ... those who were ...bene-
> ficiaries of American opportunity ... as vir-
> ulent as any Mississippian in their willingness
> to deny a place to live to a member of a race
> which had preceded them to America by many
> generations.*
>
> — Walter White (1951)

THE WAVE OF RIOTS THAT SWEPT THE United States in the mid-1960s revolutionized popular perceptions regarding the place and significance of collective violence in the nation's history. Before the sixties violence was viewed as an idiosyncratic form of behavior existing outside and apart from the American social structure and political process. Now its occurrence is seen more as a "natural" part and expression of both.[1]

The race riots, however, blinded us even as they opened our eyes. The fact that much violence was committed by blacks, for example, played no small part in the whites' sudden interest in the subject. A grim fascination for the study of black violence, and its prevention, marked much of the later literature.[2] Furthermore, the explosions of the 1960s conditioned observers to equate the significance of violence with its *visibility*. But if, in fact, violence is an expression of our social order, its judicious and less visible use by those holding power may have a more lasting impact than its open exploitation, in race riots, by the essentially powerless.

This chapter deals with a large American city in the pre-1960s, during what has been seen as a quiescent period. By exposing and examining a previously hidden though significant pattern of white-initiated racial violence in Chicago during the years following World War II, the focus is not on the discovery of a new sensational wave of riots, but rather on the revelation of a persistent form of day-to-day violence and what it can tell us about social and ethnic change in the postwar city. The examination of disorder — its frequency, discernible features, and historical context — will be used as an

From rural slum...

...to urban slum

analytical tool to lay bare the structure and workings of society in an era during which many decisions were made which shaped the modern American city.

Despite official attempts to control racial tensions, a competitive struggle for homes and "turf" engulfed portions of Chicago in the 1940s and 1950s. This battle was rooted in shifting demographic realities as the racial composition of the city underwent drastic change. White population declined while black population rose dramatically, from 8 percent in 1940 to nearly 25 percent by 1960.[3] Prior to World War II, the area in which this growing black population was compelled to live remained relatively stable; its borders were still largely those drawn during the Great Migration. After World War II, black territorial expansion began anew. Pushing out to the south and west, the growth of the old Black Belt generated violent resistance. The resulting battles for living space were carried on by local residents of contested neighborhoods whose actions, though charged by a strident emotionalism, were generally measured, limited, and purposeful. Even more important was the perception of that purposefulness by the City Council. Embarking on a program to redevelop the city, the Council's reaction to violence was to be instrumental in shaping Chicago's race relations throughout the civil rights era and into the turbulent 1960s.

The extent of postwar racial violence in Chicago, as well as the degree to which it was hidden from public view, is best illustrated by way of contrast. The most widely publicized racial disorder of these years occurred not within the city proper but at its western edge in the working-class suburb of Cicero. There, during the summer of 1951, a mob assaulted a large apartment building which housed a single black family in one of its twenty units. The burning and looting of the building's contents lasted several nights until order was finally restored by the presence of some 450 National Guardsmen and 200 Cicero and Cook County Sheriff's police.[4]

The reaction to this incident was immediate, outraged, and worldwide. Thomas E. Dewey, visiting Singapore, was

A black tenement on the South Side

"shocked" to find the Cicero riot front page news in South East Asia. News of the riot was also carried in the *Pakistan Observer* and apparently reached Africa as well; a resident of Accra wrote to the mayor of Cicero protesting the mob's "savagery" and asking for an "apology to the civilized world. . . ."[5]

At home the Chicago press provided extensive coverage of the riot, complete with editorials denouncing the violence and letters to the editor protesting racial barbarism. However, buried among those letters was one of a slightly different tone written by Homer Jack, a Unitarian minister and co-founder of the Congress of Racial Equality (CORE). The Cicero disorder "contained perhaps more vandalism than recent racial disturbances in Chicago," Jack wrote, "but fortunately there was no persistent attack on the police . . . or violence towards Negroes," as had been the case elsewhere in the city.[6] Jack was referring to two recent Chicago riots, one at the Chicago Housing Authority's (CHA) southside Fernwood Park Homes and another in the southside Englewood community. In each case the issue was the same: the introduction of black residents into previously all-white communities. Yet, though he was minimizing the level of violence seen in Cicero compared with these other disorders, it was only through his role as a social activist that Jack was aware of them at all. The Chicago press had virtually ignored these earlier riots and, as a contemporary observer noted, "the man in the street . . . is wholly unaware that a cruel kind of warfare is going on in the no-man's land around Chicago's Black Belt."[7]

The unpublicized Chicago riots dwarfed the better-known Cicero incident by every possible measure. Four or five rioters were found in the streets of Chicago for each one mobilized in Cicero. While a mere building was attacked in Cicero (there was not a black within miles of the area when the rioting started), both Chicago mobs vented their wrath on human victims. In Fernwood blacks were hauled off streetcars in a fashion reminiscent of 1919; in Englewood the crowd attacked not only blacks, but also Jews, University of

Chicago students, and anyone else labeled an "outsider." Even in terms of the size of the force needed to quell the violence, the Cicero disorder seemed less dangerous than the Chicago outbursts. One thousand police were needed in Fernwood, and 700 were kept on duty for a full two weeks in the area. At the height of the rioting the police were compelled to quarantine an area of nearly eight square miles in order to contain the incident. In comparison, there were never more than 650 peace officers on duty in Cicero, nor were they obliged to clear more than a single square mile as a precaution.[8]

National Guardsman in fighting gear, with bayonet-tipped rifles, form a cordon around the riot center, Cicero, 1951.

Courtesy of Chicago Historical Society

Not only were the Chicago riots larger and more threatening than Cicero's, but they were only two of many such incidents. The Fernwood riot was the second disorder to erupt at a veterans' housing project; the Airport Homes at 60th and Karlov suffered a riot comparable to that of Cicero in December 1946. Similarly, the block-by-block expansion of the Black Belt was not Englewood's concern alone. To the south of the ghetto, Park Manor endured its worst of several disorders in July 1949 as thousands gathered in the attempt to destroy a black family's newly purchased home. Other Chicago disturbances occurred after the Cicero episode as well. The Trumbull Park Homes, another CHA project on the far South Side, experienced chronic violence for several years in the mid-1950s; beaches and other public facilities became bones of racial contention as the neighborhoods surrounding them changed in these years. The most serious incidents ignited a large portion of the South Side around Calumet Park in the summer of 1957, lasted the better part of a week, and injured at least fifty people.[9]

More than a string of isolated incidents, these events present a pattern which shows that Chicago was undergoing an ordeal by fire in the postwar years as the spatial accommodation of the races underwent adjustment. In the mid-1940s individual attacks — arson, bombings, stonings — against homes sold to blacks in previously all-white areas reached proportions similar to those of the 1917-1921 period, when one racially motivated bombing occurred every twenty days.[10] By the fifties this form of violence was supplemented by another, related to the blacks' consolidation of newly acquired territory. Confrontations over the use of local parks, beaches, and schoolyards followed the increased migration of blacks into previously restricted areas. Large-scale disturbances became less frequent, but those that developed in this context necessarily involved many more assaults on persons than property. The connecting thread, however, was still the battle for living space and the perquisites that went with neighborhood control. The sheer force of numbers was compelling the city to alter its heretofore rigid racial boundaries. It proved to be a painful process.[11]

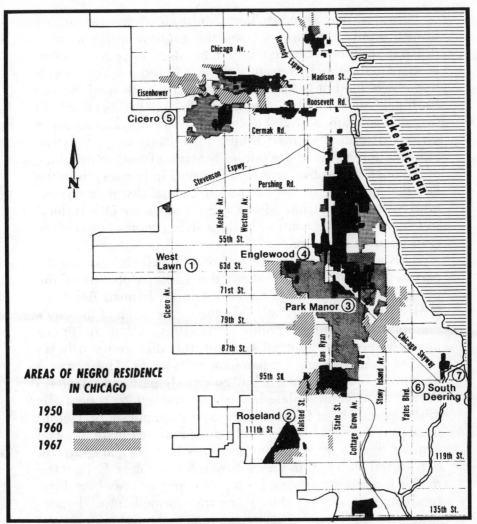

From Chicago's Widening Color Gap, *Interuniversity Social Research Committee: Report No. 2 (Chicago, 1967)*

Locations of the housing disturbances

1 Airport Homes housing project, 1946
2 Fernwood Park housing project, 1947
3 Park Manor (71st and St. Lawrence), 1949
4 Englewood (56th and Peoria), 1949
5 Cicero, 1951
6 Trumbull Park, 1953
7 Calumet Park, 1957

The question remains: how could all of this be hidden from the public at large? Again the contrast with Cicero is illustrative. When Cicero's fifty-man police force lost control of the situation and Chicago's police refused aid, the suburb had no choice but to appeal to the governor to send out the National Guard. On the other hand, Chicago had been able to dispatch as many as 1,200 of its own police to calm far more serious disorders without asking for outside help; thus the city was able to avoid the publicity arising from the presence of bayonet-armed troops. Also of critical importance was the fact that the Cicero riot was the first racial disturbance covered by local television. Most Chicagoans viewed the turmoil in Cicero from the comfort of their living rooms before they read about it in the papers.[12]

This reticence in reporting news of racial violence on the part of the Chicago press kept the earlier riots out of the public eye. The Chicago Commission on Human Relations (CHR) had successfully solicited the cooperation of the city's editors in developing a policy of "circumspection" in reporting news of racial altercations, and the latter voluntarily refrained from running "inflammatory" stories. There was a unanimity born of fear as Chicago's grisly past and uncertain future were contemplated. No one wanted to repeat the mistakes of 1919 or follow the hideous example set by Detroit in 1943. The result was severely truncated treatment of racial conflict, the most extensive accounts being a paragraph or two buried well within the dailies' interior pages. Even if the reader located the stories, he soon found that they bore little semblance to reality: riots were transformed into "demonstrations," the issue of race was never mentioned, and the lists of those arrested provided precious little in the way of explanation.[13]

The primary rationale for this policy was the belief that it kept outsiders away from the scene of disorder. It had long been postulated that "outside agitators" greatly aggravated Chicago's racial tensions. Scholarly analysis seemed to confirm that view. Allen Day Grimshaw, a leading observer of American racial violence, hypothesized in 1959 that the participants in "contested area" riots were not local residents of

those areas. Seeking an explanation for the relative absence
of violence in residential districts during major upheavals,
Grimshaw speculated that those usually operating in contested areas were "outside fanatics" who naturally gravitated
towards the "action" in large riots, thus leaving residential
neighborhoods alone.[14]

An effective way to test this hypothesis is to compile and
analyze *arrest lists* for five of the worst postwar riots.[15] Individually and collectively, such lists demonstrate clearly the
opposite of Grimshaw's hypothesis: the participants in "contested area" riots were, with few exceptions, residents of the
territory involved. Of the total of 319 persons arrested, 78.7
percent lived within one mile of their respective riot areas,
and 87.5 percent lived within one and a half miles; only
22 of the arrestees lived more than three miles away. Most
striking in this regard was the Fernwood riot, where only
7 of the 113 arrestees lived more than twelve blocks from the
officially designated riot area. Moreover, of the 22 "outsiders"
in these five riots, 10 were arrested at the Trumbull Park
Homes disorders — the only incident covered by television,
given national publicity, and of several months' duration.
But even during this disturbance, 7 of every 10 rioters arrested
lived either within the project or less than a mere four blocks
away; 86.1 percent of those arrested here lived within twelve
blocks of the project. Despite the television coverage and
the widespread publicity, the participants in the Trumbull
Park Homes uprising conformed to the pattern established
by the earlier and lesser-known incidents, a pattern which
saw nearly 90 percent of all rioters living within twelve
blocks of their riot scenes (Table I).

The seeming exceptions to these findings, on closer
examination, prove to be no exceptions at all. The Peoria
Street incident in Englewood provides the most illuminating
case. At first glance it appears that the rioters in this episode
came from all over the city; nearly a quarter of the sixty-six
arrested lived more than four miles away from the house
whose rumored sale precipitated the riot (Table II). A look at
the conduct of the police during the riot, however, reveals
that for the first two nights of the disorder police officers were

TABLE I

Residential Proximity of Arrestees to Riot Areas by Number and Percentage

Distance	1947 (a) Fernwood Park	1949 (b) Park Manor	1949 (c) Engle-wood	1953-54 (d) Trumbull Park	1957 (e) Calumet Park	Total
0-4 blocks*	89 (78.8)	9 (50.0)	10 (34.5)	76 (70.4)	35 (68.6)	219 (68.7)
5-8 blocks	13 (11.5)	3 (16.6)	3 (10.3)	5 (4.6)	8 (15.7)	32 (10.0)
9-12 blocks	4 (3.5)	2 (11.1)	9 (31.0)	12 (11.1)	1 (2.0)	28 (8.8)
13-16 blocks	0 (0.0)	1 (5.5)	4 (13.8)	3 (2.8)	1 (2.0)	9 (2.8)
17-24 blocks	2 (1.8)	3 (16.6)	2 (6.9)	2 (1.9)	0 (0.0)	9 (2.8)
25-32 blocks	2 (1.8)	0 (0.0)	1 (3.4)	3 (2.8)	1 (2.0)	7 (2.2)
over 32 blocks	3 (2.7)	0 (0.0)	0 (0.0)	7 (6.5)	5 (9.8)	15 (4.7)
Total	113 (100.1)	18 (99.8)	29 (99.9)	108 (100.1)	51 (100.1)	319 (100.0)

*Eight blocks are equal to one mile.

(a)
Though this riot started at the site of the Fernwood Park Homes, it became a more generalized conflict in which blacks throughout the community were attacked. It was thus deemed more appropriate to measure the distance between the addresses of the arrestees and the main riot area rather than the distance between those addresses and the project proper. The riot area, defined by the deployment of police patrols intended to quarantine the violence, stretched from 95th to 130th and from Michigan Avenue to Vincennes and the city limits.

(b)
All addresses were measured from the intersection of 71st and St. Lawrence; the house under attack was located at 7153 St. Lawrence.

(c)
This riot was also generalized throughout the community. The police, however, did not establish a clearly defined riot area as had been the case at Fernwood. Thus, the intersection of 56th and Peoria, the riot's point of origin, was taken as the base from which to measure the distance between the arrestees' addresses and the scene of the riot. This procedure would, obviously, *overestimate* the distance between the arrestees' homes and the locale of the disorder. Those arrested during the first two nights of rioting here were not included as it was impossible to separate rioters from victims on the arrest lists.

(d)
The project site was the base from which the rioters' addresses were measured.

(e)
This riot began at Calumet Park (95th to 102nd on the lakefront) but spread throughout the area and eventually included disorders at the nearby Trumbull Park Homes. Since the Chicago Commission on Human Relations reported numerous related incidents occurring between the park and the CHA project, the area from 95th to 109th and from Lake Michigan and the Indiana state line to Bensley was considered the riot area. All addresses were measured from that base.

sympathetic to the mob and arrested victims as well as attackers. It was only on the third night, after the Commission on Human Relations complained about police actions, that the authorities cracked down on the rioters rather than on their prey.[16] A comparison of arrests made the third night with those made the previous two nights discloses the distribution anticipated if local residents were indeed the rioters. Three out of four arrested on the third night lived within twelve blocks of the riot scene; all sixteen of those living more than four miles away were arrested during the first two nights and probably were victims. Here, as in other riots, local residents fought to prevent racial change in their neighborhood.

TABLE II

Residential Proximity of Arrestees to Riot Area at 56th and Peoria (Englewood) by Night of Arrest

Distance	All 3 Nights	First 2 Nights	Third Night
0-4 blocks	19	9	10
5-8 blocks	6	3	3
9-12 blocks	9	0	9
13-16 blocks	5	1	4
17-24 blocks	8	6	2
25-32 blocks	3	2	1
over 32 blocks	16	16	0
Total	66	37	29

The central fact that emerges from this analysis is the prominence of local defenders in each of the rioting communities. Placing these findings in the proper historical context, it appears that while there were widely shared assumptions regarding the undesirability of racial change, the various neighborhoods responded to it independently, reacting only as it actually touched them. Consequently, the housing battles, these struggles over "turf," were localized by nature. Black residence in a particular home or use of a specific park were not issues around which a city of millions could be mobilized; they did, however, have a significant local impact on those who perceived themselves to be immediately threatened by such developments. The fact that a wave of such disorders occurred testified only to the magnitude of the changes sweeping the city; it was not, apparently, due to a clique of professional race-haters or outside agitators.* The typical Chicago housing riot was thus a "communal riot" in the most literal sense of the term; each community rose up in its own defense, produced its own defenders, and proceeded to fight for its self-defined goals and interests.

The truly communal nature of these scattered uprisings can be demonstrated in a number of ways. First, though arrest lists supply valuable information regarding the most visibly active participants in any disorder, they tend to emphasize the role played by young males, that social segment from which the "soldiers" in any battle are traditionally drawn. Eyewitness accounts of these housing riots, however, bring into clear relief not only the supportive roles played by older males, but also the truly instrumental part played by women. Many housing riots were complex communal endeavors launched by a demographic cross-section of the areas involved. The division of labor which — more or less — naturally appeared during these disturbances simply placed the young males in the greatest danger of arrest. The relative absence of women, children, and older men from such lists cannot be interpreted as evidence of their nonparticipation.[18] Indeed, the whole community, or at least every segment in it, often took part in housing riots. The violent ones who were most often arrested were the community's representatives, not, as was believed by those denouncing the criminality of "hoodlums," its aberrations.

---

*Significantly, the one violence-prone racist organization that was active in some of these disorders, the White Circle League, was founded in Park Manor *after* that area's worst disorder. Representatives of the League were present at both Trumbull Park and Cicero during those disturbances, but they followed the outbreak of violence there and were the exploiters rather than the precipitators of those incidents. The CHR was well aware of the League's activities and had, in fact, been keeping watch on founder Joseph Beauharnais for months before the League was formally organized. There is no evidence to suggest they had a hand in starting any disorder.[17]

The most destructive mobs, those attacking persons as well as property, had the youngest arrestees. The average age of forty-four persons arrested during the 1957 Calumet Park riot was 22.6 years, and the average age of those arrested on the third night of the Peoria Street disturbance was only 20 years. The Fernwood riot, however, though as violent as any of the others, had rioters who averaged a mature 27.8 years of age. More important, fully 34.3 percent of the 108 arrested rioters for whom information is available were thirty or more years of age. Lending additional weight to the adult-role argument is the fact that 16.6 percent of the Fernwood rioters were over forty and that eight of those (8.3%) were at least fifty years old.

The more typical housing mobs, those that confined themselves largely to harassment and property destruction, had an age distribution similar to that of the Fernwood crowd. The average age of those arrested in the 1949 Park Manor disturbance was 27.1 years; even if one assumes that the four unidentified "juveniles" arrested there were all only 16 years old, the average age of the Park Manor rioters is still 25 years. Over one-fifth (22.2%) of the rioters were at least forty, and one-third (33.3%) were over thirty. The same apparently holds true for the Trumbull Park Homes. Although the incomplete sample suggests caution (ages were found for only 29 of 109 rioters), the data reveal an average age of 33.3 years for these arrestees. Moreover, nearly half of the rioters in South Deering (48.3%) were over thirty years of age, and more than a quarter (27.6%) of them were over forty.

Eyewitness accounts of these disorders provide further proof that they were not merely the productions of bored or uncontrollable youths. The people in Park Manor, for example, displayed their neighborhood ingenuity as police developed techniques for keeping the streets and walks clear in front of the homes of unwanted black neighbors. Families threw open their front porches and yards and furnished legal sanctuary for their friends who, in a grim parody of a community sing, hurled racial epithets and verbal abuse — along with the occasional rock or bottle — at the neighborhood's "intruders." In one 1950 Park Manor disorder, CHR observers reported that "about 150 people had gathered on the porches and in the yards" of five homes within shouting distance of a new black resident. From there "shouting and heckling became ... organized" and cries of "Bring out Bushman," "Get the rope," and "String him up" could be heard. Songs such as "Old Black Joe" and "Carry Me Back to Old Virginny" were sung in derision.[19]

The Cicero and Airport Homes incidents were communal endeavors of a similar sort. An informant for the American Civil Liberties Union mingled with the Cicero crowd and noted its "jovial mood." Another observer reported that "boys and girls," aged twelve to their "late teens," gathered rocks and broke bricks for the older boys to throw. "There was a great deal of camaraderie and spirit of fun throughout this whole group," the observer wrote, "and it was apparent that all were having a good time." Included within that group were adults who encouraged their children's actions and whose approval often "took on the form of urging and initiating the aggression." The same set of circumstances also seems to have prevailed at the Airport Homes, where, official reports state, the crowd was composed of "men and women, boys and girls of all ages."[20]

The broad community participation characteristic of most of these incidents, however, is best demonstrated by the roles played by women. It was a woman who first alerted the Englewood community to the presence of blacks in the home at 56th and Peoria; and adult women, no less than youngsters, were seen arming Cicero's brick throwers.[21] Women were certainly present, if not prominent, in the yards and porches of Park Manor, though CHR reports failed to identify members of these crowds by sex. It was the Airport Homes and the Trumbull Park disorders, though, that demonstrated that women not only supported but at times supplanted men as the most virulent and violent antiblack protestors.

At the Airport Homes the CHA tried to move in black veterans during daylight hours when most of the community's men were at work. The task of protesting, if not preventing, that development consequently fell to the area's women and older men. Both groups kept up a "constant shouting" as

A woman attempting to throw a brick at the Airport housing project loses her balance as a policeman grabs her arm.

officials tried to escort blacks into the project. One eyewitness felt the crowd was composed of "mostly women" who "booed and hissed recognized civic leaders, talked with newspaper photographers, and made numerous threats" before the fighting broke out. When the violence erupted, it was found that "a great many women were in the front ranks of the mob," and it was they who "began to fight with policemen, kicking and scratching and slapping at them." The police, for reasons unknown, made no arrests but were compelled, the *Tribune* noted with a trace of condescension, to "spank unruly housewives" with their clubs in self-defense. It proved a dangerous task: one lieutenant was struck on the head by a missile "while preventing a woman from taking away his . . . club." Thus, while no female names graced any police blotters, their protest was duly registered, and the next day several appeared at the project, pushing their baby carriages while "carrying sticks and bricks."[22]

Women were equally involved in the Trumbull Park Homes disorders. There, as at the Airport Homes, women carried on alone in the front lines when the community's men were away at work. The women seized and freed neighbors arrested by the police and battled the latter, on occasion hand-to-hand. One police sergeant had to be hospitalized after being kicked in the groin by a female rioter. The most notable incident, however, came in October 1953, when the CHA again attempted a midweek daylight move-in of blacks. It was reported that several local women

> . . . literally hurled themselves, first at a truck loaded with the newcomers' furniture, and later at a new car driven by the head of one Negro family. A gray-haired woman of about 65 fell prostrate in front of the car. . . . When the halted car began to inch ahead, the woman clung to its front bumper. Police seized her, and carried her, kicking and fighting, to a curb.

The men of South Deering were not unmoved by that display. At a later fund-raising dinner, the lawyer for the local improvement association paid homage to the three mothers arrested that day and "in tribute to them sang 'Mother Machree'." It was an accolade that could well have been given to the community's women as a group. For the first time, police were compelled to arrest women as well as men in significant numbers. Nearly one out of every five persons held by police in connection with these disturbances (21 of 109) was female.[23]

These communal uprisings and their participants were more than demographically representative of their respective communities. They were also expressions of the general feelings of the city's poorer white "ethnics." As native whites and the more mobile descendants of the "old" immigration moved to the city's periphery or to its suburbs, the children and grandchildren of predominantly Catholic Irish and South and East European immigrants were left to face a rapidly growing and territorially starved black population. Unable — or simply unwilling — to leave their old neighborhoods, the "ethnics" were reacting against their involuntary transformation into natural "buffers" between fleeing whites and inner-city blacks. This growing confrontation between "ethnic and black metropolis" is especially evident in the riots occurring during or after 1949; before then the housing shortage was unrelieved, and even those possessing the means and desire to leave the city were left no alternative to racial succession save the active physical "defense" of their homes.[24] Consequently, one of the earliest housing riots included substantial representation from the "old" as well as the "new" immigration. Once new postwar housing construction permitted the possibility of flight, however, those who wished to avail themselves of it did so and thus not only left behind those who could not similarly leave, but also, in some cases, provided the very vacancies into which blacks could move.

Blacks were fully aware of the sources of the most active and violent opposition to their movement. In each of the major riots occurring in the 1950s, black commentators noted repeatedly, and often disparagingly, the ethnic origins of anti-black rioters. Walter White compared the Cicero crowd to Southern lynch mobs, noting that he had never encountered as much "implacable hatred as I found in Cicero." Significantly, he added that "some of those with whom I talked" had "such thick Bohemian, German, Polish, or Greek accents that it was not always easy to know what they were saying. It was appalling," he concluded, "to see and listen to those who were but recently the targets of hate and deprivations, who, beneficiaries of American opportunity, were as virulent as any Mississippian in their willingness to deny a place to live to a member of a race which had preceded them to America by many generations."[25]

Similar conclusions were drawn by blacks regarding the Trumbull Park Homes disorders, the Calumet Park riot, and lesser 1950s disturbances as well. St. Clair Drake reported on the "vicious and poisonous" propaganda circulating in the neighborhood press serving the Calumet Park area. These local newspapers "boast[ed] that it was Southern and Eastern Europeans who really built this country while Negroes were 'swinging in trees,' 'eating each other'." This, plus an examination of the names of arrested rioters, led him to believe that they were "immigrants and the children of immigrants. . . ."[26] The *Defender* had much the same to say about the Trumbull Park violence and some minor West Side incidents as well. Crowds screaming in "thick foreign-accent[s]" were denounced, as was the "strange paradox" that saw "foreigners, some of them not yet naturalized, who can scarcely speak English," denying freedom and justice to others even as they themselves were seeking these rights. "Evidently the free courses in Americanism which are offered to prospective citizens have failed of their mark," the *Defender* editorialized. "Or perhaps," it concluded even more ominously, "they are taught by people who inject the venom of race prejudice into the bloodstream of the new-comer."[27] The growing sense of frustration and bitterness blacks felt toward these racially aggressive immigrants was epitomized by Chandler Owen, a black social analyst, who urged the adoption of a vigorous deportation campaign as a means of bringing the Trumbull Park violence to an end.[28]

Such impressionistic conclusions about the make-up of the white mobs proved quite accurate. The victims, or their spokesmen, had a fairly clear idea of who their immediate adversaries were. The only real flaw in their identification of antiblack rioters was their omission of Chicago's Irish, who, along with other predominantly Catholic immigrants of later arrival, combined to form the overwhelming majority of nearly every mob.

TABLE III
Ethnicity of Arrestees by Percentage* and Riot

Ethnicity	Fern-wood Park 1947 (N=113)**	Park Manor 1949 (N=18)	Engle-wood 1949 (N=29)	Trum-bull Park 1953-4 (N=109)	Calu-met Park 1957 (N=51)	Total (N= 320)
Anglo	22.4	35.3	16.6	13.6	22.4	19.6
Irish	7.7	25.5	51.2	19.6	18.4	18.2
Slav	4.4	0.0	6.0	25.5	14.5	13.0
Italian	6.5	25.5	0.0	12.0	7.9	9.0
Polish	5.3	0.0	0.0	10.7	16.4	8.2
Southeastern Europe***	6.2	0.0	1.2	6.9	4.6	5.5
Dutch	26.3	0.0	0.0	0.0	0.0	9.4
German	14.7	9.8	22.6	5.7	3.3	10.3
Scandinavian	5.6	0.0	0.0	0.3	0.0	2.1
Jewish	0.0	0.0	0.0	0.0	1.3	0.2
Spanish (surnamed)	0.0	3.9	2.4	4.7	10.5	3.7
Other	0.8	0.0	0.0	0.9	0.7	0.7
Total	99.9	100.0	100.0	99.9	100.0	99.9

* The percentages in the table were produced by averaging the findings of the three independent surveys of the arrest lists.

** N represents the number of those arrested.

***Persons of uncertain nationality but with obviously Southern or Eastern European names were included in this category.

The ethnicity of the rioters (Table III) was determined by examining the names on the arrest lists for the Fernwood riot of 1947, the Park Manor and Englewood riots of 1949, and the Trumbull Park Homes and Calumet Park disorders of the mid-1950s.[29] Only one of the five mobs studied failed to have a majority of its members drawn from Irish and "new" immigrant stock.* As expected, the earliest riot — Fernwood — had only 30.4 percent of its rioters with such surnames. After the Park Manor upheaval, however, the remaining three incidents displayed a mob composition in which approximately 60 percent or more of those arrested appear to have been of Irish or "new" immigrant ancestry. Descendants of the "old" immigration represented 41.4 percent of the more than 300 persons for whom ethnicity was determined but only 26 percent of 200 rioters arrested during or after 1949. In contrast, those of Irish or "new" immigrant origins represented 54 percent of all rioters and 67.2 percent of those arrested in the four later riots (Tables IV and V).

None of the riots is characterized by the exclusive confrontation of a single nationality group defending its ethnically homogeneous territory against a black "invader." Only the riot at 56th and Peoria, where 51.2 percent of those arrested were Irish, had even a bare majority of its participants drawn from a single group. In each of the other riots a liberal mixture of white "ethnics" seemed content to live in close proximity to each other, but not in similar proximity to blacks. Aside from persons with Anglo-sounding surnames, those of Irish and Slavic origin dominated the Calumet Park mob, representing 18.4 percent and 14.5 percent of the known rioters. An additional 24.5 percent of the Calumet Park rioters were either Polish or Italian. At Trumbull Park no group could claim more than 25.5 percent of the rioters as its own; yet the Irish, Slavs, Italians, and Poles represented at least 67.8 percent of that incident's known arrestees. Whatever the degree of white interethnic hostility (and it surely did exist: South Deering's Poles were often heard to complain about the "dago" president of the local improvement association), it was subordinated to an overriding mutual concern. The *De-*

----

*"New" immigrant stock refers to those of Slavic, Polish, or Italian ancestry as well as those of uncertain Southeast European provenance. All subsequent references to the "new" immigration, whether in the text or in tables, will refer to these groups. The descendants of the "old" immigration are considered those of Dutch, Swedish, or German origin; those of apparent "Anglo" ancestry are kept separate throughout this study. All subsequent references to the "old" immigration thus are only to the former three groups.

fender was probably characterizing most housing mobs when it said of one crowd that "although there was no unity in the language backgrounds [of the individuals in the shouting mob], they had a common communicative [*sic*] hatred for Negroes."[30]

TABLE IV
Ethnicity of Rioters by Percentage* and Riot

Ethnicity	Fern- wood Park 1947 (N= 113)**	Park Manor 1949 (N=18)	Engle- wood 1949 (N=29)	Trum- bull Park 1953-4 (N= 109)	Calu- met Park 1957 (N=51)	Total (N= 320)
Anglo + "Old" Immigration	69.0	45.1	39.3	19.6	25.7	41.5
Irish + "New" Immigration	30.4	51.0	58.3	74.8	61.8	54.0
Spanish (surnamed)	0.0	3.9	2.4	4.7	10.5	3.7
Other	0.6	0.0	0.0	0.9	1.9	0.8
Total	100.0	100.0	100.0	100.0	99.9	100.0

*The percentages in the table were produced by averaging the findings of the three independent surveys of the arrest lists.

**N represents the number of those arrested.

TABLE V
Ethnicity of Arrestees by Percentage* and Time of Riot

Ethnicity	All Riots 1947-1957 (N=320)	4 Riots After 1947 (N=207)	2 Riots After 1950 (N=160)
Anglo	19.6	18.0	16.4
Irish	18.2	24.1	19.2
"Old" Immigration	21.8	7.9	5.1
"New" Immigration	35.7	43.0	51.4
Spanish (surnamed)	3.7	5.8	6.6
Other	1.0	1.2	1.3
Total	100.0	100.0	100.0

*The percentages in the table were produced by averaging the findings of the three independent surveys of the arrest lists.

**N represents the number of those arrested.

The components of these ethnic crowds, moreover, did not appear in random fashion. Linked geographically by their proximity to the omnipresent house, apartment, or park that was about to "change" racially, they were nearly as ethnically representative as they were demographically representative of the communities involved. The Irish predominated in Englewood, with the Germans the next most populous foreign-born group. Together these two nationalities supplied 73.8 percent of those taken into custody there. Slavs, Poles, and Italians were the most numerous foreign-born groups in the Calumet Park area in 1960; in 1957 these three groups, or their descendants, provided 47.5 percent of that community's rioters. The same was true of Trumbull Park: Slavs were both the most numerous and the most arrested foreign-born group in the area; Italians and Poles were not far behind in either category. Most significant of all perhaps was the fact that the Roseland community, which supplied most of the Fernwood rioters, had been founded by Dutch farmers, who were followed into the community by Scandinavian, German, Italian, and Polish settlers. The Fernwood riot furnished all the Dutch and virtually all the Scandinavians arrested for racial rioting in Chicago; more than one-third of all the Germans arrested also came from this single disturbance. When the Poles and Italians are added to the other founding groups, fully 58.4 percent of Roseland's rioters are accounted for.[31]

Each of the housing mobs was thus broadly representative of the community in which it was located. Participation was not strictly limited by age, sex, or nationality. The social make-up of the crowd, in general, reflected that of the neighborhood in which it operated. Talk of rioting done only by "hoodlums" or "criminals," however politically satisfying it may have been, was factually meaningless in this context. These were homespun affairs and not the machinations of outside hooligans. This becomes clear when one studies the actions of the mobs; they were far more than mere mindless expressions of racial antipathy.

Despite the independent nature of the uprisings, the behavior of the crowds displayed remarkable similarity. Although often spontaneous in origin, the typical Chicago housing mob was purposeful, both in the targets it selected and in the level of violence it employed to achieve its self-defined goals. Moreover, the duration of the rioting often depended more on the mob's achievement or its prospect of success than on the magnitude and effectiveness of the police forces arrayed against it.

The spontaneity of the violence was evident in the vast majority of cases. The city's first two postwar riots, those at the temporary veterans' quarters at the Airport Homes and Fernwood Park, erupted without benefit of prior planning, despite earlier organized protests against the CHA's non-discriminatory policies. At the Airport Homes, crowds gathered in front of the apartments on the day they were scheduled to be occupied. Their protests were merely verbal until a truck carrying furniture and two black veterans tried to enter the project. At that point, attention shifted immediately to the blacks and their truck; the latter came under immediate attack. Debris found on the ground and clumps of dirt — hardly the arsenal of a mob anticipating violence — served as weapons. The attack on the black veterans was solely the result of their untimely appearance in an exceptionally tense situation; it was neither a well-orchestrated nor a previously organized onslaught. The presence of the veterans was simply the proverbial "last straw" which demonstrated to the crowd that their earlier protests had been to no avail.[32]

At the Fernwood Park Homes there was no single, clearly defined precipitating incident as there was at the Airport Homes. Augmented police forces and a minor car accident, which briefly diverted attention away from the project, permitted the handful of blacks assigned to the apartments to enter peacefully. Violence came only on the following night and, according to official reports, appeared as if by spontaneous generation from a protesting crowd gathered outside the project. Several of those supporting the CHA looked on the mysterious origins of the disturbance with suspicious eyes and charged there was a "conspiracy involved to deprive Negroes of [their] rights." An investigative report on the riot commissioned by the American Jewish Congress, however, noted that these charges came from those who became "highly emotional in condemning the Fernwood community" and concluded, after a sober second look, that "nothing ever materialized to substantiate those suspicions of organized planning behind the violence."[33]

Several other riots were even more clearly spontaneous in origin. The Park Manor disorder at 71st and St. Lawrence began after it became evident that the black man moving furniture into a newly purchased home was not a mere laborer, but the new owner. Here there was no time for planning; people simply filled the streets as word passed through the neighborhood. The ensuing rock-throwing attack on the home caught even the usually alert Chicago Commission on Human Relations by surprise. Through its "listening posts" in communities, its police connections, and its associations with local black organizations, the Commission had always had advance warning when blacks were about to move into an all-white area. This time, however, no one had been forewarned. The move-in, which had been conducted without advance publicity and as unobtrusively as possible, was followed almost immediately by rioting.[34]

Similarly, the disorders at 56th and Peoria and in Calumet Park flowed from events so patently fortuitous that any attempts to ascribe them to prescient conspirators would appear ludicrous. In the former incident, a rumor that a home was being "shown" to blacks sparked the violence. Growing out of the mere appearance of blacks in a local home (they were attending a union meeting), the rumor called forth large crowds which registered a violent protest against the presence of blacks, Jews, University of Chicago students, communists, and "outsiders" in general.[35] In Calumet Park, the attacks on blacks were precipitated by their use of a portion of the park that had previously been "reserved" for whites. It was an event to which white residents could react but not one which they could have planned themselves.[36]

Only the Trumbull Park Homes rioting, which evolved into a war of attrition intended to harass and drive out black project tenants, displayed a considerable degree of planning. But even here the origin of the disturbance was spontaneous.

A gang of whites overturns a car at the Airport Homes project.

The belated discovery that a black woman had "passed" for white in applying for a Trumbull Park apartment prompted the first rock- and bottle-throwing mobs. Only later, after the situation had become a test of wills between the community and the CHA, did the local residents, aided by the South Deering Improvement Association, plan, coordinate, and organize their violent activities.[37]

The absence of prior planning in nearly every case does not mean, however, that the actions of those engaged in them were chaotic or uncontrolled. In terms of target selection, the housing riots were virtual models of limited, purposeful violence. The crowd at the Airport Homes, for example, displayed considerable discrimination in attacking the units occupied by blacks, the trucks moving their furniture, and cars belonging to city officials. The purpose and extreme selectivity of the West Lawn residents is perhaps best shown by the fact that one official's car was overturned and looted even though it was parked several blocks away, and no other property nearby was damaged. The police also came under attack, but this was due to their efforts to protect the blacks and their subsequent position between the crowd and the objects of its anger.[38] The police became a target of the Fernwood crowd under similar conditions, and in this later riot, assaults on nearby black motorists were initially conceived as a tactic to get the police away from the project. An eyewitness to the episode described the scene:

> One of the agitators in the mob yelled that if they could stop traffic, the cops would have to straighten it out, at which time the crowd could break through the weakened police lines and rush the project. So the traffic was impeded. Then a boy shouted "Nigger, Nigger." A stone flew, a safety-glass window crunched. And there started a bloody game of "bash their dirty brains in" which continued unchecked for almost 20 minutes. Every Negro driver was attacked....[39]

The Park Manor and Cicero rioters were no less discriminating in their choice of targets. The main objective of the July 1949 Park Manor mob was the first house bought by blacks in the area south of 71st Street — a street that had been considered a tentative boundary in a changing community. Secondary targets included those homes owned by blacks in the already changing area north of 71st Street. In Cicero the crowd's sole target was the building in which the suburb's new black tenants were to move — a building which the landlord, after a dispute with her tenants, had threatened to open to blacks.[40]

Most notable, perhaps, was the generally limited nature of the violence involved. In Park Manor, as at the Airport Homes, the violence was never random, and despite the fact that the southern border of the Black Belt was a mere five blocks away, there were no assaults on black individuals or forays into the district by white gangs.[41] In Cicero, the crowd was content to merely "pull down" the building that threatened the homogeneity of the community. Indeed, the control of the typical housing mob was such that it asserted itself even when the opportunity for greater violence was clearly present. In a Bridgeport incident, crowds gathered outside a home rumored to have been sold to blacks and attacked it, while less than a quarter of a block away blacks strolled by en route to a White Sox ball game at Comiskey Park. Black transients posed no threat to the residents and were ignored; it was their permanent presence in the area, albeit only rumored, that sparked — but also limited — the mob's actions.[42]

Even in the riots where the violence was escalated to include attacks against people as well as property, the fury of the mob seemed the result of circumstances, given the rioters' perspective, which demanded more drastic action. Before the post-1950 confrontations over the use of community facilities, the Fernwood and Peoria Street disturbances were the most serious in terms of human casualties. The distinguishing feature that separated these neighborhoods from those whose defense took the form of property destruction was the fact that the residents of these areas lacked any alternative to racial succession save the most determined violent resistance. There was no possibility of escape as there was for the more well-to-do in Park Manor; the chronic housing shortage precluded the possibility of flight in 1947, and by 1949 only those with considerable means could afford the small number of relatively expensive homes being constructed. It was also important that each of these communities was being surrounded by black enclaves; their actual "invasion" thus had added significance. Both Fernwood and Englewood had a history of hostile and violent reactions to their becoming white islands in a black sea. The threat was deemed far more serious than the presence of a few isolated blacks, as was the case in the militantly all-white communities surrounding the Airport Homes, Trumbull Park, and the ill-fated building in Cicero. The level of violence increased in Fernwood and Englewood because their desperation and fear were proportionately greater and also because the very situation evoking their anxiety provided ample targets at which to lash out.[43]

The mobs perpetrating the worst violence were, additionally, methodical if not meticulous in their actions. In Calumet

Park, as dusk fell on the scene of whites attacking cars occupied by blacks, white handkerchiefs began to appear on the antennas of those driven by whites so that, in the diminishing visibility, the rioters would have no problems in selecting their targets. While similar conduct has been viewed as evidence of prior planning, it appears that such actions were more the result of common sense than conspiracy.[44]

This sort of calculation was also present in the Peoria Street incident, the one riot considered most "irrational" by contemporaries. Aroused by the rumor that a house was being sold to blacks, the Englewood residents blamed "outsiders" for their problems and attacked an array of "subversives" along with whatever blacks were in the area. Those strangers in the vicinity not identified as enemies by the color of their skin were asked to produce identification by roaming gangs; only *after* their status as an "outsider" was officially ascertained were they attacked.[45]

Ultimately, the best evidence of the control under which even the most violent mobs operated was the actual cessation of rioting on the part of the participants themselves when they felt their sought-after goals had been achieved. While ineffectual police work accompanied — perhaps permitted — many disorders, it was not always the increased exertion of the "forces of social control" which brought an end to disturbance. In at least two cases the political context of events played an equal, if not more instrumental, role than did the police in ending a disorder.

The Fernwood rioters knew well the success violent protest had enjoyed during the troubles at the Airport Homes less than a year before. Mob gatherings had frightened away the first black who was supposed to move in and had done the same to all but two families in the second group assigned. Though not driven off by the rioting, these two brave families had been compelled to leave when gunshots ripped through their apartments. At the time of the Fernwood rioting, the Airport project was, via the means of coercion and intimidation, all-white.[46] Subsequently, a delegation from the afflicted Roseland community conferred with Mayor Martin

Courtesy of Chicago Historical Society

An embattled couple in Trumbull Park tests the plywood panel that serves as a barrier against bricks and other missiles.

Kennelly while the Fernwood riot was in progress and left with the impression "that some plan would be worked out whereby Negro families would be removed from the project and that keeping quiet was the community's part of the bargain." CHR observers in the neighborhood reported that "such was the 'talk' in the community" and felt that this, in conjunction with increased police activity, produced the "sudden calm" that descended on the area after days of bitter fighting.[47]

The ebb and flow of violence at the Trumbull Park Homes

was also closely keyed to political developments. After nearly
a year of intermittent destructive protests over the presence
of blacks in the project, several clashes took place during the
summer of 1954 as black groups from outside the community
tried to use the athletic facilities within Trumbull Park.
Though white residents had failed to have the black families
removed from the area, they had been successful in denying
free access to public facilities to all blacks — including those
from the project. After a serious incident between local residents and blacks who had been using one of the park's
baseball fields, community representatives met with city
political leaders and returned claiming a "deal" had been
struck. The number of black families in the nearly 500-unit
project would be limited to twenty, the leaders said, if only
the violence would cease. When publicized, city fathers denied making any such "deal," but the next week black dem-
onstraters played ball unmolested in the same park where
they had been mobbed just a few days before. Members of
the South Deering Improvement Association had made sure
that those unwilling to compromise on a minimal black presence in the area stayed away from the park. However much a
"deal" might have been denied, it remained a fact that no
more than roughly twenty black families lived in Trumbull
Park Homes at any one time throughout the decade.[48]

This close interaction between crowds in the street,
community representatives, and city fathers reveals that not
only were the actions of these homegrown mobs purposeful
to the participants themselves, but that they were purposeful
in the broader sense of having an impact on the community at
large. Insofar as it shaped and altered public policy, the
"creative disorder" of the 1940s and 1950s benefited whites
rather than blacks.

The clearest indication of this may be seen in the public
housing controversies that swirled around the Chicago Housing Authority at this time. Not only was the CHA responsible
for providing low-cost homes for those ignored by private
builders, but, given the housing shortage, the Authority was
the key to the city's redevelopment program. Until the poor
were moved off valuable inner-city property and placed in

"relocation" housing, no land would be available for the fulfillment of the developer's dreams.[49] Since the poor involved were mostly black, the CHA had to deal directly with the problem of segregation. In the two areas where the issue presented itself most insistently — tenant selection and site selection — the CHA proved responsive to white resistance against changes in the status quo.

At first it did not appear that this would be the case. The emergency veterans' housing program saw the CHA erect temporary shelters all over the city. The fact that most were located in white areas did not prevent the CHA from selecting its tenants on a nondiscriminatory basis.[50] However, this program quickly provoked violent reactions at the Airport Homes and Fernwood Park. It was to be the last significant attempt to implement a public housing program that employed both scattered sites and a policy of nondiscrimination.

The CHA was able to embark on this limited experiment only because of its independence from the Chicago City Council. Legally, it was not responsible to the council for either its site selections or its policies. Politically, it enjoyed the sponsorship of Mayor Edward J. Kelly until the spring of 1947. With the protests at the Airport Homes, though, came the first calls for the curtailment of the Authority's power. Alderman Michael Hogan, representing the people surrounding the Airport project site, presented a petition to the city council just days before violence erupted asking that the CHA be brought under the authority of the mayor and the council. Reginald DuBois, the alderman in whose ward the Fernwood project was located, declined to introduce a similar resolution while that riot was in progress only because of an agreement with black alderman Archibald Carey, Jr.; both felt the necessity for public restraint in a tense situation. After a cooling-off period of two months, however, DuBois finally did offer the resolution that led to the subordination of the CHA.[51]

DuBois charged the CHA with inefficiency and mismanagement and called for an official investigation. His main complaint, though, was that the CHA "persist[ed] in theories of housing which are shared by no other representative governmental agencies . . . and are not in accord with those of a great majority of citizens." Though couched in such formal language, it was evident to all informed observers that the charges of mismanagement were being used as a "cover" to attack the CHA for its racial policy. The editors of the *Chicago Defender* denounced the "little bund of rabid racists" seeking the investigation, and even the genteel Board of Directors of the reformist Metropolitan Housing Council was informed that those bringing charges against the CHA "really have the Authority race policy in mind."[52] The City Council eventually cleared the CHA in a generally laudatory

Mayor Martin Kennelly congratulates CHA Chairman Robert R. Taylor (far right) at the Dearborn Homes groundbreaking. Others pictured are Dr. Edward Welters, Chairman of the People's Welfare Organization; Miss Elizabeth Wood, CHA Executive Secretary; and John Sengstacke, publisher of the *Chicago Defender*.

Courtesy of University of Illinois Library at Chicago Circle, Manuscripts Division

Dr. Edward A. Welters   Mr. John Sengstacke   Mayor Kennelly   Mr. Robert R. Taylor
Miss Elizabeth Wood

report; buried within that report, however, was a council policy statement of the greatest significance.

In issuing its findings exonerating the CHA, the council included a request that it be granted veto power over the CHA's site selection process.[53] The state legislature granted the council the powers it sought in 1949, and the CHA became the only housing authority in the state to have its prerogatives so restrained. The CHA commissioners knew at the time the law was passed that it meant "the end of public housing sites in good residential areas." Ex-commissioner Robert R. Taylor was to say later that he knew the battle to distribute public housing throughout the city "was lost" when the Illinois General Assembly acceded to the council's request — a request resulting from the desire to "prevent the influx of Negroes into white neighborhoods" and from the "pressure of public opinion."[54]

The result was predictable. Although the aldermen were compelled to provide some public housing, they granted, in effect, final approval of public housing sites to protesting whites in the outlying neighborhoods. The CHA's attempt to gain sites in accord with "sound planning principles" proved futile; the "Big Boys" in the council dictated the placement of public housing within the current ghetto boundaries, thus fixing and institutionalizing its borders as they had never been before.[55] By the mid-1950s the CHA refused to submit sites they knew would be controversial, knowing the futility of doing so; their later selections merely completed the process which enshrined a racially and economically segregated South State Street in poured steel and concrete.[56]

It was also during these years that the pressure from violent white resistance to neighborhood change made itself felt in the CHA's tenant selection policy. The CHA was on record as favoring nondiscrimination, but it faced a problem with the older Depression-era projects, which had been occupied under the federal "neighborhood composition" guideline; located in white areas, their tenants were white, and now this pattern had the weight of tradition behind it. Four such projects were kept all-white out of deference to local attitudes, and the situation was exposed only after a fair-skinned black was admitted to the Trumbull Park Homes. After that, the CHA still proclaimed its adherence to a policy of nondiscrimination and, of course, could not publicly back down. However, the commissioners spoke privately of integrating the projects only at a rate consistent with the maintenance of "law and order." The chairman of the CHA, Wilfred Sykes, summarized his own stance when he stated that the CHA had to weigh the views of three million whites against those of a half-million blacks. Such considerations proved paramount; the process of integration would take years.[57]

Thus the CHA, the one governmental agency that might have challenged the city's racial status quo, found itself responding directly and favorably to white protestors taking violent action or to those powers acting in their behalf. In terms of the CHA's tenant selection policy, the link between violent reaction and government response was clear and direct: as long as whites were willing to fight to keep blacks out of the projects already established in their areas, the CHA was unwilling to forcibly speed their integration. In terms of the more important site-selection process, the link is less direct but present nonetheless. City Council pressure, which was itself the institutional response to the violent reactions precipitated by the veterans' housing program, produced the state law that enabled the council to substitute its own will for that of the CHA.[58]

The efficacy of violence was made even more explicit during the confrontation between the CHA and the City Council over the first slate of project sites. Alderman John J. Duffy, the reigning power in the council after Kelly's retirement and the engineer of the "deal" which culminated in the CHA's acceptance of ghetto sites, seemed to have a healthy respect for those who fought. In chastising an alderman who opposed him and consequently had some public housing slated for his ward, Duffy said: "The trouble with you Jews is, when you get backed up against the wall you start crying. When we Irish were backed up against the wall . . . we used clubs, we used bricks, we used stones. But what do you Jews do? You don't fight. You start crying. Well, you asked for it and you're going to get it."[59]

It was in this fashion that the violence that was kept so carefully hidden from the general public made its most lasting impression. The parameters of social change were delimited not by those seeking it, but by the violent and purposeful actions of those challenged by it.

By the late 1950s the worst of the violence was over, as neighborhoods that had been cracked open earlier filled with new residents, and as increasing suburban construction provided alternatives for those unwilling to stay in the city. By that time, however, the key decisions shaping race relations in the city for the next generation had been made. In an era that saw the massive expansion of the old Black Belt, no fundamental alteration in the pattern of segregation was permitted; if anything, that pattern was now reinforced by government sanction and public funds. As civil rights forces mobilized in the South, and the *Brown v. Board of Education of Topeka, Kansas* decision of 1954 was hailed as a possible new beginning in American race relations, Chicago moved in the opposite direction by institutionalizing a greatly enlarged black ghetto and admonishing potential newcomers to stay away.

Speaking in 1957, Francis W. McPeek, executive director of the CHR, issued a "friendly warning" to those planning to come to Chicago looking for work. While he did not wish to discourage those with "energy, drive, and initiative" from migrating to Chicago, he emphasized the housing problems for minorities and felt compelled to remind them that "not even Carl Sandburg ever referred to this town as a bed of roses."[60] With the recent rioting in Calumet Park clearly on his mind, he held out a welcome sign which read simply: "Enter at your own risk."

Contributors

MELVIN G. HOLLI is Professor of History and Director of the Urban Historical Collection at the University of Illinois at Chicago Circle. He is the author of *Reform in Detroit: Hazen S. Pingree and Urban Politics*, and *Detroit* in the New Viewpoints' Documentary History of American Cities Series.

PETER d'A. JONES is Professor of History at the University of Illinois at Chicago Circle and the author of several books, including *Since Columbus: Pluralism and Poverty in the History of the Americas* and *The USA: A History of Its People and Society* (two volumes).

CHARLES BRANHAM is Assistant Professor of history at the University of Illinois at Chicago Circle. He was a writer and coproducer of the television series "The Black Experience," which won an Emmy from the Chicago chapter of the National Academy of Arts and Sciences. He is completing his Ph.D., a study of Chicago's black politics, at the University of Chicago.

VICTOR R. GREENE is Associate Professor of history and coordinator of the ethnic studies program at the University of Wisconsin—Milwaukee. He is the author of numerous articles and two books on ethnicity: *Slavic Community on Strike: Immigrant Labor in Pennsylvania Anthracite* and *For God and Country: The Rise of Polish and Lithuanian Ethnic Consciousness in America, 1860-1910*.

ARNOLD HIRSCH is completing a study of Chicago's racial and housing problems for his Ph.D. at the University of

Illinois at Chicago Circle, where he is a research associate and teaching assistant.

EDWARD R. KANTOWICZ is Associate Professor of history at Carleton University and the author of *Polish-American Politics in Chicago.*

LOUISE AÑO NUEVO KERR is Assistant Professor of history at Loyola University and the author of several papers and articles on Mexican-Americans in Chicago and the Midwest. She is completing a volume on the twentieth-century experience of Chicanos in the United States, to be published next year in Indiana University Press's Minorities in America series.

HUGO P. LEAMING is a lecturer in history at the University of Illinois at Chicago Circle, where he is completing a doctoral study of triracial fugitive communities.

EDWARD H. MAZUR is Associate Professor of social sciences and urban studies in the Citywide Institute of the City Colleges of Chicago. His doctoral dissertation, "Minyans For A Prairie City: The Politics of Chicago Jewry, 1850-1940," was completed at the University of Chicago.

JACQUELINE PETERSON is a research associate for the *Atlas of Great Lakes Indian History*, being prepared at the Newberry Library. She is completing her doctoral dissertation, a study of eighteenth- and nineteenth-century Indian and *métis* groups of the Great Lakes region, at the University of Illinois at Chicago Circle.

Notes

Chapter I: "Wild" Chicago

This chapter derives from research initially begun under the supervision of the late Professor Gilbert Osofsky at the University of Illinois at Chicago Circle. It owes much to his inspiration and is written in his honor.

1 Earliest descriptions of the Chicago portage, with its frozen marshes and floods, are those of Marquette, Joliet, and LaSalle, 1674-1682. See A.T. Andreas, *History of Chicago, From the Earliest Period to the Present Time* (Chicago, 1884), I, 44-45. Later descriptions can be found in Henry Rowe Schoolcraft, "A Journey up the Illinois River in 1821," in Milo M. Quaife, ed., *Pictures of Illinois One Hundred Years Ago* (Chicago, 1918), pp. 120-121; Gurdon Hubbard, "Recollections of First Year," Gurdon Hubbard Papers, Chicago Historical Society; Charles Cleaver, *Early Chicago Reminiscences* (Chicago, 1882), pp. 28, 30, 46; Edwin O. Gale, *Early Chicago and Vicinity* (Chicago, 1902), p. 105; Colbee C. Benton, in Paul Angle, ed., *Prairie State: Impressions of Illinois* (Chicago, 1968), p. 114; Bessie Louise Pierce, *A History of Chicago, 1673-1848* (New York, 1937), pp. 6-12.

2 Cleaver, pp. 28-29; Andreas, p. 192; "Remarks of Hon. George Bates," *Michigan Historical Collections*, 40 vols. (Lansing, 1877-1929), II, 180-181.

3 William H. Keating was one of the more outspoken critics of Chicago as a site for future settlement. See his *Narrative of an Expedition to the Source of St. Peter's River, Lake Winnepeek, Lake of the Woods, etc. Performed in the Year 1823....* (London, 1825), I, 162-163, 165-166. For more favorable comments, see James Herrington to Jacob Herrington, Chicago, January 27, 1831, in Alphabetical File: James Herrington, Chicago Historical Society; "Recollections of First Year," p. 20; Charles Butler Journal, Friday, August 2, 1833, in Letter File: Charles Butler, Chicago Historical Society; Benton, *A Visitor to Chicago In Indian Days*, Paul M. Angle and James R. Getz, eds. (Chicago, 1957), p. 76; Andreas, p. 129. Charlotte Erickson's "The British Immigration in the Old Northwest, 1815-1860," in David M. Ellis, ed., *The Frontier in American Development* (Ithaca, N.Y., 1969) is an interesting study of the British exception to the American farmer's aversion to prairie living during this period.

4 Gale, pp. 105-106; Cleaver, p. 28; Andreas, p. 207. Wolves were numerous on Chicago's north side as late as 1834.

5 See Cleaver, p. 30 for description of street drainage and building raising. Population estimates for the years 1833-1837 vary somewhat: Andreas claimed that the town grew from 200 in 1833 to 4,000 in 1837 (p. 142); a visitor's estimate in 1833 was 350, as cited in Angle, p. 64. Pierce (p. 14) lists 3,989 whites and 77 blacks in 1837.

6 See the Augustus Dilg Collection and the Albert Scharf Papers, Chicago Historical Society. See also Andreas, Ch. 1, and Louis Deliette, "Memoir Concerning the Illinois Country," Theodore C. Pease and Raymond C. Werner, eds., *Collections of the Illinois State Historical Library*, XXIII, French Series 1 (1934) (a copy signed "DeGannes" is in the Edward Everett Ayer Collection, Newberry Library, Chicago); Hiram Beckwith, *The Illinois and Indiana Indians* (Chicago, 1884), pp. 99-117; Raymond E. Hauser, "An Ethnohistory of the Illinois Indian Tribe, 1673-1832" (Ph.D. diss., Northern Illinois University, 1973).

7 For geographic movement and settlement patterns of the Great Lakes tribes, see George Quimby, *Indians in the Upper Great Lakes Region, 11,000 B.C. to A.D. 1800* (Chicago, 1960) and James E. Fitting and Charles Cleland, "Late Prehistoric Settlement Patterns in the Upper Great Lakes," *Ethnohistory*, XVI (1969), 289-302. For cultural variations, see W. Vernon Kinietz, *The Indians of the Western Great Lakes, 1615-1760* (Occasional Contributions from the Museum of Anthropology of the University of Michigan, No. 10, 1940; reprinted by University of Michigan Press, 1965).

8 Quimby, p. 110.

9 *Ibid.*, pp. 109-115. The 1600-1760 estimated population density of the Great Lakes tribes of one per square mile assumes that Great Lakes peoples were subsistence farmers as well as hunters during this period. A growing literature concerns the impact of the fur trade upon Indian society: see, most recently, Calvin Martin, "The European Impact on the Culture of a Northeastern Algonquian Tribe: An Ecological Interpretation," *William and Mary Quarterly*, XXXI, Ser. 1 (1974), 3-26.

10 Quimby, pp. 147-151. See also Quimby, *Indian Culture and European Trade Goods* (Madison, Wis., 1966); Harold Hickerson, *The Chippewa and Their Neighbors: A Study in Ethnohistory* (New York, 1970); Felix M. Keesing, "The Menomini Indians of Wisconsin," *Memoirs of the American Philosophical Society*, X (1939); and Arthur J. Ray, *Indians in the Fur Trade: Their Role as Trappers, Hunters, and Middlemen in the Lands Southwest of Hudson Bay 1660-1870* (Toronto, 1974).

11 Quimby, *Indians in the Upper Great Lakes*, pp. 151 and *passim*. That traditional authority was threatened is indicated by the tribal attempt to integrate British and American fathers into the patrilineal clan structure. Britishers were made members of a new clan, "the Lion," and Americans, "the Eagle."

12 Andreas, pp. 34-45; James A. Clifton, *The Prairie People: Continuity and Change in Potawatomi Indian Culture, 1665-1965* (Lawrence,

Kan., 1977); Erminie Wheeler-Voegelin and David B. Stone, *Indians of Illinois and Northwestern Indiana* (New York, 1974).

13 Quimby, pp. 147-151; John Kinzie Papers and Accounts, Chicago Historical Society; the Chicago Historical Society's collection of material artifacts, particularly the Fort Dearborn display; Arthur Woodward, *The Denominators of the Fur Trade* (Pasadena, Cal., 1970), pp. 22-23, and *passim.*

14 Madore Beaubien Papers, Beaubien Family Papers (including information on Chief Alexander Robinson) and Billy Caldwell Papers, Chicago Historical Society. See also Jacqueline Peterson, "Ethnogenesis: Métis Development and Influence in the Great Lakes Region, 1690-1836" (Ph.D. diss., University of Illinois, Chicago Circle, 1977).

15 Juliette Kinzie, *Wau-bun, The Early Days in the Northwest* (Chicago, 1932), pp. 193-194; Beaubien Family Papers, Chicago Historical Society.

16 John Kinzie Papers and Accounts, Chicago Historical Society; "Recollections of First Year," Gurdon S. Hubbard Papers; American Fur Company Papers, Letter Books, Chicago Historical Society; John Jacob Astor to Ramsay Crooks, New York, Mar. 17, 1817, in *Collections of the State Historical Society of Wisconsin* (Madison, 1854-1931), XIX, 451. See also Gordon Charles Davidson, *The Northwest Company* (New York, 1918); David Lavender, *The Fist in the Wilderness* (Garden City, N.Y., 1964); John D. Haeger, "The American Fur Company and the Chicago of 1812-1835," *Journal of the Illinois State Historical Society* (Summer 1968), 117-139.

17 Account Books, American Fur Company Papers, Chicago Historical Society. Details of the estates of the American Fur Company's competition at Chicago, William Wallace and John Crafts, are given in Ernest B. East's "Contributions to Chicago History from Peoria County Records," Part I, *Journal of the Illinois State Historical Society* (Mar.-Dec. 1938), 197-207. See especially Robert Stuart to John Crafts, Aug. 20, 1824; Mar. 2, 1825; Aug. 26, 1824, American Fur Company Papers, Chicago Historical Society.

18 John Kinzie Papers and Accounts, Chicago Historical Society; Robert Stuart to Astor, Sep. 12, 1825, American Fur Company Papers, Chicago Historical Society.

19 Quimby, pp. 1-20. In 1800, most of the land at Chicago was free of water at least half of the year. The lake continues to recede.

20 Cleaver, pp. 15-16; Juliette Kinzie, pp. 205-211; Keating, pp. 165-166.

21 Juliette Kinzie, pp. 209-211; Benton in Paul Angle, *Prairie State*, pp. 112-114; Surgeon John Cooper's description in James Grant Wilson Papers, Chicago Historical Society; Captain John Whistler, 1808, Fort Dearborn Papers, Chicago Historical Society.

22 Robert Stuart to John Kinzie, Oct. 22, 1825, American Fur Company Papers, Chicago Historical Society; Juliette Kinzie, p. 215; testimony of Mary Galloway, wife of Archibald Clybourne, in Andreas, *History of Chicago*, p. 103; Ernest B. East, "The Inhabitants of Chicago, 1825-1831," *Journal of the Illinois State Historical Society* (1944), 155.

23 Keating, in Angle, p. 84; Marshall Smelser, "Material Customs in the
Territory of Illinois," *Journal of the Illinois State Historical Society*
(Apr. 1936), 17; Andreas, p. 134; Beaubien Family Papers, Chicago
Historical Society; "Beaubiens of Chicago," MS in Frank Gordon
Beaubien Papers, Chicago Historical Society.

24 Information concerning Jean Baptiste Point du Sable is elusive. For a
brief sketch, see Lyman Draper interview with Robert Forsyth in
Lyman S. Draper Manuscripts, S, XXII (1868), 104, Wisconsin Historical Society, Madison, Wisconsin. See also Milo M. Quaife,
Checagou (Chicago, 1933), p. 90; Pierce, *A History of Chicago*,
p. 13; William C. Smith to James May, Fort Dearborn, Dec. 9, 1803,
William C. Smith Papers, Chicago Historical Society; "Beaubiens of
Chicago," Frank Gordon Beaubien Papers, Chicago Historical
Society. The Wayne County records at Detroit, Michigan show the
sale of du Sable's house to Lalime, as well as several Indian grants of
land to Kinzie at Detroit. Pierre Menard claimed to have purchased
a tract of land on the north bank of the Chicago River from an "Indian"
named Bonhomme and later sold it to the Kinzies for $50. No houses
are mentioned in these transactions.

25 Juliette Kinzie, p. 210. There is a drawing in the Augustus Dilg Collection, Chicago Historical Society, of the old Kinzie house which
fairly matches Mrs. Kinzie's description. See also John Wentworth,
Early Chicago (Chicago, 1876), p. 23, and Elizabeth Therese Baird,
"Reminiscence of Early Days on Mackinac Island," *Collections of
the State Historical Society of Wisconsin*, XIV, 25. For a description
of the "poteaux en terre" of the lower Illinois country, see John
Reynolds, *The Pioneer History of Illinois* (Belleville, Ill., 1852),
pp. 30-31.

26 Smelser, pp. 18-19; John McDermott, ed., *The French in the Mississippi Valley* (Urbana, Ill., 1965), pp. 26-40. For a description of
"half-breed" housing, see John H. Fonda in *Collections of the State
Historical Society of Wisconsin*, V, 232; Peterson,. *op. cit.*, Ch. 5.

27 Jane F. Babson, "The Architecture of Early Illinois Forts," *Journal of
the Illinois State Historical Society* (Spring 1968), 9-40; Fred Kniffer,
"Folk Housing: Key to Diffusion," *Annals of the Association of
American Geographers* (Dec. 1965); Interview by Milo M. Quaife of
Emily (Beaubien) LeBeau, Aug. 3, 1911, in Emily LeBeau Papers,
Chicago Historical Society.

28 "The water lay 6 inches to 9 inches deep the year round," according to
Cleaver, p. 30. See also "William B. Ogden," *Fergus Historical
Series*, No. 17 (Chicago, 1882), 45; Benton in Angle, p. 114; Quaife,
Checagou, p. 78.

29 John Kinzie Papers and Accounts, Chicago Historical Society; F.
Clever Bald, *Detroit's First American Decade, 1796-1805* (Ann
Arbor, 1948), p. 12. See also Eleanor Lytle Kinzie Gordon, *John
Kinzie, the Father of Chicago: A Sketch* (1910). This inflated family
history suggests that Kinzie lived in New York City and ran off to
Quebec to learn a silversmith's trade, a plausible though unsub-
stantiated story.

30 John Kinzie Papers and Accounts; Quaife, p. 95; Pierce, p. 21; Lyman S. Draper Manuscripts, S, XXII (1868), 102, Wisconsin Historical Society, Madison, Wisconsin; Clifton, "Captain Billy Caldwell."

31 Surgeon John Cooper of the first garrison at Fort Dearborn said that Kinzie was a man of "ungovernable temper," who had bitter quarrels with people; Cooper also charged Kinzie with Lalime's murder. See the James Grant Wilson Papers, Chicago Historical Society. See also *Hyde Park-Kenwood Voices*, III, No. 8 (1960), in John Kinzie Papers; Matthew Irwin to William Eustis, Chicago, July 3, 1812, in Lewis Cass Papers, II, Clements Library, Ann Arbor, Michigan.

32 Bald, p. 76; John Kinzie Papers and Accounts.

33 John Kinzie Papers and Accounts; Andreas, pp. 90-91; Lewis Cass to John Calhoun, Jan. 9, 1819, Lewis Cass Papers, Burton Historical Collection, Detroit Public Library.

34 John Kinzie Papers and Accounts; Robert Stuart to Astor, Sep. 12, 1825, American Fur Company Papers; Robert Stuart to J.B. Beaubien, Sep. 11, 1825, American Fur Company Papers; Gurdon Hubbard, Jan. 2, 1828, Gurdon S. Hubbard Papers.

35 Conway, p. 405 and *passim;* Charles J. Kappler, ed., *Indian Affairs. Law and Treaties* (Washington, D.C., 1904), II, 402-404; James R. Clifton, "Captain Billy Caldwell: The Reconstruction of an Abused Identity," paper read at the American Historical Association meetings, Dec. 1976, Washington, D.C.

36 Eleanor L. K. Gordon, *John Kinzie, Father of Chicago*, p. 28; John Kinzie Papers and Accounts; Ramsay Crooks to John Kinzie, Oct. 29, 1819 and Aug. 11, 1819 and Robert Stuart to Kinzie, 1826-1827, in American Fur Company Papers.

37 Between 1829 and 1830 alone, prominent Chicagoans Archibald Clybourne, Samuel Miller, Archibald Caldwell, Mark Beaubien, Alexander Robinson, and Russell Heacock were licensed to keep tavern. See Ernest East, "Contributions to Chicago History From Peoria County Records," Part II, *Journal of the Illinois State Historical Society* (1938), 328-329; "Beaubiens of Chicago," Frank Gordon Beaubien Papers, Chicago Historical Society.

38 Kinzie Family Papers; Gale, p. 125.

39 Juliette Kinzie, p. 209.

40 *Ibid.*, p. 205.

41 See Keating in Angle, *Prairie State*, pp. 84-86. Mrs. Kinzie's *Wau-bun*, while an important historical document, is unfortunately skewed to favor the family's social aspirations.

42 Juliette Kinzie Papers, Chicago Historical Society; Eleanor L. K. Gordon, pp. 6-7. Trader Clark's first name is listed variously as John and Alexander. Mrs. Kinzie omitted this branch of the Kinzie family in her *Wau-bun*.

43 Gordon, *loc. cit.*; Andreas, pp. 101-102.

44 Andreas, p. 100; John Kinzie Papers; Robert Stuart to John Crafts, Mar. 2, 1825, American Fur Company Papers.

45 Andreas, pp. 100-102; Wentworth, *Early Chicago*, Supplemental Notes, pp. 34-35.

46 East, "Contributions," Part II, 329-331, 336-339; East, "The Inhabitants of Chicago, 1825-1831," *passim.*

47 The canal section, platted and sold in 1831, held the only lots on the market when the Eastern speculators began to arrive in 1833. Its location, the central loop, gave it a speculative advantage over areas further away from the new harbor. The Kinzie family did not pre-empt the Point, and it went to southerners who did not have a flair for exciting the Eastern interest. See Andreas, pp. 111, 130-132; also Gale, p. 54.

48 Mark Beaubien Papers, Chicago Historical Society; Andreas, pp. 106, 288-289.

49 For the *habitant* dancing tradition, see John Reynolds, *The Pioneer History of Illinois*, pp. 52-53. Cleaver, *Early Chicago Reminiscences*, pp. 5-12; John H. Kinzie Papers; "John Dean Caton Recollections," *Reception to the Settlers of Chicago Prior to 1840, by the Calumet Club of Chicago, Tuesday evening, May 27, 1879* (Chicago, 1879), 36-37. For a discussion of the liquor problem, see Marshall Smelser, pp. 11-13; Thomas Forsyth to General William Clark, Peoria, Apr. 9, 1824, Thomas Forsyth Papers, Folder 2, Missouri Historical Society, St. Louis, Missouri.

50 Juliette Kinzie, p. 205; Beaubien Family Papers.

51 "John Wentworth's Recollections," Calumet Club, pp. 42, 48; Cleaver, p. 13. Beaubien's tavern was only 16 by 24 feet, yet in 1833-34, forty people were being boarded in shifts. No one knows how many people actually slept there in a given evening.

52 "John Wentworth's Recollections," Calumet Club, pp. 49, 71. In the winter of 1835-36, prominent Easterners and the Kinzies built the Lake House on the North Side. Gale said "they ain't going to call it no tavern," and Cleaver said there was a joke circulating that no one worth less than $10,000 would be allowed to stay there. Weekly dancing parties were held there by invitation only. At least some of the French Creoles were being included; there is an 1843 dance ticket in the Beaubien Family Papers requesting the company of the "misses Beaubien." See also "Beaubiens of Chicago," Frank Gordon Beaubien Papers; Gale, p. 118.

53 On the Beaubien farm at Grosse Pointe, see Bald, p. 35. Beaubien was early Chicago's most colorful character, according to most Easterners' recollections. He is mentioned in nearly every old settler's reminiscences, especially in Gale, Cleaver, the John Wentworth Papers, Chicago Historical Society, and "Sketch of Hon. J. Young Scammon," *Chicago Magazine*, Mar. 1857, reprinted in *Fergus Historical Series*, No. 5 (Chicago, 1876). See "Beaubiens of Chicago," Frank Gordon Beaubien Papers and Beaubien Family Papers, for particulars, and Andreas (p. 107) for a physical description. "His favorite dress on 'great occasions' was a swallow-tail coat with brass buttons. . . . He was in his glory at a horse-race."

54 Andreas, pp. 85, 174; East, "Contributions," Part I, pp. 191-197.

55 East, "Contributions," Part I, pp. 191-197; Wentworth, *Early Chicago*, p. 41.

56 *Ibid.*

57 See Jean Baptiste Beaubien Papers for original voting lists; "Beaubiens of Chicago," Frank Gordon Beaubien Papers; Andreas, pp. 600-602.

58 Andreas, p. 602; East, "The Inhabitants of Chicago," *passim.*

59 Regarding the first Board of Trustees, see Andreas, pp. 174-175; *Chicago Democrat* (Dec. 10, 1833).

60 John Kinzie Papers, Madore Beaubien Papers, and Beaubien Family Papers; for a vivid description of Reverend See, see Juliette Kinzie, p. 216.

61 For a description of private schools in Detroit, see Bald, pp. 88-91; Beaubien Family Papers.

62 "The Beaubiens of Chicago," Frank Gordon Beaubien Papers; Madore Beaubien and Billy Caldwell Papers; Clifton, "Captain Billy Caldwell."

63 John Kinzie Papers; Madore Beaubien 1881 and 1882 letters, Madore Beaubien Papers; Andreas, pp. 204-209.

64 Andreas, p. 205; Mary Ann Hubbard, *Family Memories* (printed for private circulation, 1912), p. 68.

65 Andreas, p. 205; letter from John Watkins in Calumet Club, pp. 73-74.

66 Andreas, pp. 299-301; Reverend Jeremiah Porter, *Early Chicago's Religious History* (Chicago, 1881), pp. 54-58.

67 Andreas, pp. 288-289; Gale, p. 60.

68 Andreas, p. 289; Porter, pp. 56-57.

69 Gale, p. 60; Andreas, p. 289.

70 Andreas, pp. 174, 111-124; Beaubien Family Papers.

71 Andreas, pp. 132-133; *Chicago Democrat*, Nov. 26, 1833; Wentworth, *Early Chicago*, pp. 39-40.

72 John Wentworth to Lydia Wentworth, Nov. 10, 1836, John Wentworth Papers, Chicago Historical Society; Madore Beaubien Papers; Harriet Martineau, in *Reminiscences of Early Chicago* (Chicago, 1912), p. 30; Cleaver, p. 27.

73 Charles Fenno Hoffman, in *Reminiscences of Early Chicago*, pp. 21-22; Beaubien Family Papers; Porter, p. 78; Cleaver, pp. 5, 12. According to Cleaver, large hunts of over 100 men were still being held in 1834. He describes improvised sleighs built by setting crockery crates filled with hay on two young saplings shaved at the end to create runners. See Reynolds, p. 229, for the French Creole habit of cardplaying on Sunday.

74 Cleaver, p. 12. For descriptions of the Guignolée and other French customs transplanted in the Illinois country, see Natalia Maree Belting, *Kaskaskia Under the French Regime*, Illinois Studies in the Social Sciences, XXIX, No. 3 (Urbana, 1948), J. M. Carriere, *Life and Customs in the French Villages of the Old Illinois Country* (Report of the Canadian Historical Association, 1939).

75 See Andreas, pp. 267-271, for a treatment of Chicago's role in the Black Hawk War; interview with Madore Beaubien, *Chicago Times*, May 16, 1882, in "Beaubiens of Chicago," p. 39, Frank Gordon Beaubien Papers.

76 Andreas, pp. 122-128, 174-175; Kappler, ed., pp. 402-403; Charles Royce, *Indian Land Cessions in the United States*, 18th Annual Report of the Bureau of American Ethnology (Washington, 1899), pp. 750-751; Anselm J. Gerwing, "The Chicago Indian Treaty of 1833," *Journal of the Illinois State Historical Society* (1964); Wentworth, *Early Chicago*, pp. 39-40.

77 Andreas, pp. 120-121; "Biography of Thomas Church," *Fergus Historical Series*, No. 5 (Chicago, 1876), p. 42.
78 Andreas, pp. 131-133. See Daniel Elazar, *Cities of the Prairie* (New York, 1970), pp. 153-180, for Illinois migration streams; "List of Settlers of Chicago Who Came Between January, 1831, and December, 1836," in Rufus Blanchard, *Discovery and Conquest of the Northwest, With the History of Chicago* (Wheaton, 1879), pp. 424-433.
79 See Madore Beaubien Papers. For affinity of French Creoles for the Potawatomi and Potawatomi culture, Mark Beaubien spoke of this on his deathbed in "Beaubiens of Chicago," Frank Gordon Beaubien Papers.
80 Andreas, pp. 130-131; Kinzie Family Papers; "William B. Ogden," *Fergus Historical Series*, No. 17 (Chicago, 1882); "John Dean Caton Recollections," Calumet Club, p. 35; John Wentworth to Lydia Wentworth, Nov. 10, 1836, John Wentworth Papers.
81 Beaubien Family Papers; "Beaubiens of Chicago," Frank Gordon Beaubien Papers.
82 Beaubien Family Papers; store inventory, Madore Beaubien Papers.
83 Andreas, p. 103.
84 Juliette Kinzie, pp. 227-229.
85 John Harris Kinzie Papers, 1833-1837, Chicago Historical Society; Harriet Martineau, *Reminiscences of Early Chicago*, p. 32; Martineau, "Strange Early Days," *Annals of Chicago*, IX (Chicago, 1876).
86 Cleaver, pp. 13, 24; Gale, p. 122; John Wentworth to Lydia Wentworth, Nov. 10, 1836, in John Wentworth Papers.
87 Cleaver, p. 27.
88 Andreas, pp. 122-125.
89 *Ibid.*, p. 123; Charles Latrobe, *A Rambler in North America* (London, 1836), pp. 201, 207, 210-211.
90 Andreas, p. 124; Latrobe, pp. 213-214. For the influence of mixed-bloods in Potawatomi politics and the treaty of 1833, see miscellaneous fragment, n.d., Alphabetical File: James Herrington, Chicago Historical Society; Frank R. Grover, *Antoine Ouilmette* (Evanston, 1908), pp. 12-16; Conway, pp. 410-418; Clifton, "Captain Billy Caldwell."
91 Andreas, pp. 126-128; Porter, pp. 71-73; *Chicago Democrat* (Dec. 10, 1833).
92 Andreas, pp. 126-128; Kappler, ed., pp. 402-410.
93 Porter, pp. 73-74.
94 *Ibid.*
95 Gale, p. 154; Madore Beaubien Papers.
96 In his old age Madore Beaubien said that he wanted his children to honor his name and lamented the fact that Chicago had not remembered him. See interview in *Chicago Times*, May 16, 1882, in "Beaubiens of Chicago," Frank Gordon Beaubien Papers. See also John Dean Caton, *The Last of the Illinois and a Sketch of the Pottawatomie* (Chicago, 1876), pp. 26-30; Wentworth, *Early Chicago*, pp. 35-36.
97 Pierce, pp. 57-69. See also John D. Haeger, *Men and Money: The Urban Frontier at Green Bay, 1815-1840* (Mt. Pleasant, Mich.: Clarke Historical Library, Central Michigan University, 1970) for a comparable takeover by Eastern speculators of another fur-trading town.

Chapter II: French Detroit

1 Alphonse de Tonty to ? , September 1, 1701, Cadillac Papers, *Michigan Pioneer and Historical Society Collections*, XXXIII, 131. For the question of authorship of the letter, see Jean Delanglez, "The Genesis and Building of Detroit," *Mid-America*, XXX (Apr. 1948), 94, n. 44.

2 This paradox of using the social instruments of precapitalism for capitalist ends was explained by Professor Edgar McInnis: "The forms of feudalism were to be used to stimulate the profit motive, strengthened by the added incentive of social prestige. Accompanying this, however, was the desire to use the system as an agency of discipline and authority. The central control of the royal government was to be supplemented by the creation of a small privileged class of landholders under whom the bulk of the population would form a submissive tenantry." Edgar McInnis, *Canada: A Political and Social History* (New York, 1954), p. 63; W.J. Eccles, *France in America* (New York, 1972), p. 227.

3 William B. Munro, "Introduction," in *Documents Relating to the Seigniorial Tenure in Canada, 1598-1854* (Toronto, 1908), xix, xxi, cxv.

4 Munro, *The Seigniorial System in Canada* (New York, 1907), pp. 12, 13.

5 The alienation fine on sale of lands held *en fief et seigneurie* was one-fifth, *en roture*, one-twelfth.

6 J. Williams, "Report of the Solicitor General upon Various Questions Relating to the Seigniorial System, October 5, 1790," in Munro, *Documents Relating to Seigniorial Tenure*, pp. 254, 257-258.

7 Munro, *ibid.*, liii; Donald Creighton, *A History of Canada: Dominion of the North* (Boston, 1944), p. 80.

8 Thomas Gage to Jeffry Amherst, Mar. 20, 1762 in *Michigan Pioneer and Historical Collections* (Lansing: Michigan Historical Society), XIX, 17 (hereafter *MPHC*); "A Selection of George Croghan's Letters and Journals Relating to Tours into the Western Country — November 16, 1750-November 1765," in R.G. Thwaites, *Early Western Travels, 1748-1846* (Cleveland, 1904), I, 152.

9 Land in Detroit was first granted *en seigneurie* but in 1716 changed to *en censive* (or *roture*). The latter carried the same feudal duties, with the exception already noted on alienation fines (see n. 4). Munro, *Seigniorial System in Canada*, p. 79; Sumner C. Powell, *Puritan Village, The Formation of a New England Town* (Garden City, N.Y., 1965), pp. 171 ff.

10 "Clauses and Conditions Expressed in the Concessions Granted by M. de la Mothe Cadillac at Detroit," Nov. 4, 1721, *MPHC*, XXXIII, 686-687; "Reply of Gatineau to the Petition of the Inhabitants of Detroit to the Intendant of New France, October 21, 1726," in *Collections of the State Historical Society of Wisconsin* (Wisconsin, 1857), III, 171-175; Almon E. Parkins, *The Historical Geography of Detroit* (Lansing, 1918), pp. 55, 66.

11 McInnis, *Canada*, pp. 141-143, 284.

12 F. Clever Bald, *Detroit's First American Decade, 1796-1805* (Ann Arbor, 1948), pp. 246-249; James V. Campbell, *Outlines of the*

Political History of Michigan (Detroit, 1876), pp. 242-244, 262.

13   Munro, *Documents Relating to Seigniorial Tenure*, pp. xxxix, lxx; "Reply of Gatineau to the Petition of the Inhabitants of Detroit to the Intendant of New France, October 21, 1726"; "A Selection of George Croghan's Letters and Journals Relating to Tours into the Western Country — November 16, 1750-November, 1765"; Jacob Lindley, "Expedition to Detroit, 1793," *MPHC*, XVII, 594.

14   Estwick Evans, "A Pedestrious Tour of Four Thousand Miles Through the Western States and Territories During the Winter and Spring of 1818," *Early Western Travels*, VIII, 219; Thomas L. McKenney, *Sketches of a Tour to the Lakes* (Baltimore, 1827), p. 126; Issac P. Christiancy, "Recollections of the Early History of the City and County of Monroe," *MPHC*, VI, 373.

15   Bela Hubbard, *Memorials of a Half-Century in Michigan and the Lake Region* (New York, 1888), pp. 118-120; Evans, "A Pedestrious Tour," p. 219; Lewis Cass to Secretary of War, May 31, 1816, in Silas Farmer, *The History of Detroit and Michigan* (Detroit, 1890), p. 338.

16   Assessment and Tax List, 1864, Special Income Tax for District I, Michigan (MSS in National Archives). For the 1844 Real and Personal Property Tax Assessment for the Detroit elite, see Alexandra U. McCoy, "Political Affiliations of American Economic Elites, Wayne County, Michigan, 1844, 1860, As a Test Case" (unpublished Ph.D. thesis, Wayne State University, 1965), pp. 56-61; George N. Fuller, "Detroit: Michigan's Capital 100 Years Ago," *Michigan History Magazine*, XX (Winter 1936), 9, 13; George N. Fuller, *Economic and Social Beginnings of Michigan* (Lansing, 1916), p. 131.

17   M. Carrie W. Hamlin, "Old French Traditions," *MPHC*, IV, 70; Richard C. Ford, "The French-Canadians in Michigan," *Michigan History Magazine*, XXVII (Spring 1943), 257; George Pare, *The Catholic Church in Detroit, 1701-1888* (Detroit, 1951), pp. 210, 225.

18   Farmer, *History of Detroit*, pp. 334-336; Calvin Goodrich, *The First Michigan Frontier* (Ann Arbor, 1940), p. 56.

19   Leigh G. Cooper, "Influences of the French Inhabitants of Detroit upon its Early Political Life," *Michigan History*, IV (Jan. 1920), 299-304; *Detroit Gazette*, August 8, 1817, reprinted in Farmer, pp. 715-716; Ronald P. Formisano, "The Social Bases of American Voting Behavior, Wayne County, Michigan, 1837-1852, As a Test Case" (unpublished Ph.D. thesis, Wayne State University, 1966), pp. 396, 408, 410, 414. See also Formisano, *The Birth of Mass Political Parties, Michigan 1827-1861* (Princeton, 1971), pp. 171-179.

20   Charles R. Tuttle, *General History of Michigan* (Detroit, 1874), pp. 678-680; J.A. Girardin, "Slavery in Detroit," *MPHC*, I, 416.

21   Walter March, *Shoepac Recollections: A Way Side Glimpse of American Life* (New York, 1856), p. 18; A. B. Benson, ed., *Peter Kalm's Travels In North America: The English Version of 1770* (New York, 1966), I, 534-535.

22   Friend Palmer, *Early Days in Detroit* (Detroit, 1906), pp. 437, 439; John Fitzgibbon, "King Alcohol: His Rise, Reign and Fall in Michigan," *Michigan History*, II (Oct. 1918), 742; *MPHC*, I, 394.

23   Jacob S. Farrand, "Reminiscence," *Detroit in History and Commerce*

(Detroit, 1891), p. 12.

24 Hubbard, "The Early Colonization of Detroit," *MPHC*, I, 367-368.

25 Lewis Cass to Secretary of War, May 31, 1816; *Detroit Gazette*, May 11, 1821, in Floyd Dain, *Every House a Frontier* (Detroit, 1956), pp. 139-140.

26 For precommercial subsistence farming, see Pierre J.P. DeNoyan (Detroit commandant) to the French Minister of the Colonies, Aug. 6, 1740, in *Collections of the State Historical Society of Wisconsin*, XVII, 326. Christiancy, "Recollections of Monroe," p. 373; Thomas C. Haliburton, *The Clockmaker: Or the Sayings and Doings of Samuel Slick of Slickville* (London, n.d.); Munro, *Documents Relating to Seigniorial Tenure*, p. cxvi; Eccles, *France in America*, p. 81. See also "Report of the Commissioners Appointed to Inquire into the State of the Laws and Other Circumstances Connected with the Seigniorial Tenure, March 29, 1843" (Sir Charles Bagot Commission), in Munro, pp. 254, 348, 349, 350, 355; *ibid.*, cxvi; C.E. Black, *The Dynamics of Modernization* (New York, 1966), pp. 1-34; Robert Redfield, "The Folk Society," *American Journal of Sociology*, LII (Jan. 1947), 293-308; Ann B. Jameson, "Impressions of Detroit, 1837," *Michigan History Magazine*, VIII (Jan. 1924), 64.

27 Eugene D. Genovese, *The World the Slaveholders Made: Two Essays in Interpretation* (New York, 1969), p. 5.

28 Louis Hartz, *The Founding of New Societies: Studies in the History of the United States, Latin America, South Africa, Canada, and Australia* (New York, 1964), pp. 3, 5, 7, 14.

Chapter III: The Ben Ishmael Tribe

1 The author is indebted to the late Gilbert Osofsky for his encouragement of this study.

2 J. Frank Wright, "The Tribe of Ishmael" (typewritten ms., *ca.* 1890, Indiana State Library, Indianapolis), biographical notes 1, 10, 17, 42, 64, 78, 79, 83, 86, 114, 117, 190, Addendum (hereafter cited as Wright, followed by the number of the biographical note). Benjamin Quarles, *The Negro in the American Revolution* (Chapel Hill, N.C., 1961), Chs. 2, 7-9; Herbert Aptheker, *American Negro Slave Revolts* (New York, 1969), pp. 21-22, 88, 202-208; Oscar C. McCulloch, "The Tribe of Ishmael: A Study in Social Degradation," National Conference of Charities and Correction, *Proceedings* (1888), pp. 151, 157-158; Arthur H. Estabrook, "The Tribe of Ishmael," *Eugenical News*, VI (July-Aug. 1921), 7-8, 50; Charles Benedict Davenport, *Heredity in Relation to Eugenics* (New York, 1911), p. 234. A cover note on the Wright manuscript states that it was copied from notes made by Wright between 1880 and 1890, loaned by Wright to A. H. Estabrook of the Carnegie Institute in 1917, and left by Estabrook with the Indiana Board of State Charities in 1922. There are no page numbers, but 291 numbered biographical notes, some less than a page, some several pages, followed by an addendum. Internal evidence indicates that the manuscript is a mixture of Wright's editing and reports from many charity and correctional workers, local

and state, 1840-1890. Estabrook, a national leader in eugenics, probably borrowed the collection for his article on the Tribe of Ishmael, judging from the dates of borrowing, publication, and return. The dates of compilation of the manuscript coincide with the activity of Oscar McCulloch, the state's leader in charities and corrections and in eugenics. In light of Estabrook's use, McCulloch's concurrent work, and the tendency of the collection, Wright's purpose appears to have been to compile a representative sample of Ishmaelite biographies to demonstrate the tribe's antisocial behavior, in support of McCulloch's crusade against the Ishmaelites. Indeed it may be Wright's distillation to which McCulloch refers when he speaks of 7,000 pages of information on 5,000 Ishmaelites at his disposal (McCulloch, "The Tribe of Ishmael," p. 157). There is no reason to suspect deliberate distortion in the Wright manuscript, since many of the sources would have been subject to judicial or institutional review, and Wright was apparently preparing the collection for the use of eugenicists, many of whom prided themselves on their scientific method. Much of the document then may be considered reliable when used with care, discounting the pervasive extreme bias of value judgments. Problems of interpretation are identified on p. 102 of the present study.

3 Wright, 1, 3; McCulloch, "The Tribe of Ishmael," p. 155.
4 McCulloch, p. 155; Wright, 10, 11. A date prior to 1819 is necessary for Ishmaelite settlement at the site of Indianapolis because the date of "Indian removal" from central Indiana is 1818. Therefore, 1822, submitted by Wright, is obtained from the date of the arrival of the first state officials to encounter the tribe, and 1840, submitted by McCulloch ("Tribe of Ishmael," p. 155) arises from the date of the first notice of the tribe in charity or correctional records. For the location of the White River settlements, see Thurman B. Rice, "The 'Tribe of Ishmael' Study," *One Hundred Years of Medicine: Indianapolis, 1820-1920, Monthly Bulletin of the Indiana State Board of Health,* LV (1952), 233. Real estate has traditionally been sold or rented to African-Americans where nonwhites have already resided. There were also much smaller Ishmaelite settlements near the sites of Decatur, Peoria, and Bloomington, Illinois, and other locations now unknown.
5 Wright, 10; B. R. Sulgrove, *History of Indianapolis and Marion County, Indiana* (Philadelphia, 1884), p. 8.
6 Sulgrove, p. 96.
7 McCulloch, p. 155; Davenport, *Heredity,* pp. 234-236; Wright, 1, 10, 11 and *passim.* For a few years after the move to the White River there was migration southeast to the tribe's former center north of Cincinnati. In later decades there was an occasional migration extension due east through the Quaker town of Richmond, Indiana and the predominantly black Darke County, Ohio to the vicinity of Columbus.
8 Wright, 261 and *passim;* Rice, *One Hundred Years of Medicine,* p. 233.
9 McCulloch, p. 157; Wright, 291. The change in height is stated as if statistics had been compared.
10 Wright, 10.
11 *Ibid.*
12 *Ibid.,* 1.

13 *Ibid.*, 19, 34, 78, 108.

14 *Ibid.*, 108, 230.

15 See nn. 21, 23 above.

16 Wright, 1. At least one source for the Wright compendium exhibits uncharacteristic sympathy for the Ishmaelites. The copying error suggests that this passage is not Wright's editorializing.

17 *Ibid.*, 61, 63.

18 McCulloch, "The Tribe of Ishmael," pp. 155, 157-158; Estabrook, p. 50; Davenport, pp. 234-236.

19 Wright, 2.

20 *Ibid.*, 1.

21 *Ibid.*, 109, 120, 126, 135, 162, 170, 184, 193, 205, 211, 222, 249. Except for Ishmael, family names are not generally used in this study, in deference to the privacy of Ishmaelite descendants since the diaspora.

22 *Ibid.*, 290 and *passim*.

23 *Ibid.*, 40, 62.

24 *Ibid.*, 62, 290; McCulloch, "The Tribe of Ishmael," pp. 156-158; Estabrook, p. 50.

25 Wright, 62; McCulloch, "The Tribe of Ishmael," p. 156; Davenport, pp. 234-236. The citation for the second husband is omitted in deference to the privacy of descendants. It is found among the first 108 biographies, the section on the Ishmael clan, in the Wright compendium.

26 Wright, 1-291.

27 *Ibid.*, 2.

28 *Ibid.*

29 *Ibid.*, 2, 27.

30 Rice, *passim*, photographs of cabins.

31 *Ibid.*, p. 234; Sulgrove, p. 3 (for the floods).

32 Wright, 11, 17.

33 *Ibid.*, 261.

34 Central Ishmaelite dance hall social centers were the Christian Hill Place, the Crib, and the Big Bonanza; outlying were Brighton Beach, Hop-light Station, and the Nest, which may be the present well-to-do neighborhood "The Crow's Nest," elevated ground commanding a long view up and down the river: Wright, 10, 40, 71, 139, 252. For avoidance of alcohol, see McCulloch, "The Tribe of Ishmael," pp. 155, 157; Wright mentions one light drinker and no others.

35 Wright, 2, 40, 86, 87, 105.

36 *Ibid.*, 26, 46, 71. The speed of Susan S.'s funeral procession may be related to her father's name—Jehu.

37 *Ibid.*, 108.

38 *Ibid.*, 37.

39 *Ibid.*, 206.

40 *Ibid.*, 1, 79.

41 *Ibid.*, 36. The author is indebted to the urban historian Melvin Holli for raising the question of marginality, and other helpful suggestions.

42 *Ibid.*, 27.

43 James Whitcomb Riley, "Where Is Mary Alice Smith?" *The Works of James Whitcomb Riley* (New York, 1917), II, 168, 172. For identification of the character in essay and poem as the same, see Peter Revell,

James Whitcomb Riley (New York, 1970), pp. 82, 157, n. 2. The character, in essay and poem, may be—and is likely to be—composite.

44 Edward Eggleston, *The Hoosier Schoolmaster: A Story of Backwoods Life in Indiana* (New York, 1899), pp. 18-21.

45 Booth Tarkington, *The Conquest of Canaan* (New York, 1905), pp. 79-87, 211.

46 That the Tribe of Ishmael appears in *The Prairie* was noted by the state compiler of Ishmaelite materials in the 1880s: Wright, 1.

47 Orm Överland, *The Making and Meaning of an American Classic: James Fenimore Cooper's* The Prairie (Oslo, 1975), pp. 47-49, 115-116, 149, 159-161, 166-167, 169. Sources: pp. 66-94. Quotation: p. 8.

48 Miller, *The Life of the Mind in America* (New York, 1965), pp. 115-116.

49 James Fenimore Cooper, *The Prairie* (New York, 1964), pp. 35, 42, 198. The work was first published in 1827.

50 *Ibid.*, pp. 11, 13, 69, 90.

51 *Ibid.*, p. 73.

52 *Ibid.*, pp. 96-97.

53 *Ibid.*, pp. 68, 284.

54 *Ibid.*, pp. 181, 184.

55 *Ibid.*, p. 13. McCulloch, "The Tribe of Ishmael," p. 158. Very light hair with dark skin is not unusual in young children; the combination is encountered among young African-Americans today. The hair darkens as the child grows older (author's interview with Dr. Ruth Lerner, a Chicago pediatrician with a considerable African-American practice). There are two passages, extraneous to and interrupting the progress of the plot and theme of the novel, which show that Cooper was thinking of race as he wrote of the Ishmaelites. In one, Ishmael's wife rages at the suggestion that he should take an Indian as a second wife. The other is an interpolated essay on the racial purity of the American people, which argues that western barbarism is the result of the frontier rather than any questionable ancestry of the frontiersmen: Cooper, pp. 67-69, 308-311.

56 *Ibid.*, pp. 15-16, 65, 125, 136-137, 153.

57 *Ibid.*, pp. 147-148.

58 *Ibid.*, pp. 356-357.

59 *Ibid.*, pp. 68, 91, 176, 371-372.

60 *Ibid.*, pp. 63-64.

61 *Ibid.*, p. 82.

62 *Ibid.*, p. 379.

63 Wright, 1-291.

64 McCulloch, pp. 157-158. See also n. 72 below.

65 Davenport, *Heredity*, p. 234; Estabrook, "The Tribe of Ishmael," p. 50; McCulloch, p. 151; Wright, 10, 11.

66 Wright, 17, 42, 64, 78, 79, 83, 86, 117, 190, Addendum.

67 *Ibid.*, 10, 235; Estabrook, p. 50. A member of the black or white community today who knows that he is of Ishmaelite descent may be entirely African or European in ancestry, but his ancestors belonged to a community of African, European and native American descent.

68 Rice, 233; Wright, 261 and *passim*.

69 Wright, 69, 78, 229; Sulgrove, p. 90. Except for a mob attack upon a

"colored" settlement—probably Ishmaelite—in 1839, which was beaten off by firearms, a series of attacks upon an Ishmaelite settlement between 1884 and 1886, culminating in a battle with many casualties, and attacks upon individual Ishmaelites, there are no reports of literal physical warfare. The tribe, living openly without natural sanctuaries, was in no position to consider guerrilla warfare. The continuous and increasing attacks upon the tribe by the government may have satisfied the hostilities of the majority population.

70 William A. Beavers, "Poor Relief in Marion County prior to 1860" (M.A. thesis, University of Indiana, 1933), pp. 20, 22. For Illinois, see Joseph O. Cunningham, *Historical Encyclopedia of Illinois and History of Champaign County* (Chicago, 1905), II, 735. For a community on the Ishmaelite route, see Natalia Maree Belting, "Early History of Urbana-Champaign to 1871" (University of Illinois, 1937), pp. 43-45.

71 Wright, 30, 139, 155, and *passim;* Estabrook, p. 50.

72 Wright, 1-291. For the major crimes, see *ibid.,* 37, 79, 91, 108, 246. For the ruling out of other major theft, see *ibid.,* 1.

73 *Ibid.,* 61, 100, 107, 112, 114, 121, 199. For the widow, 62.

74 *Ibid.,* 95, 99, 101; McCulloch, p. 155; Davenport, pp. 234-236. Also alleged was incest, a charge often made against isolated and poor communities. It could be related to cousin marriage, a tendency towards endogamy from tribal pride and dislike of the majority community. Estabrook, p. 50; Wright, 65, 95, 268. It was considered humorous: *ibid.,* 103.

75 Wright, 67, 226. So felicitous was the last statement found, that it was used again in 68.

76 *Ibid.,* 37, 57, 93, 100, 107.

77 *Ibid.,* 157 and *passim;* Estabrook, p. 50.

78 Wright, 178.

79 *Ibid.,* 203, 220, 221.

80 *Ibid.,* 34, 36, 66, 70, 79, 105, 283.

81 Oscar C. McCulloch, "Associated Charities," National Conference of Charities and Correction, *Proceedings* (1880), p. 123; Oscar C. McCulloch Scrapbooks, Indiana State Library, Indianapolis; McCulloch, "The Tribe of Ishmael," pp. 154, 159.

82 McCulloch, "Tribe of Ishmael," p. 159.

83 McCulloch, "Associated Charities," pp. 122-135.

84 McCulloch, "The Tribe of Ishmael," pp. 154-155. The notion of another culture in their midst seems to have been beyond the patterns of thinking of McCulloch and associated eugenicists. There is no hint of social or historical analysis, for to them there was nothing to analyze. What they called laziness, incorrigibility, vagabondage, filthy habits, licentiousness, the thieving instinct, feeblemindedness, and degeneracy was entirely inherited through the genes: McCulloch, "Tribe," *passim;* Wright, *passim;* Davenport, pp. 234-236; Estabrook, *passim.* For the population estimate, see Estabrook, p. 50. McCulloch's figure of 5,000 is for that portion of the tribe who received the official attention of the authorities of the majority society: "Tribe of Ishmael," p. 157.

85 Davenport, pp. 234-236; Estabrook, p. 50; Rice, pp. 233-235; Mark H. Haller, *Eugenics: Hereditarian Attitudes in American Thought* (New Brunswick, N.S., 1963), pp. 35, 126 (on the leadership of McCulloch), 71, 78, 108 (on the place of the Tribe of Ishmael). This last study is not concerned with the Ishmaelites except as they were conceived by eugenicists. Some writers on eugenics, perhaps not from the Midwest, or perhaps writing after the tribe's dispersal, may have assumed that the name "Ishmael" was made up, as were Kallikak and other names assigned by eugenicists.

86 Haller, *Eugenics*, pp. 65-68, 73-75, 107-108, 138-139; Davenport, pp. 234-236. For Estabrook, see also n. 2 above.

87 Haller, pp. 6-7, 50-57, 94, 144-159, 179-182.

88 Davenport, pp. 234-236; Estabrook, p. 50; Rice, p. 237. At least twenty present-day residents of Indianapolis and Champaign-Urbana, black and white, mostly natives and persons interested in history, were asked if they had heard of the Ishmaelites, a local wandering tribe. They all answered that they had not. Mass social amnesia, produced by local or regional social trauma, is suggested to explain this phenomenon. As a parallel, the author knows liberal, intellectual persons who have never heard of the historically important Ku Klux Klan domination of Indiana in the 1920s, either from formal learning, or their active, varied social and civic life as young adults in small cities of central Indiana during the 1940s and 1950s. This can be explained by lack of local contemporary reports, avoidance of related books by libraries and bookstores, and the older generation's silence on the subject, especially in the presence of the young.

89 Haller, pp. 42-50, 134-141.

90 *Ibid.*, pp. 139-140, 180.

91 Author's interview with Mr. Charles Burroughs, Curator, Du Sable Museum of African-American History, Chicago.

92 Author's interview with Mr. Abu Bakr, recent office secretary and receptionist, Chicago Institute of Islamic Culture. Black Muslims and Black Hebrews have often moved in the same nationalist circles.

93 Author's interview with Mr. Ahmad Mabarak, member, Mumin Mosque, Detroit. Black Muslims, like other Muslims, have often adhered to dietary laws similar to those of the Hebraic Law.

94 Mr. William Prothro Bey, member, Moorish Science Temple of America, Chicago. There is no separate history of Moorish Science, but brief notes are included in the two standard works on the Nation of Islam: E. U. Essien-Udom, *Black Nationalism: A Search for an Identity in America* (Chicago, 1962); C. Eric Lincoln, *The Black Muslims in America* (Boston, 1961). Note the meaning of the word "gallivant," appropriate as the name of a member of a nomadic people.

95. "Abū Bakr al-Siddīq of Timbuktu," in Philip D. Curtin, ed., *Africa Remembered: Narratives by West Africans from the Era of the Slave Trade* (Madison, 1968), pp. 163-164. For Brazil: Donald Pierson, *Negroes in Brazil* (Chicago, 1942), pp. 39-45. For the West African holy wars: Basil Davidson, *A History of West Africa to the Nineteenth Century* (Garden City, N.Y., 1966), pp. 269-286.

96 Rice, p. 233. Ishmael does not seem to appear as a family name in America except among the Tribe of Ishmael. Genealogical indexes

in the Genealogy Room, Newberry Library, Chicago, do not list the name, and the Index of Family Names, Census Files, Illinois State Archives, Springfield, lists the name only along the tribal migration route.

97 Author's interview with Mr. Reynold N. El, National President, Moorish Science Temple of America, Inc., Chicago. The author thanks Mr. El, his assistant Sister Carrie Bey, and Mr. Prothro Bey for their help in this study.

98 The information on Morocco is from personal observation. The information on the Moorish Science Temple at Pembroke is from a confidential source. A list of temples of the Nation of Islam appeared weekly in the journal *Muhammad Speaks* until 1975.

99 Milton W. Mathews and Lewis A. McLean, *Early History and Pioneers of Champaign County* (Urbana, 1886), p. 115; Godfrey Sperling, comp., "Clippings and lists concerning cemeteries of Champaign County" (Illinois Historical Library, Springfield), p. 2; *History of Champaign County, Illinois* (Philadelphia, 1878), p. 125; J. S. Lothrop, *Champaign County Directory, 1870-1* (Chicago, 1871), p. 395; Isabelle S. Purnell, *A History of the Schools of Mahomet* (Mahomet, 1962), p. 198; Purnell, *Centennial Year, The Methodist Church 1855-1955* (Mahomet, n.d.), p. 98.

100 Lothrop, *op. cit.*, pp. 232-315. The author is indebted to the immigration historian Leo Schelbert, who has made a study of immigrant name changes, for his opinion that this list does not represent that process, and for other illuminating suggestions.

101 *Rural Mail Directory, Indianapolis* (Saginaw, Mich., 1906), p. 31 and *passim*.

102 Marjorie Corrine Smith, "Historical Geography of Champaign County, Illinois" (Ph.D. diss., University of Illinois, 1957), map, p. 144.

103 D. McKenzie, *Champaign and Urbana City Directory, 1883-1884* (1883), *passim*. Champaign in the title refers to the county.

104 Mathews and McLean, *op. cit.*, p. 120.

105 Erdmann Doane Beynon, "The Voodoo Cult among Negro Migrants in Detroit," *American Journal of Sociology*, XLIII, No. 6 (May 1938), 906-907. The author states that the title, a police term, is otherwise unrelated to the subject, the Nation of Islam.

Chapter IV: "Becoming American"

1 The author received financial support for this research from the Center for Twentieth Century Studies, University of Wisconsin—Milwaukee, which he gratefully acknowledges. A recent and very rich review of American ideology concerning pluralism is John Higham's fine essay, "Ethnic Pluralism in American Thought," in his *Send These To Me: Jews and Other Immigrants in Urban America* (New York, 1975), Ch. 10. To the on-going exchange about the ethnic issue which he cites on page 228, one should add more recent left-wing critics as Andrew Hacker, "Cutting Classes," *The New York Review of Books*, XXIII (Mar. 4, 1976), 15-18, and Richard Sennett, "Pure as the Driven Slush," *New York Times* (May 10, 1976), p. 27.

2 Eric R. Wolfe, "Aspects of Group Relations in a Complex Society," *American Anthropologist*, LVI (Dec. 1956), 1075-1076; and Joseph Barton, *Peasants and Strangers* (Cambridge, Mass., 1975), p. 82, both referred me to these "broker" types.

3 It appeared in several editions over two decades; the latest is *The People's Choice* (New York, 1968).

4 As discussed below, Swedish-Americans did not on the whole support ethnic institutions. Those who did found most of their desired group identity in religion.

5 Swedish nationalism in Europe was not very popular among the masses. Sweden was a dominant power in Northern Europe in the 1800s, until Norway formally and finally broke away from its control in 1905.

6 Esbjorn even agreed not to enroll them in the local Swedish church record book in order to keep them as communicants. George Stephenson, *The Religious Aspects of Swedish Immigration* (New York, 1969; reprint of 1932 edition), p. 159.

7 *Ibid.*, p. 167.

8 *Ibid.*, p. 170.

9 *Ibid.*, pp. 167, 170; O. Fritiof Ander, *T. N. Hasselquist: The Career and Influence of a Swedish American Clergyman, Journalist, and Educator* (Rock Island, Ill., 1931), p. 26. A measure of his appeal is the movement of his Galesburg, Illinois congregation with him when he assumed the headship of Augustana College. See Conrad Bergendoff, *Augustana— A Profession of Faith: A History of Augustana College, 1860-1935* (Rock Island, 1969), p. 24.

10 Ander, *Hasselquist*, pp. 24-26.

11 Stephenson, *Aspects*, p. 325.

12 Ander, pp. 46, 58, 158-160, 224; Bergendoff, pp. 28-29; Stephenson, pp. 293, 311.

13 Stephenson, pp. 293, 311.

14 *Ibid.*, p. 397; Ander, pp. 32, 229-230.

15 See the recent work of Edward Kantowicz, *Polish American Politics in Chicago, 1888-1940* (Chicago, 1975), which indicates that while Polish immigrants were largely Democrats, they were not very active partisans.

16 Even the group's largest church body in America, Hasselquist's Augustana Synod, formally consisted of only about a sixth of all group members. Its influence, and therefore Hasselquist's, went far beyond the Synod's communicants. See Stephenson, p. 226; Ander, p. 26.

17 Admittedly, Polish and Polish-American nationalists formally did deny this monoreligious definition accepting Jews, Greek Catholics, and Protestants. But practically, they accepted the clerical definition; non-Catholic Poles were a rarity in nationalist bodies. See my history of the nationalist-clericalist struggle in *For God and Country: The Rise of Polish and Lithuanian Ethnic Consciousness in America, 1860-1910* (Madison, Wis., 1975), esp. pp. 67, 70.

18 William I. Thomas and Florian Znaniecki, *The Polish Peasant in Europe and America* (Boston, 1918-1920), I, 285, 667; II, 141-143; George Brandes, *Poland* (London, 1903), p. 138; Peter Ostafin, "The Polish Peasant in Transition" (Ph.D. diss., University of Michigan, 1948), among other authorities.

19 At Barzynski's death in 1899, about a million Poles had immigrated to the United States, and by World War I about three million. My estimates are from Donald Taft and Richard Robbins, *International Migrations* (New York, 1955), p. 505; Stefan Barszczynski, *Polacy w Ameryce* (Warszawa, 1906?), p. 119; J. Grabiec, *Wspólczesna Polska w Cyfrach i Factach* (Kraków, 1912?), pp. 12, 133.

20 Quoted in Greene, *God and Country*, p. 76.

21 T. Lindsay Baker, "The Early Years of Rev. Wincenty Barzynski," *Polish American Studies*, XXXII (Spring 1975), 29-52, is the most authoritative biography in English.

22 51st Congress, 2nd Session, House of Representatives, Report 3472, *Report of Select Committee on Immigration...*(Washington, D.C., 1891), II, 640.

23 Baker, "Barzynski," p. 29 partially justifies the worshipful memorial of Ks. Stanislaw Siatka, *Krótkie Wspomnienie o Życie...Barzynskiego* (Chicago, 1901). See also Thaddeus Majuch, "The Work of the Pioneer Polish Priests in the United States" (M.A. thesis, Mundelein Seminary, Mundelein, Ill., 1952), esp. pp. 12-13.

24 I am summarizing the numerous professions he made in various publications in the 1870-1895 era, from Greene, *For God and Country*, pp. 67, 77-79. Obviously, a few other Polish clerics and more Polish laymen did not share Barzynski's view.

25 See the interpretation offered by Rev. Andrew Greeley, *The Catholic Tradition* (New York, 1967), pp. 20-21, and my comments below on Barzynski's relations with the Chicago bishops. I do not agree with Greeley's implication that anti-Americanizers in the Church were politically anti-American.

26 From archdiocesan sources quoted in Joseph J. Parot, "The American Faith and the Persistence of Chicago Polonia, 1870-1900" (Ph.D. diss., Northern Illinois University, 1971), p. 53.

27 Kruszka, *Historia Polska w Ameryce* (Milwaukee, 1905-1908), II, 60-62.

28 By "assimilative" here I mean the belief that their desired church reform—and there was some—had to have the sanction of American Catholic leadership. Greene, *For God and Country*, pp. 128, 132, 138.

29 *Ibid.*, pp. 109, 113.

30 Rudolph Vecoli, "Prelates and Peasants; Italian Immigration and the Catholic Church," *Journal of Social History*, II (Spring 1969), 217-236 for religious attitudes; see Phyllis Williams, *Southern Italian Folkways in Europe and America* (New Haven, 1938), 9-11, for family and local ties.

31 I am indebted to George Pozzetta, "The Italians of New York City" (Ph.D. diss., University of North Carolina, 1971), for the most lucid discussion of these categories.

32 The confusion in identification, as well as the heated denunciations, are voiced by John Koren, "The Padrone System and Padrone Banks," *Bulletin of the Department of Labor*, No. 9 (Mar. 1897), 113-127; Edward Hale, "The Padrone Question," *Lend a Hand*, XII (June 1894), 449-451; and Frank Sheridan, "Italian, Slavic, and Hungarian Unskilled Laborers in the United States," *Bulletin of the Bureau of*

Labor, No. 72 (Sep. 1907), 435-438. Anna Maria Martellone, *Una "Little Italy," Nell'Atene a America* (Napoli, 1973), pp. 120-128 is of little help in clarifying the public debate, but Edward Fenton, *Immigrants and Unions* (New York, reprint edition, 1975), pp. 1, 55, 84, and Pozzetta, *op. cit.,* pp. 321-323, give valuable insights.

33 Charlotte Erickson, *American Industry and the European Immigrants, 1860-1885* (Cambridge, Mass., 1957), esp. pp. 83-84.

34 Fenton, p. 4; Pozzetta, pp. 321-323.

35 I am indebted to Luciano Iorizzo, "The Padrone and Immigrant Distribution," in Silvano Tomasi and Madeline Engel, eds., *The Italian Experience in the United States* (N.Y., 1970), pp. 43-75, and Humbert Nelli, *The Italians in Chicago* (New York, 1970), esp. Ch. 3.

36 John S. and Leatrice MacDonald, "Chain Migration, Ethnic Neighborhood Formation and Social Networks," *Milbank Memorial Fund Quarterly,* XLII (Jan. 1964), 82-84.

37 I am indebted heavily here to Robert Harney's illuminating analysis of social stratification in Little Italy, "Ambiente and Social Class in North American Little Italies," *Canadian Review of Studies in Nationalism,* II (Spring 1975), 208-210, 220.

38 Note the moral indignation of Charles Brace, *The Dangerous Classes of New York...*(New York, 1870), Ch. 17, in viewing the quarter. Adolfo Rossi, *Un Italiano in America* (3rd edition, Treviso, 1907), pp. 67-69, 81-83, has a vivid description.

39 *New York Times,* Dec. 13, 1900, p. 18; Aug. 30, 1910; Italian Chamber of Commerce, *Gli Italiani Negli Stati Uniti D'America* (New York, 1906), pp. 340-341; Federal Writers' Project, *The Italians of New York* (New York, 1938), p. 16.

40 *New York Times,* Sep. 23, 1900, p. 15. I feel Pozzetta, p. 379, minimizes Maggio's help to Italian-Americans in the area.

41 *New York Times,* Dec. 13, 1900; a written transcript by Nathaniel Miller, given to me by Professor Luciano Iorizzo.

42 In fact, *Gli Italiani,* p. 29, cites him as "Papa della Colonia."

43 *New York Times,* May 31, 1896, p. 32. He admitted that *all* such societies, especially some secret ones, were *not* desirable.

44 Fugazy's unequaled stature is evident in many sources, especially *Il Progresso,* July 20, 1890; Jan. 19, 1892; *Corriere della Sera,* Jan. 4, 1912; and his obituaries, in *New York Times,* Aug. 7, 8, 10, and *Il Progresso,* Aug. 8, 10, 1930. His distinction was exceptional, but his objectives were typical of his group's social leadership. Note a precursor, Michele Pascaldi, in Howard Marraro, "Italians in New York During the First Half of the Nineteenth Century," *New York History* (July 1945), 26, 293, and evidence presented below.

45 G. Chiada Barberio, *Il Progresso de Gli Italiana nel Connecticut* (New Haven, 1933), p. 311; Morty Miller, "New Haven; The Italian Community" (undergraduate paper at Yale University, 1969, with the courtesy of Professor Rollin Osterweis and the New Haven Colony Historical Society).

46 As quoted in Miller, *op. cit.,* p. 25. See also *New Haven Sunday Register,* Feb. 16, 1930, Sec. V, p. 7; Barberio, *op. cit.,* pp. 312-315; Joseph William Carlevale, *Who's Who Among Americans of Italian Descent*

in Connecticut (n.p., 1942), p. 343.

47 George Schiro, *American By Choice* (Utica, 1940), p. 114. I could not obtain sufficient information on other group leaders. Charles Churchill, "The Italians of Newark, A Community Study" (Ph.D. diss., New York University, 1942), cites two leading "padrone-banker-saloonkeepers" of note with no elaboration, as does Richard Juliani, "The Social Organization of Immigration: The Italians of Philadelphia" (Ph.D. diss., University of Pennsylvania, 1971), pp. 211-213.

48 Note, for example, Moses Rischin's introduction to Hapgood's *Spirit of the Ghetto* (New York, 1902; John Harvard Library, 1967).

49 Irving Howe, *World of Our Father* (New York, 1976), pp. 58-61, is the present standard on American Yiddish cultural life; however, he inadequately records the social organization of Orthodox Jewry.

50 See, for example, Moses Rischin, *The Promised City* (Cambridge, Mass., 1962; paperback edition, 1970), especially Ch. 6, the standard historical work.

51 My judgment modifies that of Rischin, pp. 192-193, and is based on Melech Epstein, *Profiles of Eleven* (Detroit, 1965), pp. 113-123.

52 Between 1900 and 1911, Sarasohn's paper increased from 40,000 to 70,000 in circulation, while Cahan's rose more spectacularly from 20,000 to 122,500. From Mordecai Soltes, *The Yiddish Press: An Americanizing Agency* (New York, 1925), p. 23.

53 See Leon Stein, et al., trans. *The Education of Abraham Cahan* (Philadelphia, 1969), I, 374; Milton Doroshkin, *Yiddish in America* (Rutherford, N.J., 1969), pp. 113-114.

54 Moses Rischin, "Abraham Cahan and The New York Commercial Advertiser," *Publications of the American Jewish Historical Society*, XLIII (1953), 10-36; other references are in "Abraham Cahan," in Higham, *Send These To Me*, pp. 88-101.

55 Sarasohn's magnificent funeral is reported in *The New York Times*, Jan. 13, 14, 1905. Note the respect given by leading Reform Jewish laymen. At least 90 cars and 2,000 mourners on foot followed the body in the cortège across the bridge to Brooklyn and the cemetery. See also Jacob de Haas, et al., *Encyclopedia of Jewish Knowledge* (New York, 1934), p. 490.

56 Soltes, p. 21, and the statements of Professor Joseph Jacobs and Maurice Weisenthal in *Yiddishes Tageblatt*, Mar. 20, 1910.

57 Samuel Niger, "Yiddish Culture," in *The Jewish People, Past and Present* (New York, 1955), IV, 270; Moshe Starkman, "Kasriel Sarasohn," *Yorbukh Ampteyl* (1921), pp. 273-274, translated by the author with the aid of Mrs. Ethel Himberg.

58 His trials are told in his memoirs, in *Yorbukh Ampteyl*.

59 *Ibid.*, p. 26.

60 His charities and organizational principles are in *Yorbukh Ampteyl*. Charles Madison, *Yiddish Literature* (New York, 1968), pp. 133-136; *New York Times*, Jan. 13, 1905, p. 6; *Jewish Daily News*, Mar. 20, 1910, sec. 4, p. 6. Note the appreciative letter from Jacob Schiff in *ibid.*, p. 2.

61 Stein, *Education*, p. 158.

62 His early life is detailed in Stein, *Education*.

63 Always the pragmatist, he felt that American immigrants were simply

too enamored of their destination to be a base for class war. *Ibid.*, p. 412.

64 Quoted in Theodore Pollock, "The Solitary Clarinetist: A Critical Biography of Abraham Cahan, 1960-1970" (Ph.D. diss., Columbia University, 1959), p. 303.

65 Howe, pp. 241-247, 524; Soltes, Columbia University, pp. 177-178.

66 Howe, pp. 442, 528, 531-537; Pollock, "Clarinetist," p. 300.

67 Elsewhere he did admit that they did have some psychological value. Robert E. Park, *The Immigrant Press and Its Control* (New York, 1922; reprint, 1970), pp. 50-51, 87-88.

68 See Higham, p. 225, who refers to Gordon; and Frederic Barth, ed., *Ethnic Groups and Boundaries: The Social Organization of Cultural Difference* (Oslo, 1970), pp. 9-10, 32-33.

69 Higham, p. 232.

70 Robert Wiebe, *The Segmented Society: An Introduction to the Meaning of America* (New York, 1975), p. 66.

71 Philip Gleason, "The Crisis of Americanization," in Gleason, ed., *Catholicism in America* (New York, 1970), p. 138.

Chapter V: Polish Chicago

1 Two recent books deal with Poles in Chicago: Victor Greene, *For God and Country: The Rise of Polish and Lithuanian Ethnic Consciousness in America* (Madison, 1975), and Edward R. Kantowicz, *Polish-American Politics in Chicago, 1888-1940* (Chicago, 1975). In addition, three unpublished doctoral dissertations document the relations of Polish Catholics with the Church authorities in Chicago: Joseph John Parot, "The American Faith and the Persistence of Chicago Polonia, 1870-1920" (Ph.D. diss., University of Northern Illinois, 1971); James W. Sanders, "The Education of Chicago Catholics: An Urban History" (Ph.D. diss., University of Chicago, 1970); Charles H. Shanabruch, "The Catholic Church's Role in the Americanization of Chicago's Immigrants, 1833-1928" (Ph.D. diss., University of Chicago, 1975). Recent work on Polish-Americans in other parts of the country includes: Victor Greene, *The Slavic Community on Strike* (Notre Dame, 1968); Frank Renkiewicz, "The Polish Settlement of St. Joseph County, Indiana, 1855-1935" (Ph.D. diss., University of Notre Dame, 1967); Carol Ann Golab, "The Polish Communities of Philadelphia, 1870-1920" (Ph.D. diss., University of Pennsylvania, 1971); William Galush, "The Polish National Catholic Church," *Records of the American Catholic Historical Society of Philadelphia*, LXXXIII (Sep.-Dec. 1972), 131-149, and "American Poles and the New Poland," *Ethnicity*, I (Oct. 1974), 209-221. Victor Greene provides a bibliographic survey of the literature on Polish, Czech, and Slovak immigrants in *The Immigration History Newsletter*, VII (Nov. 1975), 6-11.

2 See, for instance, Joseph Wytrwal, *Poles in American History and Tradition* (Detroit, 1969), pp. 75-79.

3 No one should take too seriously any population estimates for Polish-Americans, including my own. Censuses probably underestimate the

numbers of Poles and other immigrant and racial minorities; Polish sources overcompensate by giving inflated estimates. My own figures are on the conservative side and are drawn from the following sources: 1890, U.S. and Chicago—extrapolations from U.S. census totals of foreign-born; 1910, U.S.—census totals for "foreign stock"; Chicago— extrapolations from the population of minors in the 1910 school census; 1930, U.S. and Chicago—census totals of foreign stock.

4 Golab, "Polish Communities of Philadelphia," pp. 52-59.

5 See Kantowicz, *Polish-American Politics*, pp. 12-22, for details on these five settlements. Greene, *For God and Country*, pp. 31-33, stresses the mediating effect of established German and Bohemian communities in lessening the culture shock for incoming Poles.

6 Population data for this table was obtained from the Chicago Board of Education School Census, 1898. The data for calculating the 1930 index came from Ernest W. Burgess and Charles Newcomb, eds., *Census Data of the City of Chicago, 1930* (Chicago, 1933). Burgess and Newcomb used "community areas" as a base; these were generally about the same size as a city ward. The index of dissimilarity is explained most fully in Karl and Alma Taeuber, *Negroes in Cities* (Chicago, 1965), pp. 28-31, 195-245.

7 Kantowicz, *Polish-American Politics*, pp. 23-24; Kantowicz, "The Ghetto Experience: Poles in Chicago as a Case Study" (paper delivered at the National Archives Conference on State and Local History, May 1975).

8 Golab emphasizes this pattern of segregation and decentralization for Philadelphia's Poles, "Polish Communities of Philadelphia," pp. 5-7.

9 Kantowicz, "The Ghetto Experience"; statistics were calculated from the 1898 school census.

10 Historians like Humbert Nelli and Howard Chudacoff, who have argued that the ethnic neighborhood was not so common an experience as supposed, fail to take sufficient account of the social and cultural aspects of the ghetto. See Nelli, *The Italians of Chicago* (New York, 1970), p. 45; Chudacoff, "A New Look at Ethnic Neighborhoods," *Journal of American History*, LX (June 1973), 77; Kantowicz, "The Ghetto Experience."

11 Raymond Breton, "Institutional Completeness of Ethnic Communities and the Personal Relations of Immigrants," *American Journal of Sociology*, LXX (1964), 193-205.

12 Jakub Horak, "Assimilation of Czechs in Chicago" (Ph.D. diss., University of Chicago, 1924), pp. 74-75; Greene, *For God and Country*, pp. 54-56.

13 *Ibid.*, pp. 58-63; Kantowicz, *Polish-American Politics*, pp. 14-22, 165-168.

14 Sanders, "Education of Chicago Catholics," pp. 52-59, 114, 183; Parot, "Persistence of Chicago Polonia," pp. 225-226; Francis Bolek, *The Polish American School System* (New York, 1948), p. 5.

15 These figures were obtained from the annual reports submitted by the pastor of each parish to the Archbishop, Archives of the Archdiocese of Chicago (AAD). The proportions of other ethnic groups in ethnic parishes in 1930 were: Lithuanians, 38%; Italians, 36%; Yugoslavs,

33%; Czechoslovaks, 19%.

16 All the financial information in these paragraphs was calculated from the parish annual reports, AAD. See Philip Taylor, *The Distant Magnet* (New York, 1971), pp. 167-209, for estimates of immigrant wages and expenditures during various periods. In the early twentieth century several American dioceses set quotas anywhere from 4% to 10% of annual income as the Church's share. The average Polish contribution of $17.55 would be about 3% or 4% of an unskilled laborer's wage. See Michael N. Kremer, "Church Support in the United States" (Ph.D. diss., Catholic University of America, 1930).

17 The parish I attended in Chicago in 1975-76 set an official goal of $5.00 per family per week. This total of $260 yearly was about equal to one month's apartment rent. For the wage differences, see "Immigrants in Cities," *Reports of the Immigration Commission*, II, 147.

18 One important exception is the Bohemians. After 1916 their financial support equaled, and sometimes exceeded, the level of the Poles, Lithuanians, and Slovaks. Over the period 1908-1947, the Italians slowly raised their level of financial support, but at all times they remained at the bottom of the list.

19 Joseph Wytrwal, *America's Polish Heritage* (Detroit, 1961), pp. 148-259, contains the best description of the PNA and the PRCU in English.

20 Greene, *For God and Country*, pp. 61-68; Kantowicz, *Polish-American Politics*, pp. 26, 94. Among the Poles, a small socialist leadership group also existed. From 1907 to 1924 the Polish Section of the Socialist party of America published a Polish daily paper in Chicago which heaped scorn on both the Polish priests and the bourgeois nationalists. Other East European groups also had small socialist, and sometimes also communist, contingents. The role of socialism among East European Catholic immigrants cries out for historical study.

21 *Panorama: A Historical Review of Czechs and Slovaks in the USA* (Cicero, Ill., 1976), pp. 31-32; Horak, "Assimilation of Czechs," p. 84; Eugene R. McCarthy, "The Bohemians in Chicago and Their Benevolent Societies" (M.A. thesis, University of Chicago, 1950), pp. 35-38.

22 Joseph Krisciunas, "Lithuanians in Chicago" (M.A. thesis, DePaul University, 1935), pp. 42-44, 50-51, 56-62; Marion Mark Stolarik, "Immigration and Urbanization: The Slovak Experience, 1870-1918" (Ph.D. diss., University of Minnesota, 1974), pp. 228-229.

23 Patrick J. Dignan, "A History of Legal Incorporation of Catholic Property in the United States, 1784-1932" (Ph.D. diss., Catholic University of America, 1933).

24 Greene, *For God and Country*, pp. 70-71; Galush, "Polish National Catholic Church," pp. 132-133; Mark Stolarik, "Lay Initiative in American Slovak Parishes, 1880-1930," *Records of the American Catholic Historical Society of Philadelphia*, LXXXIII (Sep.-Dec. 1972), 151-158.

25 The exact nature of the Resurrectionist-episcopal agreement is uncertain. The only surviving record of it is in the memoirs of the

Resurrectionists' Superior-General, Jerome Kajsziewicz, *Pisma: Rosprawy, Listy z Podrozy, Pamietnik o Zgromadzenia* (Berlin, 1872), III, 350. Joseph Parot mounted a search for some firmer evidence of the agreement, but was unsuccessful: see Parot, "Persistence of Polonia," p. 39, n. 55. For the Holy Trinity controversy, see Greene, *For God and Country*, pp. 74-82; Parot, pp. 40-64; John Iwicki, *The First Hundred Years, 1866-1966* (Rome, 1966), pp. 10-64.

26   Greene, *For God and Country*, pp. 103-108; Parot, "Persistence of Polonia," pp. 74-75; Galush, "Polish National Catholic Church," pp. 133-134.

27   Greene, *For God and Country*, p. 109.

28   Galush, "Polish National Catholic Church," pp. 134-145; John P. Gallagher, *A Century of History: The Diocese of Scranton, 1868-1968* (Scranton, Pa., 1968), pp. 154-223; Theodore Andrews, *The Polish National Catholic Church in America and Poland* (London, 1953), pp. 18-25; Paul Fox, *The Polish National Catholic Church* (Scranton, n.d.), pp. 139-140.

29   Parot, "Persistence of Polonia," pp. 127-154.

30   Bohdan P. Prosko, "Soter Ortynsky: First Ruthenian Bishop in the United States, 1907-1916," *Catholic Historical Review*, LXIII (Jan. 1973), 513-533; Gerald R. Fogarty, "The American Hierarchy and Oriental Rite Catholics, 1890-1907," *Records of the American Catholic Historical Society of Philadelphia*, LXXXV (Mar.-June 1974), 17-28.

31   Parot, "Persistence of Polonia," p. 156; Greene, *For God and Country*, pp. 141-142. The Polish auxiliary in Milwaukee was Edward Kozlowski, no relation to the schismatic Anthony Kozlowski.

32   Greene, *For God and Country*, p. 142, misconstrues the significance of Rhode's appointment, picturing it as a successful conclusion of the Polish recognition drive and ending his book at that point. He implies that Rhode, as auxiliary bishop, shared in the archbishop's corporate, financial authority, which is erroneous. For a good example of how unimportant an auxiliary bishop can be, consult Ch. 7 of Robert I. Gannon, *The Cardinal Spellman Story* (Garden City, N.Y., 1962).

33   Shanabruch, "Church's Role in Americanization," pp. 557-569; Parot, "Persistence of Polonia," pp. 302-303, 311-340.

34   Kruszka to Pius XI, June 9, 1923 (AAD: 7-1923-P-21).

35   The rest of this section is largely derived from my uncompleted research for a forthcoming study of Cardinal Mundelein. It is based mainly on chancery records at the Archdiocesan Archives; the files of *The New World*, Chicago's archdiocesan newspaper; and a collective biography of the Chicago clergy which I have compiled. Some pertinent references to Mundelein's early years can be found in Shanabruch, "Church's Role in Americanization," pp. 554-557; Sanders, "Education of Chicago Catholics," pp. 157-164, 215-236; and Parot, "Persistence of Polonia," pp. 311-322.

36   Polish Clergy Association to George Mundelein, July 9, 1917 (Polish Roman Catholic Union Archives).

37   These figures were obtained by tracing the "cohort" of priests

ordained in 1926 and 1927 through their entire careers by means of
the official announcements of appointments in *The New World* and
the yearly listings in *The Catholic Directory*. The 1916-1917 cohort
showed a similar disparity: 22 years waiting time for Polish priests,
15.4 for Irish. However, the cohorts of 1936-37 and thereafter show
a different pattern. By this time, Mundelein's seminary was producing
such a supply of clerics that all priests of the archdiocese, Polish
and non-Polish alike, had to wait between twenty-five and thirty
years for a pastorate.

38 See Kantowicz, *Polish-American Politics*, for all references in this
    section.
39 *Dziennik Chicagoski*, Mar. 14, 1933, p. 4.
40 Sr. Lucille Wargin, C.R., "The Polish Immigrant in the American
    Community, 1880-1930" (M.A. thesis, De Paul University, 1948),
    pp. 54-55.
41 Russell Barta, "The Representation of Poles, Italians, Latins and
    Blacks in the Executive Suites of Chicago's Largest Corporations,"
    Minority Report (National Center for Urban Ethnic Affairs, Washing-
    ton, D.C.). See also the NORC study by Andrew Greeley and
    William McCready (Beverly Hills, Cal., 1977).

Chapter VI: Black Chicago

1 Edward H. Wright, the "Iron Master" of Chicago politics, came to
   the city in 1884 (*Chicago Inter-Ocean*, June 14, 1900); Dan Jackson
   came in 1892 (Works Progress Administration, "The Negro in
   Illinois," Hirsh Collection, Carter G. Woodson Regional Center,
   Chicago Public Library [hereafter cited as WPA papers]); Louis
   B. Anderson came in about 1894 (Thomas Yenser, ed., *Who's Who in
   Colored America* [Brooklyn, 1942], p. 29); DePriest came to Chicago
   in 1889 (*Broad Ax*, Apr. 18, 1903); Archibald Carey came in 1898
   (Joseph A. Logsdon, "The Rev. Archibald Carey and the Negro in
   Chicago Politics" [M.A. thesis, University of Chicago, 1961], p. 9).
2 Bessie Louise Pierce, *A History of Chicago*, 3 vols. (New York, 1937
   [I], 1940 [II], 1957 [III]), is the most comprehensive study of
   the city yet produced; unfortunately, it only goes up to 1893. The
   best general studies of black Chicago are: St. Clair Drake and Horace
   Clayton, *Black Metropolis* (New York, 1945), and the more limited
   study by Allan H. Spear, *Black Chicago* (Chicago, 1967), which
   covers the period from 1890 to 1920. The best general study of
   black politics is still Harold Gosnell's *Negro Politicians* (Chicago,
   1935), which can be supplemented with James Q. Wilson's inter-
   pretive discussion of more contemporary politics in Chicago and
   other cities, *Negro Politics* (New York, 1961).
3 Mason Fishback, "Illinois Legislation on Slavery and Free Negroes,
   1818-1865," *Transactions of the Illinois State Historical Society*, IX
   (Springfield, Ill., 1904), 414-432; *Public Laws of the State of Illinois
   passed by the . . . . General Assembly* (1853); *Illinois Revised
   Statutes* (1845).

4 *Weekly Chicago Democrat*, Nov. 3, 1846.

5 Estelle Hill Scott, *Occupational Changes Among Negroes in Chicago* (Chicago, WPA, 1939, mimeographed), p. 18. The servant class claimed 53.7% of all Negro workers: 47.3% of the males and 77.1% of the females.

6 *Ibid.*, p. 49.

7 *Ibid.*, p. 20.

8 Alma Herbst, *The Negro in the Slaughtering and Meat Packing Industry in Chicago* (New York, 1932), pp. 19-29.

9 The sewer riot received extensive coverage in the *Chicago Tribune*, Nov. 30, 1899; *Chicago Times-Herald*, Nov. 29, 1899; *Chicago Inter-Ocean*, Nov. 15, 1899; *Chicago Record-Herald*, Nov. 29, 1899 (the *Record-Herald's* headline states that the riot took place on 29th Street, but its text states that it occurred on 39th Street); *Daily Inter-Ocean*, Nov. 29, 1899; *Chicago Journal*, Nov. 29, 1899. On the teamster's strike see *Chicago Tribune*, Apr. 7-May 3, 1905; *Broad Ax*, Oct. 15, 1904; May 6, 13, 20, 27, 1905; Spear, *Black Chicago*, p. 40.

10 *Chicago Tribune*, Feb. 10, 1890. In 1888 a black man was charged $3.55 for a 35¢ order of roast beef and a 5¢ cup of coffee at the Brevort House. He sued and was awarded $15. In another case, filed by Josephine M. Curry against the People's Theatre, the judge declared that placing Negroes in a special part of the theatre on the basis of race was as discriminatory as denying a person admittance to the theatre altogether. The proprietor was fined $100 (*Chicago Tribune*, Mar. 16 and 17, 1866). These and similar cases of racial discrimination cited in Pierce, pp. 49-50.

11 Thomas Philpott, "The House and the Neighborhood: Housing Reform and Neighborhood Work in Chicago, 1880-1930" (Ph.D. diss., University of Chicago, 1974), p. 184. For a general discussion of the emergence of the "color line" in Chicago, see Ch. 4, pp. 149-184.

12 Rayford Logan, *The Betrayal of the Negro: From Rutherford B. Hayes to Woodrow Wilson* (New York, 1954), p. 9.

13 Ann Lane, "The Negro's Response: A Study in Desperation," in Frederic Cople Jaher, *The Age of Industrialism in America* (New York, 1968), p. 111; Richard Hofstadter, *Social Darwinism in American Thought* (Philadelphia, 1944), p. 148.

14 Spear, p. 61.

15 Fannie Barrier Williams, "Social Bonds in the 'Black Belt' of Chicago," *Charities*, XV, No. 1 (Oct. 7, 1905), 40.

16 Early national Negro political debates centered on assertion of Negro "manhood" rights and the explosive questions of black emigration from the United States. By the 1850s, however, the implications of national passage of the Fugitive Slave Law of 1850 became the major political question facing Northern blacks. Pre-Civil War debate is explored in Howard Holman Bell, *A Survey of the Negro Convention Movement, 1830-1861* (New York, 1969, a reprint of Bell's Ph.D. diss., Northwestern University, 1953).

17 See V. Jacque Voegeli, *Free But Not Equal* (Chicago, 1967), p. 2. Democratic and Republican jockeying over the race issue is recorded

in *Chicago Tribune*, March 6, 1862; July 15, 1862; Aug. 10, 1862; Jan. 16, 1863; Feb. 12 and 13, 1863; *Chicago Times*, Feb. 13, 1863. See also Frank L. Klement, *The Copperheads in the Middle West* (Chicago, 1960), and Norman Dwight Harris, *The Study of Negro Servitude in Illinois, and of the Slavery Agitation in that State, 1719-1864* (Chicago, 1904).

18 Drake and Cayton, pp. 44-50.

19 Certificate of Freedom, Nov. 28, 1844, William Tyler Brown, Clerk of Circuit Court of Madison County, Illinois, John Jones Collection, Chicago Historical Society (hereafter CHS); *Chicago Tribune*, May 22, 1879.

20 *Chicago Tribune*, Jan. 2, 1874.

21 Mrs. Lavinia Jones Lee to Caroline McIlvaine, Apr. 21, 1905, John Jones Collection, CHS; Genna Rae McNeil, "The Price of Redemption: The Repeal of the Illinois Black Laws, 1864-1865" (unpublished paper in possession of author), ms. p. 37.

22 *Chicago Times*, Nov. 23, 1864; *Journal of the House of Representatives, Proceedings*, Feb. 4, 1865, p. 551, cited in McNeil, p. 57.

23 *Chicago Tribune*, Dec. 9, 1864; John Jones, *The Black Laws of Illinois and a Few Reasons Why They Should be Repealed* (Chicago, 1864), in John Jones Collection, CHS.

24 The interrelationship between the repeal campaign, white abolitionism, and partisan political concerns emerged from a reading of the McNeil paper, but responsibility for the interpretation is entirely my own.

25 *Chicago Tribune*, May 22, 1879.

26 Spear, pp. 51-89.

27 Gosnell, pp. 65-66. Thomas received 11,532 votes in 1876, although the total black population was less than 7,000. See also *Conservator*, Dec. 23, 1882.

28 Thomas introduced House Bill No. 45, "An Act to protect all citizens in their civil and legal rights," *Journal of the House of Representatives of the Thirty-Fourth General Assembly of the State of Illinois* (Springfield, 1885), p. 113; *Laws of the State of Illinois enacted by the 34th General Assembly*, Jan. 7-June 26, 1885 (Springfield, 1885), pp. 64-65; Edward E. Wilson, "The Chicago Negro in Politics," *The Voice*, Mar. 1907, pp. 98-103.

29 *Journal of the House of Representatives. . . ,* 1889, pp. 181, 424.

30 Joseph J. Boris, ed., *Who's Who in Colored America: A Biographical Dictionary of Notable Living Persons of Negro Descent in America* (New York, 1927), p. 145; The Washington Intercollegiate Club of Chicago, *Intercollegian Wonder Book, or The Negro in Chicago, 1779-1927* (Chicago, 1927), p. 112 [hereafter *Intercollegian*]; *Inter-Ocean*, Jan. 14, 1900; August Meier, *Negro Thought in America, 1880-1915* (Ann Arbor, 1963), p. 178; Spear, pp. 61-63. Apparently not everyone thought so highly of Atty. Morris. A *Broad Ax* headline of March 27, 1909 read: "COL. E. H. MORRIS AT ONE TIME CHIEF ATTORNEY FOR THE "GAMBLER TRUST"; Morris was charged with defending several notorious gamblers in court. See also *Broad Ax*, July 2, 1910; May 18, 1918.

31 *Defender*, June 21, 1924.
32 *Journal of the House...*, HB 239, HB 23, p. 1509; *Journal of the House...*, 1905, pp. 80, 64, 665, 730, 744, 777.
33 *Broad Ax*, May 18, 1918; *Defender*, Feb. 3, 1933; *Journal of the House...*, 1905, HB 155, pp. 638, 645.
34 *Defender*, June 21, 1924; WPA Papers; Gosnell, pp. 111-112; Ira Katznelson, *Black Men, White Cities* (New York, 1973), p. 91.
35 *Broad Ax*, Dec. 25, 1909.
36 *Defender*, Feb. 4, 1933; *Journal of the House...*, 1895, pp. 133, 104; *ibid.*, 1897, pp. 133, 104, 183, 282; W. G. Sea, "The Eighth Illinois," *Negro History Bulletin*, VII, No. 7 (Apr. 1944), 149-150; William B. Gatewood, "An Experiment in Color: The Eighth Illinois Volunteers, 1898-1899," *Journal of the Illinois State Historical Society*, LXV, No. 3 (Autumn 1972), 293-305.
37 *Defender*, Oct. 24, 1932; Thomas Bullard, "From Businessman to Congressman: The Careers of Martin B. Madden" (Ph.D. diss., University of Illinois at Chicago Circle, 1973), p. 80.
38 *Journal of the House . . .*, 1897, HB 50, pp. 83, 420, 502; HB 263, pp. 182, 183; HB 395, p. 244. See also pp. 152, 667, 714, 907.
39 *Defender*, July 2, 1927; *Inter-Ocean*, Aug. 14, 1895; William M. Tuttle, Jr., *Race Riot: Chicago in the Red Summer of 1919* (New York, 1970), p. 113; Arna Bontemps and Jack Conroy, *Anyplace But Here* (New York, 1966), pp. 142-144.
40 James A. Roe, ed., *Blue Book of the State of Illinois, 1899* (Springfield, 1899), p. 297; *Journal of the House...*, HB 462, HB 463, and HB 686, pp. 275, 301. Martin also introduced HB 810, which would permit children of school age to attend public schools nearest their homes. The bill may have been intended as an anti-discriminatory piece of legislation — a safeguard against school segregation through district gerrymandering. *Journal*, p. 676; *Defender*, Feb. 4, 1933.
41 *Journal*, 1899, HB 577, p. 277; HB 715 and 716, p. 338.
42 *Ibid.*, HB 561, p. 275; HB 562, p. 275; HB 578, p. 277; HB 689, p. 301.
43 Spear, pp. 62-63.
44 *Journal*, 1901, HB 6, p. 46; HB 278, p. 151.
45 *Ibid.*, HB 235, p. 151; HB 400, p. 191; HB 41, p. 66; HB 482, p. 66; HB 564, p. 263.
46 *Ibid.*, HB 553, p. 208; HB 682, p. 362; *Gideon v. Wainwright*, 372 U.S. 335 (1963): 1030, 1032; *Douglas v. California*, 372 U.S. 352 (1963): 1031; *Escobedo v. Illinois*, 378 U.S. 478 (1964): 1032.
47 Mae Felts Herringshaw, ed., "Chicago Men of 1913," *Clark J. Herringshaw's City Blue Book of Current Biography* (Chicago, 1913), p. 159; *Broad Ax*, Apr. 20, 1901; *Chicago Tribune*, Dec. 9, 1900; Mar. 2, 1901; Mar. 3 and 14, 1901; *Inter-Ocean*, Nov. 21, 1900; Mar. 25, 1901.
48 *Inter-Ocean*, Jan. 4, 1891; *Chicago Tribune*, May 6, 1897; Gosnell, p. 112; *Broad Ax*, Dec. 25, 1909.
49 Buckner died in 1913, two years before DePriest became the city's first black alderman. The Buckner funeral cortège was one mile long;

DePriest was in charge, and Madden delivered the eulogy. A John Buckner Memorial Association was incorporated in 1925, with DePriest as president. See *Defender*, Nov. 12, 1932; Dec. 26, 1913; May 30, 1925; Sep. 15, 1928; Apr. 3, 1926.
50 *Broad Ax*, Dec. 30, 1905; Aug. 15, 1908; Drake, pp. 361-362.
51 *Defender*, Feb. 5, 1938.
52 Members of the assistant corporations council were Franklin A. Denison and Earl B. Dickerson; State Representatives Buckner, Bish, R. R. Jackson, William Warfield, George W. Blackwell and Charles Jenkins; State Senator Jackson; Aldermen Jackson, Earl B. Dickerson, and William L. Dawson; and Congressman Dawson.
53 Gosnell, pp. 216-217.
54 Logsdon, "The Rev. Archibald Carey and the Negro in Chicago Politics," pp. 36-39.
55 *Ibid.*, pp. 24-25.
56 Mark Miles Fisher, *The Master's Slave: Elijah John Fisher* (Philadelphia, 1922), pp. 75, 145.
57 Deneen to Fisher, April 9, 1904; "A Word to Colored Voters, Endorsing Charles S. Deneen for Governor of the State of Illinois, in the primary of May 6, 1904," Dunne to Fisher, June 14, 1905; Deneen to Fisher, Aug. 17, 1908 (thanks for endorsement); letter, National Taft Bureau, 1908, in Fisher, pp. 75, 76, 93, 107, 145-146. In 1905, Fisher needed $20,000 to complete his church in time for a Chicago meeting of the National Baptist Convention. He got financial help from Frank O. Lowden, later Governor of Illinois, and George Dixon of Borden Milk Company, and from Republican judges McEwn and Hanecy. Fisher, pp. 95-96.
58 Albert L. Kreiling, "The Making of Racial Identities in the Black Press: A Cultural Analysis of Race Journalism in Chicago, 1878-1929" (Ph.D. diss., University of Illinois, Urbana-Champaign, 1973).
59 Ralph Nelson Davis, "The Negro Newspaper in Chicago" (M.A. thesis, University of Chicago, 1939), p. 30; Kreiling, p. 165.
60 *Defender*, Apr. 3, 1926; Davis, pp. 42-43; I. Garland Penn, *The Afro-American Press* (Springfield, 1891), pp. 256-258.
61 Davis, pp. 31-32.
62 *Broad Ax*, July 15, 1899; Jan. 6, 1900.
63 Taylor's economic radicalism can be found in *Broad Ax*, July 15, 1899 and Jan. 6, 1900. His Democratic allegiance was, however, not unswerving. On occasion he would commend or even endorse a Republican, usually a black Republican, for elective office. He was particularly partial to Ed Wright (*Broad Ax*, Feb. 10, 1900) and Oscar DePriest (*Broad Ax*, Dec. 27, 1904).
64 The paper's political views are revealed in *Conservator*, Dec. 23, 1882; Davis, p. 16.
65 Wilson, p. 100.
66 *Inter-Ocean*, Oct. 28, 1892; Nov. 13, 1893.
67 *Ibid.*, June 10, 1894.
68 *Defender*, July 5, 1930; *Intercollegian*, p. 103; Gosnell, p. 154.
69 *Defender*, Nov. 5, 1932; *Intercollegian*, p. 135; *Defender*, Jan. 4, 1913.
70 Gosnell, p. 154; *Defender*, Nov. 5, 1932.

71 *Defender*, Nov. 5, 1932.
72 *Defender*, July 5, 1930; Gosnell, p. 155; *Intercollegian*, p. 135.
73 Gosnell, p. 154.
74 Ellen Josephine Beckman, "The Relationship of the Government of the City of Chicago to Cook County from 1893 to 1916" (M.A. thesis, University of Chicago, 1940), p. 608; *Chicago Daily News*, Aug. 20, 1900.
75 *Chicago Tribune*, Mar. 1, 1895; Jan. 5, 1896; Apr. 8, 1896; *Chicago Daily News*, Apr. 2, 1910; Beckman, p. 14.
76 The Republican nominee in 1900 was Daniel M. Jackson, a South-side funeral director with gambling interests, who was defeated, in part, by the use of the race issue in the white press. *Broad Ax*, Feb. 9, 1901; May 4, 1907; Gosnell, pp. 83, 131, 156.
77 *Defender*, Apr. 20, 1929; Drake, p. 361; Gosnell, p. 164.
78 *Broad Ax*, Dec. 30, 1905; Gosnell, p. 168.
79 *Broad Ax*, Apr. 18, 1903; Dec. 30, 1905.
80 *Broad Ax*, Dec. 30, 1905; Gosnell, p. 169.
81 *Inter-Ocean*, "The Rise of the Sumner Club," Jan. 14, 1900. Both Harding and Madden were members of the Hamilton Club. *Blue Book, 1911*, pp. 68, 72.
82 *Defender*, Feb. 12, 1910; June 6, 1929; *Chicago Whip*, May 10, 1929; July 6, 1929; Gosnell, pp. 111, 316, 318; Spear, p. 781.
83 *Defender*, Mar. 4, 1910.
84 *Defender*, Feb. 5, 1910.
85 *Defender*, Feb. 3, 1912; *Broad Ax*, Nov. 28, 1914.
86 The extent of Wright's concern for the independence of political organizations representing black Chicagoans is perhaps over-emphasized in eulogies and articles written by Wright partisans after his death. Yet his activities between 1900 and 1915 seem to bear out this general interpretation. See *Defender*, Dec. 24, 1932; Dec. 31, 1932; *Chicago Whip*, Aug. 16, 1930. Wright is credited with having Anderson appointed assistant county attorney, with getting Dr. Daniel Hale Williams appointed to the Cook County Hospital Staff and F. L. Barnett as the first assistant states attorney while Wright was County Commissioner. *Intercollegian*, p. 103.
87 *Inter-Ocean*, Jan. 23, 1895; Alfreda M. Duster, ed., *Crusade for Justice; The Autobiography of Ida B. Wells* (Chicago, 1970), xxix, 352.
88 *Broad Ax*, Nov. 2, 1907; Nov. 9, 1908; May 21, 1910.
89 Merriam Papers, University of Chicago, Box LXXIV, Folder 4; *Interim Report*, Municipal Voters League, Thirteenth Year, 1926, p. 1. Criticisms of Anderson and Jackson can be found in *Twenty-Sixth Annual Preliminary Report*, MVL, 1912, 1919, 1920, 1925, and 1927.
90 Author's interview with Mae C. Barnett, Jan. 2, 1972.
91 Heinz Eulau and Kenneth Prewitt, *Labyrinths of Democracy: Adaptations, Linkages, Representation, and Policies in Urban Politics* (Indianapolis, 1973), p. 262.
92 It was the geography of Chicago ward politics that allowed

blacks to advance so rapidly. Chicago used the ward system with relatively small, ethnically homogenous political units, which, coupled with residential segregation, enabled blacks to maximize their numbers. On the other hand, New York blacks had to contend with large political units gerrymandered to protect Italian and Jewish political power.

93 Katznelson, pp. 102-103.

94 *Ibid.*, pp. 196-197.

95 Wilson, pp. 169-185.

96 Martin Kilson, "Political Change in the Negro Ghetto, 1900-1940's," in Nathan I. Huggins, Martin Kilson, and Daniel M. Fox, eds., *Key Issues in the Afro-American Experience* (New York, 1971), pp. 167-174.

97 *Ibid.*, pp. 174-182.

98 *Ibid.*, pp. 182-183.

99 "Diary," John Jones Collection, CHS, no pagination.

100 *Ibid.*

101 *Broad Ax*, Nov. 2, 1907.

102 *Defender*, Sep. 7, 1912.

103 In 1938, Democrat Edward M. Sneed, the first black Democratic ward committeeman was elected to the county commission.

104 A fuller understanding of the interrelationship between black economic nationalism, laissez-faire capitalism, and black political conservatism can be found in Meier, *Negro Thought in America*, and Louis Harlan, *Booker T. Washington: The Making of a Black Leader, 1856-1902* (New York, 1972).

105 *Chicago Chronicle*, Nov. 8, 1906.

106 *Chicago Tribune*, Jan. 2, 1874.

107 *Ibid.*, Mar. 12, 1875. The article, which described a party given by Jones for his daughter Lavinia, was headlined "Chicago's Favorite Colored Citizen."

108 *Chicago Whip*, Mar. 29, 1924.

109 Henry McGhee, "The Negro in the Chicago Post Office" (M.A. thesis, University of Chicago, 1961), pp. 7-8, cited in Katznelson, pp. 96-97.

110 Robert L. Factor, *The Black Response to America* (Menlo Park, Cal., 1970), pp. 48-58.

111 *The Appeal*, Aug. 28, 1888, cited in Spear, p. 125.

112 *Chicago Daily News*, Apr. 6, 1895; *Inter-Ocean*, Apr. 6, 1885.

113 *Broad Ax*, Oct. 1, 1898; Aug. 12, 1899. The Colored Democratic League established its permanent headquarters on Oct. 1, 1898.

114 *Broad Ax*, Aug. 12, 1899. Newby edited the *Indianapolis Courier* from 1892 to 1893, and when he came to Chicago he also served as editor and owner of two short-lived papers, the *Chicago Leader* (1896-1897) and the *Chicago Plaindealer* (1916-1918). *Who's Who in Colored America*, 6th ed., 1941-1944, p. 384.

115 *Broad Ax*, Oct. 1, 1898; May 26, 1900; Apr. 20, 1901; Spear, p. 125.

116 *Broad Ax*, Apr. 6, 1900; Apr. 20, 1901; May 18, 1901.

117 Harrison's popularity with blacks gave rise to the overly optimis-

tic prediction that "the social ostracism that made in former days the life of a 'nigger democrat' as he was termed, a burden, has been obliterated." *Broad Ax*, Oct. 1, 1898. See also *Broad Ax*, Apr. 6, 1911; Gosnell, p. 252. The *Conservator* endorsed Carter Harrison II in 1878 and 1880. Nelson, p. 14.

118 Wilson, p. 101.
119 Spear, p. 125; Meier, p. 274. The traditional anti-Democratic argument is presented in Henry Rucker, "Why Colored Men Cannot be Democrats," *Voice of the Negro*, I, No. 9 (Sep. 1904), 386-390. The article makes a special reference to the treatment of blacks at Democratic political conventions and cites Southern demagogues like Tillman and Vardaman.
120 I am particularly impressed with Kilson's analysis of the "modernization" of black politics. The experience is similar in many important ways to those of a West African political elite. See his *Political Change in a West African State: A Study of the Modernization Process in Sierra Leone* (Cambridge, Mass., 1966), especially the sub-chapters "A Note on the 'Mass Factor' in Political Change," pp. 117-122, and "The 'Mass Factor' in Political Change," pp. 284-286.
121 Wilson, pp. 102-103.

Chapter VII: Jewish Chicago

This chapter partly derives from research undertaken for the Ph.D. degree in History at the University of Chicago, supervised by Prof. Arthur Mann, for whose guiding counsel the author is deeply grateful.

1 *The Occident*, Dec. 21, 1886.
2 Nathan Glazer, *American Judaism* (Chicago, 1957), p. 23; Marshall Sklare, ed., *The Jews: Social Patterns of an American Group* (New York, 1958), p. 11; Walter LaQueur, *A History of Zionism* (New York, 1972), pp. 3-6, 21-25; Eric E. Hirshler, ed., *Jews From Germany in the United States* (New York, 1955), pp. 22, 34-36, 116.
3 Hyman L. Meites, *History of the Jews of Chicago* (Chicago, 1924), pp. 37-39.
4 *Ibid.*, p. 46.
5 *Ibid.*
6 Louis Wirth, *The Ghetto* (Chicago, 1928), pp. 257-261; Meites, pp. 37-39, 41, 46.
7 Bernard Felsenthal and Herman Eliassof, *History of Kehillath Anshe Maariv* (Chicago, 1897), p. 12; Jacob J. Weinstein, *A History of K.A.M. Congregation of the Men of the West* (Chicago, 1951), p. 3.
8 Morris A. Gutstein, *A Priceless Heritage* (New York, 1953), pp. 27, 31; Meites, pp. 53, 78-79.
9 Gutstein, pp. 28-29.
10 Meites, pp. 100-107, 149, 155, 407-416; Wirth, p. 174.
11 *Ibid.*, pp. 172-174.
12 Philip L. Bregstone, *Chicago and its Jews: A Cultural History* (Chicago, 1933), pp. 143-144; Erich Rosenthal, "Acculturation Without Assimilation? The Jewish Community of Chicago, Illinois," *American Journal*

of Sociology, LXVI (Nov. 1960), 279; Vivien M. Palmer, *History of Chicago Communities* (typescript, Chicago Historical Society, 1930), V, Document 6.

13 Gutstein, p. 283; Meites, pp. 45-46.

14 Sinai Executive Board Minutes, Dec. 28, 1885; Gutstein, pp. 172-173.

15 *The Reform Advocate*, I (26 Sep. 1891).

16 *Ibid.*, p. 21; XXI (May 4, 1901), 305; Harold Korey, "The History of Jewish Education in Chicago" (Master's thesis, University of Chicago, 1922), p. 40.

17 Wirth, p. 170.

18 *Hull House Maps and Papers* (New York, 1895), pp. 17, 93; Wilfred Carsel, *A History of the Chicago Ladies Garment Workers' Union* (Chicago, 1940), p. 237; Wirth, p. 180.

19 Carsel, pp. 5-6.

20 Charles S. Bernheimer, *The Russian Jew in the United States* (Philadelphia, 1905), pp. 136-137, 321-322; Robert Hunter, *Tenement Conditions in Chicago* (Chicago, 1901), pp. 60, 64, 97, 108; Melech Epstein, *Jewish Labor in the United States* (New York, 1942), I, 104; Rosenthal, pp. 278-279.

21 Florence Kelly, *First Special Report of the Factory Inspectors of Illinois on Small-Pox in the Tenement House Sweatshops of Chicago* (Springfield, Ill., 1894), pp. 6, 8-10, 40.

22 Oscar Handlin, *Adventure in Freedom* (New York, 1954), p. 92.

23 Bernheimer, p. 140.

24 *Yiddishe Arbeiter Welt* (Yiddish), May 10, 1910, p. 3; Epstein, I, 94; Kelly, pp. 10-11; *Hull House Maps and Papers*, p. 41.

25 "The Immigrant," *Council of Jewish Women Monthly Bulletin*, IV (Sep. 1912); Joel A. Tarr, *A Study in Boss Politics: William Lorimer of Chicago* (Urbana, Ill., 1971), pp. 13-14; Bernard Horwich, *My First Eighty Years* (Chicago, 1939), p. 126. Horwich observes that "crime was rampant and no one was safe. Especially Jews, they were constantly the recipients of well aimed missiles being thrown at them and their long beards made welcome targets for youths who delighted in pulling those beards. These men of Israel carried packs on their backs filled with notions and light dry goods. . . . There was hardly a streetcar where there were not to be found some Jewish peddlers with their packs riding to or from their business."

26 *Sentinel History of Chicago Jewry, 1911-1961* (Chicago, 1961), pp. 79-85; Simon Rawidowicz, ed., *The Chicago Pinkas* (Chicago, 1952), pp. 125-126.

27 *The Occident*, Sep. 28, 1889.

28 *Report of the Senate Vice Committee* (Springfield, Ill., 1916), p. 402; Esther Kohn Papers (Jane Addams Hull House Museum, Chicago), III, n.d., "Speeches and Articles"; Bernheimer, pp. 251-254.

29 Wirth, p. 205.

30 *The Occident*, Dec. 31, 1886.

31 *Ibid.*, May 29, 1891.

32 Gutstein, p. 37.

33 Erich Rosenthal, "This Was North Lawndale," *Jewish Social Studies*, XXII (1960), 68-69; Wirth, p. 191.

34 Louis Wirth and Eleanor H. Bernert, eds., *Local Community Fact Book of Chicago* (Chicago, 1949), p. 29; Rosenthal, "Acculturation Without Assimilation," pp. 276-282; "The Jewish Community of Albany Park," Sec. II of *Report of Study of the Jewish People's Institute, Chicago, Illinois* (New York, Jewish Welfare Board, 1937), pp. 2-3, 6.

35 *Ibid.*, pp. 32-40; Meites, p. 535; *History of Chicago Communities,* I, Documents 57, 67, 68, 69.

36 Wirth, pp. 257-261; Bregstone, pp. 143-144; Rawidowicz, *Chicago Pinkas*, p. 79; Paul R. Conway, "The Apartment House Dweller: A Study of Social Change in Hyde Park" (M.A. thesis, University of Chicago, 1926), pp. 214-215.

37 *Sentinel History of Chicago Jewry*, p. 27; Ernest W. Burgess Papers, IV, Box 48, University of Chicago.

38 For an extended and comprehensive examination of the politics of Chicago Jewry, see Edward H. Mazur, "Minyans for a Prairie City: The Politics of Chicago Jewry, 1850-1940" (Ph.D. diss., University of Chicago, 1974). See also Joel A. Tarr, *Boss Politics;* Carter H. Harrison II, *Stormy Years* (Indianapolis, 1935); W.J. Abbott, *Carter Henry Harrison: A Memoir* (New York, 1895); Adolf Kraus, *Reminiscences and Comments* (Chicago, 1925).

39 *Reform Advocate*, XXIII, No. 6 (Mar. 15, 1902), 476.

40 In 1914, Horner's victory margin was 32,633 votes; in 1930, his margin was 691,854. Tom Littlewood, *Horner of Illinois* (Evanston, 1969), pp. 29, 33-35, 44.

41 Adolph Sabath, a Bohemian-Jew, was elected U.S. congressman of the 5th District in 1906 and served until his death in 1952. His aide-de-camp and chief liaison with the Jewish community, Harry Fisher, became a municipal court justice in 1912. Michael and Moe Rosenberg were the chieftains of the 24th Ward, the Lawndale Jewish ghetto. Under their tutelage the ward became one of the leading Democratic bastions in Chicago. Michael was ward committeeman from 1923 until his death in 1928. His brother Moe succeeded him and governed the ward until he died in 1934. The committeemanship was assumed by Alderman Jacob Arvey, who had served in the city council since 1923. Under his leadership, the 24th Ward, the most Jewish election district in Chicago, became known as the number one Democratic precinct in the United States.

42 *Sunday Jewish Courier*, Apr. 10, 1934, p. 10.

43 A survey of twenty-five precincts with at least a 50% German-Jewish majority indicates that Horner received 77.2% of the German-Jewish vote. A similar survey of 111 Eastern European-Jewish precincts with at least a 55% East European-Jewish majority indicates that Horner received 86.2% of the East European vote.

44 Charles E. Merriam Papers, Apr. 7, 1934, University of Chicago, Box 99, Folder 6.

45 Littlewood, p. 182; *New Republic*, CXVI (Mar. 24, 1947), pp. 20-23. Horner averaged 71.8% of the vote in 30 German-Jewish precincts, compared to 51.6% in 114 precincts with at least a 55% East European-Jewish majority.

46 In the general election, Henry Horner's vote in the 30 German-Jewish precincts averaged 68.3%. The slight decline in German-Jewish support from the primary was more than offset by his 81.3% of the vote in the 114 precincts with at least a 55% East European-Jewish majority.

Chapter VIII: Mexican Chicago

1 See especially Paul S. Taylor, *Mexican Labor in the United States: Chicago and the Calumet Region*, University of California Publications in Economics, VII, No. 2 (Berkeley, 1932); Anita Edgar Jones, *Conditions Surrounding Mexicans in Chicago* (San Francisco, 1971); Mark Reisler, "The Mexican Immigrant in the Chicago Area During the 1920's," *Journal of the Illinois State Historical Society*, LXVI (Summer 1973), pp. 144-157.

2 See Edward Jackson Baur, "Delinquency among Mexican Boys in South Chicago" (M.A. thesis, University of Chicago, 1938), and "Mexican Migration to Chicago," WPA Research Library, Records of the Works Progress Administration, Record Group 69, National Archives. See also Louise Año Nuevo Kerr, "The Chicano Experience in Chicago: 1920-1970" (Ph.D. diss., University of Illinois at Chicago Circle, 1976). For further information about population changes in the Chicano population of Chicago, see Louis Wirth and Eleanor H. Bernert, ed., *Local Community Fact Book of Chicago* (Chicago, 1949).

3 Arthur Corwin, "Causes of Mexican Emigration to the United States: A Summary View," in Donald Fleming and Bernard Bailyn, eds., *Perspectives in American History* (Cambridge, Mass., 1973), VII, 567-568.

4 For a reliable account of the riots, see Carey McWilliams, *North from Mexico: The Spanish-Speaking People of the United States* (1949; reprint ed., New York, 1968), pp. 244-258.

5 Frank Tannenbaum, *Mexico: The Struggle for Peace and Bread* (New York, 1950), pp. 277-281.

6 Howard F. Cline, *The United States and Mexico* (Cambridge, Mass., rev. ed., 1962), p. 268.

7 Robert C. Jones, *Mexican War Workers in the United States: The Mexico-United States Manpower Recruiting Program and Operation, 1942 to 1944 Inclusive* (Washington, 1945), p. 1.

8 See, for example, George Messersmith to Secretary of State, Aug. 20, 1943 (two telegrams), Records of the War Manpower Commission, Record Group 211, National Archives, Washington, D.C.

9 Manuel Gamio, *Mexican Immigration to the United States: A Study of Human Migration and Adjustment* (1930; reprint ed., New York, 1971), pp. 170-196. See also "Agreement for the Temporary Migration of Mexican Workers" (Aug. 4, 1942), p. 1, Railroad Retirement Board Papers, Chicago. The second point listed under "General Principles" is instructive: "In accordance with the principles enunciated in executive order no. 8802, issued at the White House on June 25, 1941, *Mexican Nationals* [italics mine] who enter the United States as a

result of any understanding between the two governments shall not suffer discriminatory acts of any kind."

10 Robert C. Jones, *Mexican War Workers*, p. 2.

11 Messersmith to Secretary of State, Nov. 6, 1942, Records of the War Manpower Commission, Record Group 211.

12 Claude Wickard to Harold D. Smith, Nov. 5, 1942, Records of the Secretary of Agriculture, Record Group 16, National Archives, Washington, D.C. Speaking of the August 4 agreement, Secretary of Agriculture Wickard reported that "the Mexican government . . . insisted upon the asking by the United States of certain minimum guarantees to its nationals who would be so transported" [*sic*].

13 Conference on Mexico's Role in International Intellectual Cooperation, Albuquerque, 1945, *Mexico's Role in International Intellectual Cooperation*, University of New Mexico, School of Inter-American Affairs, Inter-Americana Series, Short Papers, no. 6 (Albuquerque, 1945), p. 43.

14 Churchill Murray to John D. Coates, Jan. 4, 1945, Records of the War Manpower Commission, Record Group 211. Murray wrote of the projected need for 1,000 Mexican nationals in heavy industry. In John D. Coates to Churchill Murray, Dec. 1, 1944, Coates had announced the need for an additional 25,000 Mexican nationals in the forge, foundry, tire, and other industries.

15 "Employment Situation in Important Labor Market Areas" [1943], p. 8, Records of the War Manpower Commission, Record Group 211.

16 "Estimate of Percentage by Which Unfilled Openings Could Be Reduced at Wage Rates Indicated," Railroad Retirement Board Papers, n.d.

17 "Mexican Placements, May 1, 1943 Thru September 30, 1945," Oct. 1945, Records of the War Manpower Commission, Record Group 211.

18 *Ibid.*

19 "Mexican Program—Status Tabulation," Aug. 18, 1945, Railroad Retirement Board Papers.

20 "Relations with Immigration and Naturalization Service," Nov. 13, 1944, Railroad Retirement Board Papers.

21 "Unfilled Openings, Referrals and Placements from Oct. 1 to Oct. 25, 1945," Railroad Retirement Board Papers, n.d.

22 W. H. Spencer to Executive Director, War Manpower Commission, Sep. 7, 1945, Records of the War Manpower Commission, Record Group 211.

23 E. J. Brock to Director of the United States Employment Service, Jan. 30, 1946, Records of the War Manpower Commission, Record Group 211.

24 H. B. Lautz to Mario Lasso, Consulate General of Mexico, Chicago, Dec. 11, 1944, Records of the War Manpower Commission, Record Group 211.

25 F. M. Wilson to Operating Officers of Member Roads, Mar. 16, 1944, with six-page attachment, "Hints on the Employment of Imported Mexican Laborers," Railroad Retirement Board Papers.

26 Director of Employment and Claims to Washington Representative

of the War Manpower Commission, Sep. 2, 1943, Records of the War Manpower Commission, Record Group 211.

27 *Chicago Tribune*, Aug. 17, 1945; Mar. 21, 1945. The program was initiated by Mexico for all interested teachers in the United States and Canada. Courses were to be taken at the National Autonomous University of Mexico. The language program was designed to teach the teachers a non-Castilian way of speaking Spanish. For details, see Conference on Mexico's Role in International Intellectual Cooperation, *Mexico's Role in International Intellectual Cooperation*.

28 *New York Times*, June 10, 1943.

29 Messersmith to Laurence Duggan, June 21, 1943, Records of the State Department, Record Group 84, State Department, Washington, D.C. Messersmith, Ambassador to Mexico, outlined the extensive coverage given to the zoot-suit riots by the Mexican press. Included in Messersmith's files is a bound volume of clippings from Mexican newspapers referring to the riots. See also *Business Week*, Jan. 1, 1944, p. 82; *New York Times*, June 11, 1943; June 16, 1943; June 17, 1943.

30 Frank X. Pax to the Mexican Patriotic Committee, Aug. 20, 1943, Chicago Area Project Papers, Chicago Historical Society (hereafter CHS).

31 David J. Saposs, "Report on Rapid Survey of Resident Latin American Problems and Recommended Program," Apr. 3, 1942, Chicago Area Project Papers, CHS.

32 "Request to Coordinator of Inter-American Affairs for Grant to Aid Latin Americans in Chicago," n.d., Chicago Area Project Papers, CHS.

33 *Ibid.*

34 *Chicago Tribune*, Aug. 12, 1945.

35 See Corwin, "Causes of Mexican Emigration," p. 570. In 1946, 91,456 illegals were returned to Mexico; 45,215 in 1950; 1,075,168 in 1954.

36 U.S. Bureau of the Census, *U.S. Census of the Population: 1950*, IV, *Special Reports*, Part 3, Chapter C, Persons of Spanish Surname (Washington, D.C., 1953), 3C-16.

37 U.S. Immigration and Naturalization Service, *Annual Reports, 1946-50* (Washington, D.C., 1946-50).

38 *Chicago Tribune*, Sep. 16, 1947.

39 Anita Edgar Jones, *Mexicans in Chicago* (San Francisco, 1971), p. 25.

40 U.S. Immigration and Naturalization Service, *Annual Reports, 1950-70* (Washington, D.C., 1950-70).

41 U.S. Bureau of the Census, *U.S. Census of Population: 1950*, IV, *Special Reports*, Part 3, Chapter A, Nativity and Parentage (Washington, D.C., 1954), 3A-265.

42 *Ibid.*

43 *Ibid.*

44 U.S. Bureau of the Census, *U.S. Census of Population: 1950*, IV, *Special Reports*, Part 4, Chapter B, Population Mobility — States and State Economic Areas (Washington, D.C., 1956), 4B-32.

45 U.S. Bureau of the Census, *U.S. Census of Population: 1950*, IV, *Special Reports*, Part 3, Chapter A, Nativity and Parentage, 3A-265.

46 *Ibid.*
47 Herman P. Miller, *Income of the American People* (New York, 1955), p. 99.
48 *Chicago Sun-Times,* Oct. 19, 1953.
49 James W. Wilkie, *The Mexican Revolution: Federal Expenditure and Social Change since 1910,* 2nd ed. (Berkeley, 1970), pp. 218-219.
50 Pan American Council, "Mexicans in Industry in Chicago" (1942), p. 85, Immigrants' Protective League Papers, Urban Collection, University of Illinois at Chicago Circle.
51 Adena Miller Rich to Nelson Rockefeller, July 15, 1944, Immigrants' Protective League Papers, Urban Collection, University of Illinois at Chicago Circle.
52 "Loyal South America," *Chicago Tribune,* Feb. 11, 1942.
53 Clifford Shaw, Frederick M. Zorbaugh, Henry D. McKay, and Leonard S. Cottrell, *Delinquency Areas: A Study of the Geographical Distribution of School Truants, Juvenile Delinquents, and Adult Defenders in Chicago* (Chicago, 1929), pp. 204-206.
54 Shaw and McKay, "Rejoinder," *American Sociological Review,* XIV (Oct. 1949), 617.
55 "Mexicans in Chicago Industry: A Survey of Leading Employers of Mexicans in Chicago," Apr. 1, 1944, pp. 4, 6, 9, 17, Immigrants' Protective League Papers, Urban Collection, University of Illinois at Chicago Circle.
56 Adena Miller Rich, "Educational Requirements for Naturalization — Do They Need Revision?" *Social Service Review,* XVIII (Oct. 1944), 382-385.
57 *Ibid.,* p. 385.
58 Interview with Encarnacion Chico, Jan. 5, 1974, taken by James Garvey as part of his research on Mexicans in Back of the Yards for a Loyola University class in Chicano history. See also F. M. Wilson to Operating Officers of Member Roads, Mar. 16, 1944, Railroad Retirement Board Papers.
59 Pan American Council, "Mexicans in Industry in Chicago," p. 3.
60 Rich to Rockefeller, July 15, 1944.
61 "Summary of the Development, Activities, and Future Plans of the Mexican Civic Committee of the West Side," n.d., Chicago Area Project Papers, CHS.
62 *Chicago Tribune,* Aug. 12, 1945.
63 See copies of "Broadcast" and "A B C" in Chicago Area Project Papers, CHS.
64 Frank X. Pax to Most Reverend Samuel A. Stritch, July 14, 1943, Chicago Area Project Papers, CHS.
65 Pax to Mexican Patriotic Committee, Aug. 20, 1943, Chicago Area Project Papers, CHS.
66 Victor Borella to Ernest Burgess, n.d., Chicago Area Project Papers, CHS.
67 *Chicago Tribune,* June 16, 1946. See also "Mexican Welfare Council Brochure" (Oct. 27, 1945), Chicago Area Project Papers, CHS.
68 "Broadcast" 1 (n.d.), Chicago Area Project Papers, CHS.
69 Pax, "Mexican Americans in Chicago — A General Survey" (Jan.

1948), Metropolitan Welfare Council Papers, CHS.
70 *Ibid.*, pp. 22-24.
71 *Ibid.*, p. 16.
72 *Ibid.*, p. 19.
73 *Ibid.* See also *The Railway Conductor*, Mar. 3, 1930, and Director of
    Publicity, NAACP, to Editor, Apr. 9, 1930, both in NAACP Papers,
    Library of Congress, Washington, D.C.
74 Pax, "Mexican Americans in Chicago," p. 10.
75 "Illinois Federation of Mexican Americans Report — 1950," Mexican
    Community Committee Papers, Special Collections, University of
    Illinois at Chicago Circle.
76 *Chicago Tribune*, June 13, 1948.
77 Committee on Division III, "Contract Laborers/Social Service"
    (1947), Metropolitan Welfare Council Papers, CHS.
78 Pax, "Mexican Americans in Chicago," p. 21. See also *Chicago
    Tribune*, May 1, 1947.
79 "Data Book for 1950-51" (Aug. 1, 1951), Chicago Area Project Papers,
    CHS.
80 *Christian Science Monitor*, Oct. 13, 1951.
81 *Ibid.* See also "Monthly Report of the Director" (Aug. 1951), Chicago
    Area Project Papers, CHS.
82 *Chicago Sun-Times*, Oct. 19, 1953.
83 Salvador Herrerra to Martin Ortiz, n.d., Chicago Area Project Papers,
    CHS. Herrerra's undated letter makes specific reference to the
    Chicago Sun-Times story of Oct. 19, 1953.
84 Martin Ortiz to Clinton White, n.d., Chicago Area Project papers,
    CHS. Reference is made to a *Chicago Sun-Times* story of Mar. 8,
    1954, which cited Ortiz as a "representative" of the Mexican-
    American community. Jose Chapa had subsequently condemned
    Ortiz and the Mexican-American Council on radio station WCRW.
    Ortiz wrote to White, WCRW's president, to complain.
85 Milton R. Konvitz, *Civil Rights in Immigration* (Ithaca, N.Y., 1953),
    pp. 147-148.
86 "Broadcast" 1 (n.d.), Chicago Area Project Papers, CHS; "Bulletin
    of the Midwest Committee for the Foreign-Born" (Sep. 27, 1953),
    Chicago Area Project papers, CHS.
87 Mexican American Council to Dear Friend, n.d., Chicago Area Project
    Papers, CHS. Reference is made to a report of Dec. 5, 1955, evidently
    intended to be sent with the letter.

Chapter IX: Race and Housing

1 Pauline Maier, "Popular Uprisings and Civil Authority in Eighteenth-
   Century America," *William and Mary Quarterly*, XXVII, Ser. 3
   (1970), 3-35; Maier, *From Resistance to Revolution* (New York,
   1972); Gordon S. Wood, "A Note on Mobs in the American Revolution," *William and Mary Quarterly*, XXIII, Ser. 3 (1966), 635-642;
   Leonard Richards, *Gentlemen of Property and Standing: Anti-
   Abolition Mobs in Jacksonian America* (New York, 1970); Michael

Feldberg, "Urbanization as a Cause for Violence: Philadelphia as a Test Case," in Allen F. Davis and Mark Haller, eds., *The Peoples of Philadelphia* (Philadelphia, 1973), pp. 53-70.

2 National Advisory Commission on Civil Disorders, *Report* (New York, 1968); Stanley Lieberson and Arnold R. Silverman, "The Precipitants and Underlying Conditions of Race Riots," *American Sociological Review*, XXX (Dec. 1965), 887-898; or any of the studies produced by the Lemberg Center for the Study of Violence at Brandeis University, to cite just a few of the better-known examples.

3 In 1940 the white population of the city was 3,114,564; by 1960 it had declined to 2,712,748. The black population, meanwhile, had risen from 277,731 to 812,637.

4 *Chicago Daily News*, July 12, 1951; *Chicago Sun-Times*, July 13, 1951; *New York Times*, July 14, 1951 and Oct. 21, 1951.

5 *New York Times*, Aug. 1, 1951; *Chicago Defender*, Aug. 11, 1951 and Sep. 15, 1951.

6 *Chicago Daily News*, July 17, 1951.

7 The Fernwood riot occurred in Aug. 1947 at a veterans' emergency housing project bordered by 104th Place, 106th Street, Halsted, and Fernwood Park. The Englewood disorder took place in November 1949 and was centered around the intersection of 56th and Peoria. For the effect of the press's silence, see William Peters, "The Race War in Chicago," *New Republic*, CXXII, No. 2 (Jan. 9, 1950), 12.

8 *New York Times*, July 14, 1951; Homer Jack, "Chicago Has One More Chance," *The Nation*, CLXV, No. 11 (Sep. 13, 1947), 252; Chicago Commission on Human Relations (hereafter cited as CHR), "Memorandum on Fernwood Park Homes" (mimeographed, n.d.); "Peoria Street Incident" (mimeographed, n.d.).

9 CHR, "Memorandum on Airport Homes" (mimeographed, n.d.); "Documentary Report of the Anti-Racial Demonstrations and Violence Against the Home and Persons of Mr. and Mrs. Roscoe Johnson, 7153 St. Lawrence Ave., July 25, 1949" (mimeographed, n.d.); "Tuley Park Incident" (mimeographed, n.d.); *The Trumbull Park Homes Disturbances* (Chicago, n.d.); CHR, "A Preliminary Report on Racial Disturbances for the Period July 21 to August 4, 1957" (mimeographed, n.d.).

10 For the period 1917-1921, see Chicago Commission on Race Relations, *The Negro in Chicago* (Chicago, 1922), p. 122; for the period 1944-1946, see Chicago Council Against Religious and Racial Discrimination, "Arson-Bombings and Other Terrorism Against Negro Households in Chicago, Documented Memorandum No. VII" (Aug. 3, 1946; mimeographed).

11 Counting only the largest disturbances, at least eight separate major racial disorders have been documented for Chicago (including Cicero) from 1946 to 1957. The incidents were: Airport Homes, 1946; Fernwood Homes, 1947; Park Manor, two separate incidents in 1949 and 1950; Tuley Park, 1950; Cicero, 1951; Trumbull Park beginning in 1953; and Calumet Park, 1957. None of the disputes over the use of community facilities occurred before 1950. The analysis that follows is based on an examination of all these incidents

as well as several lesser disorders.

12   *Chicago Sun-Times*, July 14, 1951; Charles Abrams, *Forbidden Neighbors* (New York, 1955), p. 105.

13   See, for example, *Chicago Daily News*, December 3, 1946, or *Chicago Tribune*, August 15-17, 1947; although these stories are limited, their coverage is extensive compared to that given later riots. One can search the press in vain to find any significant mention of the troubles in Park Manor during the last week of July 1949 or of the Peoria Street incident of November 8-12, 1949. For the attitudes of race relations officials and the press, as well as for details of their cooperation, see CHR, *The People of Chicago* (Chicago, n.d.), p. 3; *Fourth Chicago Conference on Civic Unity* (Chicago, 1952), pp. 77-78; "Memorandum on Airport Homes," p. 15; "Memorandum on Fernwood Park Homes," pp. 5, 8; "Peoria Street Incident," pp. 22, 28; "Documentary Report of the Violence. . . ," p. 20.

14   Allen Day Grimshaw, "A Study in Social Violence: Urban Race Riots in the United States" (Ph.D. diss., University of Pennsylvania, 1959), pp. 207-208.

15   CHR research memoranda and the daily press were used to compile arrest lists for the Fernwood riot of 1947, the Park Manor disorder of 1949, the Peoria Street incident in Englewood in 1949, the Trumbull Park disturbances of the mid-1950s, and the Calumet Park uprising of 1957. The lists for the first three episodes appear to be comprehensive, or nearly so. The Trumbull Park outbreaks, however, lasted for years, and the list compiled for that disorder covers arrests made from Aug. 1953 through Aug. 1954; though the CHR reported 120 persons arrested in the Calumet Park rioting, no list of arrestees was found. The 51 names obtained for this riot were gleaned from press reports and represent, apparently, 42.5% of all Calumet Park arrestees.

16   CHR, "Peoria Street Incident," pp. 32, 35; "Notes on Special Meeting of the Board of Directors," Dec. 5, 1949, Chicago Urban League Papers, Manuscript Collection, The Library, University of Illinois at Chicago Circle.

17   CHR, "Documentary Memorandum, The White Circle League" (mimeographed, n.d.), *passim.*

18   George Rudé warns against treating violent crowds as "militant minorit[ies] to be sharply marked off from the larger number of citizens . . ." and notes that a "bond of sympathy and common interest" may link "the active few with the inactive many." See his *The Crowd in History: A Study of Popular Disturbances in France and England, 1730-1848* (New York, 1964), pp. 211-212.

19   CHR, "Documentary Report on Recurrence of Anti-Racial Disturbances in the 7100 and 7200 Blocks on St. Lawrence Avenue" (mimeographed, n.d.), pp. 15-16, 22.

20   William Gremley, "Social Control in Cicero, Illinois" (mimeographed, n.d.), p. 8, in the Catholic Interracial Council Papers, Box 2, Chicago Historical Society (hereafter CHS); ACLU Observers' Report for July 13, 1951, American Civil Liberties Union—Illinois Division Papers, Addenda, Box 13, Folder: Cicero Riot—1951, Joseph Regenstein Library, University of Chicago; CHR, "Memorandum on Airport

Homes," p. 4.
21 Thomas Rook, Report, Nov. 17, 1949, 1 in Catholic Interracial Council Papers, Box 1, CHS; ACLU Observers' Report, July 13, 1951.
22 CHR, "Memorandum on Airport Homes," p. 14; Homer Jack, "Documented Memorandum VIII, The Racial Factor in the Veterans' Airport Housing Project" (mimeographed, n.d.), pp. 2, 4; *Chicago Tribune,* Dec. 12, 1946.
23 CHR, *The Trumbull Park Homes Disturbances,* pp. 12, 19, 23, 30, 32, and 49.
24 Joseph Parot, "Ethnic vs. Black Metropolis: The Origins of Polish-Black Housing Tensions in Chicago," *Polish American Studies,* XXIX (Spring-Autumn 1972), 5-33; Pierre de Vise, *Chicago's Widening Color Gap* (Chicago, 1967), pp. 71-73. De Vise shows that Poles and Italians were the "whites" found in the greatest numbers in areas adjacent to the expanding Black Belt.
25 *Chicago Defender,* July 28, 1951.
26 CHR, "Report on Press, Radio, and Television Coverage of Racial Disturbances in Chicago from July 28 to August 15, 1957" (mimeographed, n.d.), pp. 5-6.
27 *Chicago Defender,* Apr. 18, 1957.
28 Chandler Owen, "A Program for the Solution of the Trumbull Housing Conflict" (1954?), p. 13, in the Robert E. Merriam Papers, Box 23, Folder 2, Joseph Regenstein Library, University of Chicago.
29 It is understood that such a method is imprecise at best and it is not intended to reduce each ethnic group to exact percentages of rioters. It was simply deemed appropriate to go beyond the *assumption* that the local residents arrested during a riot were ethnically representative of the community involved; and the attempt to establish, in broad terms, the general ethnic composition of the various mobs was thus desirable. The arrest lists were surveyed independently by the author (a Jew) and two colleagues (a Polish-American and a scholar of French-Irish extraction) who are specialists in urban history. The results, which were highly corroborative in almost every case, were then combined to minimize possible error. The percentages in tables III, IV, and V represent the averages produced by that collaboration.
30 *Chicago Defender,* Apr. 18, 1957.
31 Evelyn M. Kitagawa and Karl E. Taeuber, eds., *Local Community Fact Book: Chicago Metropolitan Area, 1960* (Chicago, 1963), pp. 112, 116, 118, and 150.
32 CHR, "Memorandum on Airport Homes," pp. 13-14.
33 CHR, "Memorandum on Fernwood Park Homes," pp. 2-5; The Community Relations Service, "Housing and Race Relations in Chicago" (Sep. 22, 1948), pp. 50-51, in the Archibald J. Carey, Jr. Papers, Box 5, Folder 34, CHS.
34 CHR, "Documentary Report of the Anti-Racial Demonstrations . . . ," p. 1 and Appendix A.
35 CHR, "Peoria Street Incident," *passim.*
36 CHR, "A Preliminary Report . . . ," p. 6.
37 CHR, *The Trumbull Park Homes Disturbances,* pp. 10-11; *Chicago Daily News,* Apr. 10, 1954.

38 CHR, "Memorandum on Airport Homes," p. 14.
39 Homer Jack, "Chicago Has One More Chance," p. 251.
40 CHR, "Documentary Report of the Anti-Racial Demonstrations . . . ,"
    pp. 1, 30; For Cicero, see Homer Jack, "Cicero Nightmare," *Nation*,
    CLXXIII, No. 4 (July 28, 1951), 64-65; Mary Yedinak, "Cicero: Why
    it Rioted" (B.A. thesis, University of Illinois—Champaign, 1967), p. 13.
41 Despite the proximity of the Black Belt and the apparent availability
    of black targets, there were only reports of three cars being stoned by
    white teens and only a single injury was recorded. CHR, "Documentary
    Report of the Anti-Racial Demonstrations . . . ," pp. 11-12.
42 CHR, "Emerald Street Incident" (mimeographed, n.d.), pp. 19-20.
43 American Civil Liberties Union, Chicago Division, "Report" (mimeo-
    graphed, n.d.), Chicago Urban League Papers, University of Illinois
    at Chicago Circle. The ACLU report on the Englewood disorder noted
    that the neighborhood around 56th and Peoria "has been known for
    some years as one of the most dangerous spots" in the city insofar as
    race relations were concerned. The black enclaves of Morgan Park,
    Lilydale, and the wartime developments in Princeton Park and West
    Chesterfield surrounded and worried white Roseland residents. See
    the Minutes of the Regular Meeting of the Board of Directors of the
    Metropolitan Housing Council, April 1, 1943 and August 3, 1943, in the
    Metropolitan Housing and Planning Council Papers (hereafter MHPC),
    Manuscript Collection, The Library, University of Illinois at Chicago
    Circle.
44 "White drivers without white flags were warned by white bystanders
    to keep their dome lights on to avoid damage to their automobiles."
    CHR, "A Preliminary Report . . . ," p. 11; Richards, *Gentlemen of
    Property and Standing*, p. 120.
45 CHR, "Peoria Street Incident," p. 31.
46 *Chicago Bee*, Feb. 23, 1947; CHR, *The People of Chicago*, p. 7; Com-
    munity Relations Service, "Housing and Race Relations in Chicago,"
    p. 37.
47 CHR, "Memorandum on Fernwood Park Homes," pp. 19-20.
48 Edward H. Palmer served as Director of Tenant and Community Rela-
    tions at the Trumbull Park Homes from 1960 to 1962; during that time
    he had "direct personal knowledge" of CHA placement procedures at
    the project and swore that he received "oral instructions" to permit
    no more than 25 black families to reside in Trumbull Park Homes at
    any one time. His affidavit of June 7, 1968 is in the Business and
    Professional People in the Public Interest Papers (hereafter BPPPI),
    Box 3, CHS. For reports of the original "deal," see CHR, *The Trumbull
    Park Homes Disturbances*, p. 50.
49 Holman D. Pettibone, president of the Chicago Title and Trust Com-
    pany and a key figure in the city's redevelopment program, felt that all
    plans "rise and fall on public housing for relocation." Holman D.
    Pettibone to Martin Kennelly, Sep. 18, 1952, Holman D. Pettibone
    Papers, Box 8, CHS. See also Martin Meyerson and Edward C. Banfield,
    Politics, Planning, and the Public Interest (New York, 1955), p. 19.
50 Meyerson and Banfield, p. 124.
51 CHR, "Memorandum on Airport Homes," p. 9; "Memorandum on

Fernwood Park Homes," p. 31; Chicago City Council, *Journal of the Proceedings* (Oct. 15, 1947), p. 1032.

52　Chicago Housing Authority, untitled typewritten statement, Oct. 24, 1947 in the MHPC Papers; *Chicago Defender*, Dec. 6, 1947; Minutes of the Board of Governors Meeting, Nov. 5, 1947, MHPC Papers.

53　Chicago City Council, *Journal of the Proceedings* (Mar. 15, 1948), p. 2040.

54　Meyerson and Banfield, pp. 83-87; "Memorandum of Record" of an interview with Robert R. Taylor, June 27, 1956, in the BPPPI Papers, Box 1, CHS.

55　Meyerson and Banfield, *passim*.

56　After a second group of project sites had been selected, Ferd Kramer, president of the MHPC, met with Mayor Richard J. Daley and informed him that it was bad planning to "relegate all low rent projects to the South Side." Daley "took note of the argument, but made no commitments." Later, the MHPC Board was warned that "if Alderman (Emil V.) Pacini (10th) appraises the local temper correctly, the mayor cannot help very much to reverse the situation": "Memorandum of Conclusions of the Special Board Meeting on Public Housing in Chicago" (n.d.), MHPC Papers, UICC.

57　Meyerson and Banfield, pp. 122-136, 135n.; Meyerson and Banfield emphasize the decision made to open all projects to nonwhites, "as soon as consistent with the maintenance of law and order," after rioting broke out at Trumbull Park; it should be noted, however, that no time constraint was placed on the CHA, and the reference to "law and order" opened the door to indefinite delay. As of June 1959 there were still no blacks in the Bridgeport Homes and only two black families in Lawndale Gardens; twenty-one black families occupied the 925-unit Lathrop Homes and twenty of Trumbull Park's 462 units were occupied by blacks. At that time CHA Chairman Alvin Rose spoke of non-discrimination as a "goal" rather than a policy and stated that he would not take any "further steps in integration . . . until he was sure it could be done without violence": *Chicago Defender*, May 2, 1953; Memorandum from Judy Miller and Kale Williams to Bill Berry, et al., June 16, 1959, and Kale Williams to Ken Douty, June 26, 1959, in the ACLU Papers, Box 11, Folder 8, Joseph Regenstein Library, University of Chicago.

58　The aldermen, closely attuned to developments within their wards, thus knew that the violent opposition to the CHA was rooted in the local residents and not a roving band of agitators; the latter could have been safely ignored—the former could not.

59　Meyerson and Banfield, 199.

60　Francis W. McPeek, "Human Relations: Imperatives for Public Action" (speech delivered at the Chicago Commission of Human Relations Twelfth Annual Awards in Human Relations Luncheon, Dec. 10, 1957).

INDEX

417